DOLLS' HOUSES IN AMERICA

Historic Preservation in Miniature

DOLLS' HOUSES IN AMERICA

Historic Preservation in Miniature

FLORA GILL JACOBS

CHARLES SCRIBNER'S SONS · NEW YORK

Copyright © 1974 Flora Gill Jacobs

Library of Congress Cataloging in Publication Data

Jacobs, Flora Gill.
    Dolls' houses in America.

    Includes bibliographical references.
    1. Doll-houses—United States. I. Title.
NK4894.U6J32   745.59'23'0973   73-1100
ISBN 0-684-13583-3 (cloth edition)
ISBN 0-684-15627-X (paper edition)

THIS BOOK PUBLISHED SIMULTANEOUSLY IN
THE UNITED STATES OF AMERICA AND IN CANADA
COPYRIGHT UNDER THE BERNE CONVENTION

ALL RIGHTS RESERVED. NO PART OF THIS BOOK
MAY BE REPRODUCED IN ANY FORM WITHOUT
THE PERMISSION OF CHARLES SCRIBNER'S SONS.

3 5 7 9 11 13 15 17 19 M/C 20 18 16 14 12 10 8 6 4

1 3 5 7 9 11 13 15 17 19 M/P 20 18 16 14 12 10 8 6 4 2

PRINTED IN THE UNITED STATES OF AMERICA

*For Ephraim, Amanda
and "the lady from Philadelphia"*

In small proportions we just beauties see,
And in short measures life may perfect be.
                          BEN JONSON

ACKNOWLEDGMENTS

Such a book as this owes a great deal to the numerous museums, historical societies and private collectors who provided photographs and information, and although my debt is great to all of those whose names and treasures are to be found in these pages, among them are those to whom my gratitude must be particularized.

Many museums extended special privileges, and I wish to extend special thanks to Bart Anderson, West Chester Historical Society; Lawrence L. Belles, Evanston Historical Society; Rose Briggs, Plymouth Antiquarian Society; Mrs. John Crosby Brown, Lyme Historical Society; Susan E. Burns, Oakland Museum; Mildred Compton, Indianapolis Children's Museum; Irene Dodge, Wenham Museum; Mrs. Louis H. Dorr, Milan Historical Museum; Dr. Richard H. Howland, Smithsonian Institution; Mrs. J. M. Hughes, Metropolitan Toronto and Region Conservation Authority; Barbara Luck, Abby Aldrich Rockefeller Folk Art Collection, Watt Marchman, Rutherford B. Hayes Library; Helena McCormack, Missouri Historical Society; S. W. Milligan, Wayne County Historical Museum; Hazel F. Morse, Ashburnham Historical Society Museum; Patrick Murray, Museum of Childhood, Edinburgh; Joseph Noble, Museum of the City of New York; Eleanor L. Nowlin, Shelburne Museum; Richard Nylander, Society for the Preservation of New England Antiquities; Doris L. Perry, Allen County-Fort Wayne Historical Society, Rodris Roth, Smithsonian Institution; H. J. Swinney (also Thomas E. McFarland and Ann Hotra), Strong Museum; William L. Warren, Litchfield Historical Society; Kenneth E. Wheeling, Shelburne Museum; and Grace Wells, Valentine Museum.

A number of collectors have ventured even beyond the bounds of collectorship to provide aid and information, and although an alphabetical listing seems ungracious and mechanical, earnest thanks are so offered to Mrs. Joseph Andrews; Mrs. John M. Archer; Mrs. Ernest Bruder; Mrs. Claude Callicott; Mrs. Roderic Davison; Mrs. Lytton W. Doolittle; Mrs. Clayton H. Englar; Mrs. Myrtes Fallon; Mrs. W. Franklin Farnsworth; Mrs. George Glasson; Colleen Moore Hargrave; Mrs. John Harrell; Miss Ethel Howard; Miss Eleanor Hosie; Herbert H. Hosmer; Barbara Whitton Jendrick; Mrs. George Kephart; Raymond Knapp, Mrs. Walter Kueffner; Mrs. Ralph H. Krueger; Sister M. Lenore; Mrs. Arthur LaVove; Charles T. Lennon; Mrs. Gordon MacLaren; Miss Anne McCaughey; Mrs. J. W. McKennon; Miss Marguerite Mumm; Mrs. Raymond Norris; Miss Marshall Norris; Mrs. A. M. Ray; Miss Florence Redman; Mrs. Philip Ross-Ross; Miss Gertrude Sappington; Mrs. Harry Spencer, Jr.; Mrs. Frank Steele; Mrs. George Evans Steinmetz; Mr. and Mrs. Alfred H. Stiles; Mrs. B. H. Thornton; Mrs. James Timpson; Mrs. Homer Lee Twigg and Miss Hazel Whitaker.

For extraordinary contributions I shall forever be beholden to Mrs. John H. Grossman, Mrs. Richard Robbins Kane and Mrs. Donald Mar-

ACKNOWLEDGMENTS

ion. I wish also to make special note of the considerable aid and comfort provided by my friend and fellow laborer in a related vineyard, Dorothy Smith Coleman.

In any study of objects of the past, the value of illustrated trade catalogues is axiomatic. Toy catalogues are rare, as one can attest who has hunted for them, and even advertised for them (with small success) for nearly thirty years. My fellow members of the Antique Toy Collectors of America have ferreted out and reprinted a surprising number in recent years, and they have my gratitude. Among them, I am especially in the debt of Margaret and Blair Whitton, who not only are responsible for some of the reprints, but also furnished rare original material. Mrs. Paul Giles and Mrs. Henry Erath, who gave me access to catalogues in the files of F. A. O. Schwarz, also have my gratitude; as do G. William Holland and Louis H. Hertz, who also made available valuable catalogue illustrations; and Mrs. Preston Weatherred, who lent her *Tynietoy* catalogue. I also wish to acknowledge the kindness of Mrs. William Maunder and William H. Green, both of whom supplied catalogue material relating to the Whitney-Reed Chair Co.

As valuable as trade catalogues, are the files of *Playthings*, the toy trade magazine. I am indebted to Geyer-McAllister Publications, Inc. for access to these.

Although most of the pictures from "author's collection" were excellently taken by Allen Bress, I am grateful to my friends Margaret Stevenson and Emily and Cecil King who, out of friendship, provided others.

My warmest thanks are to my editor, Elinor Parker, who graciously, as always, bore up under the weight of a manuscript of tomelike proportions, betraying no sign of sinking under its weight.

Finally, I wish to salute my husband, Ephraim Jacobs, a demon with a comma, and perhaps the only lawyer in the United States who, willy-nilly, knows as much about dolls' houses as about the anti-trust laws (and undoubtedly far more than he has any need—or wish—to know).

CONTENTS

ACKNOWLEDGMENTS ix
Introduction 3

PART ONE

HISTORIC PRESERVATION IN MINIATURE: Unique Examples

Dolls' Houses from New England 15

Dolls' Houses from the Mid-Atlantic Region 62

Dolls' Houses from the State of New York 106

Dolls' Houses from the South 139

Dolls' Houses from the Mid-West 165

Dolls' Houses from the West 186

Dolls' Houses from Canada 196

PART TWO

HISTORIC PRESERVATION IN MINIATURE: Factory-Made Buildings

"Commercial Property" 207

CONTENTS

PART THREE

RELATED MATTERS

Furnishings 289

Chairs 332

Dolls' House Occupants 340

PART FOUR

CONTEMPORARY MATTERS

The Philosophy of Restoration, or, the Horrors of Urban Renewal in Miniature 351

Contemporary Craftsmen 360

APPENDICES

A Brief Bibliography 367

Museums with Dolls' Houses 369

Inventory of Wheeler Dolls' House 371

Inventory of Fair-y Villa 375

Note on Metric System 379

Scale Plan of Hayes House No. 1 380

Scale Plan of Hayes House No. 2 381

INDEX 383

COLOR PLATES BETWEEN PAGES 338 AND 339

DOLLS' HOUSES IN AMERICA

Historic Preservation in Miniature

Introduction

For a number of years, a variety of concerned antiquarians have been shouting from the housetops about the disappearance of some of the very houses whose tops they are shouting from—too many of which are removed even before the shouting dies away.

With the buildings of the past going down like tenpins, and the wrecker's ball frequently sending landmarks to oblivion despite the assiduous efforts of the National Trust for Historic Preservation and smaller, local groups struggling to preserve them; with atrocities committed again and again in the name of urban renewal, and the flavor of the past, its variety and vitality, being snuffed out like so many gas-lamps at dawn on a Victorian lane, the preservation of old dolls' houses has become considerably more than a footnote to the architecture and furnishings of days gone by.

As the following pages hope to reveal, there are many collections of highly architectural and/or historical dolls' houses and related miniature buildings in museums, historical societies, and in private hands, which are not only disarming relics but documents of their times, three-dimensional miniature supplements to printed records and old photographs of architecture and furnishings. In combination, the miniature buildings which remain form an astonishing cross-section, not only of houses but of shops, stables, warehouses, churches, and almost every conceivable structure, and in virtually every nineteenth-century style—Greek Revival and Victorian Gothic through High Victorian and Colonial Revival, along with a remarkable variety from the early twentieth.

Unlike the landmarks designated by the National Trust, the miniature architecture which has been preserved is not all historic. It is not all "important" from either an architectural or a historical point of view. Even in the case of "replica" houses, miniature buildings which traditionally are copies of actual ones in full size, the "replicas" are nearly always approximations, withal most informative ones.

It is also true that, as this book goes to press, only one colonial "baby house" is known to me—the same Van Cortlandt miniature mansion which research disclosed more than twenty-five years ago,* plus a scant few houses from the Federal period. Until very recently, the full-sized buildings of the eighteenth century, with a few historic exceptions, were the only ones with which preservationists were actively concerned. Whole neighborhoods of early-, mid-, and late-Victorian houses have been, and continue to be, bulldozed, and whole neighborhoods of those architectural (and now verbal) clichés, the "cubes," have been angularly and monotonously substituted. Most of the cubes are office buildings and apartments which are sparsely represented in miniature (Fig. 112), but if the houses and shops of the mid-twentieth century are not

---

* Almost the moment the galley proofs for this Ms. were returned to the publisher, I learned of another, (See pp. 139–140)

INTRODUCTION

all bad (and of course they are not), they often needlessly replace houses and shops built with a variety, a craftsmanship, and a richness which we cannot afford today, nor possibly ever can again. It is reassuring to have miniature examples of these rapidly disappearing structures, mercifully of no interest to those enemies of history, the land speculators and the developers. Dolls can fill only miniature shoes, and dolls' houses only miniature foundations, but the amount of surviving material is formidable.

This quantity (and quality) is also extraordinary when one considers that old dolls' houses and related buildings have met with demolition problems of their own. Apart from the exigencies of play, the survivors often are packed away in attics for generations, only to meet sorry fates when finally they emerge: they may be turned over to latter-day children and swiftly demolished; or, if they survive, they may be subjected to miniature urban renewal projects by misguided adults* or, even if the houses themselves are not abused, their furnishings may be sold off in deference to the practicalities of the antiques business.

The number which remain, despite these hazards, is overwhelming. At least the compiler of the assortment described in the following pages has been overwhelmed. Friends who have heard reference to a "bottomless book" have also been subjected to a summary which has become almost a catechism: "When a history of dolls' houses is written, there is a chapter about Dutch dolls' houses, one about English houses, one about German . . . But when the dolls' houses of *one* country are considered, there is an obligation to be reasonably comprehensive. The United States is a sizeable country."

It is because of this formidable size, and the great number of examples even a relatively modest sampling has discovered, that an effort has been made to group the one-of-a-kind houses, which are to be found in Part One, into regions. Most of these divisions are usual, but there are a few exceptions. Most noticeably, the dolls' houses of New England are numerous and, like the full-sized structures they resemble, have a character uniquely their own. The vast state of New York, not unexpectedly, has supplied a similarly formidable selection, and a highly diversified one. To have lodged these two areas, as in a tour booklet, under the broader "Northeastern" heading seemed inappropriate and, therefore, they are listed separately.

In several instances, it was impossible to know whether the dolls' house originated in the state in which it was found. When there was doubt, as there was, for instance, with respect to a few examples in the Strong collection, the house in question has been placed in the area (in this case, New York) in which it is presently located. Conversely, it is known that the magnificent dolls' house now in Williamsburg was found in Long Island. Despite the fact that this recently acquired treasure is likely henceforth to be identified as the Williamsburg dolls' house, it necessarily has been placed with houses from the state in which it originated (again, New York). The two White House dolls' houses are similarly classified: Though they are on permanent display in the Hayes Museum in Fremont, Ohio, they are shown here with the Mid-Atlantic group, one of them having been made in Washington, D.C., and one in Baltimore.*

While coping with such technical matters, it might be well to mention, at least, the tricky subject of measurements. In such a far-flung country as this, it has not been possible to visit all the collections represented in these pages. In the absence of visits, overall measurements have been requested, and it is *hoped* that overall measurements have been sent, unless additions of chimneys, turrets, etc. were specified. Such

---

* See pages 351–353

* Inasmuch as all other Baltimore houses are considered with those of "the South," "Mid-Atlantic" is a compromise between the South and the Mid-West!

INTRODUCTION

measurements, of height, width, and depth, offer, at least, a fairly specific idea of the size and scale of a dolls' house, and it seemed an imposition, as well as unnecessary, to ask for more.

Scale is another technical area. Although there are many variations, a comparison of the two Hayes (White House) dolls' houses may serve to illustrate the possibilities. "Hayes House No. 1" (Fig. 87), the turreted mansion built in Baltimore, is smaller in scale—$\frac{1}{12}'' = 1''$—than "Hayes House No. 2" (Fig. 90) which is $\frac{1}{8}'' = 1''$.* Most customarily referred to as "an inch to a foot," the $\frac{1}{12}''$ scale is the size most popular today, and it is well to remember that commercially made dolls' house furniture was usually manufactured in a choice of several sizes, and so, too, were commercially made houses and related toys. I have gone on elsewhere, and shall not again here, about the piquancy of slightly assorted scales versus the rigidities of the maker of model rooms. The dolls' house was (and still is), after all, a toy; when an old dolls' house is found, out-of-scale objects often accompany it, and help to give it part of its not inconsiderable (said the collector) charm.

Even though the sizeable assortment which is offered here has at times seemed overwhelming, what remains unfound and unknown seems more overwhelming still. It would be possible, seemingly, to spend the rest of one's life, however long that might be, delving into this quite bottomless subject. The number of dolls' houses which must still be tucked away in attics, and even in museum attics, in addition to those on display which are not, for one reason or another, included here, is awesome to contemplate. Many houses in museums or private collections, with respect to which more than one letter was exchanged (or ignored), continued to elude this summary, whether owing to a photographic problem, or to one completely baffling, and frequently frustrating, to the researcher.

Other dolls' houses, some of them important and well known, have been purposely omitted. Their very celebrity, plus space limitations, have excluded such celebrated specimens as Miss Bradford's dolls' house at the Smithsonian, Miss Stettheimer's at the Museum of the City of New York, and the fabulous (a word not used lightly) collection given by Dr. Fritz Rosenberg to the Denver Art Museum. The same considerations applied to Mrs. Longworth's French dolls' house which she played with as a little girl in Oyster Bay, and which is still in her possession. All of these houses, including a number in the writer's collection, have been sufficiently illustrated and described elsewhere. It may appear arbitrary that a selection of other houses which *have* been dealt with in earlier publications (mostly by this writer) have not been similarly excluded. When they haven't, there is usually a compelling reason; the house is an architectural type which seems essential to such a compendium, or one so important and early (the Brett, for instance) that it cannot be omitted.

Occasionally a relatively modest house has

*"Blueprints"—scale plans for both doll's houses—may be found in the Appendices.

Figure 1. From *The House Beautiful*, 1903

(5)

INTRODUCTION

been admitted in lieu of a more impressive specimen because it represents an area of architecture, or an area of the United States, of which examples are otherwise in short supply. Regrettably, relatively few dolls' houses from the Southern states have been located and, as a result, one or two which might otherwise have been omitted have been included. It is possible only to muse about and to mention a glorious Charleston dolls' mansion, ca. 1860, with a typical portico, the only Charleston dolls' house known to me; and a marvelous Baltimore townhouse with iron balconies at the windows, and with a black-and-white checkerboard marble walk in front to match the marble steps. Both of these miniature residences are unforgettable (though I saw them more than twenty-five years ago), but lamentably, they have been behind the locked doors of a full-sized Baltimore mansion for many long years.

The houses that got away, the pictures that have been promised which never came, information that has been sought but never found—all of this has been tantalizing, even though it is clear that to include more would have amplified a space problem already formidable. A few of these elusive ones must at least be mentioned, for perhaps a future dolls' house historian to pursue.

It was through Mrs. Myrtes Fallon of New Jersey that I learned of one of the most irresistible representatives of this category: "An elaborate dolls' house behind a sliding panel" in the library of Henry Adams in Washington, which was "always ready for any little girl that might be brought to see him." It has not been possible to amplify this account, by Mrs. Winthrop Chanler, who mentioned it in a memoir* published in 1937; and at this writing, I do not know if this historic dolls' house is still in existence. Investigation into this small and intriguing mystery continues.

* *Roman Spring.*

Another puzzle is suggested by one miniature object in the sizeable and elegant dolls' house collection of Mrs. Wilson (Figs. 41–2 and 149–51). This is a small secretary said to have belonged to a dolls' house copied from Stevens Castle, Hoboken. "The castle is gone," Mrs. Wilson once wrote. "Where is the little house?"

Where indeed?

The exclusion of another fine old dolls' house, on display in its original residence of which it was a copy, in Alexandria, Virginia, is for the most curious of reasons. The owner, who conducted an antiques and gifts business on the premises, and permitted customers to view the dolls' house, on display in an upstairs room which was part of her shop, had "recently" suffered a burglary in her own Alexandria residence. Even though she was going out of business, and was taking the dolls' house to her home, she was unwilling to have it "publicized" in a book, for fear of stimulating further thievery. One can hardly picture a burglar reading a book entitled *Dolls' Houses in America*, though dolls' house burglaries are not entirely unknown. (The celebrated seventeenth-century cabinet house at Utrecht was, of course, burgled in 1831. The items stolen, however, included such treasures as an amber chest inlaid with gold and ivory, the sort of thing no self-respecting

Figure 2

INTRODUCTION

burglar can resist in any size. There was nothing of the sort in the Alexandria dolls' house.)

Because it has been a matter of considerable pride to be able to present in these pages a selection of dolls' houses which are copies of full-sized ones, this incident was especially frustrating. Those "replica" dolls' houses which *are* illustrated, along with old photographs of the houses of which they are copies, most dramatically demonstrate the role of dolls' houses in historic preservation, and they may be found scattered through Part One.

Many of the other dolls' houses shown, whose histories have been lamentably lost or mislaid,* clearly are copies of actual residences, often more explicit or otherwise impressive than some of the modest examples whose histories have been carefully treasured and recorded. A striking example is the marvelous Cresson-Dickey baby house in Philadelphia. Even though much of its history is known, and it bears every sign of resembling an actual house, with the remarkable presence of the rare, possibly unique, Greentree fire marks to furnish a clue, the house of which it may well be a copy is unknown. (It is true that in the case of a baby house which goes back to the beginning of the nineteenth century, as this one does, it is not altogether surprising to discover that bits of its history have been chipped off along the way.)

The theme of "historic preservation in miniature" may be applied not only to the one-of-a-kind carpentered dolls' houses which crowd Part One of this compilation, but also to the "commercial property"—the houses and related buildings commercially made in the United States which are considered in Part Two. In some instances, the often small dolls' houses, stables, stores, and other buildings which were made in such variety and detail, many of them in the New England states, are frequently more precise records of past architecture than some of the more imposing and beautifully made one-of-a-kind houses.

In the Victorian era, ideas which led to "creative playthings" had not been advanced and, as we know, little was left to the child's imagination. In 1901, Bliss, with his marvelously-detailed gingerbread houses and related buildings (Figs. 255–79), proudly advertised a line of dolls' houses "designed and modeled by a practical architect." Sometimes a specific and historic building was copied by a commercial firm: Although I have never seen such an incredible item, Louis Hertz* describes a wooden "replica of Mount Vernon complete with its various outbuildings *and* Washington's tomb!"

The Bliss 1901 catalogue advertises a skyscraper, an early reference to an architectural style which had been launched in full size only a few years before. As skyscrapers go, the Bliss model was inexpensive: Complete with twelve stories and a chimney, it came set up, for ten cents. Its dimensions are descriptive, 5⅛" by 17", and its inspiration was readily at hand. The Flatiron Building, in which many toy makers and jobbers had their offices, was completed, like the catalogue, in 1901.

Along with skyscrapers, Bliss and other toy manufacturers supplied many types of buildings, apart from houses. Komlosy & Company (after 1904 known as Martin & Co.), a New York manufacturer whose handsome dolls' houses are known to me only through their advertisements, in 1904 referred to (in addition to dolls' houses): "lighthouses, farms, stables, stores . . . theaters, ball booths and bowling alleys." A news story in a 1905 issue of *Playthings*, showing a mansion with arched windows and an imposing portico, pointed out:

It should be an interesting fact to any toy buyer that

---

* One dreams of receiving letters, following publication, which begin: "About the house on page x in your book, I recognize it as one given by my late-great aunt, born in 1817, to . . ."

* *The Handbook of Old American Toys*, Mark Haber & Co., 1947.

INTRODUCTION

Figure 3. From *Playthings*, 1904

Figure 4. From *Playthings*, 1904

right in this city there is a factory which turns out all kinds of wooden toys, the kind that delight the hearts of boys and girls at Christmas time. No machinery is used in this factory, the work all being done by hand. . . . The doll house illustrated . . . is an example. . . . Everything . . . is complete; stairs, doors that open, glass windows, lace curtains, imported wall paper, etc. . . . The house can be taken apart so as to be conveniently packed for shipping. . . .

The same firm advertised, also in 1905, a "well-equipped" boathouse. Boathouses were "shown in several sizes and styles" and could "be had with the names of different well-known yacht clubs on them." The "Nonpareil Boat Club" shown was well named. If one could be found today, it would be a toy without equal; at least I have never seen or heard of another.

The microcosmos is complete, and in the pages which follow, the "miscellaneous structures" which were factory-made may be found, along with factory-made houses, in Part Two. The one-of-a-kind species, like the one-of-a-kind houses, will be discovered in the regions in which they were made in Part One.

Figure 5. From *Playthings*, 1905

The title *Dolls' Houses in America*, thoroughly unoriginal, has been chosen with deliberation. Although it is now clear, after nearly three years of hard labor, that a book entitled *American Dolls' Houses* would have been possible, the multitude of commercially made houses and the tidal wave of furniture and accessories which have come to our shores suggest that perhaps it is just as well such a work was not attempted.

INTRODUCTION

It has been necessary to make arbitrary choices here, as well as among the regional houses. The number of dolls' houses from abroad which have been admitted to these pages have been relatively few, and they have been kept largely to species which have been imported in such numbers that excluding them would disappoint many collectors. (Many of the houses collectors inquire about prove to be imports.) Such a series as the French houses described on pages 258–9, which continued to be imported well into the 'twenties, were made essentially in the same styles as they were earlier, with the result that they are frequently found and "collected" and inquired about.

With one-of-a-kind houses, the examples represented are even fewer. The beautiful English baby house (Fig. 73) built in 1816 by a known architect has, as the summary suggests, been in this country for so many years that it most certainly has qualified for citizenship by now.*

Although while these pages were in progress, a folder had been set up marked "South—and North—of the Border," and it had been hoped to include a selection of South American dolls' houses, examples from our Latin neighbors continued to be elusive, though miniature objects from Mexico are known to be made in multitudes, and a few chairs are illustrated here (Plate 11).† A well-known line of well-made dolls' house furniture has been manufactured in Colombia for a decade or so and it would seem that other miniatures would have been made there in earlier days.

Canadian dolls' houses are another matter, and a small selection is offered.

With reproduction houses, it has been especially necessary to set limits. The great craft revival, as we know, has been in progress for some time, and the making of dolls' houses and their furnishings has not been exempt. Never before have so many craftsmen been building dolls' houses and/or furniture, either for themselves or, on a large scale, for the multitude of collectors who have made miniatures the number three collecting pursuit after dolls (number two), and coins and stamps (number one).* This tidal wave is briefly discussed, and the names of some of the leading craftsmen and suppliers mentioned. Someone should do a book about the houses and furnishings being made today and (as I have said more than once), surely someone, at any moment, will.

There has been an effort in these pages to emphasize the furniture of the United States, but because American dolls' houses have contained a cross-section of imports along with the native product; and perhaps because less of it was made, especially in the final quarter of the nineteenth century and the beginning of the twentieth, when German furniture, and especially accessories, flooded the market, much of the American furniture to be found is rare or, like the Pia metal pieces, limited in style.

Such relatively modern dolls' house furniture as Tootsietoy, Arcade, and Kilgore, most of it metal, is the "antique" dolls' house furniture which now is to be found in shops and at shows

---

* It is shown with the houses of Pennsylvania because it has resided there for so many years.

† Years ago, by mail, I bought a variety of painted metal dolls' house furnishings, part of which, according to the California dealer who sold them, had come from the stock of an old store in Mexico City, and were "about forty years old." Since that was in 1955, these can be considered, if he was accurate, pre-World War I. Others he believed to be about fifteen years old. All were unused, and clocks, desks, umbrella stands, etc. in several scales were included. A figure of a woman holding a mirror (3⅞" tall) is marked "Nacional." The pieces are similar, but more crudely made than German pieces from which some of them, including a Singer sewing machine, were copied. Others, such as a gilt flower stand, with a removable pot and painted metal flowers, have a charm of their own.

* For this information I am indebted to John Blauer of San Francisco, who should know. Mr. Blauer, a collector-dealer on the grand scale, has for a number of years dispensed an enormous variety of miniature objects to an ever-widening mass of collectors (see page 360).

INTRODUCTION

Figure 6

and is, according to pessimistic collectors, all that is likely to be available.

For a price, of course, one can still come by the lovely old Biedermeier, the German furniture of imitation rosewood, delicately decorated with gilt patterns, for which Vivien Greene* coined the term "the Dolls' Duncan Phyfe," and which has sometimes been described in nineteenth-century periodicals as "imitation ebony and gold." It is known that Mrs. Greene has been writing a book about this lovely furniture with its several scales, silk upholstery, and infinite variations; and that she has discovered its origins, heretofore vaguely identifiable as "made in Saxony." In an English publication in 1971, she referred to this as "the beautiful Waltershausen† furniture" which she dates as

* *English Dolls' Houses of the 18th and 19th Centuries*, Batsford, 1954.

† Waltershausen appears to have been a center for dolls' house furnishings of all kinds. The Gebrüder Schneegass firm, established in 1845, was in that Thuringian town (see pp. 314–17 and 335), and so, too, were makers of dolls' house inhabitants. The Colemans assert that "the finest grades of dolls were made in Waltershausen . . . Next to Sonneberg in importance as a doll center."

1820–80, and which she reports was "made in hundreds of designs and was exported in many thousands of crates to England as well as to the Continent." And, as she might well have added, to the United States.

An informative description relating to the making of what is apparently this furniture, the most coveted by all collectors, was given ca. 1874, by "W. H. Cremer Jun" in *The Toy Kingdom*, a small book, unfortunately with no illustrations, about the marvelous wares whose manufacture he was describing. Mr. Cremer, of the celebrated English toy shop family, described "the very simple process" the "Saxons" had invented

of giving Dolly's furniture a rich antique semblance. A drawing-room suite is displayed before me. Carefully made in white-wood, the several pieces of furniture are covered with designs printed on paper and coloured. It is a novel and cunning process. The sideboards and pianos seem like the real things, so well are the minutiae brought out. In some of the panels there are elegantly-coloured designs of birds and flowers, and sofas and chairs are covered with pink and blue silk.*

In addition to many different types of furniture illustrated in black-and-white and described in the text, more than two hundred chairs, each one different, and grouped in an attempt at chronology, country of origin, or purpose, are illustrated in color. The writer is pardonably (she hopes) proud of this assortment, all from her collection; the selection is offered with the realization that with one chair, it is usually possible to identify an entire set.

This type of grouping, in color, has also been utilized, to a more limited degree, with dolls'

* It is true that the reference to "elegantly-coloured designs of birds and flowers" more accurately describes the "French" furniture with its gaily multi-colored patterns, than the considerably more sedate "imitation ebony and gold." Perhaps Mr. Cremer's summary applies to both varieties.

INTRODUCTION

house dolls, those bisque immigrants who came to our shores in large numbers, and who deserve a book of their own. (Happily, I know of at least two, entirely different in character, which are in progress, and both of which are bound to be glorious.)

Dolls' house collectors, as well as the objects they collect, may be found in great variety. There are many kinds, collecting in various ways and to different degrees; and many of them like to examine dolls' houses from every possible vantage point, not only from the angle of a roof or the style of a window. Some of them are building their own houses and are looking for ideas; others are antiquarians, recapturing the past in miniature; still others are scholars, searching for relationships between small architecture and large, full-sized furniture and diminutive. Many of them are absorbed by all aspects of the subject, and are as arrested by the knowledge that Colleen Moore, for instance, had a dolls' house in 1924 which was not unlike her Bel Air mansion, as by the information that Whitney-Reed, in 1897, advertised a miniature coal yard.

Many collectors mix reproductions and antiques but are particular about period. Others will use only antiques (although this has become a costly method),* and will research carefully not only which pieces of furniture and accessories were to be found together at a given period,† but the manner in which they were arranged in the room.

The collectors who build their own houses and furniture have the pleasure of creating, but those of us who collect have the pleasure of discovery. Vivien Greene has noted that every dolls' house offers its own surprise, and all collectors must agree: every dolls' house of the

---

* The Augsburg Dolls' house collector Frau Negges who, in the seventeenth century collected so assiduously that she "did hurt to her estate," would have considerable company in the twentieth!

† An inventory of "Fair-y Villa," a lost dolls' house which must have been the most sumptuous of Victorian dolls' houses, should be helpful to all conscientious decorators of dolls' houses of the 1860's. Another, of a surviving house in the Newark Museum, although not as comprehensive, may be a useful guide to the furnishing of dolls' houses of the 1880's. Both inventories may be found in the Appendices.

Figure 7. One of a series of miniature stereopticon slides (1½ x 3″), early twentieth century, by the Metropolitan Syndicate Press, Chicago.

INTRODUCTION

past appears to have something special or engaging to recommend it. Such delights as sliding doors in Mrs. Fraser's ca. 1920 house (Fig. 64–5) come to mind,* or perhaps the flight of backstairs, provided for a retinue of bisque servants, in a huge dolls' house on the lawn of the late Mrs. Homer Strong in Rochester.

Osbert Lancaster, in *Here, of All Places*,† a marvelously funny compendium of architecture which he hilariously illustrated as well as wrote, included the following "Author's Note": "All the architecture in this book is completely imaginary, and no reference is intended to any actual building living or dead."

In the pages which follow, the converse of this objective is attempted: Only part of the architecture in *this* book is imaginary, and much of it is actual. Reference to any actual building "living or dead" is seized upon, and, if a resemblance is otherwise untenable, *imagined*.

However, one need only flutter through the illustrations in these pages to see that many dolls' houses resemble full-sized houses; just as conversely, by looking through books about life-size architecture, it is possible to see that many full-sized houses resemble dolls' houses.

Our theme of "historic preservation in miniature" may be well chosen, if it persuades a few additional antiquarians to add old dolls' houses to the list of "landmarks" to be preserved, and if it persuades even a few custodians to cherish these miniature three-dimensional documents, and to restore them (only) with moderation and love.

---

* There is a pair in the dolls' house in Williamsburg, and another in the Crane house in the Museum of the City of New York.

† Houghton Mifflin, 1958.

PART 1

HISTORIC PRESERVATION IN MINIATURE: Unique Examples

DOLLS' HOUSES
From New England

A "1780" HOUSE FROM MASSACHUSETTS

DATE: CA. 1810
HEIGHT (OVERALL): 50"
WIDTH: (INCLUDING BALCONIES) 51"
DEPTH: 18"
OWNER: MR. AND MRS. RAYMOND KNAPP (RHODE ISLAND)

Because of its architectural style, Mr. and Mrs. Knapp refer to this as their "1780 house"; the dealer from whom they acquired it told them it had been in the possession of the same Massachusetts family since *before* 1810. He also said that the family's name must remain unrevealed. Such regrettable silences, sometimes imposed by the owner of a treasure (not wishing other family members to know of its departure), and sometimes by the purchasing dealer (not caring to have the original owner learn details of the transaction), are hard on history. And it is especially unfortunate with respect to this unusual baby house.

If it is indeed ca. 1810, or before, and if it *was* made in the United States (for there is always the possibility that it crossed the ocean early on), it is, along with the pre-Revolutionary Van Cortlandt baby house, and the recent Cresson-Dickey discovery in Philadelphia (page 62), one of the three earliest American examples known to dolls' house history.

However, even without its genealogy, this is a charming and unusual house with its multiplicity of arched windows, and with its exquisitely turned balusters which comprise the cornice. The latter could assuredly relate to balustraded cornices to be seen on more than one four-square mansion designed by Samuel McIntire. The numerous arched windows seemed a figment of some exuberant dolls' house architect's imagination till a book about the architecture of the neighboring Piscataqua* yielded up, in Portsmouth, New Hampshire, a similar multiplicity of arched windows on a house traditionally attributed to no less an architect than Bulfinch. The five windows and door on the façade of the latter are not merely arched but Palladian, with narrow side openings on each side of the arched window. The Portsmouth Athenaeum, built in 1803 by John Peirce, also features arched windows (more frequently seen, on eighteenth-century houses, singly and over stair landings).

Although there is no entrance door on the façade of the dolls' house, there are glazed arched pairs of doors on the sides, each opening on to a small balcony. There are also arched wooden doors between the two lower rooms, and the Knapps have noticed a "faint outline under the wallpapers on the second floor" which leads them to suspect similar arched doors there.

It is known that the original owners refurbished the dolls' house for a charity exhibit

* *The Architectural Heritage of the Piscataqua* by John Mead Howells, Architectural Book Publishing Co., Inc., 1965.

Figure 8

Figure 9

"forty or fifty years ago," and much of the decoration and furnishing were presumably added at that time. The decoration of the two majestic downstairs rooms with their "twenty-foot" (twenty-inch) ceilings is quite beautiful, and the papers most unusual. The blue-and-white drawing-room is embellished with Wedgwood medallions on the walls and a Wedgwood strip on the face of the mantel. The paper panels fit the room space so exactly that the Knapps suspect it may have been hand-blocked. Not visible in the photograph are sixty-nine stars of a white enameled metal in the ceiling and upper walls. Mr. Knapp observed that the striking scenic wallpaper in the dining-room has always interested visitors, and he surmises that it may have been "cut down" from full-sized paper. An array of pictures hangs around the top of this room above a "plate rail" so high that dolls fond of art would be hard put to gaze upon them without a ladder.

These pictures came with the house along with an estimated 60 per cent of the furniture.

DOLLS' HOUSES FROM NEW ENGLAND

Among the latter are a number of Eric Pearson pieces, including most of the dining-room furniture.

Of particular interest is the handsome tester bed in the left-hand bedroom which has beneath it a paper label with the name and town of its maker in incised gilt letters: "Edwin B. Dutcher. Sheffield, Mass." (Mr. Knapp says the second line would do for the final line of an optometrist's test chart!) There are vestiges left of similar labels on the corner washstand, the chest of drawers, and the shaving mirror on top of it, all of meticulous workmanship. "At least ten years ago," after the house was acquired, Mr. Knapp succeeded in reaching by phone Mr. Dutcher's daughter-in-law who told him that although the craftsman was still living "at a very advanced age, he had not been active . . . for 'many years.' " Mr. Knapp feels that Mr. Dutcher's work of necessity would have preceded the charity exhibit, and believes that his contributions to the dolls' house would have been added by the middle or late 'twenties at the latest.

There are many treasures in the house, including crystal chandeliers reportedly brought from France several generations ago. There are two harps, one of them an Irish harp (often used to teach beginners). The "1780" house has its original lock, though a key had to be found for it. One wonders if it might not have been an approximation of the family mansion, built a generation or two after the latter was constructed. This would account for the discrepancy in the "before 1810" date associated with it (presumably not much before) and its earlier architecture.

"FOLK ART" AT THE SHELBURNE MUSEUM

DATE: EARLY NINETEENTH CENTURY
HEIGHT: 23¼"
WIDTH: 25¼"
DEPTH: 13"
OWNER: THE SHELBURNE MUSEUM (SHELBURNE, VERMONT)

It is not surprising that in addition to collecting full-sized buildings for her marvelous

Figure 10

HISTORIC PRESERVATION IN MINIATURE: UNIQUE EXAMPLES

museum at Shelburne, the late Mrs. J. Watson Webb was also attracted to miniature ones. There are many dolls' houses and shops and much miniaturia of all kinds in the collection, but somehow, in all her years of collecting, Mrs. Webb found only one American dolls' house. It is displayed unfurnished, labeled as "Folk Art," and it assuredly has the lovely naïveté of the genre.

Its history is regrettably lost, but the house clearly speaks for itself as a modest reflection of Federal architecture, a toy representation of a classic one might have found on a street in New York or Philadelphia early in the nineteenth century. Although it is essentially a square wooden box with a door and windows painted on the removable front, the effect is an appealing approximation of trompe l'oeil. The façade is framed like a picture (the molding is its only extra-dimensional aspect), and the "picture" itself, as the illustration suggests, consists of a panelled door with pilasters and a fanlight, a sizeable bull's eye window, and four twelve-light windows with tall lintels. In the windows are painted curtains and shades as evanescent as the past itself.

The interior is similarly unassuming with simply painted fireplaces, two of them black "marbled" and two white, the one in the kitchen somewhat larger than the others. But what gives the interior additional distinction are the recessed arches (two-dimensional like the exterior frame), one to each room, with their own free-hand decoration—a simple gilt vine on a dark green background.

Everything has the patina and the dim beauty of extreme old age—we long to know when the house was made and where. Assuredly it is early nineteenth century. It may owe its survival unrestored to the fact that children prefer more realistic toy houses, as anyone knows who has heard a child complain (as I have more than once) of the lack of a staircase in even quite a grand house with proper windows and doors.

Perhaps this one lay hidden, for generations, in some obscure attic. Whatever its story, we can be grateful that no one felt the need to "freshen" its painted walls—a faded rose in one room, a faded green in another, with colors equally modified by time in the remaining two.

Once this winsome house must have contained furniture, highly prized, behind a lock to which the key, alas, is forever lost.

THE WARREN HOUSE AT SALEM

DATE: CA. 1852
HEIGHT: 6'
WIDTH: 5'
DEPTH: 20"
OWNER: THE ESSEX INSTITUTE (SALEM, MASSACHUSETTS)

This formidable baby house, infused with history, was planned by Annie Crowninshield Warren,* and it contains among its furnishings such historic treasure as a mahogany drop-leaf table in the dining-room "said to have been captured from a British ship in the War of 1812 by the Crowninshield privateer ship *America*." The hapless British vessel was "all fitted with furniture, brocades, and even toys for a family going to India, and this little table was going to India."

This arresting notation is part of a detailed history of the dolls' house which Mrs. C. H. Gibson, one of Mrs. Warren's daughters, thoughtfully provided when she presented her childhood possession to Essex in 1925. Mrs. Warren had had the house built for her four daughters about 1852 by a Salem cabinetmaker who had done a great deal of work for her. The façade is not shown here, but when it is in place, each of its deep glazed windows corresponds to a room inside. A door with top light and sidelights opens into the downstairs staircase

* Mrs. J. Mason Warren.

Figure 11

hall. (This door originally bore a brass plate with "Warren" on it * which had disappeared when I first saw the house many years ago,† and a doorbell.) Even without its façade in place, the pointed dormers, like the peaks of witches' hats, seem appropriate to Salem, and give the dolls' house a special flavor.

* Such name plates seem to have been to some degree traditional on dolls' houses of that period and region; in the Society for the Preservation of New England Antiquities in Boston, one small door bears a silver plate marked "Estelle." A later house, in the author's collection, has a silver plate on each of the doors; one with the owner's name, "Gertrude," and the other "1904" (Fig. 59).

† I remember being told that years before there had been a regrettable dolls' housebreaking, with books from the library among the stolen goods.

The house is a faithful reflection of an aristocratic Boston residence of its day, and the library is actually copied from the one in the Warren house at 2 Park Street, Boston, which was torn down about 1876, "for business purposes," with only this dolls' house replica to commemorate it, along with Mrs. Gibson's description:

Tall oak bookcases on either side of the fireplace reaching nearly to the ceiling, with marble busts on top. Red silk curtains cover the front, as there were not enough books to fill them. A red velvet valance with gold fringe hung from the mantel, over which was a mirror with beautiful carved gold frame. A

HISTORIC PRESERVATION IN MINIATURE: UNIQUE EXAMPLES

quaint English grate with coal in it, and clock and figures on the mantelpiece. On left of room a little real square piano, and sofa on opposite side, the furniture being the same color as the bookcases and covered with rich velvet. A round table in middle of room with a tiny pack of cards on it, and equally small books bound in red leather printed in French and (I think) dated 1825. In front of the fireplace stood a small chess table carved in black and white ivory with legs like a stag's antlers, and on it a little green box containing the chessmen no larger than a grain of rice.

"The affection the Warrens felt for their dolls' house," as I once wrote, "as well as the years of attentive interest they must have lavished upon it, is apparent to the most cursory inspection. There are monograms, exquisitely worked, on approximately everything entitled to a monogram: tablecloths and napkins in the pantry; sheets and pillowcases in the bedroom—all are marked with "W." Mrs. Warren worked the drawing-room carpet to represent Aubusson; roses and leaves on a white ground. But this and a handsome firescreen nearby are only a fraction of her contributions, which undoubtedly included such gossamer needlework as bedspreads and matching curtains, blue satin in the 'Mother's room,' and cherry satin in the 'Eldest daughter's'—with satin slippers to match!"

Doll hands as well as doll feet were provided for. Inside a tall desk in the dining-room, Mrs. Gibson recorded, is "a walnut shell with white gloves enclosed which was handed to Mrs. Warren at her engagement dinner." This bit of intelligence suggests that Mrs. Warren was caught up in miniatures well before her four daughters appeared on the scene, a fact oft-noted with respect to parents, prospective or existing, of dolls' house owners.

Although few dolls may be seen in the illustration, the house was originally well populated, including "black Dinah," who may be seen in the kitchen on her own settee. Dinah undoubtedly needed to rest after her climb to the strangely located pantry in the second-floor hall. This curiously located pantry is perhaps the only feature of the dolls' house not quite typical of a proper Boston mansion of the period!

The Essex Institute has a splendid collection of dolls' houses, including Bessie Lincoln's (Fig. 31), and a somewhat later one, dating from the turn of the century, with gables, turrets, bays and a very American front porch.* It seems of special interest in these pages that this dolls' house was built by a local carpenter from the plans of a Salem house believed to have burned in the Salem fire of 1914. Mrs. Lawrence S. Philbrick, to whom the house was given when she was a little girl, many years ago supplied the picture given here, along with some amusing details regarding the early history of her toy. The dolls' house, it seemed, was occupied by a family named Sterling, "for the very simple reason," Mrs. Philbrick wrote, "that that was one of the first words I learned to spell (from the back of spoons), and thought 'Mr.' Sterling a very remarkable man to have made so many pretty things!"

* The porch is not in view in the illustration shown.

Figure 12

DOLLS' HOUSES FROM NEW ENGLAND

THE PICKERING-DODGE-DEVEREUX BABY HOUSE

DATE: (HOUSE) 1860
(FURNISHINGS) EIGHTEENTH AND NINETEENTH CENTURIES
HEIGHT: 5'
WIDTH: 4'
OWNER: SOCIETY FOR THE PRESERVATION OF NEW ENGLAND ANTIQUITIES (BOSTON)

In 1860, a foresighted woman named Marianne Cabot Devereux Silsbee decided that there were so many things of historic interest in her family baby house, hitherto arranged in a bookcase, that she commissioned Paul of Boston, a well-known cabinetmaker of that time, to build a proper miniature residence to contain them.

Her wisdom resulted in the preservation of four generations of dolls' house furnishings, some of it the earliest documented dolls' house furniture in the United States. This includes a Chippendale settee and four matching chairs (illustrated) played with by Lucia Pickering, born at Salem in 1747.* The house and its contents were presented to the Society in 1921 by Frederick Silsbee Whitwell, in memory of his daughter Gertrude, the last child to play with the house, who died aged twelve, in 1908.

Mr. Whitwell wrote that his daughter had added nothing to the house "except one little pair of pewter candlesticks which are copied from old ones, and are on the dining-room table. The contents of this dolls' house has been played with from 1750 down to 1908, and its historical interest is great on that account. The furniture of each period is marked in its style and dates from the actual period when that kind of furniture was made."

The house itself is architecturally unassuming. The glazed front which protects the six rooms makes only one concession to exterior architecture; the two bedrooms on the third floor are contained beneath a deep mansard roof. Although the windows, one in each room, are merely suggested by black paint rather than glass within the well-constructed framing, they are of particular interest since they were made to fit the curtains used in the original "desk-bookcase." * The dotted net curtains in the two bedrooms are undoubtedly later additions, but the green moiré draperies in the dining-room, and the delicately brocaded pair in the drawing-room may well be originals, along with the green upholstery on the chairs.

The floor coverings include two needlepoint carpets, worked by Mrs. Silsbee when she commissioned the house in 1860, one of them in the drawing-room and the other in the library. At that time Mrs. Silsbee also had family portraits photographed and framed, and these early examples of miniature photography, several of them visible on the dining-room walls, were, in 1921, still in the possession of the Silsbee, Crowninshield,† and Whitwell families. The one of Eliza Devereux is by Stuart. Also on the walls, are numerous small landscapes, obviously framed and photographed at the same time.

Well-made wooden cornices crown the draperies, especially an elegant gold-leaf specimen in the drawing-room; and Paul of Boston was also clearly responsible for the tall arched over-mantel mirrors which are built in and framed with harmonizing moldings, including one of gold leaf ornately carved to match the drawing-room

---

* She was married in Salem in 1776 to Israel Dodge of Salem and died there in 1822.

* Undoubtedly what we think of today as a "secretary," or as it is known in English cabinetwork, a secretaire. This piece was still in the family when Mr. Whitwell wrote the history of the baby house in 1921, being then in the possession of Miss Natalie Whitwell.

† Mrs. Silsbee's daughter, born at Salem in 1840, was Mary Crowninshield Silsbee. It is of interest to note that the Warren house was also built by a Salem cabinetmaker in 1852, and that Mrs. Warren was born Annie Crowninshield. Clearly there was much dolls' house activity in Salem at mid-century, especially amongst Crowninshields!

Figure 13

Figure 14

Figure 15

(22)

Figure 16

Figure 17

pear to date from the 1860 period of the house.

We are indebted to Mr. Whitwell's 1921 summary for the history of the furniture to be seen in this house. Mr. Whitwell's grandmother had told him that a dining-room table and sideboard originally had accompanied the Chippendale chairs and settee, but "through the length of years," had disappeared. Although there is danger in oral traditions, the accuracy of this one appears to be borne out by the style of the replacements Mrs. Silsbee had commissioned. These two pieces, which can be seen in the photograph, bear the substantial proportions to be found in a substantial household at mid-century, and one suspects that Paul of Boston, or someone apprenticed to him, may

HISTORIC PRESERVATION IN MINIATURE: UNIQUE EXAMPLES

have fashioned these. In a lesser dolls' house, such handsome pieces, with a known history, would receive ecstatic acclaim. Unfortunately, in the company of the delicate Chippendale, and the numerous treasures to be seen in all the rooms, one tends to overlook them, though with their generous proportions they are not easily overlooked.

However, it is necessary to challenge Mr. Whitwell's belief that the "Chinese Chippendale" bedroom furniture (in the left-hand bedroom) originated in the eighteenth century along with Lucia Pickering's dining-room furniture. This set, which (as its photograph suggests) is most unusual and appealing, consists of a two-drawer chest, a commode, a secretaire, four chairs, and a sleigh bed, all charmingly lacquered with pagodas, trees, and Oriental personages, in shades of rust and gold on black. As Mr. Richard Nylander, Curator of Collections at the Society, points out, the furniture is not Chinese Chippendale in style. He admires the sleigh bed which is "a true sleigh bed," to fit against the wall, with no design on the back. However, the American sleigh bed did not appear till ca. 1820.*

As for the chairs, in the writer's collection are Victorian chairs of identical shape with upholstery in lieu of the unusual lacquered design on the backs and seats of these. One suspects that this set is a mid-nineteenth-century reference to Admiral Perry's treaty with Japan, and the resulting deluge of Oriental objects in the United States, rather than to the mid-eighteenth-century popularity of "Chinese Chippendale."

Despite this lapse, it is of interest to consider the remainder of Mr. Whitwell's summary: The next owner of the early dolls' furniture was the daughter of Lucia Pickering, Eliza Dodge, born at Salem, December 14, 1785. To find the second owner as well as the first born in the eighteenth century is extraordinary in American dolls' house circles! She was married at Salem in 1809 to Humphrey Devereux, and died there in 1828. The pink Empire drawing-room set, the Empire bedroom set with the Empire curtains were all added by her. In the drawer of the bureau is a cork doll, about an inch long. The doll was always kept in that drawer, and Mr. Whitwell's grandmother . . . told him that the doll was there when she was a little girl in the first of the nineteenth century and had one arm gone then. Mr. Nylander was kind enough to open the drawer and the tiny doll was still there. It is not cork, but actually the most perfect of "peg woodens," fully articulated and, as described, the arm was missing.*

The lovely Empire furniture has survived in a remarkable state of preservation. The bed, of the type the French might have described as a "lit à couronne," and which was made, in miniature, in many later versions, is rare with its brocaded upholstery and net curtains stretched from the small canopy to the ends of the bed (placed lengthwise against the wall). The bed unfortunately cannot be seen in the illustration, but there is an elaborate gilt paper ornament at the crest of the canopy, and an unusually wide gilt paper strip across the base. Seemingly pristine gilt paper embellishments are on the chairbacks, and gilt strips edge the pillows (Fig. 16). The shapes in this make of dolls' house furniture were evidently made the same way, with only minor variations, during several decades of the nineteenth century. The form of the chairs is especially constant. A mirror is fastened to the back of the bed.

---

* According to the Bogers (*The Dictionary of Antiques and the Decorative Arts*), "the design for this type of bed was inspired by contemporary French Empire models."

* These tiny, early peg woodens are rare but can be found. One in the writer's collection was wearing a baby dress when found which perhaps helped prevent so small a doll (not preserved in a drawer as this one was) from slipping out of sight entirely.

DOLLS' HOUSES FROM NEW ENGLAND

The Whitwell account continues: "It is easy to see what furniture was added by Marianne Cabot Devereux. The early Victorian, between 1830 and 1860; the red plush and black chairs, the blue tufted furniture, the wax flowers under glass, etc., were all Victorian and Louis Philippe things, added by her, for her daughter, Mary Crowninshield Silsbee. . . ."

The dating of these pieces appears to be entirely reliable. There is a variety, they are choice indeed, and all of them are rare. In more than twenty-five years of collecting, I have not previously seen the Biedermeier* chairs and sofa with blue-tufted seats and backs. This curious tufting, set within the usual gilt-patterned dark frame, appears to be of some embossed and painted composition. It is very pretty and, like the Empire furniture, is beautifully preserved. The plush furniture with its black-washed filigree metal frames is likely to be found in dolls' houses dating from the second quarter of the nineteenth century. The sofa seen here in "pink" is also known in dark blue. The "easy chair" is unusual, but the chair with circular padded back most certainly is rarer still.

Apart from its considerable historical aspects, this is a house laden with treasures. Never before has this collector encountered the lighting fixture which hangs in the dining-room, a clay (?) chandelier on chains, with three fonts in the Greek Revival idiom, and undoubtedly inspired by that early-nineteenth-century predilection. The house is abundant with mid-nineteenth-century Biedermeier, including a pair of bookcases in the library, and a cabinet rich in the familiar gilt embellishment of the genre in the drawing-room. Candy-box furniture is frequently found in old dolls' houses, but the elaborate prie-dieu of this origin in one of the bedrooms is a beguiling and certainly early example.

Similar choice pieces undoubtedly have wandered away, along with the two dining-room pieces, over the years. Since more than two hundred years are involved, as well as generations of children, this is not surprising. What is remarkable is that so much remains, and in such a glorious state of preservation, and that, as in a "real" house, generations of furniture mingle.

One usually avoids the patronizing "real" to differentiate a house built for people rather than for dolls, but here the word is used to emphasize the reality of time as well as objects which exist in this choicest of heirlooms. The mark of several generations is frequently found upon dolls' houses of the past, but here the span has been most marvelously lengthy and, therefore, most marvelously historic.

More marvelously still, this history was cherished and preserved.

THE BREWSTER CUPBOARD HOUSE

DATE: CA. 1860's
HEIGHT: 80″
WIDTH: 40″
DEPTH: 19½″
OWNER: PLYMOUTH ANTIQUARIAN SOCIETY (MASSACHUSETTS)

Certainly no such frivolity as a dolls' house came over on the *Mayflower*, and therefore such a specimen as this is as close to Plymouth Rock as dolls' house history is likely to come. Not only is this huge house permanently, and appropriately, ensconced in Plymouth, but its history, ancestrally speaking, is impeccable. It was played with by two generations of the Kingston, Massachusetts, branch of the Brewster family, descendants of the *Mayflower*'s Elder William Brewster.

As its photograph indicates, the simple cup-

---

* The German term here is a reference to the German manufacture, although it is also a term this writer prefers to assign to the imitation rosewood which was made in so many styles. The Empire toy furniture which has been described was certainly made in France.

HISTORIC PRESERVATION IN MINIATURE: UNIQUE EXAMPLES

board-style house with its hipped roof is properly Puritan in spirit, although many generations of Brewsters had come and gone before it came into being in the 'sixties. (One says "came into being" because somehow it is difficult to picture the actual building of such a curious structure, with its storage drawer casually inserted between the first and second floors.) Glass windows on the sides are the only concession other than the attic roof to "architecture."

The old wallpapers in each of the rooms, possibly from the 'eighties when the house was "refurbished for a second generation," supply a great deal of warmth and character, and it is a pity that the house cannot be shown in color. A mustard gold with Indian red print in the kitchen and pantry provides a handsome background for pots and andirons reportedly made in a local foundry. Miss Rose Briggs, the Curator at Plymouth, thinks this may have been Cobb & Drew's in Kingston, which still exists. She notes that in the first half of the nineteenth century the area was "full of iron works."

A floral print with a rusty red background sets off green tufted furniture in the parlor, and the bedroom, with lettuce green walls, is bordered with a most unusual mustard pattern. One of the finest pieces of furniture in the house is in this room, the tester bed with rope spring and delicately reeded posts. The scale of this bed which could engulf two such Biedermeier secretaries as the one in the parlor give a true dolls' house character to a miniature residence with an unmistakable New England flavor.

A duplicate of the iron stove in the kitchen* may be seen more clearly nearby in Fig. 207.

THE DEXTER MANSION

DATE: CA. 1860's
HEIGHT (INCLUDING CUPOLA): 40"
WIDTH: 32"
DEPTH: 17"
OWNER: HISTORICAL SOCIETY OF OLD NEWBURY (NEWBURYPORT, MASSACHUSETTS)

The history of the Dexter dolls' house is known: who built it and for whom, as well as, approximately, when. All the details are available except for the one we most long to possess: Why is this called "the Dexter dolls' house"?

Figure 18e

* Author's collection.

Figure 19

"Lord" Timothy Dexter, a self-styled nobleman and eccentric of Newburyport, Massachusetts, acquired, in 1798, a splendid estate on High Street. He added a formidable cupola to the mansion itself, and some extraordinary "improvements" to the grounds. As the early postcard view indicates, these included fifteen-foot pedestals on which stood motley statues, all brightly painted from the gaudy palette of a young ship's carver. Among these were Washington, Franklin, Napoleon, Jack Tar, Louis XVI, George III, a unicorn, Adam and Eve in the Garden, several lions (with a lamb to lie down beside them!), and, of course, one of Lord Timothy himself.*

Perhaps it is possible to perceive why, with such a colorful figure looming on the miniature horizon, a dolls' house historian might long to make a less tenuous connection between the Dexter dolls' house and the Dexter house than the fact that both have captain's walks and cupolas with weathervanes.

However, apart from these two features in common, there is no recorded fact to relate the eighteenth-century mansion and the nineteenth-century plaything.

---

* Novelist John Marquand wrote a life of Timothy Dexter.

It is known that a Newburyport druggist named Charles M. Hodge, who lived at 126 High Street, and had his apothecary shop at the corner of State and Charter Streets, built the lovely dolls' house for his daughters, Effie Carolina and Annie. Effie was born in 1857; and it may be assumed that he built it within the next ten years. Although the Hodges were High Street neighbors of the Dexter house and Mr. Hodge might readily have copied the mansion, neither the arched windows nor the dormers bear the slightest resemblance to the rectangular windows on the Dexter house, and although it has for a very long time been known as the Dexter dolls' house, no one seems to know why.

Nevertheless, it is, as its photograph suggests, charming, and we must be grateful for its survival as well as for a portion of its history. The pleasing lemon yellow exterior with white trim appears to be the original. Not visible in the photograph is the weathervane on the cupola. "The latter is an arrow which swings," says Frieda Marion, who also furnished this incidental intelligence: "The ceilings of the upper rooms are made of slats, painted white, a fact which is really noticeable only to dolls living in the house, and to curious dolls' house collectors."

Figure 20

Figure 21

The façade lifts off, and although there is relatively little of an architectural nature within, barely in view, between the windows in each room, is a small shelf. Mrs. Marion's theory is that these were the intended location for a small Franklin stove, and she points out that the placement of the chimneys "would bear out" her theory, along with the presence, in the parlor of such a stove (not visible in the photograph). She also observed that the windows have glass which slides into place on the inside of the house (this practical method of "glazing," also to be seen in more than one house, may be a useful tip to present-day builders in miniature).

As the photograph indicates, the furniture is mostly of the Gebrüder Schneegass variety,* and is considerably later than the house. The outstanding piece, in the parlor and not as visible as might be wished, is the piano with green

* See Figs. 388–90.

DOLLS' HOUSES FROM NEW ENGLAND

plush-seated stool which was made by Mr. Hodge, and which is so marked (upon a long-ago label stuck on). The top folds back to show the harp with tiny threads stretched in the manner of proper pianos.

Mrs. Marion notes that "Mr. Hodge must have been a joy to his daughters as there are other pieces of furniture in the museum which he made for them, although these are too large for the dolls' house." In 1876, he built an attractive model of Independence Hall which came to the society in 1913 through his daughter, who was recorded as "Effie Carolina Hodge Currier," a member of the Boston Tea Party Chapter of the D.A.R., and it may be seen, along with the dolls' house, at the Society's headquarters in the Cushing House. It is possible that Mrs. Currier gave the dolls' house and other toys to the Society at the same time.*

Since my visit to the museum, a new curator has taken over, and has discovered two other old dolls' houses on the premises, one in the cellar and one in the attic. They are large and rather plain, according to Mrs. Marion, but they have been set up with furniture owned by the Society, and a future dolls' house historian may wish to investigate *their* histories.

A CIVIL WAR RESIDENCE

DATE: CA. 1863
HEIGHT (WITHOUT STAND): 45″
WIDTH: 36¼″
DEPTH: 18¼″
OWNER: FAIRFIELD HISTORICAL SOCIETY (FAIRFIELD, CONNECTICUT)

Although the rather unassuming, no-nonsense façade of the Glover house will win no

Figure 22

Figure 23

---

* It is remembered that Mrs. Currier used to visit the Society, then at a different location, and dust the dolls' house furniture with a piece of fur! (An excellent tip to dolls' housekeepers, and supplemental to the Chicago Art Institute's use of watercolor brushes to clean the Thorne Rooms.)

HISTORIC PRESERVATION IN MINIATURE: UNIQUE EXAMPLES

prizes for its proportions, it has "real" rain gutters, and a history.

Members of Company K, 17th Regiment, Connecticut Volunteers, built the house while they were confined in a Confederate prison. They had been sent things from home by Mr. Samuel Glover in wooden packing boxes. The appreciative soldiers used the boxes to construct the house, and returned Mr. Glover's favor by sending the result to his daughter, Miss Deborah Anna Glover.*

There are six rooms and a hall, and one admires the charming bravado of the elaborately carved floral spray with which the soldiers crowned their handiwork.

A HOUSE FROM PORTSMOUTH, NEW HAMPSHIRE

DATE: MID-NINETEENTH CENTURY
HEIGHT (NOT INCLUDING CHIMNEYS AND CAPTAIN'S WALK): 35½"
WIDTH (NOT INCLUDING BAYS): 25½"
DEPTH: 24½"
OWNER: THE STRONG MUSEUM (ROCHESTER, NEW YORK)

Bereft of its foundation, if it ever had one, and with a pair of bays on each side of its upper story projecting like a pair of ears, this brown sandstone house has other comic aspects, including the tiny widow's walk perched like a small tiara upon the head of a two-hundred-pound widow. Actually, one might better refer to a captain's walk with respect to a dolls' house which hails from the seacoast town of Portsmouth, New Hampshire. Since Portsmouth is celebrated for its eighteenth-century architecture, one can only hope it will not be embarrassed by identification with this blatant piece from the mid-nineteenth century.

* The aunt of Miss Deborah Norris Glover and Mrs. Allen Johnson who presented the house to the Society.

Figure 24

It is a dolls' house with a great deal of vitality, and one of very few to contain a vestibule. Inside the strangely patterned double doors, there is space enough for a doll or two to come in out of the rain and wait for the inner doors to be opened.

There is red glass in the light over this front entrance, and red glass may also be seen in the lower sashes of the windows in the concave mansard roof. Perhaps this stained glass prevented glare from the sea one might well have viewed from such a height.*

The doors and fishscale-patterned roof are painted gray. The cornice and coigning embellish a house which has been somewhat coarsened by many coats of paint, but which like most buildings of its era, full-sized or miniature, has a personality entirely of its own.

* Mrs. James Timpson has a house with a blue glass window in the gable and observes that she has seen blue lights in seaside houses, but has not found the reason.

DOLLS' HOUSES FROM NEW ENGLAND

A SOMERVILLE, MASSACHUSETTS, MANSION

DATE: MID-NINETEENTH CENTURY
HEIGHT (INCLUDING CORNICE, NOT INCLUDING ROOF AND CHIMNEYS): 50¼″
WIDTH (INCLUDING EAVES): 44″
DEPTH (INCLUDING EAVES): 23½″
OWNER: AUTHOR'S COLLECTION

The idiosyncrasies of old dolls' houses are endlessly fascinating to those who study them. This example from New England offers more than its share of possibilities, especially when it is compared to the Tiffany-Platt (see page 116) from New York.

When it was offered, it was described as a copy of "an existing house" * in Somerville, Massachusetts. When it arrived, it was clear that its plans, its proportions, and even its very dimensions bore a striking resemblance to the Tiffany-Platt. "It was almost," I once wrote, "as though a cousin in Massachusetts had sent a sketch to a cousin in New York." And I might have added that there is always the possibility that a dolls' house plan was published in a periodical of the day, inspiring subscribers in different regions to reach for their hammers (or to send for their carpenters).

In both houses, there is the same arrangement of rooms; and, with minor differences, of windows; and such details as bracketed cornices under the eaves and double chimneys on the pitched rooftops are common to both. The two houses also diverge in striking ways.

Where the Tiffany-Platt has its charmingly over-scaled stoop (with sitting-room for owner and friend), Somerville substitutes a practical feature of another sort: a storage drawer which flanks each side of the well-scaled stairs and double doors. Despite their panelled perfection, these doors are no more operable than the gray-green trompe l'oeil entrance door of the Tiffany, but there is a doorbell and a red glass toplight above them. The windows, as well as these doors, are made with more elaboration than those of the Tiffany-Platt, on which the sash bars are painted. Here the framework and sash bars are stained (walnut, I think), with outer frames and pedimented lintels painted dark brown as they are on the Tiffany-Platt. Another similarity: both houses are buff with dark brown rooftops to match the trim.

In their interiors, the differences are even fewer, though the Tiffany has an English

*With the passage of time, of course, the likelihood of this possibility diminishes.

Figure 25

HISTORIC PRESERVATION IN MINIATURE: UNIQUE EXAMPLES

basement while the first floor ceilings of the Somerville are of normal height. The Somerville's rooms are papered, while the Tiffany's are painted.

Although this is one of the few houses (in more than twenty-five years of collecting) which have come to this collector purportedly with original furnishings, most of the contents when it arrived were either damaged, or of considerably later vintage than the house itself. The elegant double drawing-room,* with its twin fireplaces, contains several of the most important pieces which were salvaged, including one of a pair of twin chandeliers and, between the fireplaces, the early Biedermeier marble-topped chest.

Two partial sets of iron parlor furniture have been added; combined to supply twin sofas, a pair of "easy chairs" (which we now call "gentlemen's chairs"), a pair of ottomans, and a set of side chairs in the popular balloon shape. All of these pieces retain their red flocked "upholstery." The center table with its lyre-shaped pedestal supporting a top "marbled" with paint, and the cheval glass with the patent date of "Feb. 8, 1867" on the back of the frame, are also part of this parlor set.

The pair of "looking-glasses" over the mantels, a square pianoforte (with black and white keys reversed, as they frequently were on full-sized pianos in earlier days), and many pictures and accessories have been added.

The most remarkable piece of furniture which came with the house is the unpainted card table with its original label, that of Samuel Hersey of Hingham, Massachusetts. This rare table, placed in the third floor sitting-room, may be seen in Fig. 351–2.

---

* This room is shown, and the story of the furniture described in detail, on pages 301–2.

A HISTORIC "REPLICA" FROM PROVIDENCE

DATE: CA. 1870
HEIGHT: 4'7½"
WIDTH (BELOW ROOF): 3'7½"
DEPTH (BELOW ROOF): 2'3½"
OWNER: MRS. LYTTON W. DOOLITTLE (RHODE ISLAND)

This big oak* house from Providence, Rhode Island is unassuming architecturally, but it is substantial, to say the least, and it is accompanied by the tradition, always intriguing, that it is a "replica" of an actual house. It is also a historic dolls' house, having been in the family of Henry Lippitt, a former Rhode Island governor, for longer than any of its members can remember. Mrs. Doolittle, a granddaughter of the Governor, believes it to be "a model of the Lippit-Bowen house on Benefit Street built by Tefft † which happens to be the same as the . . . house (also Tefft)" next door to her on Hope Street.

* The oak is stained, again in the tradition of a number of nineteenth-century dolls' houses built in New England (Figs. 31, 32 and 35).

† Mrs. Doolittle helpfully supplied the following information about Thomas A. Tefft who "was born in 1826 and died in Florence, Italy, in 1859. Very young. He practiced in Providence around 1853."

Figure 26

DOLLS' HOUSES FROM NEW ENGLAND

Although the third story to be seen on both the Benefit and Hope Street houses is absent on the dolls' house, there are several resemblances. The Hope Street windows with their flat lintels are similar to those on the dolls' house, while part of the Benefit Street lintels are pedimented; but the Benefit Street entrance door, with simple cornice and flat pilasters, more closely resembles the dolls' house entrance than does the one with its small columned porch on Hope. Both the Hope Street house and the miniature one have dentelated roof cornices.

Perhaps it would be conservative to say that the oak dolls' house bears a family resemblance to both brick houses, and that if Tefft had built a dolls' house, this is the one he might well have built. Perhaps he did! "None of us can remember much about exactly where it came from"; according to Mrs. Doolittle "it has been here all my life. My mother was born in 1861 and it must have been built during her youth."

Vivien Greene* has coped with the matter of "replica houses" in England and has, "in most instances," found the tradition "that they were . . . copies of family houses . . . to be a fable." As an alternative, she has come up with a

* op. cit.

Figure 28

Figure 29

Figure 27

(33)

charming theory: "In most cases this is merely a most natural assumption. Perhaps it is only a remembrance of some nursery game played by great-aunts and great-uncles long ago ('This was grandpapa's house and this is Aunt Florence . . .')." However, even though most of the so-called replica houses are, as I have mentioned elsewhere, "approximations," often, in many details, if not in all, they bear sophisticated resemblances; and with our full-sized houses disappearing before our eyes, we must be grateful for these. Frequently, alas, when the dolls' house remains but the history is gone, a piece of architecture so specific survives that one knows the house, to a substantial degree, *was* a copy, a replica, and we long to discover whether the original still stands or, more frequently, where it stood.

Unfortunately, the interiors of *this* miniature house cannot be seen in any detail on the available photographs. There is a good staircase, and the rooms, as the measurements suggest, are unusually deep, allowing the one at the lower left to be divided by double panelled doors, and the others with curtains. There are wooden mantels in the back rooms on both floors, with mirrors above. The original furniture has not remained with the house, but Mrs. Doolittle has been furnishing it "gradually with Victorian,

Figure 30

which has been great fun, finding odd pieces here and there." Echoes from multitudinous kindred spirits may be heard.

Mrs. Doolittle has in her possession another miniature house which is highly architectural, even more historic, and undoubtedly a truer model than this one. It is a copy of her own house, next door to the Hope Street house which is described, and it was built by Governor Lippit in 1860–64.* However, she insists that this small house "is just a shell and was used in back generations in which to keep white mice"! This is a most beautiful "shell" indeed, with an exquisite entrance porch above circular stairs, an elaborate pedimented roof, and a sizeable and elegant oval wing. It is to be hoped that the mice were comfortable.

THE BESSIE LINCOLN HOUSE

DATE: 1876
HEIGHT: 69″
WIDTH: 52″
DEPTH: 23″
OWNER: ESSEX INSTITUTE (SALEM, MASSACHUSETTS)

Elsewhere† I have referred to the fact that dolls' houses often reflect a regional type of dolls' house architecture as well as regional architecture in full size. This has been especially evident in Massachusetts and Rhode Island where the wood of which a dolls' house was built was sometimes left unpainted both inside and out. The sizeable Bessie Lincoln house is a striking example.

The house was built in the Centennial year of 1876 for young Bessie Lincoln of Salem, Massa-

---

* Several letters had been exchanged with Mrs. Doolittle, over a period of several months, before, with a question about this "mouse house," I learned that her grandfather had been "at one time" a Rhode Island governor. (A dolls' house associated with another Rhode Island governor is described in *A History of Doll's Houses*, Scribner's, 1965.)

† See page 40.

DOLLS' HOUSES FROM NEW ENGLAND

Figure 31

chusetts, who had been born in 1868, and who, at the age of eighty-five (in 1953), presented her treasured plaything to the Essex Institute. In her letter offering the dolls' house to Essex, Bessie Lincoln Potter wrote that the dolls' house had been built by a carpenter by the name of Ayers, or Ayres.

"Some of the Salem ladies joined with my mother in furnishing the house," she recalled. "It would give me great pleasure to know that the dolls' house was in Salem—where I had a happy childhood."

The Salem ladies who joined Bessie's mother in furnishing the house were thorough indeed. From the nursery on the top floor (which can be reached logically by a flight of stairs) to the downstairs hall, there are many choice objects. Especially rare in dolls' house scale is the "toy perambulator" in the front hall. This is the type one associates with the Vermont Novelty Works and Joel Ellis. A number of toy manufacturers were turning these out in the 'sixties and 'seventies, but in large sizes. In Ellis, Britton & Eaton's 1869 "Illustrated Price List," a very similar four-wheeled perambulator is advertised as "a new article, just brought out." Clearly these were far larger than the one in the dolls' house since the catalogue states that it "is large enough for a mammoth doll."

For comparison with the Bessie Lincoln house, the author's Massachusetts house, smaller in scale (46″ high, 45″ wide, and 19″ deep) seems of interest. Although this house has been "decorated" with old papers and a true feeling for period, presumably in recent years, the exterior was left as found. In addition to the

HISTORIC PRESERVATION IN MINIATURE: UNIQUE EXAMPLES

Figure 32

unpainted wood, there are several other striking similarities to the Bessie Lincoln house, notably the same open front plan with an identical arrangement of rooms. The attic room on this smaller house has a lift-out section with stained glass window. Both houses have bases incised to resemble stone foundations. (See Fig. 35.)

The principal difference between them, apart from scale, is the rooftop: a mansard complete with chimneys on the Bessie Lincoln, and a pitched roof surmounted by a captain's walk on the anonymous house in the author's collection. The latter roof would have been, of course, much at home in Salem, and it is agreeable to speculate that it, too, may stem from Salem and the hand of Mr. Ayers or Ayres.

The tiny two-room house (13″ high, 13¼″ wide, and 11″ deep) was found in a Boston antiques shop. It is wallpapered within, with papers which appear to be original, but the exterior is of dark, varnished wood very like the house with the captain's walk. The owner has always wondered whether this small house, not much more than a square box with windows on three sides and a charming arched front door (with a keystone above the frame) might not once have had a roof section which lifted off, and perhaps even a foundation which the main section sat upon. (Whether or not it did, one offers this as a rather purposeful plan for constructing a portable dolls' house!)

"46 HUNT," BEVERLY, MASSACHUSETTS

DATE: MID-NINETEENTH CENTURY
HEIGHT: 39″
WIDTH (INCLUDING EAVES): 18¼″
DEPTH (INCLUDING EAVES): 18¼″
OWNER: AUTHOR'S COLLECTION

Because this winsome house has "46" and "Hunt" painted on its double doors, these hieroglyphics were construed, when it arrived from Massachusetts in 1963, as an address. Clearly, it seemed, the "46" was the house number and "Hunt" the street, but this has proved to be a misconception.

Although the delighted owner had long intended to visit Beverly, Massachusetts, the North shore town from which the dolls' house came, and hunt for Hunt Street, it is just as well that the opportunity had not been found. While going through old correspondence in preparation for this book, I came upon a 1963 letter from the dealer from whom the house had been bought by mail. As always, an attempt had been made to learn something of its history, and though such attempts are usually unproductive, in this case the dealer was most cooperative:

"Regarding the inscriptions of '46' and 'Hunt' on the doors of the house," she wrote, in reply to an inquiry, "we believe it relates to the 'Hunt' sisters who had a large waterfront estate on Ober Street in Beverly. This whole estate was bought and given to the City of Beverly for a recreation park and is now known as the 'David Lynch Park' (the name of the man who bought the Hunt estate). We bought the house in Beverly and believe our assumption to be correct."

Perhaps the fact that the information, though intriguing, was to some degree inconclusive, caused it to become out of focus, and finally to blur. The house was to me "46 Hunt Street" until recently, when the evidence was re-examined, and the information more logically re-interpreted.

Since "Hunt" is a family name rather than a street, a question remains about the "46," which seems less likely to be a house number than it did before. A date is a possibility, but "1846" though not out of the question seems a bit early for the house.

In any case, this is an unusual and agreeable dolls' house, tall and slender under its pitched roof. There is evidence that it may once have had a central chimney, making it taller still. The roof is veneered, and this fact, along with the presence of a lock on the front, suggests a mid-nineteenth-century date. The windows and doors have been painted on the hinged front with the same assurance and style as some additional painted embellishment which may be seen inside the façade when it is swung open. The double doors, in addition to the "address," have been painted with charming trompe l'oeil panels decorated to resemble cut glass. There is no question that the original paint survives; even time has realized that to repaint this house would be barbarous. It is difficult to give a name to the apricot trim which has undoubtedly mellowed along with a darkened buff. The same colors serve, along with the black of doors and sash bars, to decorate the inside of the hinged façade.

Inside, there is a simple arrangement of three square rooms, one to a floor, given light by the presence of glass windows on both sides. This is in realistic contrast to the painted windows on the front, which have three-dimensional bracketed lintels exactly like their glazed counterparts, but are otherwise sham.

Also within, early if not original papers and carpets are intact, along with dotted swiss curtains tied back with ribbons. The key to the lock did not accompany the house, and except for a few pretty lithographed pictures glued to the walls, and a small "ogee" mirror with a gilt liner (in the smallest Biedermeier scale), the contents, obviously once treasured, are gone. The house, which is on casters, has been refurnished in the small scale the room dimensions require.

Figure 33

HISTORIC PRESERVATION IN MINIATURE: UNIQUE EXAMPLES

Figure 34

A MAINE COTTAGE

DATE: CA. 1879
HEIGHT: 25½″
WIDTH: 25″
DEPTH: 37½″
OWNER: FORMERLY IN THE COLLECTION OF MRS. DELANNE LOPEMAN DUBOIS (TEXAS)

Since full-sized houses are sometimes uprooted and moved blocks, or even miles, it is not surprising that dolls' houses often wander far from their original regions.

Inasmuch as this straightforward cottage from Maine now resides in Texas,* we are grateful that its new owner has taken care to preserve the brief history that accompanied it: This unassuming house was built by a man with the unassuming name of Harry Smith, for his two daughters, ca. 1879. Although the photograph suggests a small house, the substantial measurements, and especially the depth, indicate otherwise. There are two rooms, one behind the other, each with its original wallpaper, and they are BIG.

With its rugged simplicity, this cottage is

* The house has changed hands, and possibly states, since these words were written.

appealing for the regional fact that it reflects the Maine pinewoods—which provided its exterior. The aged pine has never been stained nor painted, though the house has changed hands a number of times. There are five glass windows, including two at each side. The roof lifts off for play.

HIGH VICTORIANA FROM MASSACHUSETTS

DATE: CA. 1880
HEIGHT: 46″
WIDTH: 49″
DEPTH: 18″
OWNER: AUTHOR'S COLLECTION

This straightforward house was acquired from a dealer in Massachusetts, and is believed to have originated there. It may be compared to the Bessie Lincoln house from Salem (Fig. 31). Although the latter has a mansard roof with chimney and this one is hipped with a captain's walk, even these have an important resemblance —the attic room in each.

Other resemblances include the unpainted wood, often seen on dolls' houses from the New England states, the exact arrangement of rooms and stairs, and even the incised "masonry" foundation. The fundamental difference is revealed in the lush Victorian wallpapers, draperies, carpets, and beaded chandeliers, a veritable compendium of mid-Victorian decor. These, however, seemingly have been superimposed in recent years on walls, floors, and ceilings which for decades may have been as unadorned as those in the Bessie Lincoln house.

It is impossible to tell because old materials were used and the artful designer was either of the period, or had such a feeling for it, along with taste and style, that high Victoriana emerges. This is not as evident in black and white as one might wish, but an emphasis on crimson and gold in the wallpapers, most of

DOLLS' HOUSES FROM NEW ENGLAND

which have suitable borders, and on velvets, laces, braids, tassels, bows, and fringes for the curtains and draperies, illuminate an era of interior decoration that was popular decades before it became fashionable to refer to it as "interior design." The beaded chandeliers are themselves a minor art form—a triumph of tinted beads and dangles in intricately composed patterns.

The same gifted hand that fashioned these adornments was clearly responsible for some furnishings which every Victorian dolls' house should contain. Among these are an hourglass stool of net over pink tied at the "waist" with blue, and a crimson velvet-draped table fringed at the base and swagged near the top with garnet beads and garnet-and-gold silken tassels.

The decorator, who evidently could see no scope for her tassels or her talents in a kitchen, dispensed with the one which the architect probably intended. The latter's (anonymous) fame will have to rest on his prepossessingly reeded newel posts, which match the posts on his captain's walk; and on his fitted attic compartment, with stained glass dormer, which lifts out for attic snooping.

Figure 35

Figure 36

THE WOODMAN HOUSE FROM PROVIDENCE

DATE: 1880
HEIGHT (INCLUDING CHIMNEYS): 58″
WIDTH: 64″
DEPTH (NOT INCLUDING FRONT STEPS AND PORCHES): 28″
OWNER: WAYNE COUNTY, INDIANA HISTORICAL SOCIETY (RICHMOND, INDIANA)

"There is not only regional architecture," one has found oneself murmuring from time to time. "There is also regional *dolls' house* architecture." Years ago, one of these patterns began to be discernible in Massachusetts,* and more recently, in neighboring Rhode Island.

* See Fig. 31.

The characteristic most often noted in the dolls' houses of these New England states was a preoccupation with unpainted wood, both on interior and exterior walls. The effect was to give these houses a rich, dark, panelled and somewhat somber appearance like that of this majestic mansion in the Indiana Historical Society.

When its photograph arrived from Richmond, Indiana, another theory seemed about to evaporate. It was gratifying indeed, therefore, to turn to the well-documented history of the house and discover that, after all, it had been built in Rhode Island! A professional carpenter and wood carver named Allen Weeks of Providence was clearly proud of the dolls' house he built in 1880 for a ten-year-old girl named Caroline R. Jones; his name with the date of construction may be seen over the balconied window on the top floor.* The ten-year-old recipient obviously treasured his work: when she married and became Mrs. Charles M. Woodman, of Richmond, Indiana, she took her dolls' house with her.

It is not surprising that she cherished her possession. It was not only handsome, but its furnishing had been clearly a family effort. We are not told who made the lace curtains, some of them with brocade valances, but logically this would have been Mrs. Woodman's mother since she also worked the needlepoint for the firescreen, piano stool, and several chairs. The rosewood piano was made by her Uncle William; and the andirons, extraordinarily, by her grandfather. (Since the hardware of the house was "mostly hand-made," one wonders if he was also responsible for that.) Over the head of the bed in the nursery is a painting on glass, an heirloom from Mrs. Woodman's grandmother's dolls' house.

Among the commercially made furnishings, one notes the presence, in the dining-room, of iron chairs to be seen in the Stevens & Brown 1872 "price list."† Perceivable with a magnifying glass are a pair of side chairs, referred to as "parlor chairs," and what we refer to today as a "gentleman's chair" (called in the price list an "easy chair"). Also of interest are the brass chandeliers, for candles, bought at the World's Fair in 1893. Since Caroline Jones would have been twenty-three at the time, this suggests that she went on furnishing the house into adulthood.

The plan of the house itself is logical and handsome—and one seldom seen. As the photograph reveals, the fixed center panel includes a flight of stairs which lead to the front door and remain in place whether the front is open or closed. Doors lead properly off the center (staircase) halls to connect the rooms. There is an attic for storage of doll clothes under the mansard roof.

Among the documents that belong to the house, a letter written in 1961 to Mrs. Woodman by Elisabeth Weeks of Providence tells of her "Cousin Allen's coming to our house" when she was a little girl. Since he made the house, she wrote, "I had a sense of pride in the craftsmanship." She mentioned "what a kindly man" she thought him, and added that she owned "a number of his carved pieces."

It is not astonishing that such a craftsman and artist chose to leave unpainted a house which he built of black walnut and tulip, with amaranth and white wood for trim. The amaranth sounded marvelously exotic, and it is disappointing to learn from Webster that the name applies to a tropical American timber tree as well as to "an imaginary flower supposed never to fade."

THE CHAMBERLAIN HOUSE AT WENHAM

DATE: 1884
HEIGHT (INCLUDING CUPOLA): 38″
WIDTH: 43½″
DEPTH (NOT INCLUDING STEPS): 14½″
OWNER: THE WENHAM MUSEUM, (WENHAM, MASSACHUSETTS)

Since this dolls' house is one of the most beautiful, imaginative, and complete Victorian examples to be found on either side of the ocean, it is merciful that when it was offered for sale at the Wenham Exchange in 1938, "interested friends," far ahead of most of their contemporaries in their appreciation of such treasures, acquired it for the Wenham Museum.

It is historical as well as beautiful, having been made by Benjamin H. Chamberlain, a Salem silversmith and jeweler, who worked on the dolls' house from April 1884 to December 24, as a Christmas surprise for his two small daughters, Mamie and Millie. He built it at his

---

* AWWEEKS with metal hand stamps.

† See page 303.

HISTORIC PRESERVATION IN MINIATURE: UNIQUE EXAMPLES

Figure 37

shop, and it was undoubtedly his daughters, who lived to "a ripe old age," and often visited the museum to admire their old toy, who remembered that much of the furniture (some brought from abroad) was given to their father by customers "who knew of the project going on at his store."

Since he was a silversmith, it is not surprising that his work is to be found in the dolls' house, beginning with the small silver plaque on the front door (engraved "Mamie-Millie"), and continuing with a sterling silver tea-set inside. However, it is likely that his gifts as a jeweler were called upon to a greater degree in his work with cruder metals on the house itself. His hand-wrought metal embellishments can be found throughout, and are especially evident in the gilded railings on the cupola, central bay, and kitchen wing. The delicate grille-work pattern is also repeated on the dormers. All of these metal embellishments, including a fanciful pediment over the front door, give the house much of its personality. The exterior, of the stained wood often seen in New England dolls' houses of the period, has some painted trim, on the dormers and elsewhere, of a lovely rusty red which, with the gray painted roof and dark green base, give the house an appearance both mellow and warm. There is also carving of considerable charm on the wood itself.

DOLLS' HOUSES FROM NEW ENGLAND

Although the detail picture, made many years ago, is impaired, to say the least, by the artificial snow, it serves to illustrate some of this carving, including the decorative vergeboard and the lovely medallion (to be found on both sides of the house) beneath it.

The parts of the façade which have been removed for display contain arched windows similar to the others in the house. The section which slides into place on the kitchen wing includes another door. This house is very real—truly habitable. It is logical in plan as well as charming. In the parlor, dining-room, and upstairs sitting-room, the fireplaces are on sidewalls with windows on the rear walls. Perhaps the architect wished one of his handsome carved and marbleized arched mantels (with built-in arched mirrors above, and with metal grates below) to be visible from the front—and to provide a variation in the lay-out of the rooms. In the bedroom (upper right), he placed the fireplace against the rear wall, with the bay above the kitchen wing sufficient to light the room.

The numerous bays—upstairs and down, on each side, as well as on the front—add to the gemütlich effect of the whole. Behind the green window shades and draperies, they afford appealing nooks—a place to sip a cup of tea, or to take a nap. Draperies with fringed valances hang at the room entrances to these bays. Mrs. Chamberlain who, it is said, made the curtains, linens, and doll clothes, working till the last possible moment on Christmas Eve, must also have been responsible for the portières which hang from rings on metal rods between the rooms.

Although, as the sisters remembered, much of the furniture in the house was given to Mr. Chamberlain, and we can recognize the familiar Biedermeier and other manufactured pieces, it is quite clear that inside the house he became an interior designer *and* a cabinetmaker. The rusty reds and the gilt he used on the exterior are also to be found within: on a metal newel post ornament, on chairs and tables, and even on the chandeliers—all unmistakably of his devising. Much red was used, giving an effect of warmth and richness.

His work is also to be found in the kitchen which contains a commercially made iron stove (it appears to be one of the Bay State models in the Stevens & Brown 1872 catalogue), and even this has been logically "connected". An outlet above the stove leads to the chimney with lid which is visible on top of the kitchen wing. Also built-in are the dresser with a faucet, to be seen at the rear, and the sconce which matches the chandeliers in the other rooms. (The large pink pearls used as globes are the only false note in the whole house.)

There are many details to represent the era of which the house is such an effective representative. The windows in the cupola are glazed with red; even the rooms behind the attic dormers

Figure 38

contain furniture; a shell collection is displayed in the parlor; the stairs are carpeted. An address—the number four—is on the glass above the front doors, but it does not appear to be known whether this small residence represents an actual house. If it does, it was very likely in Salem, and perhaps the Chamberlains' own. Dolls' house builders occasionally write to ask for information about a dolls' house they wish to copy. For such a purpose—or for any worthy purpose whatsoever, this delightful dolls' house is highly recommended.

A RHODE ISLAND MANSARD

DATE: CA. 1885
HEIGHT: 38"
WIDTH: 28"
DEPTH: 25"
OWNER: MRS. JOHN R. WHEELER (CONNECTICUT)

This powder blue house with gold and white trim is, unfortunately, not as photogenic as it might be. A photograph fails to do justice to its special charm, a most original open plan with handsomely turned columns front and back on the first floor, and with pilasters above them on the second. Just this suggestion of architectural detail, combined with the carefully clapboarded sides, the shingled mansard roof with its elaborate cornice, and the imposing chimney, contrives to make the absence of windows (there is only one) and doors (none) seem unnoticeable.

This is another effective variation in the small but diversified world of dolls' house architecture, and it also affords an opportunity for small sisters, perhaps, or friends to play in the seven rooms, six of them arranged back to back. They could meet, appropriately, when their work was done, in the long parlor which runs the length of the house.

Though exterior architecture is only suggested, endless time must have been spent in fashioning such details as parquet floors of oak

Figure 39

Figure 40

on the first floor and elaborate wainscoting in the parlor. The one window may also be found in this big room.

Mrs. Wheeler, the owner of the house, is also impressed by its weight, which requires two men to move, and was, for this obvious reason, originally on rollers.

The dealer who found the house believed it to be from the vicinity of Providence, Rhode Island. There was no furniture in it, and its new owner felt obliged to re-do the walls because someone, presumably very young, had attacked them with alarming colors. The rooms have been handsomely furnished with pieces of the proper vintage.

AN "UPHOLSTERED" HOUSE

DATE: 1890
HEIGHT (AT PEAK, NOT INCLUDING 15″ STAND): 55″
WIDTH: 46″
DEPTH: 19″
OWNER: MARIANNE VAN RENSSELAER WILSON (CONNECTICUT)

Figure 41

Built in a day when the upholsterer and the cabinetmaker were sharply differentiated, this house is one of which it may be said the upholsterer reigned supreme.

It is a pity that its photograph fails to do it justice, because it is not only completely original, but completely irresistible.

Its owner refers to it as her "New Orleans house," but its background is a mystery. The woman from whom Mrs. Wilson bought it "has disappeared," but before she vanished she related that the person from whom *she* bought it asked that it not be changed from "the way it was when she was given it in 1890."

The way it was in 1890, and happily *is* still more than eighty years later, is all gilt, fringe, lace, plush, and brocade. Everything that can be tufted is tufted. There are cushions, lambrequins, and Brussels carpet, and more silk tassels than

Figure 42

the imagination can grasp—even in miniature. It is a "fancy house" in every sense of the phrase. The dolls are pretty fancy, too—as upholstered, be-laced and be-tasseled as their house.

(45)

HISTORIC PRESERVATION IN MINIATURE: UNIQUE EXAMPLES

Figure 43

A HAUNTED HOUSE FROM CONNECTICUT

DATE: CA. 1898
HEIGHT: 23″
WIDTH: 17½″
DEPTH: 12″
OWNER: MRS. PATSY POWERS (GEORGIA)

Following the appearance of this small, late Victorian house from Connecticut at a dolls' house show in Atlanta in the spring of 1972, a newspaper clipping which included its picture arrived in the mail. This revealed an astonishing degree of reality and the first miniature tombstones on record. The dedicated antiquarian who gazed upon it was quite overcome.

When, somewhat later, it was learned that the tombstones had been carved from Ivory soap not long before the show, and that even the cobwebs were artful additions, one's temperature dropped a degree or so, but when the history of the house was disclosed, it began to rise again.

Mrs. Powers acquired the house in 1970, and because of its great fragility (the wood is "matchbox thin"), she put it in her attic for "safekeeping." The following year, she related, "my home was almost totally destroyed by fire. Everything in the attic that had not been reduced to ashes was literally smashed to the ground by firemen. Two days later, when I came to my senses, I found a ladder and climbed into the attic. In the middle of the empty and charred room sat the house exactly where I had put it, and in exactly the same condition as when it came to me. I brought it down with much joy and have kept it near me ever since."

When the doll's house show evolved, Mrs. Powers found it easy to decide which of her houses to display. "It was now quite clear to me that this house, although haunted, charmed or whatever, was not unhappy and . . . wanted to stay around awhile longer."

Mrs. Powers' description of the "exceptional"

Although the interior is satin and urban, the outside has the innocence and, to some degree, the style of a peasant chest. In contrast to what goes on under the pitched roof with its brick chimney, and what may be glimpsed through the glazed windows, the façade is cupboard style, with doors, lintels, and miscellaneous embellishments painted in a trompe l'oeil manner, and in luscious colors. The foundation color is described by Mrs. Wilson as a fierce greenish mustard. The trim is olive green and a once-red now faded to pink.

In addition to the four rooms visible, there is an attic which opens from the rear.

The workable chandelier (with wicks) is similar to a much-photographed example in the author's collection. To have a pair of matching workable sconces in the same room is impressive indeed. But everything about this house is impressive, bewitching, and—*upholstered*.

(46)

Figure 44

Figure 45

Figure 46

Figure 47

(47)

Victorian furnishings she added to the house is also highly quotable:

Unfortunately, they were not overlooked by the wrath of the fire. Now even the upholstery has lost its deep green color; the old varnish has bubbled on the wood surfaces. This, of course, has added greatly to the atmosphere of the two rooms and much to the distress of this collector who found the pieces in mint condition.

They came to me in a shoe box via an honest-to-goodness town-to-town peddler (except this one drove a Volkswagen van and had boxes of depression glass he was peddling at flea markets)—a sign of the times, I suppose. He had lived most of his life in Savannah, Georgia, and was selling the miniature furniture for an eighty-eight-year-old friend of his, a woman he had known for many years. Supposedly, the furniture was made for her by her grandfather and dated in the early 1890's. The small alabaster urns by the graves were in this box of treasures.

The bed and bureau may appear a trifle out-of-scale in the low-ceilinged house (though Mrs. Powers believes them to be "inch-to-the-foot," with the parlor furniture somewhat smaller in scale). In any case, they are marvelously real with what must be the smallest, hand-carved, tear-drop handles ever made. There are also infinitesimal, hand-carved escutcheons on the drawers, and these pieces may well have been made by the grandfather. When Mrs. Powers re-glued them, she discovered they had been made of cigar-box wood, long a favored lumber for craftsmen working in miniature.

It is clear that the same gifted hand fashioned the tufted parlor chairs and mirror-back sofa. "Only two chairs survived the fire entirely (they had been tucked safely away in a drawer.)" A snapshot (unfortunately not reproducible) shows this pair in their original green; the others appear to have taken on the red of the fierce element which failed to consume them.

Clearly an artist, Mrs. Powers added the base and the trees as well as the gravestones. The front and side fencing is old, of the type used around Christmas gardens. "An old wooden parquet floor salvaged from one of the Candler estates here in Atlanta" served to restore the back fence and gate.

Perhaps this wood also supplied another notable "first"; the only boarded-up window so far recorded, one believes, in dolls' house history.

THE LONGFELLOW-CRAIGIE HOUSE

DATE: LATE VICTORIAN(?)
HEIGHT: 27"
WIDTH: 36"
DEPTH: 25"
OWNER: MRS. JOHN R. WHEELER (CONNECTICUT)

Here is a copy not only of an actual house, but of a historical house, and one that is still standing. Craigie House, with its Chippendale-Georgian features, was old when Longfellow lived in it,* and Mrs. Wheeler, the owner of the miniature version, does not know the age of her handmade copy, but the clapboards appear to have been done with a chisel in the old manner, and there is some crudely laminated wood which also suggests a degree of antiquity.†

The hinged front that opens in two sections is so similar to the façade of the full-sized house that one would not be surprised to learn that the house in Cambridge does the same! There is the identical quartet of two-story pilasters, and even the small ones that frame the front door are embellished with similarly reeded brackets. The widow's walk, dormers, and window arrangement resemble the originals, and only the side

* Also known as the Vassall House, it was built by Major Vassall in 1759, and occupied by Longfellow from 1837 to 1882.

† Mechanical production of plywood was invented in the 1880's in Russia, but handmade efforts go back to antiquity.

DOLLS' HOUSES FROM NEW ENGLAND

Figure 48

piazzas (added in a remodeling of Craigie) are missing from the dolls' house.

More than many, this resembles an actual house, with front and back doors, and a total of twenty-seven windows on four sides. The rooms are arranged with similar realism; there is a long parlor on one side of a wide central hall and a proper staircase with a landing.

When she found the house, the walls of all eight rooms were covered with a sort of lightweight canvas, and Mrs. Wheeler, an expert craftswoman who has built and furnished a variety of miniature rooms and shops, re-did them. When she first saw the house it was "in a shed with a tractor hanging over it," and she had to crawl on her hands and knees, in tractor oil, to see her prospective purchase. There was no furniture in it except for a small brown upholstered sofa with lots of little finger marks on it which she reluctantly removed.

Upstairs, there are four rooms plus a small one which has been made into a bathroom. Mrs.

Figure 49

Wheeler has logically furnished one of the bedrooms as Washington's inasmuch as the General was quartered there during his stay in New England during the Revolution. In his bedroom, the "stenciled" paper is a fitting

Figure 50

Figure 51

DOLLS' HOUSES FROM NEW ENGLAND

Figure 52

Figure 53

background for the Biedermeier washstand and dressing table which clearly arrived, along with the Empire chest and the ogee mirror, two generations or so after the troops departed. But the reproduction bed and the Carver chair, and the accessories Mrs. Wheeler has supplied, including a portrait of George Washington in a daguerreotype frame above the mantel, give the room an atmosphere which suggests that George Washington, even if not in this particular bed, *did* sleep here.

There is a rather elaborate postscript to Mrs. Wheeler's model of the Longfellow-Craigie house. In *A History of Dolls' Houses*, I mentioned a Chicago woman, Miss Elizabeth Gordon, who, in 1900, marketed a series of "Cranford" dolls' houses, several of which were copies of historical houses. Since these included the Longfellow-Craigie house, it seemed possible that Mrs. Wheeler's house might be one of them.

When the illustrations were re-examined, this did not prove to be the case, but it seems appropriate to reproduce the Cranford version of Craigie house, as shown in *House Beautiful* in 1900. As the pictures indicate, this is an even more elaborate version than Mrs. Wheeler's, with finer detailing, including the beautifully dentelated cornice and Ionic capitals. Miss Gordon chose to reproduce the remodeled Craigie. The original, like Mrs. Wheeler's, did not have piazzas "and the doorway was more elaborate. The toy house, like the Cambridge one, is a deep cream color, with dark green blinds and white trimmings." The house came furnished and inhabited: "Mrs. Longfellow sits with much dignity in a high-back chair. . . ." Other members of the family were also present.

A "skillful cabinetmaker" who worked under Miss Gordon's supervision did the building, and his work was meticulous: "clapboards are clapboards and shingles are shingles," *House Beautiful* reported.

Also illustrated were an Evanston house, a one-room bungalow, and two other historic houses: the Whittier house and Mount Vernon. The latter was "a little smaller" (unfortunately no measurements were given), but the detail lavished on all the houses is plain to see in the illustrations.

If any of the Cranford houses survive today—and it is impossible to imagine that any have been given to orphanages or used as firewood or have met any of the horrible fates often related of fine old dolls' houses—it is to be hoped that they are treasured, because treasures they assuredly are.

HISTORIC PRESERVATION IN MINIATURE: UNIQUE EXAMPLES

THE LAWLER HOUSE FROM LOWELL, MASSACHUSETTS

DATE: CA. 1900
HEIGHT (NOT INCLUDING LOST FOUNDATION ABOUT 15"): 69"
WIDTH: 52"
DEPTH (NOT INCLUDING BAYS): 21"
OWNER: MRS. J. HARRY SPENCER, JR. (MARYLAND)

Although this superior dolls' house from Lowell, Massachusetts, can best be described as a towering edifice, it is comely as well as bulky. At about the turn of the century, Dr. William P. Lawler of Lowell had an architect draw up plans for it and a French carpenter build it for his three very small daughters, Virginia, Bawita, and Mary. Although it was moved from Lowell years ago, the house is still in the possession of the latter (Mrs. Spencer) where it is cherished and occasionally played with by grandchildren.

At some point the original deep foundation

Figure 54

Figure 55

Figure 56

(52)

with a balustraded porch was lost and a lower base and stairs substituted, but otherwise this splendid residence is intact, and since it is said to resemble—withal approximately, as is usually the case—the family residence on Nesmith Street in Lowell, one regrets that a picture of the latter is unavailable.

Beneath the pair of twin gables with their arched windows, the hinged bays swing open, giving access to the six rooms beneath them. The central section is also detachable for play, and a good staircase with double newel posts climbs logically to the third floor. (This was at some point altered to allow for a bathroom.) When the central section is in place, it is still possible to reach these hall rooms through wide doorways. There is also a spacious attic, accessible from a rear opening, which Mrs. Spencer and her sister, Mrs. Baker, recall was a perfect place for placing extra furniture and bad dolls—and for "hiding things." The bays, which give the exterior of the dolls' house a great deal of its character, are also a useful and attractive addition to the interior, forming, in effect, window seats which seem to invite plants, pillows, and "young" dolls.

This is another dolls' house furnished by Schwarz (one suspects the Boston brother), and though some of the contents have gone, quite a lot remains, including two items not previously encountered by me in nearly three decades of searching. One of these is a small hanging lamp with a gilded lead font, a glass chimney, and a wick which, under careful supervision, the sisters once lighted with coal oil. (Workable table lamps of this ilk have been sighted, but not hanging lights of this particular make.) The other item is a gilded lead fishing pole with windable reel, an item so fragile that it, along with the small flounder-like fish at the end of its line, may be the only such reel—and fish—that didn't "get away."

The most remarkable piece in the house, however, must be the formidable iron stove in the kitchen which may be unique. At least it appears to be custom made, resembling none of the many familiar types manufactured in quantities in iron or tin. It has a roll-top hood in which plates could be warmed as well as pans made for it; and, under the same careful supervision that prevented conflagration when the hanging lamp was lighted, the little Lawler sisters actually cooked *in* their dolls' house, building a wood fire in this small stove. A sad but vivid footnote to this fact is that young Mary Lawler (Mrs. Spencer) boiled the dolls' house curtains in the copper boiler on the stove so assiduously that she "over-cooked" them and they had to be replaced.

The wallpapers were also replaced, in recent years, by Mrs. Spencer, who found them too dingy, and clearly is still the zealous housekeeper she was as a child.

Two flags fly from the dolls' house roof, a Confederate one for Mrs. Spencer's mother, who was from Virginia, and the Union flag for her father (from Lowell). A seagull on the roof is also in honor of her Massachusetts father.

A "COLONIAL REVIVAL" FROM MASSACHUSETTS

DATE: CA. 1900
HEIGHT (NOT INCLUDING CHIMNEYS): 32"
WIDTH (INCLUDING EAVES): 24"
DEPTH (INCLUDING EAVES): 16"
OWNER: AUTHOR'S COLLECTION

A New England kitchen displayed in 1876 at the Philadelphia Centennial, the architectural firm of McKim, Mead and White, and Edward Bok (the celebrated editor of the *Ladies' Home Journal*), have all been given credit, in various measures, for the Colonial Revival. "The interest that was awakened," Marshall Davidson writes, "sprang partly from nostalgia, partly

HISTORIC PRESERVATION IN MINIATURE: UNIQUE EXAMPLES

Figure 57

from a quest for a new and indigenous style of American architecture and partly from a form of ancestor worship." *

This small dolls' house is a modest example of the genre, but it summarizes with clarity as well as simplicity the houses "beginning to spot the countryside as early as the 'eighties with columned houses with Palladian details in the windows and cornices." † This house has no columns except for the rounded pilasters which flank the doorway, but it has an implied (unglazed) fanlight with a pediment and the conventional number and arrangement of windows on its façade. It is the style of the windows and the doors, however, which are a dead giveaway of the late-nineteenth-century origin of the house. The dark varnished doorway with its vertical glazed panes is to be found on many a late-Victorian residence. And although there is one concession to a Colonial multi-paned window above the door, the others are of the

* *The American Heritage History of Notable American Houses*, New York, 1971.

† *The Tastemakers* by Russell Lynes, Harper's, 1949.

triple-paned style to be seen on many a house built in the 'nineties in New England (and especially in Massachusetts).

This small house is entirely habitable; some of the most elegant dolls' houses are whimsical about such practicalities as stairs and back doors. This house has both; its back is almost identical to the front, except for the style of the door which is wood-panelled rather than glazed and has a tiny projecting roof in lieu of the pediment.

Made with Yankee ingenuity, the façade is a sliding section which may be slipped off entirely, revealing the inevitable "center-hall plan" of such houses. All interior woodwork, including window frames, the one fireplace, and the staircase, with its nicely turned newel posts, is dark varnished—another suggestion of era. The original curtains and draperies still hang at the windows, all of which have paper shades (half way down for all eternity) with bead pulls. Green velvet portieres hang between the rooms.

The house is deep cream with green trim and red chimneys and, with its excellent proportions, is an appealing representative of "ancestor worship" in miniature.

A TURN-OF-THE-CENTURY INTERIOR

DATE: CA. 1900
HEIGHT: 31¾"
WIDTH: 42"
DEPTH: 13"
OWNER: FAIRFIELD HISTORICAL SOCIETY (FAIRFIELD, CONNECTICUT)

Although this house, little more than a shell, lacks architectural interest, its interior is a marvelously accurate summary of the room decoration of the period.

Made at about the turn of the century for Miss A. Elizabeth Jennings of Fairfield, Connect-

DOLLS' HOUSES FROM NEW ENGLAND

icut, by her father, the house is filled with the German dolls' house furniture so readily available at the time. But what is of significance is that not only were the carpets and curtains made by the young owner's mother from remnants of material used in the Jennings household, but the luscious late Victorian wallpapers were scraps from the same source. It is fortuitous that such a dolls' house has eight rooms rather than the more usual four or six, thus affording a marvelously diversified sampling of the papers and floor coverings to be found in a comfortable house in the Eastern United States at the turn of the century. It is also fortunate that the original papers remain. Most dolls' houses of this vintage have been re-papered by several generations, or sometimes by a well-meaning latter-day "collector."

It is more than a footnote (the pun is inadvertent) that the floor coverings in this carefully preserved miniature household are supplemented by summer grass rugs.

Figure 58

HISTORIC PRESERVATION IN MINIATURE: UNIQUE EXAMPLES

GERTRUDE'S HOUSE FROM HALIFAX, MASSACHUSETTS

DATE: 1904
HEIGHT: 35½″
WIDTH (NOT INCLUDING 5½″ PIAZZA): 22″
DEPTH (BASE): 25½″
OWNER: AUTHOR'S COLLECTION

A classic example of the pitfalls to be avoided in the dating of dolls' houses is supplied by this self-assured specimen.

When it was offered (by mail) by a Massachusetts dealer, years ago, she mentioned a house number on the door. "Such cryptography," as I've written elsewhere, "is always alluring (one dreams of discovering the street name and locating the full-sized original), but in this case the description was inferior to the actuality." When the house arrived, there was no address, but each of the pair of entrance doors bore an infinitesimal silver plate. One of these said "Gertrude" and one said "1904."

Given its true mansard roof and other mid-Victorian details, Gertrude's house might have been thought several decades earlier. Supplied the specific date, even the most casual amateur of architecture cannot fail: Presumably this was a copy of the house in which young Gertrude lived when the miniature replica was given her, perhaps on her birthday, possibly at Christmas, but unquestionably in 1904!

Although, by error,* this house was elsewhere described as from Maine, the dealer from whom it was purchased had in fact said that it came from Massachusetts, and she had even supplied the name of the town: Halifax, on the South shore of Boston, not far from Plymouth. With its population of eight hundred and sixty-seven (at least this was the total in an elderly, 1946 edition of the *Britannica*), perhaps a poll of Halifax residents, along with a survey of Halifax houses, might yield more information.

Even without a shred of history, this would be a notable dolls' house. From its arched piazza, which runs the depth of the house, to the cupola, glazed with four different tints of stained glass, Gertrude's is a most realistic miniature residence. Beneath the mansarded roof, the front, with its upstairs and downstairs bays, lifts off to disclose a staircase, one devoid of the eccentricities of many dolls' house staircases. This one ascends realistically to the attic, and there is an attractive balustrade for a doll of uncertain age (and joints) to cling to. The floor plan is similarly real: Back rooms open off of front rooms. There are three each on the first and second floors in addition to the staircase halls. A bathroom with a built-in tub and commode, and what remains of a bit of "windowphanie" at the

Figure 59

---
* My own, which I hereby confess: *A Book of Dolls and Doll Houses*, Tuttle, 1967.

DOLLS' HOUSES FROM NEW ENGLAND

window (in a geometric pattern of yellow, black and red), is logically located above the kitchen.

Handmade furniture came with the house, possibly made by the dolls' house builder, but, except for a parlor set upholstered in crimson and blue velvet, and a hall tree with three minuscule hooks, the best that can be said of it is that the maker was a clever carpenter, but not a dolls' house cabinetmaker.

The house has its original wallpapers and, under some rather coarse modern draperies which appear to be of relatively recent vintage, part of the almost inevitable, and probably original, net curtains. The house exterior is white with black trim, and the paint is applied not to wood, but to the heavy paper which is affixed to the exterior from foundation to roof.

THE LORD DOLLS' HOUSE

DATE: 1908–9
HEIGHT (NOT INCLUDING BASE): 51½"
WIDTH: 36¾"
DEPTH (OF ROOMS): 19"
OWNER: THE CHILDREN'S MUSEUM, BOSTON (on view at the Norwood, Massachusetts, Historical Society)

It is known that Mr. Foley, a carpenter of Cohasset, Massachusetts, built this substantial house for the daughter of Mrs. Frederick T. Lord of Boston. Although the exterior is barnlike, with the gambrel roof the only concession to architecture, the interior is thoroughly decorated, furnished, and inhabited, and there is even an arresting, and rather dominating, elevator.

In a four-story house, an elevator was clearly essential, and on this the architect seemingly lavished much of his interest, as well as considerable space. As the illustrations indicate, there are wooden guard rails in three upper rooms that match the cage which is manually activated by a pulley in the left-hand room on the fourth floor. There is no doubt in the world that if more dolls' houses had, or were to include, such a feature, they might become as popular among the brothers of dolls' house owners as among the owners themselves.

The eight rooms appear to have their original wallpapers and floor coverings, and these, along with lace-edged net curtains on the windows at the back of each (side windows appear only on the two lower floors), are an excellent setting for the glorious array of pre-World War I furnishings.

Views of the dining-room and what appears to be a music room are shown with the attractive German furniture, with applied brass decoration, which is often seen in houses of this period. All of the furniture in the music room is unusual, including the highly embossed upright piano with brass sconces.

Figure 60
Figure 61

HISTORIC PRESERVATION IN MINIATURE: UNIQUE EXAMPLES

Figure 62

Figure 63

DOLLS' HOUSES FROM NEW ENGLAND

MARY'S HOUSE

Date: ca. 1920
Height (not including chimneys and stand): 36"
Width (not including 5" porch): 38"
Depth (not including 5" porch): 25"
Owner: Mrs. Robert W. Fraser (Massachusetts)

Three years of work and, obviously, of love went into the building of "Mary's House." Although one visualizes such substantial dolls' houses in the possession of substantial families, it is clear from what is known of its history that this one came from a modest background.

In September of 1970, my friend Mrs. Donald Marion wrote of a visit to a Boston auction gallery where her sister, Mrs. Fraser, bought "a wonderful, large, ugly, dolls' house. . . ."

A neighbor had told Mrs. Fraser of the house which had been in storage since 1943, and was to be liquidated with "dead storage" in a warehouse sale. One can do the house no better justice than to quote Mrs. Marion's letter, with its spontaneity and pleasure:

The house is large, made with many openings (hinged), stairways to the third floor, and [it] is wired for lights. It has window glass throughout, and is fearfully and wonderfully painted, with the rugs painted on the floors. There is a porch across the front, large dormer windows on the third floor front, and [it] has much of the "original" furniture, some homemade and quite a bit commercially made, of the 1920s period when the house was built. (The style is earlier, perhaps around 1910.)

There is some fascinating, exasperating and rather touching documentation in the form of a couple of sheets of paper written in pencil by "Mary's father," who built the house, and consigned it to "the next generation" when he partially dismantled it and it was stored in the warehouse. (Why? Who knows!) He says he built it at a cost of over $100 for material excluding the paint, which is washable (and now needs a good scrubbing). He includes a list of some of the children who played with the house, last

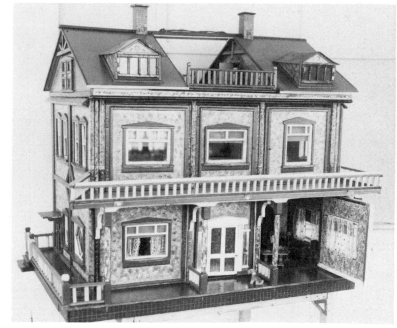

Figure 64

Figure 65

names only, and says that most of them are now grown up and graduated or in the war. (World War II.)

HISTORIC PRESERVATION IN MINIATURE: UNIQUE EXAMPLES

Oh, yes... one fascinating feature which got me—to the right of the front door there is a large double parlor, with sliding doors between the front and back rooms.

When the new owner later sent her own beguiling description, she also referred to the sliding doors which, she wrote, "delight me so that I am forever opening and shutting them." A roof garden is another unusual feature.

"I can well believe," Mrs. Fraser wrote, "that [the house] took three years to build. All the walls are double, each room is wired for electricity including the two attic rooms and the 'roof garden' itself.... The house seems to be well-scaled for 1" to 1' and is laid out so nearly like a full-sized home that I feel it must have been a copy."

The floors are also of vintage interest, with real linoleum inlaid in neat strips in the downstairs hall and all other floors "hand painted to resemble Congoleum rugs," which, as Mrs. Fraser pointed out, were meant to resemble Orientals. She saw almost identical patterns in a 1922 Montgomery Ward catalogue reprint.

The exterior of the house "is painted by a sort of sponge or daub method which suggests stucco very nicely. The walls of each room are painted, in varying terrifying combinations of color, to resemble heavens knows what!"

Four boxes of furniture came with the house, about fifty or sixty pieces, some handmade, some commercial, and all of 'twenties vintage. A Strombecker walnut dining-room set with buffet, server, six-legged table and four chairs, Mrs. Fraser noted, is also to be seen "people-size in the 1922 M-W catalogue and is termed 'Renaissance.' "

Only a few tattered pieces of ecru net curtains remain in the house, but window shades cut from an old green shade in full size may be found at each window.

Mary's house appealingly represents the vernacular of its segment of ca. 1920 society.

AN AUTHORITATIVE COLONIAL COPY

DATE: CA. 1930
HEIGHT: 41"
WIDTH: 41"
DEPTH: 26½"
OWNER: FAIRFIELD HISTORICAL SOCIETY (FAIRFIELD, CONNECTICUT)

The Colonial Revival dolls' houses of the late-Victorian era are more distant, and therefore rarer and more appealing than the colonials—mostly Southern Colonials—of the 1920's. Examples of both styles are to be found in later pages. Owing to the shortage of authentic colonial baby houses which preceded these styles, it is irresistible to include this relatively recent but handsomely authentic reproduction.

Since the house and its furnishings were made by Henry Hammond Taylor of Easton, Connecticut, author of the book *Knowing, Collecting and Restoring Colonial Furniture*, and was therefore built by an authority, it may be considered (within the limits of authorities) authoritative!

Even a glance confirms the fact that the builder knew his subject. Mr. Taylor built the house for his granddaughter, Molly Taylor,* and he built it in such detail that there is mortar between the panelled walls of the interior and the clapboarded sides of the exterior. This is true even on the hinged front where the diversified panelling of the thick walls of each room is meticulously continued. Thus when the front is open, as Mrs. John H. Grossman† has pointed out, the variations in wall decor and structure throughout the house may be seen at a glance.

There are fireplaces in each of the rooms (not visible in the photograph) beyond the doors which lead from the hall. There are beamed ceilings, timbered floors, and nineteen windows.

* Mrs. S. M. Vincent.

† Mrs. Grossman has generously provided photographs and information about all the dolls' houses in the Fairfield Historical Society.

DOLLS' HOUSES FROM NEW ENGLAND

Figure 66

Figure 67

One of the latter, in the lower left-hand room, in the manner of members of ancient houses, and with due deliberation, has been made crooked.

Except for the fact that this is not a "saltbox," one would suspect that Mr. Taylor had copied the 1690 Ogden house in Fairfield.* Although these central-chimney houses tend to resemble one another, most of them, like Mrs. Wilson's example, have nine windows on the front.† The five here are identical in number and arrangement to those on the Ogden house (Fig. 66).

There are many details to delight connoisseurs of the colonial period—from the tin chandelier in the hall to the wooden bolt on the kitchen door.

The period furniture was also made by Mr. Taylor, who died in 1932. How long before his death the small house was made is not known.

* This can be seen in *The Treasury of Early American Homes* by Dorothy and Richard Pratt, Hawthorn Books, Inc., 1959.

† Since no adequate photograph of the façade of Mrs. Wilson's house was available, only a snapshot is shown, but her house is considerably more sizeable than the Taylor house, and made in a similarly meticulous manner. In a splendid collection (see Plates 41-3 and 149-51), Mrs. Wilson considers it her "best" house.

Figure 68

There are four front rooms and, as in the Taylor house, the panelling is different in each. There are additional rooms at the back of the house—three upstairs and two down. When Mrs. Wilson acquired the house, it was accompanied by the following letter:

"The scale model of an old house was the model of an old house that I took apart and brought to my antiques shop in 1930. It was known as the old Warren homestead in Marlboro on State Road or Post Road and golf course corner of road to Gleasondale. The house was originally built about 1780 or thereabouts according to my opinion." (This letter was signed, "Leonard P. Golding, South Sudbury, Mass.")

DOLLS' HOUSES
From the Mid-Atlantic Region

A FEDERAL BABY HOUSE FROM PHILADELPHIA

DATE: CA. 1810
HEIGHT: 42½"
WIDTH: 32"
DEPTH: 16½"
OWNER: INDEPENDENCE NATIONAL HISTORICAL PARK COLLECTION (MERCHANTS' EXCHANGE BUILDING, PHILADELPHIA)

Although museums and stately homes in England are well-supplied with eighteenth-century "baby houses," * and several museums on the Continent are provided with dolls' houses of even earlier vintage, students of these beguiling microcosms of domestic history have sought almost vainly in the United States for examples from Colonial times, or even from the Federal period.

In more than twenty-five years of searching, the writer has discovered only one eighteenth-century dolls' house made in the colonies, the well-known and well-documented pre-Revolutionary house at the Van Cortlandt mansion in New York.† All other houses of early vintage to be found on this side of the ocean have sailed across it at some point in their history.

American dolls' houses from even the first quarter of the nineteenth century are virtually unknown, and therefore it was with a sense of true discovery that one learned of the charming example illustrated; a house that never has wandered far from its original family or city. It is not surprising that the latter is the historic city of Philadelphia, in the late eighteenth century considered the center of luxury and affluence in America,* and it seems fitting that when this heirloom was relinquished in the early 1960's by its family (the Dickey family, in which this rare piece descended), it was given to the Independence National Park Collection in Philadelphia.

The house is comely, as its photographs reveal, fashioned with great fidelity to detail inside as well as out, and it has the lovely simplicity of a proper Quaker house. It is possible that an architect built this correct and graceful baby house, and it is lamentable that his name has not come down to us. Luckily much of the family history is known. But, in addition to its early date, and the rarity of its architecture in miniature, the most striking feature of this small house, the detail which sets it apart from every other, is the pair of Green Tree fire marks, one at each side of the upper façade. On a full-sized

---

* This term was in common use till the middle of the nineteenth century both in the United States and Britain.

† Made in 1744 for the Homans family of Boston. This date is on the front of the house. A second date, 1774, on the opposite side, may refer to the year it descended to the Greenough family of Long Island. See page 106.

* And where "relatively little was destroyed" during the Revolution. S. W. Woodhouse, Jr., in *Antiques*, May 1927.

DOLLS' HOUSES FROM THE MID-ATLANTIC REGION

house, such marks would represent a policy issued by the Mutual Assurance Company of Philadelphia.*

Because the "1000" on this pair of miniature fire marks sounds contrived, as though the builder had arbitrarily chosen a good, round number for what was, after all, a toy, neither the family nor the curators accessioning the baby house for the Park attached any significance to the number, nor to its possible relationship to a pair of full-sized fire marks, till badgered by a dolls' house researcher, who prefers to leave no

---

* Such fire marks, of course, were affixed to the houses of policy holders by various insurance companies with varying marks. There is an old saw to the effect that if a house were aflame and a hose company rode past and recognized the fire mark of a rival insurance company, they'd let the house burn down.

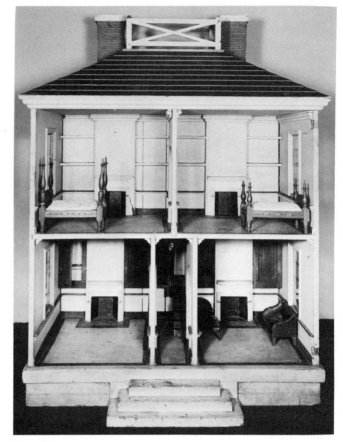

Figure 69

Figure 70

miniature stone unturned (and no miniature fire mark unchecked).

It was when a member of the family * began her own investigation that the original holder of the Mutual Assurance Company's Policy No. 1000 (corresponding, of course, to the fire mark number) was discovered, and that a fascinating coincidence, which also introduces the possibility of a different early history for the dolls' house, was disclosed.

Before this possibility was investigated, and at the time the house was given to the Park by Miss Helen Shaw of Oxford, Pennsylvania, the earliest history of the house was vague, although

---

* Mrs. Louise Dickey Davison who, along with her cousin, Miss Eleanor Hosie, made this summary possible. For the copy of the insurance policy reproduced here, I am in the debt of another family connection, Mr. Clifford Lewis III.

(63)

HISTORIC PRESERVATION IN MINIATURE: UNIQUE EXAMPLES

most of its heritage was quite thoroughly documented. Miss Shaw, probably basing her attribution on information from her aunt, Mrs. Cresson Dickey, from whom she had received the baby house, said that probably it had been made for Sarah Emlen Cresson, the wife of John Miller Dickey, both born in Philadelphia in 1806.* (This, of course, furnishes only a clue to the precise dating of the house. Sometimes, of course, dolls' houses were made "for" infants, and such a handsome specimen as this might well have been presented at birth. Certainly it was made early in the century—very likely before 1815.)

Before her death in 1929, Miss Shaw's aunt lived for many years on Locust Street in Oxford, some fifty miles from Philadelphia, in a substantial residence which had been built in the 1840's by her father-in-law, John Miller Dickey. At the time of her marriage, the dolls' house had been among the Miller, Dickey, and Cresson furniture there.

* Mr. Dickey founded Lincoln University, near Oxford, Pennsylvania, in 1854.

In any case, when the No. 1000 Green Tree policy (and its corresponding fire mark number) was located in the ancient files of the Mutual Assurance Company (records carefully preserved from fire, flood, or other damage!), the policy holder proved to be Edward Shippen, who, on February 4, 1800, had had three adjoining houses insured by "Green Tree," all on the north side of High (the original name of Market Street), between Eleventh and Twelfth.

On the corner of Tenth and High Streets, somewhat more than a block away from the Shippens', was a "marble house" built by John Miller, who had been born in Scotland in 1764. Jane, the eldest of his four daughters, was the mother of John Miller Dickey.

The proximity of Mr. Shippen's house, with its full-sized "1000" Green Tree fire mark, to the Miller house, which temporarily may have contained the dolls' house, with its corresponding miniature fire mark, is a coincidence indeed, whether the two houses, large and small, are or are not related.

It had seemed likely, when the alternative history was first considered, that the Shippens, having been neighbors of the Millers, might also have been their friends. John Miller kept a day book, still in the possession of a family member,* who looked through it carefully, in the hope of finding a reference to the dolls' house. Although none was discovered, there *was* mention of Edward Shippen, relating to a financial transaction in 1797.†

In any case, if the evidence of the fire mark is accepted, the baby house may conceivably have been made for a Shippen daughter and, somewhat later, given to the three younger Miller girls. Dolls' house history records numerous instances in which valuable dolls' houses are

Figure 71

* Miss Janet Preston of Baltimore.

† This was listed under "Bills Receable" [sic], but the "400" entered is not elaborated upon.

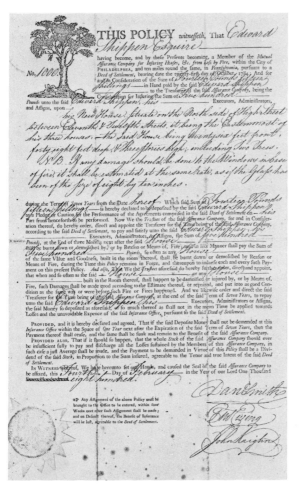

Figure 72

presented to friends, as well as handed down to relations.

Being younger than their sister, Jane Miller Dickey, the three other Miller daughters may have played with the house around 1810. Since the miniature fire marks are the only ones dolls' house history has so far discovered, it is tempting to hope that this is the case.

If this assumption is accurate, the move of the baby house to Oxford can be easily explained, since Jane's mother later moved to Oxford, to be near her daughter, and brought many Miller heirlooms with her.

The dolls' house was clearly an heirloom, and Miss Eleanor Hosie, who was allowed to play with it (ca. 1900–5) only under supervision, remembers that her cousin Cresson Dickey

treated it as one. It was not only an "important" dolls' house; it is obviously a replica of an "important" life-sized house.

From its "simulated water table above the basement," as it has been architecturally described, to its hipped roof, this is a copy of no mere lower-middle-class row house. There are windows on the sides, and we may imagine a garden. The roof also sets the house apart from the modest row houses that lined old Philadelphia. Between two red "brick" chimneys, each containing a pair of flues, there is a balustraded deck, or captain's walk. This is more than a picturesque embellishment; at the rear, a small door at a little distance from the top opens into a small room. (Of three adjoining houses insured for Edward Shippen on February 4, 1800, Policy No. 1000 was for the front of the "easternmost" of these,* and the only survey to survive is for the "westernmost." It seems worth noting here that this survey refers to a "trap door" on the third story.)

Beneath the canted, shingled green roof, the hinged portion of the façade, of simulated sanded gray stone, with cream trim, swings open. This section, arranged with the typical symmetry of Philadelphia architecture of this time, contains five twelve-light windows,† and a graceful arched and panelled mahogany door, fitted with its own brass lock. The façade also has a lock, and of course the best baby houses traditionally have been fitted with locks, indicating what prized possessions they were. Unfortunately, the front door key is lost.

Surprisingly, the muntins of the windows are

---

* Mr. Lewis mentioned that the policy "was for £500 Pennsylvania Currency. In terms of United States Federal money, this was $1333.33, a large amount for a single fire policy. For this reason, as was customary with the Company, the back of the house was insured under another policy, this being No. 1001, also for £500."

† *The Carpenters' Company of the City and County of Philadelphia Rule Book* shows only twelve-light windows. (Reprinted by The Pyne Press, Princeton, N. J., 1971.)

simulated in leather, a most unusual material to be employed for this purpose. Miss Hosie remembers that when she played with the house in her childhood, these were backed with a sheet of mica to simulate glazing.

The interior detail of the small mansion is worthy of the handsome exterior. Painted rugs are on the floors of the four rooms and the stairhall, more realistic than one might suppose since painted floor cloths were often used in full-sized houses at this time. There are also painted hearths. A winding staircase leads to the second floor, and each of the rooms, upstairs and down, contains a fireplace and mantel, properly located to correspond to the chimneys. (In lesser dolls' houses these are sometimes erratically situated.) The original brass tool holders are still in place, attached to each side of the four mantels.

Downstairs, the fireplace walls contain raised mahogany cupboards. Upstairs, painted shelves fill the walls at both sides of the two fireplaces. Chair rail of mahogany, its lower section painted white, defines the walls of all the rooms.

A few pieces of the lovely early furniture survive, notably a pair of rope four-poster beds and two black hair-cloth sofas, one of these with a curved Hepplewhite back.

Because the dolls' house spent a century and a half in Oxford, and relatively few years in Philadelphia, perhaps Oxford has as much of a claim to this treasure as has the city in which it was built. But it is so perfect a copy of an actual Philadelphia house, that it is unfortunate that an original plan to locate it in the Bishop White house (part of the Society Hill Restoration)* had to be abandoned. The Bishop had four daughters, and since they may very well have played with (or at least visited) the dolls' house before its departure for Oxford, this was an appropriate choice.

It seems more than a footnote, perhaps a proper post mortem, that the house at Tenth and High stood on a site now occupied by part of Strawbridge & Clothier. Thanks to the baby house, it is possible to see what manner of house stood there before. Owing to the nature of dolls' houses, no one can tear this one down to build a department store, or any other building whatsoever. Unfortunately, it *is* possible to destroy dolls' houses, even without miniature bulldozers, and to mislay their history.

All dolls' house partisans must be grateful that this one survives in such an excellent state of repair, along with its fire marks and enough family information to indicate that, whether Cresson or Shippen-Miller in origin, it was unquestionably made in—and "insured" in—Philadelphia, most certainly not too many years after 1800. If ever it becomes possible to *prove* that fire marks on a baby house have indeed furnished even a footnote to "life-sized" history, so much the better.

THE VICKERMAN BABY HOUSE

DATE: 1816
HEIGHT: 37"
WIDTH: 45"
DEPTH: 18"
OWNER: MRS. CHARLES G. SUNSTEIN (PENNSYLVANIA)

When the owner of this elegant baby house first wrote to me in the spring of 1971, she referred to a furnished dolls' house she had recently acquired, "built in 1816 by Vickerman, an architect of that period." Mrs. Sunstein had been told that this treasure had been in a private museum. With it she was given pictures of the interior as it had appeared in 1931 when it had been shown at an antiques exposition, and a

---

* Owing to the degree of traffic rattling by in the neighborhood, a plan to furnish the upper floors of the Bishop White house, on one of which the dolls' house would have been placed, was relinquished. The house is (in 1974) in the Merchant's Exchange Building, at the corner of Third and Walnut Streets, as a visual exhibit for school children, in a program administered by the Philadelphia public school system.

Figure 73

Figure 74

news story from a Scranton, Pennsylvania, paper detailing its history and contents.

Whether or not "Vickerman" was an American or an English architect was not mentioned, and one sent off a letter daring to hope (in view of the shortage of early dolls' houses in the United States) that both Vickerman and his handiwork were American. When this hope proved to be false (which a later examination of the Georgian façade made clear), one did not have to search unduly for rationalizations to justify its inclusion in a book called *Dolls' Houses in America*. A house which had been in the United States since 1931 (at the latest), had surely taken out citizenship papers by the 1970's. Indeed, if this miniature Georgian mansion had been a log cabin, one might have said it had squatter's rights to the bit of Pennsylvania it occupied.

As its pictures reveal, the house bears more than a passing resemblance both to Denton Welch's baby house, and to "Amelia's,"* although both are at least a generation earlier, and both have certain superiorities. This lovely house, however, has a few superiorities of its own.

Although it lacks the pedimented roof of the other two houses (and the fine balustrading of the Denton Welch), and bears a simple painted façade rather than the "dressed stone" and tall pilasters of the one, and the "painted red bricks" and coigning of the other, it alone of the three has a fine curving interior staircase—and, like Amelia's, most of its original furnishings.

All three houses have fanlights above handsomely panelled front doors, and our elegant immigrant has a similar but more elaborately mullioned Palladian window above it than the one on the Denton Welch.

There is lovely Georgian wainscoting in the three principal rooms, beautifully panelled interior doors with pink and blue china knobs,* and a most remarkable likelihood that the old buttermilk paint on the interior walls has been, like the red damask (cracking with age on the walls of the dining-room), present since 1816.

The magnificent grates are shown separately (Fig. 75). It is regrettable that the tester bed and a clock under glass were stolen some time after the house was exhibited in 1931, but so much is left, that the contents might serve to catalogue a Regency house in full size. Specifically Regency are the painted wooden chairs and the magnificent looking-glass on the chimney-breast of the upper-left-hand room, and there are Leeds figures, a rare metal knife box, and, earlier, hall-marked pewter dating from 1795. The pictures are wonderfully diversified, including hunting prints in the drawing-room, silhouettes (five) of the original family, and steel engravings, one of them, over the fireplace in the dining-room, of a jousting scene in a village. Another depicts Marcus Curtius, the legendary hero of ancient Rome, a timely classical reference.

Of particular note are two signed pieces, pictured separately (Fig. 76). Incised on their underside is "J. Bubb Maker."

There have clearly been American additions to the baby house: the late Victorian Carver chairs in the kitchen (Plate 7) for one, and the "American Newspaper Directory, 1776." The latter was published in 1876 and appears to be a Philadelphia Centennial item.

The 1931 news feature which accompanied the dolls' house referred to Mr. Vickerman's creation as "furnished in the taste of the early nineteenth century, with the assistance of his friends the cabinetmaker, silversmith and ironworker." Perhaps the silver had been sold off, or was stolen along with the bed and the clock, but so much remains that this small mansion, long hidden away, is a most important addition to

---

* Both of these houses may be found in *English Dolls' Houses of the 18th and 19th Centuries*.

* The doors of Amelia's house have white china knobs.

DOLLS' HOUSES FROM THE MID-ATLANTIC REGION

dolls' house history on both sides of the Atlantic.

THE VICKERMAN FIREGRATES

HEIGHT (OF FIREPLACE AT LEFT): 8¼″
WIDTH (OF FIREPLACE AT LEFT): 7″

Figure 75

Figure 76

In the Vickerman baby house (Fig. 74), the beautiful fire grates, different in each room, have magnificent cut steel fenders and fire tools. Matching repoussé brass medallions trim both grates and fenders, and there are painted embellishments of red and gold and green as well.

These grates are of salesman's sample (if one will pardon the expression) quality. The kitchen grate (center), according to the proud owner, has "perfect draughts" (though presumably she has not ventured to cook upon it), and the dining-room fireplace (left) "will hold a fire." Four chimney pots in the flat roof would lead properly from these fixtures, which have movable dampers.

FURNISHINGS FROM THE VICKERMAN HOUSE

HEIGHT (OF CHEST): 4¼″
WIDTH (OF CHEST): 3¾″
DEPTH (OF CHEST): 1½″

There are many unusual and beautiful furnishings in the Vickerman baby house (Fig. 74), and although they are not as elegant as some of the other pieces, the three-drawer chest and the drop-leaf table* illustrated are of particular interest because they are signed. Incised beneath each of these two pieces is "J. Bubb Maker."

In her book about several English dolls' house collections,† Jean Latham shows what appears to be the identical drop-leaf table, a tilt-top table, and a four-drawer chest (escut-

* Measurements, open: 6¼″ × 6½″.

† *Dolls' Houses: A Personal Choice*, A. and C. Black, 1969.

cheons on the drawers have seemingly been added), which she says are signed "J. Bebbe, Maker." This appears to be an error. Since signed dolls' house furniture of any date is rare indeed, we shall hope one day to learn more about "J. Bubb."

On the table are rare pieces of bristol, a candelabrum, and a rare pair of cordial glasses with air-twist stems. The porcelain candlesticks and bowl on the chest are part of a white porcelain toilet set, with gold and floral trim, which includes bowl, pitcher, soap dish, sponge bowl, and flower bowl. (There is no mark.)

HISTORIC PRESERVATION IN MINIATURE: UNIQUE EXAMPLES

THE VOEGLER HOUSE IN WEST CHESTER

DATE: CA. 1836
HEIGHT: 7'10"
WIDTH (BENEATH PROJECTING CORNICE): 73"
DEPTH: 32"
OWNER: CHESTER COUNTY HISTORICAL SOCIETY (WEST CHESTER, PENNSYLVANIA)

Like "Mrs. Bryant's Pleasure" * in the Bethnal Green Museum, and the great seventeenth- and eighteenth-century cupboard houses in the Netherlands, this magnificent house was clearly an adult's toy rather than a child's. Even so, three dolls inhabit the four elegant rooms, and it is no mere model.

* With respect to Mrs. Bryant's, Vivien Greene alludes to "the continuity of this tradition, of the houses or furnished rooms, kept in vestibules or drawing-rooms, not playthings but planned and furnished to please an adult."

Figure 77

It is known that the house was "in the Price family," * and that it was made, ca. 1836, by a Philadelphia cabinetmaker and upholsterer named Voegler. In view of his calling, it is not surprising that the larger part of his work is to be found on the interior of the immense house.† Again like the Dutch houses, the exterior is largely a cabinet, with glass doors (a replacement, for viewing purposes, of the original wooden ones). There is only a suggestion of façade, but what there is reflects, as a member of the Society's staff once pointed out, "The Greek Revival Temples in vogue at that time."

He referred to the imposing pedimented roof, and to three classical pilasters which adorn the front. There is also a reference inside: classical ruins are painted above the wainscoted dining-room walls. It is tempting to suspect neighboring influences: Thomas U. Walter, perhaps a few years before, had added a classical portico to nearby Andalusia, the riverfront estate of Nicholas Biddle, the man given most credit for bringing the classical revival to America. It may be only a coincidence that his architect was a native of West Chester where the Price family resided, but clearly the classical revival was in the air, to say the least, of the Philadelphia countryside.

The furnishings of this miniature mansion are what might be expected of a master craftsman of full-sized furniture. Most of the late Empire furniture is of mahogany (veneered on pine and poplar), and large in scale—perhaps two inches to a foot. The dining-room chairs, including their backs, are seven inches tall. (The patrician lady standing in the dining-room holds her porcelain head ten inches high.) The furniture

* The house was given to the museum by Mrs. Susan Price Sever, a member of the family, and Mrs. Julia T. Darlington, an antiques dealer who early on appreciated the house, and was instrumental in its preservation.

† Because of the great size of the doll house, and its location, it is presently impossible to photograph it as a unit.

comprises, in the phrase so dearly beloved of antique furniture dealers and collectors, "important antiques" in miniature; pieces which would be noteworthy indeed in full size, but are perhaps even rarer in miniature.

One of these is a tall case clock by Thomas Wagstaff, who according to Mr. Bart Anderson, a former director of the Society, was an English eighteenth-century clockmaker who visited the United States at least once, and made clocks for his fellow Quakers on this side of the ocean. Mr. Anderson, who knows of half a dozen Wagstaff clocks in Chester County alone, believes this to be the only known example made for a doll, and it is actually a Wagstaff watch, hanging on a hook inside the "tall" case (in the form often taken by watch holders). In this dolls' house version, engraved gold spandrels inside the wooden case surround the face.

Several of the most beautiful pieces are in the bedroom,* including a bed with exquisitely carved posts (and a crocheted tester), and a chest of drawers with glass knobs and perfect and infinitesimal keyholes. There is also a beautiful set of bedsteps of delicate design with rose velvet panels.

Also in the bedroom is an "important" accessory: a marked Tuckerware bowl and pitcher. Since the celebrated Philadelphia porcelain factory was in business very little more than a decade (ca. 1826–38), all of it is rare, but miniature Tuckerware is rarer still. This bowl and pitcher with its floral decoration and gilt edging appears to have been made during the last few years of the factory, when European workers were employed and imitations of Sèvres wares were made.† Several small pieces, including a soap dish, appear to belong to the chamber set, but they are too small to bear a mark.

* As Mr. Anderson suggests, it is puzzling that this bedroom is alongside the kitchen on the lower floor, with dining-room and parlor above.

† Boger, *The Dictionary of Antiques and the Decorative Arts*, Scribners, 1957.

The arts of the needleworker as well as the upholsterer are evident throughout the house (in tandem, as they so often are), and one wonders if a member of the Price family had a hand in working the many pieces of petitpoint with which the sofas, chairs, and ottomans are upholstered. A graceful pole screen in the drawing-room is also worked in petitpoint, adjustable on its Empire standard; nearby, on the center table, is a marvelous hand-worked cover with tasseled corners. Most probably by the same hand, two carpets are also worked in needlepoint, rose with a darker border in the dining-room, and a floral pattern in the drawing-room. All types of hand-worked floor coverings are represented, including a minutely hooked

Figure 78

HISTORIC PRESERVATION IN MINIATURE: UNIQUE EXAMPLES

rug in the bedroom and a braided one in the kitchen. One might hazard a guess that the house was built for an expert needlewoman, and the house was a showcase for her talents.

It is undoubtedly the upholsterer rather than the needlewoman who is responsible for the handsome, lined taffeta draperies with gilded wood cornices in the three principal rooms. These hang in the twelve-light windows at the sides of the house—its only architectural element besides the roof and pilasters. These draperies are fringed or edged with braid, a different style or color in each of the rooms, and behind them hang workable Venetian blinds, fashionable in the eighteenth century, but perhaps a laggard style in such a house as this.*

To catalogue all the treasures in the Voegler house is an impracticality, but it is necessary to allude at least to a dining-room piece of the type referred to by Blackie† as a slab sideboard (this one has a marble top), a corner cupboard containing a gilt-edged white porcelain dinner service, a wooden butler's tray, a pair of gilded pewter chandeliers with workable wicks, silver napkin rings, and even a pair of silver serving dishes, rare, in miniature, certainly, with their openings for hot water.

Perhaps the kitchen was an insufficient challenge to the upholsterer's art; at least the furnishings in this one are relatively simple. Still, there are two drop-leaf tables, the larger one painted green, with a matching set of handsomely turned chairs.

It may be pertinent to note that this Pennsylvania mansion is contemporary with the Brett house in New York (Fig. 122), and although no two dolls' houses could be less alike in style or scale, both were made with taste and skill and elaboration, and both reflect their times with precision and grace.

* According to Frances Lichten, the style began to subside ca. 1840. (*The Decorative Arts of Victoria's Era*, Scribners, 1950.)

† Blackie and Sons, *The Victorian Cabinet-Maker's Assistant*, Dover Publications, 1970. (Reprint of the 1853 original.)

A HOUSE FROM ENGLEWOOD, NEW JERSEY

DATE: CA. 1865
HEIGHT (NOT INCLUDING 10″ BASE): 40″
WIDTH: 29″
DEPTH: 17″
OWNER: PIXIE GROSSMAN PREWITT (CONNECTICUT)

There is something beguiling about the exterior of this mid-nineteenth-century house from Englewood, New Jersey, even though its builder clearly disdained architectural frippery except for the windows with their bold lintels which he provided multitudinously on both front and back.

Since the windows are so important, it seems fortuitous that the twenty-one pairs of original net curtains have survived. Diaphanous and fringed, they embellish the rear wall and lend

Figure 79

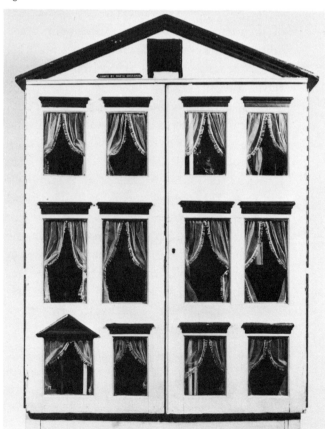

DOLLS' HOUSES FROM THE MID-ATLANTIC REGION

the façade a fanciful dimension. The architect clearly thought about the windows, making those on the second floor larger than the others, as befits drawing-room windows, and providing one on the bottom floor with a glazed pediment. The latter corresponds to the staircase hall, and appears to be the builder's concession to a front door.

The front opens in two sections, on piano hinges, and it may be locked. A locksmith called in by the owner to provide a missing key told her that the lock was handmade and of the type used in the mid-nineteenth century. Its presence indicates what a prized possession this house was considered to be, which is not surprising when we hear its story.

Figure 80

A Mrs. Miller, the daughter of the original owner, was eighty-five years old in 1957 when she sold it to a Hillsdale, New Jersey, antiques dealer (whose name is known). This dealer sold it to a friend of the present owner who then presented it to her. Although this generous friend bought the house without most of the furniture, she had examined the original contents. Many of the pieces bore metal labels on backs or bottoms marked "MASTER FURNITURE MAKER—1858" or "MASTER FURNITURE MAKER—1860." So many toys are referred to as salesman's samples by unknowing collectors and dealers, that it seems sad indeed to learn that these, which appear to have been clearly entitled to the term, were parted from the house which was built to contain them.

The house was reportedly built by Mrs. Miller's grandfather, about 1865, expressly for this miniature sample furniture given to his daughter by a traveling furniture salesman. A photograph of the house with these original furnishings was supplied by the dealer, but unfortunately this has been mislaid.

However, some of the furniture that accompanied the house, though none of the rare marked pieces, were in it when it was presented in 1957 to young Miss Pixie Grossman, now Mrs. Prewitt.

THE SANITARY FAIR HOUSE OF U. S. GRANT

DATE: 1864
HEIGHT (OVERALL): 66" (Including chimney) 72"
WIDTH: (Including eaves) 74"
DEPTH: (Including eaves) 59"
OWNER: HISTORICAL SOCIETY OF DELAWARE (WILMINGTON, DELAWARE)

One of the most historic—and patriotic—of American dolls' houses has "1776" emblazoned on the glass panel above its entrance, and "U. S. Grant" on a silver nameplate attached to one of its pair of entrance doors. The 1776 is purely nostalgic: this splendid dolls' house was exhibited at the "Sanitary Fair" held in Philadelphia in 1864. The name of General Grant (whose very initials were patriotic) was purely symbolic: in 1864 the General's name was a household word (in Union households, at least); he resided in the dolls' house only in spirit before he moved to the White House five years later.

The imposing house and its elaborate furnishings, made by Philadelphia craftsmen, and exhibited at the Great Central Fair as a fund-raising project for sick and wounded Civil War soldiers,* is five-and-a-half feet tall, contains three stories above a windowed suggestion of a basement, and beneath a roof crowned by an abbreviated widow's walk. A splendid staircase (not visible in the illustration) connects the nine rooms, realistically arranged one on each side of the center hall in front, plus an additional room on each floor at the back. It is possible to see in the illustration the connecting doors to the rear rooms (on the left-hand side of the house).

In addition to the customary parlor, dining-room, kitchen, and bed chambers to be found in a proper house of the period, this remarkably complete miniature mansion contains a library, a game room, a maid's room, and—the most extraordinary room in the house—an art gallery. The paintings which hang in this rare miniature gallery were listed in a Philadelphia newspaper of June 13, 1864, *Our Daily Fare.*

Several well-known Philadelphia artists are represented, including E. D. Lewis, who after exhibiting at the Pennsylvania Academy in 1854 "and subsequently at the National Academy and Boston Athenaeum . . . quickly became one of the most popular painters in Philadelphia."† Inasmuch as his subjects were chiefly scenes in

---

* A 1956 history of this house in *The Spinning Wheel* relates that the fair was a great financial success, realizing the sum (which must have been fantastic at the time) of more than $1,000,000.

† *Dictionary of Artists in America,* Yale University Press, 1964.

DOLLS' HOUSES FROM THE MID-ATLANTIC REGION

Pennsylvania, New York, and New England, it is not surprising that among the four Lewis landscapes in the dolls' house, one was of Mt. Washington, and one of Lake George. Another Philadelphia artist included is Peter Frederick Rothermel, "historical and portrait painter" and, for a number of years, director of the Pennsylvania Academy. After the Civil War he devoted almost five years to his most ambitious work, "The Battle of Gettysburg," now in the State Capitol at Harrisburg. Presumably, for the dolls' house, he devoted a fraction of that time to a picture a fraction of its size, and one with a less ambitious theme. This was entitled "Look at Dolly," and is a rare Rothermel, to say the least.

Figure 81

Dolly could also look at the picture—in comfort. In the center of the art gallery, there is a large, circular ottoman,* the ultimate piece of Victorian furniture (and the only antique miniature example known to me).

Among the twenty-five diminutive works of art, the largest of which measures three by five inches, landscapes predominate. An international treasure mingles with the "contemporary" American pictures: "Ruins of a Temple of the Sun," by the Neapolitan seventeenth-century

---

* In *Decorative Arts of Victoria's Era* (Scribners, 1950), Frances Lichten calls this "an ottoman or causeuse." In the *Dictionary of Antiques and the Decorative Arts* (Scribners, 1957), the Bogers refer to it as a "borne."

master Salvator Rosa. Even this is well documented; the Rosa was presented to the dolls' house by a Miss Mary Wilcox.

Perhaps Miss Wilcox was a friend of "Miss Biddle," whose name lends additional Philadelphia flavor to the Delaware treasure, and who contributed the house, valued at $1,000, to the Fair. This sum seems modest, even for its day, when some of the details of the house are considered. There were, for instance, three marble fireplaces, one of which gave an expert marble cutter three days of employment. There were also handsome curtains, draperies, and carpets (some of these replaced during a 1965 refurbishing).*

One account relates that, at the Fair, "subscriptions at $10 [which] . . . brought in $2,300 to the Treasury" gave subscribers "the privilege of deciding what disposition to make of the model house." It seems more likely that this sum entitled each subscriber to participate in a lottery. The details are obscured by time, but Colonel Henry S. McComb of Wilmington became the owner, and he just happened to have a seven-year-old daughter named Nellie, and she appears to have taken good care of her dolls' house, one of the most historic and beautiful in the United States.

A NEW JERSEY MANSION AND GARDEN

DATE: CA. 1870 (?)
HEIGHT (NOT INCLUDING BELVEDERE): 39"
WIDTH (NOT INCLUDING BAYS): 26½"
DEPTH: 26"
(ON A BASE 8' LONG AND 66½" WIDE)
OWNER: THE STRONG MUSEUM (ROCHESTER, NEW YORK)

In a collection of nearly eight hundred dolls' houses, it should be difficult to single out the most imposing, but owing to the presence in the Strong collection of this mansion from Haddonfield, New Jersey, with its formal garden and working fountain, there is no problem!

Regrettably, as with most of the material the late Mrs. Strong collected, the history of this formidable edifice (a word used advisedly) is lost, but at least the place name of Haddonfield has remained, and perhaps a New Jersey resident will recognize the photograph and supply the missing information.

The perfection to be seen here suggests a model as much as a dolls' house, and it is of interest to compare this house from Haddonfield with the architects' model from Philadelphia in Fig. 86. The latter, with its porches and architectural gas-light fixtures at the base has more elaboration, but the dolls' house has a windowed cellar which the model lacks, and both have dormered mansards, belvederes, and bays. Even the green-flocked base on which the dolls' house rests is similar in character to the shaped bases usually to be seen on architectural models. (Unfortunately, this base was removed at the time when the photograph of the model was made.)

Since Haddonfield is just a few miles across the Delaware from Philadelphia, it is not surprising that the two miniature houses should share regional similarities. Because the possibility always lurks that the dolls' house was made as a copy of an older house, it is risky to infer that it is as old as the Centennial model, but it *is* clear that it represents a house built in the 'seventies.

The interior is "roomy"—there are eight rooms plus central halls, attic, and the rare cellar, previously mentioned, with window screens and a laundry. This interior is not shown because it does not compare in quality and detail to the exterior, and one wonders if at some point in its history the back was sheared off what may also have been a model, and the rooms added.

Whatever the case, the Haddonfield house,

---

* The photograph was made prior to this refurbishing.

DOLLS' HOUSES FROM THE MID-ATLANTIC REGION

Figure 82

HISTORIC PRESERVATION IN MINIATURE: UNIQUE EXAMPLES

with its elegant garden laid out in walks and balustraded parterres around the central fountain, and the handsome fence with its panelled base and prettily turned posts, is a most impressive addition to miniature architecture.

THE "SOUTH JERSEY"

DATE: CA. 1870's
HEIGHT: 44"
WIDTH (INCLUDING EAVES): 41"
DEPTH (INCLUDING EAVES, PLUS BAYS, AND STAIRS): 25"
OWNER: AUTHOR'S COLLECTION

Figure 83

Because the South Jersey mansion has been described and pictured in several books about dolls' houses, as well as in a magazine article reprinted in many languages, and is also the "central character" in a juvenile mystery which it inspired,* it seemingly requires little additional comment here.

As a splendid example of post-Civil War "sandstone" architecture, however, it is illustrated, with the essential information that a bit of roof above the convex mansard, obviously

* *The Dolls' House Mystery*, Flora Gill Jacobs, Coward-McCann, 1958.

(78)

DOLLS' HOUSES FROM THE MID-ATLANTIC REGION

Figure 84

missing when the house was found, and the original foundation with its elaborate staircase, are restorations and/or additions. (One section of the original foundation remained, establishing the correct style and depth for the replacement.) It is tempting to imagine that the original roofline might have included a central turret!

A few other details may also be essential: The house opens in back in three sandstone sections at the rear (carefully preserved, but replaced by Plexiglas doors for viewing purposes). Behind the kitchen and bath (the latter an improvisation rashly added early on by the inexperienced collector), staircase halls, up and down, large enough to contain furniture, are additional rooms which cannot be seen in the interior view. The iron Christmas tree fence is, of course, an addition, and so is the pair of French toy street lamps with workable wicks and "Deposé JS Paris" molded on their bases.

The house, the first this collector found—and clearly beginner's luck—came in 1945 from an antique dealer's barn in Malaga, New Jersey, where layers of dust had nearly obscured its beauty; and time (eight years) had entirely obscured its history, apparently, alas, forever.

A PHILADELPHIA TOWN HOUSE

DATE: CA. 1870'S
HEIGHT: 6'
WIDTH: 38"
DEPTH: 24"
OWNER: MRS. JAMES TIMPSON (NEW JERSEY AND MASSACHUSETTS)

Having frequently confessed to a partiality for collecting coincidences as well as dolls' houses, one finds this splendid *dolls' house* especially appealing because it relates to a splendid *coincidence*.

While these pages were in progress, I ordered the Hopkinsons' compendium* about the celebrated 1970 auction of their "dolls and miniatures," and, when it arrived, was enraptured with the portrait of this tall town house on the back cover. When I wrote to Mr. Hopkinson to attempt to learn where the house had gone, he promptly forwarded the name of the Bolton, Massachusetts, auctioneer who had presided at the sale, but the latter did not reply to my inquiry.

That was in April of 1971. Some months later, Mrs. Timpson, whose charming collection in Chatham, Massachusetts, has delighted many visitors to the "Ten O'Clock Scholar," happened to include, with pictures she'd promised of several of her houses, one which was unexpected. Its identity can be guessed: one was this house, the very one which seemingly had dropped from sight!

As the photograph indicates, the house is not, as it was described in the catalogue, a row house. There are windows on both sides, but it is, as

---

* *Dolls and Miniatures with their Prices at Auction* by Isabella and William Hopkinson.

HISTORIC PRESERVATION IN MINIATURE: UNIQUE EXAMPLES

Figure 85

Mrs. Timpson referred to it, a copy of a Philadelphia town house, ca. 1850–60. Although this is very likely the date of the actual house, the dolls' house, as often happens, may be later, since many a dolls' house was made as a copy of a family house which had been occupied for a period of years.

The façade of the house opens in two sections. The attic is false, but there are two rooms on each of the other three floors, and the exterior is painted to represent brick, carefully delineated in a mellow red. There is "a simple fireplace" in each room. The house has its own lock, indicating that it was prized in the early years of its lamentably lost history. The "08" on the glazed panel above the right-hand door may be a clue to the latter. (Unfortunately, the left-hand door, along with the important part of the address, was missing and had to be replaced.)

AN ARCHITECT'S MODEL FROM PHILADELPHIA

DATE: 1876
HEIGHT: 60″
BASE: 34″ SQUARE
OWNER: THE SMITHSONIAN INSTITUTION (WASHINGTON, D.C.)

At Christmas 1971, this invincibly Victorian architect's model was displayed at an entrance of the Smithsonian's Museum of History and Technology with a tree and a group of antique toys, so perhaps one may be allowed a similar juxtaposition of this model and some dolls' houses.

The model, which I have further taken the liberty of comparing with a dolls' house to be seen in Fig. 82, was made in the Centennial year of 1876 in the Centennial city of Philadelphia, and therefore it was possibly made for Centennial display. The name of its maker, Leonard Roth, is known, but no other history is available.

This glorious example of Victorian eclecticism is interpreted in metal as well as wood: The shingled wooden mansard with its cast metal railing "shows the influence of the French Second Empire mode" while the pagoda-styled cupola upon the belvedere was inspired by "the Oriental designs then just beginning to come in from China and Japan." Embellishment upon embellishment: This is topped by a metal weather vane. There is more metal in the curlicued stems of the gas fixtures with their white glass globes which have been electrified to illuminate the several flights of exterior stairs. The wooden lace fretwork valance that drips prettily from the porch cornice is a lingering reminder of "Steamboat Gothic."

DOLLS' HOUSES FROM THE MID-ATLANTIC REGION

Figure 86

THE WHITE HOUSE DOLLS' HOUSE (I)

DATE: 1878
HEIGHT: 57"
WIDTH (NOT INCLUDING BAYS): 30¾"
DEPTH (NOT INCLUDING STAIRS): 28¾"
OWNER: THE RUTHERFORD B. HAYES LIBRARY (FREMONT, OHIO)

Rich both in history and architectural detail, this piece of high Victoriana with its three bays and towering belvedere, was made for ten-year-old Fanny Hayes when her father was president. Except for fortunate Fanny's other house (Fig. 90), it remains the only White House dolls' house to come to light.*

Because it was made for the daughter of a president, the presentation of this stately toy, was, like all matters relating to a presidential family, properly documented. We are indebted to Mr. Watt Marchman, Director of the Rutherford B. Hayes Library in Fremont, for information from several contemporary news stories.

On February 21, 1878, President and Mrs. Hayes attended the Methodist Fair at the Masonic Temple in Baltimore, for the benefit of the Emory Grove Camp-Meeting Association. "After the reception," the Cincinnati *Commercial* reported the next day, "Mrs. Hayes was presented by the lady managers (of the Fair) with a handsome doll playhouse for her daughter, Miss Fanny Hayes."

When the dolls' house was restored in 1959–60, the name of the maker and his address were found modestly inscribed inside the belvedere: "Made by George C. Brown, Baltimore, Md." The date, "February 13, 1878," was added. According to Mr. Marchman, a Baltimore directory for 1878 showed that George C. Brown, a

Such continuous porches as these surrounded the four sides of more than one Victorian mansion, affording, like the deck of a ship, an after-dinner constitutional for one who wished a convenient stroll.*

The model contains sash windows, and a double interior staircase from the first floor to the cupola. Both of these assets are sometimes found in the best dolls' houses, but might not have been expected in a model. In any case, there is a fine line between a fine dolls' house and an architect's model, and it has been irresistible to include this one glorious specimen.

---

* The writer lives in a Maryland Colonial Revival house to which such porches had been added late in the 'nineties by an occupant who was said to like his evening promenade. They were subtracted, alas, in the 1930's.

* Mrs. Longworth's dolls' house (see *A History of Dolls' Houses*) was hers when she was a little girl in Oyster Bay, and is therefore in a somewhat different category. A dolls' house made for the Cleveland children said to be a miniature copy of the White House has seemingly vanished without a trace.

Figure 87

carpenter and builder, was living at 186 Saratoga Street.

(Mr. Brown, in signing his work, may have been conscious of the fact that in building for a presidential daughter he was building for posterity, though less notable dolls' houses occasionally bear signatures.* In any case, dolls' house collectors should include a strong magnifying glass among their supplies!)

Although the furnishings were lost, at the time the house was restored, Mrs. Webb C. Hayes, whose husband is a great-grandson of the nineteenth president, spent two years collecting antique replacements with great care for fidelity and scale.

In March of 1878, Miss Grundy (Austine Snead), a female Washington correspondent,

* A modest house in Fig. 157 was signed on the bottom, and there must be many more.

Figure 88

Figure 89

after a tour of the White House living quarters, wrote an article entitled "How Presidents Live—Description of the White House at Washington."

"Most agreeable reminders of the presence of children," she wrote, "are the two large 'baby houses' standing in the hall, in which the president's only daughter, little Fannie, between ten and eleven years of age, and the youngest child, Scott, some three or four years younger, take great delight. . . ."

HISTORIC PRESERVATION IN MINIATURE: UNIQUE EXAMPLES

One can well believe it. The house built by Mr. Brown, with its staircase hall, attic rooms, and four chimneys, is the ultimate in Victorian dolls' houses—it even has a skylight—and it would figure prominently in dolls' house history even if its history weren't so illustrious.

THE WHITE HOUSE DOLLS' HOUSE (II)

DATE: 1877
HEIGHT (INCLUDING CHIMNEYS): 48"
WIDTH (OVERALL): 50"
DEPTH (NOT INCLUDING BAYS): 21½"
OWNER: THE RUTHERFORD B. HAYES LIBRARY (FREMONT, OHIO)

Only two White House dolls' houses are known to be extant, and the descendants of President Rutherford B. Hayes appear to have a monopoly. One was built for young Fanny Hayes in Washington in 1877, and the other was built for her in Baltimore in 1878 (Fig. 87). Since the 1877 house did not come to light till a few years ago, perhaps there is still hope of discovering others.

In 1965, in the new edition of *A History of Dolls' Houses*, I mentioned an 1878 newspaper reference to the "two large 'baby houses' standing in the hall" of the White House, and alluded to the belief of Mr. Watt Marchman, Director of the Rutherford B. Hayes Library in Fremont, that this second house had not been preserved. "It was made for the Hayes children in Washington for $15, and is remembered by one of President Hayes' grandsons, Walter S. Hayes, of Perrysburg, Ohio, as more of a frame house for rooms of doll furniture."

Curiously, not long after these words were printed, I received a phone call from New York from one who purported to have the second Hayes house for sale. I relayed the information to Mrs. Webb C. Hayes, whose husband is a great-grandson of the nineteenth president, and who had been responsible, along with Mr. Marchman, for refurbishing Hayes dolls' house I with such authenticity and care.

Before the Hayes Library purchased this Hayes dolls' house II, the probability of its being Fanny Hayes' 1877 "play house" was taken up with Walter S. Hayes, the presidential grandson mentioned above, who remembered playing with both houses, in his youth, in the Hayes' Ohio residence. "When he saw it, he definitely remembered it as . . . the missing one. '. . . That is the dolls' house we played with as children [along] with the one in the Museum. They were located in the unfinished attic over the drawing-room, and it was on rainy days that we trooped up there to play. . . .'"

This is the record of a conversation Mr. Marchman had with Mr. Hayes in December 1966, and the unfinished attic Mr. Hayes referred to was in the Spiegel Grove residence, which is

Figure 90

(84)

DOLLS' HOUSES FROM THE MID-ATLANTIC REGION

still in the possession of the Hayes family. Both dolls' houses were, of course, removed to Ohio after the family left the White House.

"It seems," Mr. Marchman writes, "that the 1877 dolls' house was acquired by the family of Mrs. Charles Gordone of New York, when they were living in Columbus, Ohio, from Hayes relatives in Columbus." One can understand why this second house may have taken second place to the miniature mansion from Baltimore, but although less architectural detail was lavished upon it, it would have, both from a dolls' house point of view, and a historical point of view, a larger share of the limelight if it were not obliged to stand in such a majestic shadow.

Less imposing in height and style, but larger in scale ($\frac{1}{8}'' = 1'$), it is, as its portrait shows, also a three-story house with attic and staircase; and there are well-designed bays on each side of the entrance—double doors with a rectangular light above them. The bays are surmounted by dentelated cornices which match the one beneath the green mansard roof; and the embossed brick surface, the coigning, the decorative lintels above the windows, and the twin chimneys make the bill which Madison Magruder, a Washington carpenter-contractor rendered to Mrs. Hayes, seem reasonable even for 1877: "For one play house, $15.00." But perhaps Mr. Magruder was pleased to be asked to build a "play house" for the White House, and he had no way of knowing that he'd be outdone the following year by a present from Baltimore. The only piece of Fanny Hayes' dolls' house furniture which survived, along with the two empty houses, is a tin bathtub which is the proper scale for this house II.

In recent years, both dolls' houses have returned to Washington for visits. The Baltimore house was on view at the Smithsonian for some months, following its refurbishing in the early '60s, and the house shown here was lent to the White House at Christmas 1971, where, embellished with live boxwood shrubbery in front, and with evergreen wreaths on the doors and in all the front windows, it beguiled many a White House visitor.* See Appendix for plans.

A NEWARK HOUSE DATED 1882

DATE: 1882
HEIGHT (NOT INCLUDING CUPOLA): 29¾"
WIDTH: 42¾"
DEPTH: 30¾"
OWNER: THE NEWARK MUSEUM (NEWARK, NEW JERSEY)

"The house is a Newark product. It was built by a Newark carpenter in 1882 for a Newark girl's Christmas. It was decorated with papers

---

* The writer and her daughter saw it at this time, at a reception for Washington Press Club members and their children, and very charming it looked. This White House view was illustrated in the December 1971 issue of *House and Garden*.

Figure 91

HISTORIC PRESERVATION IN MINIATURE: UNIQUE EXAMPLES

Figure 92

and carpets made in Newark, and the furniture was bought in shops here and in New York." These lines appeared in *Playthings*, the toy trade publication, in 1927. Since the dolls' house described had been given to the museum the year before, undoubtedly this information was fresh in the mind of the curator who furnished it to *Playthings*, and the notation about the papers and carpets having been made in Newark seems of particular interest.

It is necessary to study the two pictures of this pleasing house carefully in order to realize that one is of the front and one of the back, and that both open in an identical manner. Variations in pediments and panels of the front and rear doors are the only discernible differences. As we might in an actual house, we glimpse the dining-room through the kitchen, and the front rooms upstairs through the two in back. The parlor is double, and it is unfortunate that since it may be seen from either front or back, this is the one section closed in the photograph of the rear.

When I visited the Newark Museum many years ago this most realistic house was in storage (as it is at present), but floor plans shown to me further suggested an actual house. There is an alcove off the upstairs sitting-room, for instance (presided over by a parrot in a gilded cage), a bathroom (thoroughly furnished), and a back hall with an ice box.

It is clear that the house was restored at some stage in its long history, and repainted. The degree of "restoration" is puzzling: looking closely, it is possible to see that arched windows painted on the cupola, totally out of character with the colonial revival style of the rest, have been painted over. Obviously, the many windows, realistically placed on all four sides of the house, were always rectangular, and unlike the painted ones on the cupola, could not have been obliterated or altered; but there is something not quite right about the front door with its strangely proportioned panels. Both the brass name plates, which say "Wheeler" and "82" to commemorate the family and the date, and the brass knocker seem stuck on, and the writer would take odds that they originally graced a Victorian door which some "restorer" found outmoded.* If only it would transpire that Rant Stewart, the Newark carpenter who built the house, has left behind some miniature elevations which one of his descendants would kindly locate in an old trunk!

However, it may seem carping to point out defects in a doll residence which has so much to admire. The aforementioned Newark wallpapers and carpets are intact, along with most of the furnishings, the curtains, and even the curtain pins. The latter are included in a marvelous inventory of the contents of this house. I could not resist quoting the description of these curtain pins in 1953,† and I can't again: "13 quatre-foil, 7 bouquet-shaped." In any case, the full inventory is reproduced on page 370, together with the inventory of a lost New York dolls' house of 1864, and these two inventories, nearly a generation apart, should be an invaluable guide to anyone refurnishing a Victorian dolls' house (or even a Victorian house!) of either period.

It need only be added that each room in the dolls' house is papered differently, except the kitchen which has painted walls, and the dining-room which is covered in red silk with paper borders. The latter again bears out Osbert Lancaster's statement* that in the Victorian dining-room the walls were covered "nine times out of ten" in crimson, "that colour being considered, quite rightly, as stimulating to the appetite."

A LUTHERAN CHURCH IN PENNSYLVANIA

DATE: CA. 1885
HEIGHT (INCLUDING STEEPLE): 36"
WIDTH: 17"
DEPTH: 30"
OWNER: MRS. DANIEL RHOADS (PENNSYLVANIA)

Churches, like houses, frequently were made as models. This one, a "replica" of St. John's Lutheran Church in Columbia, Pennsylvania, is also, clearly, a toy.

A bell in the tall steeple can be rung, and there are not only wooden pews (twelve of them) inside, but there is also a "clergyman," a wooden preacher who, when the key is turned, pounds on the lectern in front of him. This rare toy was made by Ives† and even if the history of

---

* See Fig. 53 for the colonial revival house in the author's collection. It is the dark-stained, Victorian style door, along with the arrangement of window panes, which helps to date the house.

† *A History of Dolls' Houses.*

* *Here of All Places*, Houghton Mifflin, 1958.

† In an Ives, Blakeslee & Williams Co. catalogue, ca. 1893 (reprinted in 1965 by L. C. Hegarty), the Bridgeport, Connecticut, firm showed a very similar toy with "Our New Clergyman" on the base. The lectern was square rather than round and the clergyman was dressed in a robe. Blair Whitton, a past president of the Antique Toy Collectors of America, says that Ives made these with different bases and titles.

HISTORIC PRESERVATION IN MINIATURE: UNIQUE EXAMPLES

Figure 93

Figure 94

Figure 95

the church were not known, "Our New Clergyman" would help to date it.

The latter was made, probably in the late 'eighties, by the late Charles Kuntz, a resident of Columbia, for his son, now a very old man. Since it was only brought out at Christmas when the son was a child, and had been stored in the attic ever since, it is not surprising that both clergyman and church are in excellent condition.

The wooden minister is ten inches tall (including platform), and his black cloth coat has tails. His costume is elegant with a white vest, high collar, and trousers of black and white check. Since he is black, this clergyman was clearly not a replica of the minister at St. Paul's.

There is a front door and a large rear door on the church, both of which open wide for a proper view of his performance.

Also illustrated is a second toy church from Pennsylvania. Unfortunately its history is unknown, but it was most probably constructed in the early twentieth century. It has double doors at front and rear, and vivid "stained-glass" windows, through the courtesy of "window-phanie," on all four sides. Inside, there are half a dozen upholstered "pews," actually imported dolls' house settees of a suitable simplicty. When rung, the bell in the steeple chimes impressively. (AUTHOR'S COLLECTION)

A HOUSE FROM PLAINFIELD, NEW JERSEY

DATE: CA. 1880'S
HEIGHT (TO TOP OF GALLERY): 18"
WIDTH: 34"
DEPTH (NOT INCLUDING DOUBLE PORCH ON BACK): 16"
OWNER: MRS. JAMES TIMPSON (NEW JERSEY)

Window for window, and there are fifty on the dolls' house, give or take a few, these two residences, full size and miniature, are very much alike, as their portraits suggest.

Although the actual house, in North Plainfield, New Jersey, is now divided into apartments—a fact not surprising in view of its hotel-like proportions—the dolls' house remains a family residence, as the actual Victorian house was in 1917 when this miniature version was made of it. It also retains its shutters, which were probably removed from the house it imitates for the same problem of economics which altered the latter's residential character.

The wooden gallery which surmounts the mansard roof of the dolls' house is present on the full-sized house but does not show in the photograph.

An assortment of porches, including the one to be seen on the front and a large double one on the back, are also present in duplicate. The house is not finished inside, rooms being indicated by low divisions, but although there is no

Figure 96

Figure 97

interior decoration, there are interior staircases. Though she bought the small house as a dolls' house, Mrs. Timpson wonders if it wasn't planned originally as a model. However, as in her Dyckman Street house (Fig. 147), this one has an accessibility which models generally lack: The entire front of the main section and the front of the wing lift off. So does the back of the main section.

A TRUE "PRISON" HOUSE FROM PITTSBURGH

DATE: CA. 1890
HEIGHT: 38"
WIDTH: 44"
DEPTH: 19"
OWNER: MRS. BLAIR WHITTON (CONNECTICUT)

Although it has not been possible to prove or disprove the prison origin of the series of "mystery" houses (Figs. 243–5) which rumor has attempted to assign to them, Mrs. Whitton's miniature mansion is both a "mystery" house and a true "prison" house.

The "mystery" is minor. The family for whom the dolls' house was built, as occasionally happens, does not wish its identity revealed. But with delving, Mrs. Whitton has been able to learn the essential facts from the great-niece of the child for whom the house was built in the 1890's:

My grandfather was the publisher of a newspaper in Pittsburgh. He was very interested in working in prisons. One prisoner whom he befriended, to show his gratitude to my grandfather, made the dolls' house for my grandfather's young sister, my great aunt. Subsequently, for reasons of health, my father moved to California where my mother grew up and played with the house. She came East to Newton, Massachusetts, where she married and we played with the house in our home there. My daughter enjoyed it in our rectory in Essex, Connecticut.

Figure 98

Figure 99

DOLLS' HOUSES FROM THE MID-ATLANTIC REGION

This then is an individual "prison" house—not related to a wholesale operation such as imaginative collectors have attempted to relate to the series of houses advertised by Schwarz in the late nineteenth century. Even without its nameless pedigree, it would have been clear that this handsome structure had no ordinary origin. With its lovely reeded pairs of arched windows on all four sides, its winding cantilevered interior staircase, and an abundance of exquisitely carved detail, it is clear that the prisoner who built this small mansion not only had time on his hands, but that the latter were gifted hands.

His plan was as ingenious as his workmanship. It is unusual to find a lift-off façade which reveals an attic room as well as those on the lower floors. But this attic room is no afterthought; it not only contains its own pairs of arched windows, front and back, but it may be reached by the winding stairway. It is entirely "liveable" by the standards of the most claustrophobic doll. (The rear of the stairwell curves from first floor to attic, and, as Mrs. Whitton points out, this was a careful addition to the straight exterior.)

The iron Christmas tree fence was added at some point in the history of the house. Made to surround the base of a holiday pine or balsam, this type of fence was manufactured in varying patterns till well into this century.

REGIONAL ARCHITECTURE FROM YORK, PENNSYLVANIA

DATE: SECOND HALF OF NINETEENTH CENTURY
HEIGHT (NOT INCLUDING CHIMNEYS): 22½"
WIDTH: 19¾"
DEPTH: 15¾"
OWNER: AUTHOR'S COLLECTION

Although this small townhouse from York, Pennsylvania, is in need of repairs, it represents its area architecture so fairly that it is shown without further apology. The lintel over the front door is missing, and the front steps are a temporary substitution, but the absence of a window shutter or two is no more than what might be expected on any house of this vintage, especially when the shutters are workable, and therefore loseable. These, on leather hinges, with shutter pins to keep them in place, are white-panelled on the first story, green-louvered on the second.

What the vintage may be is not precisely known, but the arrangement of sash bars on the windows and the type of detail in the workmanship suggest the mid-Victorian era. The elegant bracketed cornice is surmounted by a roof of a pattern almost identical to the one on the

Figure 100

(91)

HISTORIC PRESERVATION IN MINIATURE: UNIQUE EXAMPLES

mammoth Harding sisters' house from neighboring Frederick, Maryland (Fig. 170).

Except for lace curtains at the windows, there is no interior detail. There is evidence that a partition between the first and second floors was once present, but it was missing when the house was acquired. As an example, however, of miniature regional (exterior) architecture this small gray house, with its pair of red brick chimneys and green and white shutters, warrants recognition.

AN AMISH FARMHOUSE

DATE: CA. 1895
HEIGHT: 32″
WIDTH: 25½″
DEPTH: 39″
OWNER: MRS. DANIEL RHOADS (PENNSYLVANIA)

With its bright red "brick" and emerald-green shutters and dormer, this farmhouse presents a lively appearance somewhat at variance with one's impression of the Amish farmers (some of whom have been known to paint the chrome on their cars black to avoid ostentation).

This beguiling dolls' house is Amish nevertheless, and it was purchased from the elderly occupants of a full-sized farmhouse in which it had been stored, in a barn, for more than fifty years. Mrs. Rhoads relates that though the old couple from whom she bought it "deep in Pennsylvania Dutch Country, near Safe Harbor," were in their eighties, they were still "sturdy enough to take care of their small farm."

Reflecting the architecture to be seen in farmhouses in the Lancaster area, the house was handmade, before 1900, obviously with care, by a member of the family for one of the children.

Figure 101

DOLLS' HOUSES FROM THE MID-ATLANTIC REGION

There is a hand-split shingle roof, and smaller matching ones on the three small porches which are supported by columns. The shutters on the glass windows have raised panels and workable hinges.

The left side of the house opens and there is a large door to the small kitchen wing. On the first floor there is a living room with rafters supporting the ceiling as well as the kitchen. On the second floor, a large bedroom with a tall ceiling extends to the eaves and a smaller room above the kitchen.

Just as there was no indoor plumbing in the full-sized farmhouse, there is none in the miniature one. Mrs. Rhoads has provided furniture of the proper vintage. "A little Amish man sits lazily on one of the side porches near a butter churn and an iron kettle for making apple butter."

A PUZZLING PAIR FROM PHILADELPHIA

DATE: LATE NINETEENTH CENTURY
HEIGHT (OF HOUSE AT LEFT): 28½″
HEIGHT (OF HOUSE AT RIGHT): 27″
WIDTH (OF HOUSE AT LEFT): 15″
WIDTH (OF HOUSE AT RIGHT): 17½″
DEPTH (OF BOTH): 23″
OWNER: MRS. B. H. THORNTON (GEORGIA)

These houses are an enigma, and a most sophisticated jigsaw puzzle for addicts who like a challenge. The heads of the rest of us are likely to swim when this puzzling pair is contemplated.

Although the Pennsylvania dealer who sold it to Mrs. Thornton sold it as one house, the Thorntons believe they have two. But these fit together ingeniously (as the second picture indicates). In any case, the new owners returned home with nine boxes of pieces, and this is what they put together!

Mrs. Thornton's description of her treasure suggests that the puzzle aspect is not the only astonishing feature of this structure:

> Each [house] is made of tiny blocks of wood glued on separately. Each has a porch with "gingerbread" railings, carved corner posts and cornices. Each has a corner tower or turret with railing; one has a balcony. The porches are completely different from each other—in shape and design. The houses are not duplicates, but are made of the same types of woods. The double-hung windows open. There is a captain's walk on top of each. One has a . . . bay window. The doors are hand carved into panels with brass knobs. There are three stories in each with the railings and towers on top of these. The backs are not finished. One is boarded up except for a small opening on the first floor. The other is open in back. . . .

The left-hand sections blend together, making a single complex unit. Asked for an opinion of this curiosity, I suggested that these might have been copies of semi-detached houses built separately for maneuverability; perhaps copies of full-sized semi-detached houses belonging to relatives—cousins or sisters, the most usual recipients of twin houses.

In any case, although the first floor is "good," parts of the second and third floors are missing. The interior is lined in wood, some of it cigar-box type. On one of the porches the floor is of parquet, but of irregularly shaped segments of wood, not unlike flagstone. The windows may be opened, and there is a drainpipe down the side of each house. There is 160″ of tall fencing in pieces which apparently was intended to fence in this uninhibited structure, but which was never completed. Mrs. Thornton suggests that thousands of hours must have gone into the building of this complex piece, and one is prepared to believe it.

Unfortunately, the dealer from whom the Thorntons bought the dolls' house at a Pennsylvania auction in 1970 knew nothing of its

HISTORIC PRESERVATION IN MINIATURE: UNIQUE EXAMPLES

Figure 102

Figure 104

Figure 103

history. The auctioneer told him that he'd bought it with the contents of a Philadelphia household which had belonged to a very old lady. She had died in a nursing home, and he knew "*nothing* about *anything*" among her possessions.

A TURN-OF-THE-CENTURY HOUSE FROM PENNSYLVANIA

DATE: CA. 1898
HEIGHT: 35"
WIDTH: 36½"
DEPTH: 28"
OWNER: THE SMITHSONIAN INSTITUTION (WASHINGTON, D. C.)

Although no such claim accompanied its presentation to the Smithsonian, this is seem-

DOLLS' HOUSES FROM THE MID-ATLANTIC REGION

ingly the copy of an actual house. It was given to Beatrice Johannah Grieb Johnstone as a child in Overbrook, Pennsylvania, in about 1898; and viewed from the narrow front with its small porch and bay, it has the look of many a semi-detached house one sees driving through the towns which are strewn across the Pennsylvania countryside. Conceivably, the long open side, giving access to the interior, may have been joined there by the wall of the second house.

The interior has an appealing quality best seen in person inasmuch as the four bays on the front and side add beguiling alcoves which provide a degree of cozy reality difficult to perceive in a photograph.

Figure 106

Figure 105

HISTORIC PRESERVATION IN MINIATURE: UNIQUE EXAMPLES

Something is not quite right about the roof line of the house (though this does not show in the illustrations), possibly owing to a "restoration" by Mrs. Johnstone in 1965 in which she made "repairs and replacements." According to her husband, who presented the house to the museum, "All the shingles were hand-cut and made" by his wife, and so was "the entire stair railing."

Luckily, most of the original furnishings are still with the house, although it was also played with by the Johnstones' daughter between 1928 and 1932 when the family lived in Short Hills, New Jersey. These include the light wood German dining-room furniture which was still being made in 1914 (Figs. 388–9), and a set of bedroom furniture with a charmingly draped dressing table and bed. Since Overbrook is near Philadelphia, it seems likely that at least some of the furniture came from G. A. Schwarz.

A COTTAGE FROM CAPE MAY

DATE: LATE VICTORIAN
HEIGHT: 30"
WIDTH: 24"
DEPTH: 29"
OWNER: MRS. JAMES DOUGLAS BAILEY (MARYLAND)

Seaside cottages, and especially Victorian seaside cottages, have a way of resembling Victorian dolls' houses. Dolls' houses, and especially Victorian dolls' houses, have a way of resembling Victorian seaside cottages. One can almost—but not quite—invent a syllogism based on these premises, but instead shall settle for the thought that both Victorian and seaside architecture share the exuberance to be found in an ocean wave, and that perhaps it is this exuberance which their admirers find so difficult to resist, in full size or in miniature.

In full size, a mecca for Victorian architecture buffs is Cape May (New Jersey) which, despite its share of the many fires (fanned by ocean breezes) which have periodically ravaged seaside resorts, has managed to retain a considerable amount of its Victorian architecture.

The small house pictured is an example in miniature. Unfortunately, no history came with Mrs. Bailey's dolls' house, but she bought it in Cape May and was assured it was from the area. Like a true seaside cottage, it has three-window bays at the sides, to offer an ocean view and/or breeze to occupants of back rooms, and there are attic windows to provide additional ventilation and viewing. The windows on the sides open onto small balconies which surmount the bays on which, presumably, a doll could take a sunbath or dry a bathing suit.

Spinach green and what Mrs. Bailey calls

Figure 107

DOLLS' HOUSES FROM THE MID-ATLANTIC REGION

"dirty yellow" trim the maroon "sandstone," the textured finish which also may be found on the "South Jersey house" (Fig. 84). Here it is divided properly into blocks.

The four screened basement windows which, along with a chimney, cannot be seen in the picture, and the three flights of porch steps (one of which has rubber treads) are other unusual features of this ingratiating cottage.

Even though the house is open at the back, and the two floors are not divided into rooms, the bays form nooks which convey a homey quality. The ceilings are painted yellow and the one on the first floor has smoke marks where children, risking another resort conflagration, have lighted lamps or a stove. Mrs. Bailey washed the original curtains and "rehung" them, but the yellowing window shades seemed too far gone to restore, though the ones at the attic windows remain. Window shades must have been an important accessory of seaside cottages, to protect the occupants from the summer sun, always more intense near the sea.

A LIGHTHOUSE WITHOUT A LIGHT

DATE: CA. 1900 (?)
HEIGHT (NOT INCLUDING 5" BASE): 30"
BASE (NOT INCLUDING STEPS): 22¼" SQUARE
OWNER: AUTHOR'S COLLECTION

Seemingly, if one is going to collect dolls' houses, stables, stores, and other miniature buildings, the whole microcosmos might just as well be considered. At least one lighthouse seemed plausible, especially when one turned up, shortly before this book went to press, in so appropriate a spot (for a lighthouse) as Cape May, New Jersey.

Unfortunately, both the light and the history of the lighthouse are missing. It was possible to learn only that it was from northern New Jersey. The stucco exterior surrounds a structure divided into two levels, forming a tall-ceilinged area below and a small room above. A large central opening on the flat top with four smaller ones in the corners suggest where the light was attached, and a door with a porcelain knob in the rear of the upper room indicates *how* it was attached. The front door, glazed above and panelled below, does not appear to open despite its ostentatious black hinges.

The style of the ornamental green fence implies a late Victorian origin,* and the new owner hopes someone will recognize the lighthouse and supply further information.

---
* If so, the light may have been an oil lamp. By 1881 there were only twelve electrically lit lighthouses in all the world. It was not until 1909 that the filament lamp of ductile tungsten was made practical.

Figure 108

(97)

HISTORIC PRESERVATION IN MINIATURE: UNIQUE EXAMPLES

A HOUSE IN ALTOONA

Date: ca. 1900
Height: 38"
Width: 36"
Depth: 34"
Owner: Mrs. Daniel Rhoads (Pennsylvania)

If this house looks real, it isn't surprising. It is a copy of a full-sized house at 19th Avenue and 11th Street in Altoona, Pennsylvania, and it was built by Mr. William Brandt, a foreman for the Pennsylvania railroad shops there. Since Mr. Brandt's specialty was wooden railroad cars, and he liked to work with wood, one might almost have anticipated this attractive replica of a house on his own street.

Both sides of the dolls' house are hinged, revealing, when they are opened, four rooms on the left side of the front door, and three rooms, a stairway, and hall on the right.

Figure 109

Figure 110

DOLLS' HOUSES FROM THE MID-ATLANTIC REGION

The former president of the Lancaster County Historical Society, a nephew of Mr. Brandt, gave this information to Mrs. Rhoads—along with the completely furnished house! Including, of course, the marvelous old wooden porch swing . . .

(The donor of the dolls' house does not believe the original is standing today, and it has not been possible to check this out in advance of publication, but visitors to the famed Horseshoe Curve may make a slight detour and check it out for themselves.)

A "TRAMP ART" HOUSE

DATE: CA. 1900 (?)
HEIGHT: 40½"
WIDTH (OF BASE): 36"
DEPTH: 27"
OWNER: MRS. W. GRAHAM CLAYTOR, JR. (DISTRICT OF COLUMBIA)

According to Webster, a tramp is "a foot traveler." According to a 1969 magazine piece on the subject,* tramp art is "a name applied to numerous articles turned out by gentlemen of the leisure set [which] appears to have had its heyday between 1880 and 1914."

The numerous articles were fashioned, usually, with a "good sharp pocket knife," small nails and glue, mostly from discarded wooden cigar boxes, and then varnished. The results, frequently traded by the itinerant for food and lodging in farm areas, are found "throughout Pennsylvania and New York and surrounding areas, including Canada." The writer, Mr. Breininger, pointed out that such objects are among "the last remnants of American folk art still available to the average collector."

Jewelry chests, comb-and-brush holders, picture frames, and other accessory pieces of moderate size are most commonly found. Mrs.

* *The Spinning Wheel*, by Lester P. Breininger, Jr.

Figure 111

Claytor's fanciful dolls' house is gargantuan in relation to most of these, although a hanging comb case with a mirror twenty-five-inches tall* is illustrated in the article. Certainly this is the only tramp-art dolls' house which seems to have surfaced, and even though it appears to be a combination dolls' house and jewelry chest, it seems to warrant inclusion in these pages.

The dual-purpose aspect of the house is suggested by the presence of small drawers, fitted carefully beneath windows and above porches into the sides and back of the highly

* From the collection of A. C. Revi, the editor of *The Spinning Wheel*.

architectural exterior, which perhaps may best be described as boathouse baronial. One drawer, on the lower-right-hand side, is lined with navy velvet. The same velvet forms a carpet in the one big room, on the bottom floor, to which access is gained by a sizeable hinged section in the rear. This room extends to the front of the house on which may be seen glazed windows at each side of the front door, which contains panels and toplight of blue glass.

The drawers, being knobless, are virtually secret drawers, and the windows into which they extend are shielded with paper. This is especially noticeable (in the photograph) in the left-hand turret, fitted from behind with three such drawers. Remnants of cigar-box labels may be found in some of the drawers, paper ones still firmly affixed, or words incised in the wood. A student of the subject might infer from such notations as "Factory No. 500, 3rd District NY 50," or "Factory No. 19 Dist. of Conn. 50," how late the house may be. How early, needless to say, would remain a mystery—since the boxes might have been old when taken over by the folk artist.

Cigar-box wood also liberally encrusts the exterior, which is covered with the typical diminishing layers of cigar-box wood, each with the chip edge carving frequently found on the works of tramp artists. Most of the drawers are embellished with three layers, but Mr. Breininger mentions articles made with anywhere from six to ten. On the house there are unusual shapings to this layering, including the diamond-pattern shingles on part of the roof. The fish-scaled central roof section is a variation.

Since the house, with its assortment of turrets and porches, has a warm varnished cedar finish, painted simulated red brick chimneys and the white painted stone foundation are a startling contrast. Matching white pathways are part of a lawn with painted green grass which forms the base. With the flagpole which sits atop the double-decker porches, the effect is pleasing.

From the flagpole, a flag once flew which could be raised and lowered; the evidence is a peg, below the turret, on which the cord was to be wound and fastened. If the original flag were extant, it might help to date the house which, whatever its age, is a treasure.

Mrs. Claytor found this curiosity in the Lancaster-York area of Pennsylvania where, since it was covered with snow, it had evidently been part of a Christmas garden. The snowflakes proved to be soapflakes when its new owner, washing it down, found the snow bubbling enthusiastically.

A SIX-STORY BUILDING FROM NEW JERSEY

DATE: 1903
HEIGHT: 33"
WIDTH: 33½"
DEPTH (INCLUDING TERRACE): 16½"
OWNER: AUTHOR'S COLLECTION

If the heading for these paragraphs had been written a year or two before it actually was, it would proudly and unhesitatingly have read: "A New Jersey Seaside Hotel." When this six-story building was acquired in 1965, the dealer who sold it was relatively specific. He had been told that it was a dolls' hotel from New Jersey—he thought from Asbury Park.

Unfortunately, there was no documentation, and only two facts were positive. One was the date, 1903, unmistakably placed, in metal numerals, on the cornice, and one was the condition of the small building which was sadly rundown indeed—as rundown as the original may well be, or have been, if it has not given way to the wrecker's ball, or to some other catastrophe.

But even disrepair could not dim the vitality of this small structure with its imposing cornice, balustraded balconies, elegant coigning, and multitudinous windows.* The interior, with a grand staircase leading to the top story, is equally imposing, and especially appealing is the fact that this is clearly a building for dolls, and no mere model. There are rooms opening off each side of the central staircase on each floor; and the back of the hotel opens in three hinged sections to give access to these. There are curious framed rectangles on the insides of these rear "walls" on each floor, evidently to resemble rear windows when seen from the front. Within these frames, some rather stylized (especially for 1903) doodling with a paint brush had led a few viewers to guess that these may be intended to resemble "paintings" on the walls, but this theory is suspect. An old lighting system, probably contemporary with the building, would have served to illuminate these.

When first this charming puzzle was acquired, no formal efforts were made to learn which Asbury Park hotel it might be. Asbury Park post cards were sought out at antique shows, New Jersey visitors were questioned. After a slide program in Connecticut in which the owner showed a view of the "hotel," two listeners volunteered information, one mentioning an Asbury Park Hotel on the boardwalk which had been torn down a few years before; one describing an off-the-boardwalk hotel still, at that time, standing. Both promised to send further details. Neither has. An Asbury Park friend† took this miniature riddle to Mr. Malcolm Swan, who for years had provided a feature, "Down Memory Lane," for the *Asbury Park Press*. Although he had reproduced pictures of many a local landmark, Mr. Swan could recall no six-story, ca. 1903 hotel in the neighborhood of Asbury Park or Long Branch. He suggested the Atlantic City area.

Figure 112

Figure 113

* In all, 172: 154 rectangular, 18 arched. Some are glass, most are celluloid; and the numerous casement windows, which swing open, have metal frames.

† Mrs. George H. Smith.

HISTORIC PRESERVATION IN MINIATURE: UNIQUE EXAMPLES

Appealed to, the State of New Jersey Library pursued many possibilities. The Archives and History Bureau made "a thorough check" of all their publications of the Atlantic City and Asbury Park areas, and they checked *their* post card collection of Jersey shore resorts. "Actually, we spent some time with the people of the New Jersey State Museum, and even consulted a local architectural historian in discussing this interesting problem," Mr. David C. Munn, the archivist, wrote. "Although we can offer nothing definite, I thought you may be interested in what the consensus opinion was."

This opinion sent the building detectives off into a new direction: "We thought," Mr. Munn continued, "that it was the model of an apartment house rather than a hotel, that it was most probably from an urban area, and would not have been found in New Jersey resort communities. At the time this building was erected (1903), the big hotels at Asbury Park, Atlantic City and Cape May were frame. Masonry hotels began to appear in the teens and 1920s."

The white building with green trim has been restored,* and the search for its identity, amended and considerably widened, goes on. Meanwhile, the owner of the building continues to collect matching beds,* having begun when the conviction that they were to furnish a hotel was unquestioned. Perhaps some long-ago resident, guest, or neighbor will come upon these pictures and solve the mystery.

A 1904 BAKERY FROM NEW JERSEY

DATE: 1904
HEIGHT: 32¾"
WIDTH: 30¾"
DEPTH: 24"
OWNER: MRS. B. H. THORNTON (GEORGIA)

This incredible structure is a bakery, and perhaps one of its admirers will be forgiven for calling it a confection. But such it is, a shimmering, gable-roofed fancy, iced with layers of stained and mirrored glass; hundreds of glazed segments applied in divers patterns upon a frame gilded, silvered, and/or encrusted from base to chimney.

Mr. and Mrs. Thornton discovered this many-faceted gem in the window of a New Jersey antique shop. (There are those of us who would have capsized at the sight.) A bit of its biography is blazoned in gold lettering (in a style which identified many a shop front of its day) upon the glass triangle beneath its gabled roof: "Madeline A. Harms" and "1904." The only other notation, handwritten with black paint in a corner of a triangular wedge of glass on the upper-right-hand side, is "G. H. to M.

---

* See page 354.

Figure 114

* The metal bed pictured, made in France, has proved to be perfectly scaled (length, 2½") and is approximately of the correct vintage. The tiny chairs (2⅛" high), tables, and settees in this bronze (sometimes gilded and occasionally green-painted) metal are also made in inch-to-the-foot scale (Plate 12). F. A. O. Schwarz's antique toy department had for sale some years ago a set of this filigree furniture still sewn into its original box. I've alluded elsewhere to this set with respect to the idiosyncrasies of scale.

The fireplace I believe to be rare, but the beds were evidently imported in great quantity, and the small hotel, as this is written, has fourteen. This furniture, finished in gilt, was advertised in 1911 by the Baltimore Bargain House.

DOLLS' HOUSES FROM THE MID-ATLANTIC REGION

Figure 115

Figure 116

H." The Thorntons think "Grandfather Harms" might be a possible amplification of the giver's initials; certainly a member of the Harms family seems likely. "Grandfather" may be questioned; this seems more a model to beguile an adult than to entertain a child. It seems possibly a display piece which moved (with possible storage time between) from a full-sized bakery window, which it resembled, to the antique dealer's window in which it was found.

Whatever its original purpose, it is a most glorious survival. From its blue glass front steps to its red brick chimney, it is the essence of mercantile decor, Edwardian, or earlier.

Beneath what must be the only corrugated glass roof in America (green glass tile with black striping may approximately describe it), the fantasy continues. The floor, tiled in a diamond pattern, is overlaid with shaped glass segments. The walls are tiled in multi-patterned sections to the ceiling, with only the ceiling and the wainscoting of a different material, and again one which speaks most eloquently of the period. This is Lincrusta, which Webster describes as "a variety of fabric made of canvas treated with layers of thickened linseed oil, stamped with decorative patterns. . . ." * Here the ceiling is delicately impressed with a floral pattern, and the wainscoting in a rather lumpy design resembling stonework.

Two pairs of frosted windows on each side are surrounded with small squares of stained glass in alternating shades; and the maker, who clearly could leave no surface unadorned, mounted sheets of mirror between the windows and at each side.†

Even the stove, mundanely of iron, a child's stove with "O K" on the door and a stovepipe which leads logically to the exterior chimney, stands on a sheet of blue glass. This stove is framed with brick paper which also covers the exterior. Other realistic and practical furnishings

---

* Webster defines "Lincrusta-Walton" (also Lincrusta) as a trademark which takes its name from Frederick Walton, its inventor.

† Mrs. Thornton, who supplied the photographs, alluded to the difficulties of photographing something "all glass and mirrors." The photographer performed heroically.

include sinks with pipes and faucets, a hot-water tank with pipes, and—whatever else—a baker's rack.

There is a fancy beaded chandelier suspended from the ceiling, and supplemental lighting (which doesn't work) in the form of four tiny pointed light bulbs dangling from wires in the corners.

Only the aroma of this bakery, obviously irresistible, is lacking.

A "ONE-OWNER" HOUSE FROM PHILADELPHIA

DATE: 1911
HEIGHT (NOT INCLUDING CHIMNEY): 38¼"
BASE: 39 × 13¼"
OWNER: MISS FLORENCE REDMAN (WASHINGTON, D. C.)

Like a one-owner car, a one-owner house is a cream puff, richly satisfying. Miss Redman's three-story dolls' house was made in Philadelphia in 1911, by her father and uncle. It seems peculiarly appropriate that both were pediatricians, who might have been supposed to know what children like. These two clearly did: They remembered, for instance, to include stairs (a lack of which children always notice even in otherwise splendid dolls' houses). They added another feature even more likely to intrigue the young—an elevator. They further left their mark as pediatricians on their work by constructing a balcony of tongue depressors and applicators (to be seen on the right). On learning of this, young patients might well have come to think better of such weapons.

Although this three-story house is not as photogenic as it deserves to be, it has many appealing aspects. Like many dolls' houses, it was a Christmas present, for Miss Redman and her sister. So that it could be kept a secret, it was built at their uncle's house at 16th and Christian in Philadelphia, and carried the eight blocks or so to the Redman residence at 316 S. 15th Street by a most ingenious means. To facilitate this eventual move, and as part of its construction, the house was fitted with an opening beneath the peak of the roof which ran across the width. When Christmas Eve approached, the inventive builders ran a pole or broomstick through this opening and, suspending the house between them, carried it the eight blocks or so to 15th and Spruce. (Such a device might be helpful to latter-day dolls' house builders, not necessarily for moving a house eight blocks, but for moving it across a room.) Another thoughtful addition was the pull-out slide to be seen at the base of the dolls' house, allowing space for furnishings in the process of rearrangement and play.

Perhaps the cleverest contraption of these two creative gentlemen was their elevator, with three pegs on the right-hand side of the house to permit stops at each of the three floors. (The elevator, to the right of the stairs, cannot be seen in the illustration.)

Miss Redman's mother made her own special contribution—of an order which more mothers of dolls' house owners past might well have employed. She put labels on the bottoms of most of the furnishings, indicating their origins. The charming set of lithographed-paper-on-wood furniture in the third floor sitting-room, for instance, was given in 1874 to "Aunt Sally Redman in Philadelphia." This furniture, which I believe to be French, and which was made in a variety of patterns, each one prettier than the next, may also be seen in another version in Fig. 434. Also of interest, although they are not in view, are a pair of chairs with paper seats which correspond to ones in Fig. 381. These belonged to a Redman family friend who died in 1971 at the age of ninety-five, and they are the only others of this type known to me. The bit of documentation which accompanies them confirms my impression that their rarity might be owing to an early date as well as to great

DOLLS' HOUSES FROM THE MID-ATLANTIC REGION

fragility. This information is of particular interest for these pages because, though no proof is available, I think this furniture might well be of American make—the principal clue being the presence of the stars and stripes to "upholster" the sofa!

As one might suppose, much of the furniture in the house (including dining-room and bathroom pieces, came from G. A., the Philadelphia Schwarz.* Another proper Philadelphia touch is the presence of the *Evening Bulletin* in the rural mailbox made by Dr. Redman, who thought of *everything*—even a broom closet.

* Through the courtesy of Miss Redman, the dates of the Philadelphia firm are given on page 316.

Figure 117

Figure 118

(105)

DOLLS' HOUSES
From the State of New York

THE VAN CORTLANDT BAY HOUSE

DATE: 1744
HEIGHT (INCLUDING 5½″ CHIMNEY): 48″
WIDTH: 22″
DEPTH: 18″
OWNER: THE VAN CORTLANDT MUSEUM (NEW YORK CITY)

More than a quarter of a century has fluttered past since 1945 when the author of this book began delving into the history of dolls' houses. At that time, the only American baby house dating from colonial times which research disclosed was the precisely dated 1744 example at the Van Cortlandt Mansion. When *A History of Dolls' Houses* was, at last, published in 1953, the Van Cortlandt house was still the only example known to me, and this was still the case when the new edition, greatly revised and augmented, appeared in 1965.

As this volume goes to press in 1973, the same lonely fact emerges.* If there was one colonial baby house, there must have been others, but meanwhile we are grateful to the Homans family of Boston which saw fit in 1744 to have this unusual toy constructed; and to the Greenough family of Long Island, to whom, presumably in 1774, the house descended. We are grateful to the Greenoughs because they did not give this heirloom to an orphanage, nor to a family of young children, to be ultimately destroyed, nor to an antique dealer, to be sold, nor to any of the other possible recipients in whose hands such treasures frequently meet their extinction.

One writes "presumably in 1774," with respect to the date that the house moved south to Long Island, because that year is painted on it along with the earlier one, as the illustration reveals, and with equal prominence.

As the photograph also suggests, the house is distinctly Early American. With its simple façade, it bears no resemblance to English baby houses of the period which were often small, carefully detailed copies of the stately homes of England. Just over four feet tall, it stands on casters in the nursery at Van Cortlandt among a collection of other ancient toys.

Although the house appears in the illustration to have only two rooms, it is actually an ingenious arrangement of four, back to back, with palings partially separating the ones upstairs. In *A History of Dolls' Houses*, I had suggested that the palings admitted extra light. Katharine Morrison McClinton, in *Antiques of American Childhood*,* more sensibly observes that the palings permitted two children playing with the house at the same time to see one another. (This practical device has been observed in no other dolls' house.)

Both downstairs rooms have fireplaces with

---
* Shortly before publication, I learned of another. (See pp. 139–40.)

* Clarkson N. Potter, 1970.

DOLLS' HOUSES FROM THE STATE OF NEW YORK

hooded chimneys. With their surrounding shelves, one of which extends the length, and the other also the width of the rooms, they resemble eighteenth-century toy kitchens—and, of course, actual ones as well. However, there are no fireplaces upstairs to indicate how the dolls in the bedrooms were to keep warm, even though the single chimney in the middle of the roof is logically placed to correspond with the fireplaces below.

Although there is an attic with a hinged opening, the only proper windows are painted on, four of them, on the left side. This once may have been an implied façade: vestiges remain of other architectural details which had been indicated in paint—a door with pediment, another window above it, and stairs below the door. These were obviously painted over at some point, and one wonders who did this and why. A bail handle at each side provided a means of moving the bulky toy.

The drawers at front and back at the bottom of the house were obviously provided for storing extra furnishings, but unfortunately none of the original pieces, except for a tiny basket in the attic, has survived. Acceptable reproductions, such as a gateleg table, a tester bed, and ladderback chairs, have been substituted. As in

Figure 119

Figure 120

(*107*)

the Cresson-Dickey house in Philadelphia, rugs are painted on the floors. Since rugs or floor cloths were so-painted in full-sized houses of the period, this may be esteemed an original furnishing which, having been left untouched, is thereby miraculously preserved.

It seems worthy of note that the dolls' house is a bit older even than the ancient mansion in which it has long resided, the Van Cortlandt house having been built in 1748–49. With its Indian red roof and olive green trim, the baby house is beautiful as well as rare, but one longs to discover that it is not, with respect to its era, unique.

THE BRETT HOUSE, 1838–40

DATE: 1838–40
HEIGHT: 3′
WIDTH: 4½′
DEPTH: 1½′
(ON A BASE 49″ WIDE, 89″ LONG, AND 75″ HIGH)
OWNER: THE MUSEUM OF THE CITY OF NEW YORK

The two years which the Rev. Dr. Philip Milledoler Brett spent in the building of this extraordinary dolls' house were important ones in dolls' house history. "The fact that he built it in the Sail Room of the family shipping firm on South Street is a picturesque detail that heightens in our imaginations a dolls' house that could hold its pitched roof high (if an anthropomorphic reference may be forgiven), even if its distinguished and picturesque pedigree were missing." *

These words were written in 1965, and the passage of time has only heightened one's admiration for a miniature residence notable not only for its history, its furnishings, its collections of silver and books, its garden, and its architecture, but also for its structural originality and ingenuity. Where architects of conventional

* *A History of Dolls' Houses.*

dolls' houses (and conventional houses) frequently are unimaginative in their boxlike plans, the young Philip Brett, who built this exquisite plaything when he was in his early twenties, was creative. As the photograph of his house reveals, on each side of the two-and-a-half story central section, there are two one-story wings. The attic story is sham (though nothing else about this marvelous house warrants that word), and there are only four principal rooms in the house, but they give an impression of elegance and spaciousness beyond that of any four-room house before or since.

Beyond the four principal rooms, it is true, there are a staircase hall and a basement room, but both are so unobtrusively placed that, despite numerous visits to the Brett house since its 1961 presentation to the museum, it was not till a more comprehensive examination in 1972* that this admirer was entirely aware of these subtly-placed chambers.

There is much to notice about this small mansion which stands on a desirable, and most unusual, piece of miniature real estate, surrounded by a wall† which matches the house and which encloses an olive green velvet lawn and a garden. (There is garden furniture, and there are many plants: the inventory mentions, among many other bits of miniature horticulture, "47 vari-colored pots planted with various species of flowers," and most of these are Austrian bronze.) There is a side entrance to the house with a charmingly designed portico, and a latticed area which screens laundry and out-door plumbing facilities. (The outhouse, most rare, contains a triple privy.) So much to see, plus

* In defense of one's erratic powers of observation, it might be noted that the house is now in its own glass case, and is placed where it may be observed from angles difficult before.

† The simulated brick, once described by the museum's Toy Curator, John Noble, as "Indian red," is marked off in sizeable blocks, and it seems possible that an early imitation of sandstone may have been intended. The color contrasts handsomely with the dark green (workable) shutters.

DOLLS' HOUSES FROM THE STATE OF NEW YORK

Figure 121

Figure 122

what seems an infinitude of early and rare furnishings inside, may account for the fact that both the staircase hall, behind an understated panelled door in the dining-room, and the basement room beneath it, had previously eluded the sympathetic eye. Both the stairs, which lead logically to the basement room, and the basement itself, are lighted by logically placed windows, one of which contains eighteen panes and is crowned by a fanlight.

(109)

HISTORIC PRESERVATION IN MINIATURE: UNIQUE EXAMPLES

Figure 123

Figure 124

Figure 125

DOLLS' HOUSES FROM THE STATE OF NEW YORK

But everything about this house is logical and handsome. Although, regrettably, the façade has been packed away,* the complete and elegant rear elevation indicates the perfection with which this dolls' house was made. Among the logical elements to be seen are the three exposed chimneys (one possessing two flues), which correspond perfectly to the handsome fireplaces within. Two pairs of steps with handrails lead into the garden from the two pairs of French doors at the rear of the parlor.

The façade of the house was once described in *Antiques* as "neo-classical," and apart from the absent façade, several of the features which have been mentioned make one wonder if the young Philip Brett perhaps had visited or read about the house of that great neoclassicist, Thomas Jefferson. The decorative neoclassical elements are relatively few, but one can build quite a case to relate them and, more particularly, several structural practicalities of Jefferson's own devising, to Monticello.

The Brett house lacks Monticello's dome, but it is essentially a one-story house plus a bedroom beneath a pedimented attic. Jefferson wanted Monticello to resemble a one-story house "crowned with a balustrade and a dome." † The four pairs of French doors in the Brett drawing-room are reminiscent of those in the entrance hall of Monticello. The doors in the Brett house have eight lights rather than Monticello's twelve, but the fanlights above them are identical in pattern. The understated stairs in the Brett house have been noted. In Monticello, "Jefferson did away with central stairs‡ and replaced them with unobtrusive stairs and halls." In addition, "The entire service system was placed out of sight below the main floor." This included the kitchen which, since it is not represented abovestairs in the Brett, is very likely intended for the basement space which has been described. Even the bull's-eye windows beneath Monticello's dome are echoed beneath the gables of the Brett's wings.

With the Dutch door on the porch side of the house, one also looks for a resemblance to the old Dutch houses of New York, and particularly to the Brett family's ancestral home. Another Philip Milledoler Brett who, with his sister, Mrs. Tenney, gave the dolls' house to the museum, does not believe there is any resemblance. Inside the house, however, there are a number of arresting reminders of the Brett family. Since four generations played with the house, this is not surprising.

On one of the drawing-room walls there is, as there might well be, a portrait of the builder of the dolls' house,* and over the mantelpiece in the library there hangs an aquatint of "Rutgers' College, New Brunswick," of which the Rev. Dr. Brett's grandfather was president from 1825–40. (He is said to have been responsible for changing the name from Queen's College to Rutgers following a gift of $5,000 to the school from Henry Rutgers.) The Brett coat-of-arms hangs in the dining-room. Also in the dining-room is a framed engraving of "a Sailing Vessel lying in New York Harbor with land's end in the background," a most appropriate addition to a dolls' house built in a sail room.

Seventy boxes were required to transport the contents of the dolls' house to the Museum of the City of New York, and one could write a whole book about the contents alone. It is a formidable task even to summarize them

---

* This may be as appropriate a spot as any to make a plea to museums and collectors who, for entirely practical reasons, replace façades with glass: Frequently, there is an empty wall above the house where such a façade might be hung; its presence would add immensely to the interest of the wall as well as to the architectural value of the house.

† *The American Heritage History of Notable American Houses.*

‡ *Ibid.*

* The dolls' house inventory indicates that this "Federal Bronze framed ivory miniature . . . may well be a portrait of . . . the *father* of the builder. . . ." In any case, the portrait is unquestionably of a Brett.

adequately, and there is insufficient space in the house to display all of them. (The inventory, for instance, lists several dozen dolls; only recently have a few of these been placed in the house, to which they contribute vivacity and warmth.)

The collection of silver might alone warrant a learned essay: More than three dozen items, all of them sterling, are described in the inventory. Most of the pieces are of English or continental make, and some of them are hallmarked; but it seems most pertinent here to mention the few which are American. These include an early nineteenth-century chamberstick ($\frac{3}{4}$" high) and a late-Victorian handwrought well-and-tree platter.

Miniature book collectors may also find much to interest them in the collection of early nineteenth-century miniature volumes, among them a Bible printed in 1780, a 1786 "First Edition" of Robert Burns' *Poems*, and a *Lilliputian Folio Edition of a Description of England*. Books of the size of these are usually—and aptly—compared to postage stamps; and to spare the printer their highly fractional dimensions, they will be so compared here. There is also a songbook on the music rack (with its handsomely turned stand), a volume of British songs with distinguishable printed notes.

Undoubtedly this music is meant to be played on the exquisite harp, the only one ever encountered by me, in the marvelous imitation rosewood furniture (Waltershausen, Biedermeier, Dolls' Duncan Phyfe—call it what you will). This is of the familiar black finish with gilt tracery, but only the inventory of the house* can do it justice: "Sheraton carved black and gold laquer† harp [with a] serpentine valanced crest rail terminating on a reeded columnar standard at one side and lateral tapered support on opposite side. Fitted with strings and foot pedals. $7\frac{1}{8}$" high." There are other pieces of early "Biedermeier" in the rooms, and perhaps in this most American house, Vivien Greene's term the Dolls' Duncan Phyfe is especially suitable.

There is no denying that much of the furniture is "important," in the most awesome sense of that antique dealers' term. It would be "important" in full size, and one is not certain that it isn't even more "important" in miniature. There is, for instance, in the bedroom, a "Dutch style decorated pine trousseau chest, sarcophagus form; rectangular domed and hinged cover with rectangular sides all painted with scenic motifs." This tiny chest, ca. 1753, is not only considerably earlier than the house itself, but there is an attribution: The name of Lois Sexton of Somers, Connecticut, comes down to us, solely because of her toy.

There is almost no area of antiques unrepresented in the Brett house, and the list is long. There are early Victorian gros point and petit point carpets as well as hooked rugs for the connoisseur of needlework. To mention Bristol glass and Sèvres porcelain and framed silhouettes is only to alight momentarily on fields of interest which are represented in great variety and multiplicity.

The visitor to the Brett house never fails to find something else to admire: Possibly it was ESP which impelled this one to kneel and examine the drawing-room ceiling during the "eye-opening" visit which has been alluded to. There, blushing unseen, were wreaths of roses among olive green foliage, engagingly painted probably by the same brush that created the tall pair of gilt-framed floral panels on the parlor walls. The Rev. Dr. Brett's brush? Mrs. Brett's?

If one were reduced by some accident to a five-inch height, but were permitted, by good fortune, to choose one's house, one's choice,

---

* This inventory was made, I was told, when the house was exhibited at Georg Jensen's, by a professional maker of such, and the resulting terminology gives the Brett furnishings the importance they so richly deserve!

† This "term," found frequently in the inventory, seems to be an abbreviation of lacquer. One wonders if the writer realized he was describing a toy.

DOLLS' HOUSES FROM THE STATE OF NEW YORK

among many delightful miniature alternatives, would be clear.

THE PETER GOELET BROWNSTONE

DATE: CA. 1846
HEIGHT (NOT INCLUDING CHIMNEYS): 57"
WIDTH: 44"
DEPTH: 30"
OWNER: THE MUSEUM OF THE CITY OF NEW YORK

Other New York brownstone dolls' houses are shown here (Figs. 129 and 154), but none is more perfect, nor more redolent of nineteenth-century New York history than this miniature mansion, a "modified reproduction" of Peter Goelet's house which once stood at 890 Broadway on the northeast corner of Broadway and Nineteenth Street and where, "even in recent years," according to an 1895 clipping, "a cow has grazed placidly in the dooryard."

The 1895 clipping, accompanied by a sketch of the house, was a sort of pre-obituary of the mother of Commodore Elbridge T. Gerry, the widow of the third son of a signer of the Declaration of Independence. "Commodore Gerry's Mother Dying," the headline read, but the paragraphs which followed offered as much information about the house, built "when Broadway above 14th Street was little more than a country road," as about its departing owner. In 1848, the *Times* related, the house had been purchased by Peter Goelet, Mrs. Gerry's brother. More than a century later, another *New York Times* man, Meyer Berger, writing about the dolls' house a few years after it was given to the Museum of the City of New York, referred to Peter Goelet as "New York's most eccentric nineteenth century bachelor."

Mr. Berger's summary is of special interest since it suggests that Peter Goelet may have built the dolls' house himself. "He maintained a forge and a full workshop in the brownstone's

Figure 126

Figure 127

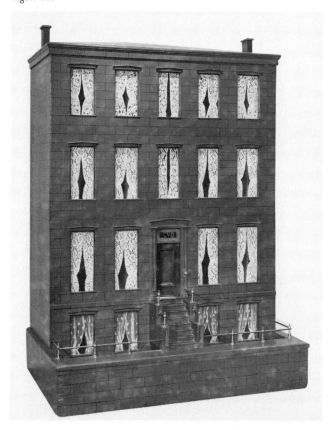

(113)

basement, did all the repair work on the place and even bound books for the family library. He had a knack with iron which wasn't astonishing —his great-grandfather, John G. Goelet, was an ironmonger and hardware manufacturer at the Sign of the Golden Key in Hanover Square in the eighteenth century." (Metal is metal, and the elegant brass rails which embellish the front of the dolls' house come immediately to mind as a possible contribution of Peter Goelet. It is not positively known whether he or the family carpenter did the building.)

The 1846 date which has always been associated with it is a bit puzzling if the 1895 clipping about Mrs. Gerry is accurate. This relates that Peter Goelet bought "890" in 1848, and it seems unlikely that the miniature "replica" would have been built two years before the purchase of the house itself! However, even if this information is a few years off, the dolls' house bears a remarkable resemblance to the original, as the woodcut, ca. 1860–70, suggests. Copied in miniature for the sitting-room of the dolls' house, the original woodcut has a nostalgic origin: It was "given to the family by Miss Dean of the famous establishment very near to 890 Broadway which supplied ice cream, jellies, and cakes for all the family parties and weddings." *

The exterior of the miniature brownstone, which has its number, "890," on the stained glass panel over the door, contains only four floors rather than the five to be seen on the woodcut, and it lacks the cornice and shutters of the original, but it has the same high stoop and the general aspect of the "severely plain structure of brick and brownstone" which the *Times* described in 1895. ("The brick walls are about two feet thick. The woodwork throughout the house is of solid mahogany—except the floors.")

---

* Janet Pinney Archer, a former Toy Curator of the museum, years ago recorded this delectable glimpse of old New York; one can picture the parties and weddings which must have been re-created in miniature in the dolls' house as a reflection of the full-scale events.

The dolls' house was sturdy in its own fashion. There are eight rooms on the four floors, connected by a winding staircase (circular in the original house) which begins in the English basement and continues to the attic. The Victorian doll occupants could cling, during this upward journey, to a balustrade of a most Victorian origin—one made of bonnet pins.

Unfortunately, none of the original furniture survived the activities of its numerous young owners, but one of them undertook to refurnish the house as she remembered the full-sized "890" to be. This reminiscence includes a pier glass between the parlor windows, inevitable accessory in its day. This glass reflects another decorating cliché in mid-century circles, an alabaster Venus. Since the double parlors of "890" had been hung "with great crystal chandeliers of prisms and wax candles," a similar specimen may be found in the dolls' house, this one a copy of a chandelier in the Trianon.

In addition to the woodcut of the house that hangs in the sitting-room, there is a photograph, taken from a daguerreotype, which shows the original owners, Almy,* Jean, and Elbridge Gerry. It seems appropriate that one of the children grew up to found a Society relating to children: Elbridge founded the "Gerry Society," the Society for the Prevention of Cruelty to Children.

"When Peter Goelet . . . died at the age of seventy-nine in 1879," Mr. Berger wrote, "peacocks, pheasants and a stork still had free run of its lawns behind iron fences." A "towering loft building" replaced "890," which was gone long before Historic Preservation became a hopeful phrase and a slender possibility. As he added, "The doll house copy of 890 . . . brings back the whole picture . . . of a greener, better age."

Thus the *New York Times*, in 1956, acknowledged the role assumed by a historic dolls' house in preserving the past.

---

* Mrs. Frederic Gallatin, whose descendants gave the house to the museum.

Figure 128

HISTORIC PRESERVATION IN MINIATURE: UNIQUE EXAMPLES

THE TIFFANY-PLATT HOUSE

DATE: CA. 1860
HEIGHT (INCLUDING CORNICE, NOT INCLUDING ROOF AND CHIMNEYS): 52″
WIDTH (INCLUDING EAVES): 40¼″
DEPTH (INCLUDING EAVES, NOT INCLUDING 14″ PROJECTING STEPS): 22¼″
OWNER: AUTHOR'S COLLECTION

When this mid-nineteenth-century mansion was acquired in 1957 from a New Jersey antique dealer, it was accompanied by the information that it had been made for a member of New York's Tiffany family. There was no doubt that it resembled a New York townhouse and that, with its windows on three sides, it was no row house, however imposing, such as the ones which lined Fifth Avenue for blocks even before the Civil War.

It did, however, have the "vaguely Italian detail"* to be seen on such houses; and, even with its absurdly underscaled front door in a façade of otherwise noble proportions, it was clearly a toy worthy of a family as illustrious as the Tiffanys.

The New Jersey dealer who had sold the house, which had been in her own collection, cooperatively furnished the name of the Kingston, New York, antique dealer from whom she'd acquired it about eight years before. This dealer promptly replied to an inquiry, verifying his belief that the house had been made for a Tiffany, and offering to seek additional information from the original source.

No further word was received, and an indirect inquiry, some years later (through a family connection) to two venerable Tiffany ladies who might have been supposed to recall such an heirloom, withal long departed, was also fruitless.

While these pages were in progress, the 1957 letter of the Kingston antique dealer surfaced and inspired a phone call. Remarkably, the

* *The Gingerbread Age* by John Maass, Rinehart, 1957.

dealer was at the same address and new information resulted.

In the light of this conversation, it appeared that the information relating the dolls' house to the Tiffanys was, at its best, possible; at its worst, hearsay. The Tiffany name had been "dropped" (to employ a contemporary usage) at a sale of possessions of the Platt family, "an old Hudson River family," in the words of the antique dealer, from New Hamburg, New York. He believed the owner's uncle had been a United States Senator in the 1880's. He added the seemingly gratuitous detail that the family "had an account at Tiffany's for about forty years," buying such things as Russian porcelains and Russian enamels.* (He did not mention

* This detail proved to be corroborative rather than gratuitous when it was learned that Senator Platt and his family moved to New York City in 1880, making Tiffany purchases convenient and a Tiffany-Platt acquaintance possible.

Figure 129

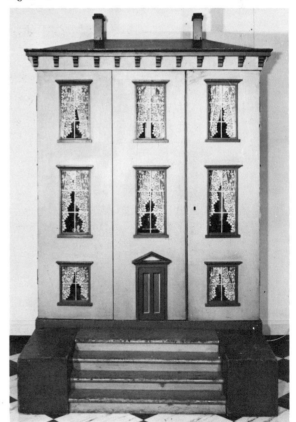

(116)

DOLLS' HOUSES FROM THE STATE OF NEW YORK

Figure 130

HISTORIC PRESERVATION IN MINIATURE: UNIQUE EXAMPLES

family heirlooms.) An attempt to reach a Platt descendant whose name and town he provided proved fruitless.

Investigation revealed that there had indeed been a Senator Thomas Platt, born in 1833 in Owego, New York, and first elected to the Senate in 1881. A biographical account relates that his mother was a member of "a Long Island family represented in the Colonial and Revolutionary wars," * but unfortunately fails to mention any Hudson River connections.

Although a reason for the acquisition by the Platts of a dolls' house belonging to the Tiffanys is by no means clear (there appears to be no

* *Dictionary of American Biography.*

family connection), it seems more appropriate to refer to the dolls' house thenceforth as the Tiffany-Platt.

So much for the history of the dolls' house, which is arresting but vague. (It is presented in full in the hope that some Tiffany or Platt descendant will step forward and clarify it!)

The house itself has the proportions and, in a far less complex way, the architectural integrity of the Goelet dolls' house (Fig. 127); but where the latter may serve, with its true basement, interior staircase, and fine woodwork, almost as an architect's model, this is basically a toy house. The unusual set of steps, although wildly out of proportion to the house as steps, provides

Figure 131

seating at each side in perfect proportion for a young owner and her companion. Nevertheless, where the Goelet has windows on front and back and, in the manner of a row house, none on the sides, this has windows on the sides, but none on the back.

The front swings open in a double-hinged section to the left and a single section to the right. A lock remains on this right-hand panel, suggesting the esteem in which the furnishings originally were held.

Happily, some of these remain. The New Jersey owner had been told that five of the pieces were original, and certainly they are of the mid-nineteenth-century Biedermeier, the imitation rosewood one would associate with a house of this vintage and quality. These include the tester bed, with its original gossamer pink silk bed curtains, and a marble-topped dresser, with the familiar gilt tracery on the mirror frame, doors, and drawer. Age has taken its toll of the green silk curtain on the commode where it no longer quite conceals the article of convenience within. The same green silk has met a similar fate on the sofa. The secretaire, to be found in many sizes and variations throughout the nineteenth century,* contains the customary drop-front writing compartment with three minuscule drawers at each side of a bit of mirror. Above this compartment there is one wide drawer and there are three below; and since the lowest, unlike the others, has no embossed pewter knob, it may be intended as a secret drawer.

It is not possible to know how much of the other furniture which came with the house was with it originally. Turn-of-the-century electric fixtures, obviously a later addition, have been replaced by gaslight. A rare three-branch lamp on the parlor table has a bristol shade pretending to shield an oil font; early pointed electric bulbs sheathed by fluted bristol shades complete a type of transitional fixture which was also to be found in full-size lighting of the time. (I have been told of similarly transitional ceiling and wall fixtures in which outlets were provided both for gaslight and electricity.)

A most unusual dining-room set, consisting of a sideboard, oval table, and four chairs,* lavishly carved in a black wood clearly meant to represent teak, appears to be Chinese, and since I have never seen another set (only a chair or two), it may be presumed rare and early, and therefore possibly original to the house. When the "Tiffany" was acquired, this dining-room was placed on the top floor, and since it was too elegant to install in the English basement, it has been left in this improbable location.

Built-in black mantels, probably meant to represent marble, in the drawing-room and the two upper rooms, are unquestionably original. Although there are no other interior architectural details, the abundant windows and the noble proportions of the rooms, and of the house itself, contribute to the splendor of the Tiffany-Platt.

A BROOKLYN "SANDSTONE"

DATE: 1861
HEIGHT: 23½"
WIDTH: 14½"
DEPTH: 10¾"
OWNER: THE NEWARK MUSEUM (NEWARK, NEW JERSEY)

This small sandstone house from Brooklyn is modest, and its cornice bold. The writer saw it many years ago and has elsewhere described its lace curtains, carpets, and wallpapers. In a field where "circa" is a word which often has to be accompanied by a great deal of wishful thinking, it is extraordinary to have so specific a date as "October 25, 1861" for the dating of a dolls' house, but that was the third birthday of Georgiana Davey Maslin, whose father, Robert Davey, built the house for her as a birthday present.

* See Fig. 364.

* See Fig. 131.

HISTORIC PRESERVATION IN MINIATURE: UNIQUE EXAMPLES

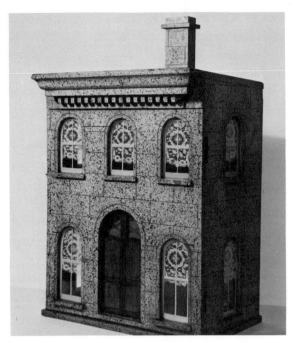

Figure 132

Figure 133

The front swings open to reveal two modestly furnished rooms presided over by a china doll in a blue taffeta dress. An elegant supplement to the two rooms of parlor furniture (there is no bedroom) consists of gold window cornices with tassels at the first-floor windows. The doll and most of the furniture are the original contents of the house, and it is not surprising that these include the framed photograph of a Civil War soldier.

It is irresistible to compare this small house with another, somewhat larger,* in the collection of Mrs. Marianne Van Rensselaer Wilson of Connecticut. Although the history of Mrs. Wilson's house is unknown, it seems pertinent that she refers to this small brownstone as her Brooklyn Heights house.

As the small illustration indicates, her house has two fairytale finials on the roof and a windowed cellar. It also has four rooms rather than two, but there are many resemblances to the Maslin house: arched entrances with double doors; an identical arrangement, on the façade, of arched windows; the bold Italianate cornice beneath the roof of each; even the location of the chimney is similar. (The brass nameplate visible over the door was added by Mrs. Wilson who had her husband's name engraved on it and gave him the house as a birthday present. Perhaps endless speculation on the part of future dolls' house historians can be lessened by recording this fact.)

THE IMPOSING HOUSE IN WILLIAMSBURG

DATE: MID-NINETEENTH CENTURY
HEIGHT: 6'
WIDTH: 11'
DEPTH: 42"
OWNER: ABBY ALDRICH ROCKEFELLER FOLK ART COLLECTION (WILLIAMSBURG, VIRGINIA)

Although *the* dolls' house in eighteenth-century Williamsburg, Virginia, is neither eight-

---

* Height: 27½", Width: 20", Depth: 17".

eenth century nor from Virginia, it seems, for several reasons, appropriate that it should be there. Owing to a curious happenstance, a hypothesis relating to the date of the house has been suggested which, even if it cannot be positively established, makes the presence of the dolls' house in "the Abby Aldrich" especially plausible.

Before disclosing this small discovery, it seems essential to relate the small amount of history which is known. The writer, who saw pictures of this huge, magnificently furnished house, and had the opportunity of acquiring it before it was purchased by F. A. O. Schwarz, had the pleasure of admiring it in the autumn of 1969 in the toy firm's big Fifth Avenue window, which it handsomely and amply filled. Since the scale of the furnishings is a bit over two inches to a foot, and since the house contains eleven rooms plus a tool shed, its great bulk is understandable.

What little is known of the house before it moved to Fifth Avenue is short and curious. A Long Island contractor acquired it from the owner of a mansion he was demolishing. Fortunately, he recognized its worth, or at least he recognized it to some degree and, mercifully, he found sympathetic hands to receive it. An antiquarian dealer less dedicated than Schwarz might have sold off its contents (the sad fate, as we know, of the majority of dolls' houses which reach the market).

The curious happenstance which may suggest some additional background relates to the choice by the Washington doll club of "The Doll Sampler" as the theme for a regional meeting it sponsored in Williamsburg in 1972. The writer, having agreed to provide an article about the dolls' house for the booklet, had acquired numerous photographs of it, to supplement a fading recollection seen through Fifth Avenue plate-glass several years before. Studying the photograph of the upstairs hall, I was suddenly confronted with the presence on the wall of an item I'd never before seen in an old dolls' house—a doll sampler!

In the picture (not shown here), the view of the sampler is oblique, and neither the initials nor the date is legible. A letter of inquiry went off to "the Abby Aldrich," along with one about a towel bearing the monogram "B" in one of the bedrooms. I asked if both items had come with the house, and learned that they had. (The only additions to the original furnishings are a few paintings from the Williamsburg Collections.)

Beneath the customary alphabet are the initials "H. A. B." and the date "1876." It seems providential indeed to have the "B" on the towel confirmed, and though the evidence may be circumstantial, one may treasure the thought that both dolls' house and sampler were made for (the latter, perhaps, by?) a Long Island daughter whose surname began with a "B." (It is also possible, of course, that both sampler and towel were made for a later generation, and that the house and part of its contents were made before 1876.)

If demolition records are kept in New York State, perhaps it would be possible to search them for Long Island mansions presumably demolished in 1968, which had belonged to families whose surnames started with "B." Of course, the house could have descended through a female line, and the "B" surname may have vanished from Long Island long before 1968. But this is a possibility for some future scholar of the Williamsburg house.

The 1876 date, corresponding as it does with the Centennial year, also appears to be of more than passing interest. Although, it is true, events other than the Centennial occurred in 1876, and the date may be purely coincidental, there are other reasons to link the dolls' house with the Centennial, notably the style of the house and its furnishings.

In the Folk Art Collection, the official dating is the second half of the nineteenth century— "probably during the Civil War period." Much

HISTORIC PRESERVATION IN MINIATURE: UNIQUE EXAMPLES

Figure 134

of the furniture is believed to be from this same period, and some from later years, but all is from before the turn of the century. The house itself is made of plywood, which one tends to think of as a modern material, but which has been fashioned in one form or another by builders or cabinetmakers since the beginning of time. (Plywood was not made commercially till the 1880's when the first factories were established, curiously enough—till one recalls the vast forests—in Russia.)

The façade of the house is only partial, unless more existed which was lost along with the history, or earlier, but there are distinctively Victorian four-paned rectangular windows, as well as small square ones on the third "attic" story (which is unfurnished and purely architectural). Attractive lintels with keystones surmount all windows. Except for the rectangular window panes, the architecture, both inside and out, appears to be pure Colonial Revival. Inasmuch as this style was inspired by the 1876 Centennial, but did not really take hold on a large scale till the 'eighties, one wonders when this pitched roof with captain's walk above and dentelated cornice below was, in fact, constructed. If the sampler is not a clue, and the dolls' house was not made as a Long Island contribution to the Centennial, there is the possibility that it was a Victorian copy of an existing eighteenth-century house (the one in which it was found), and there is good reason for a Long Island house to have a captain's walk. (The small, single, fan-shaped window appears lonely in the vast roof.)

Twin chimneys correspond logically to the handmade fireplaces in the rooms. The interior is also handsomely supplied with Colonial Revival details. There is a dentelated molding beneath the plate rail in the splendidly panelled

DOLLS' HOUSES FROM THE STATE OF NEW YORK

Figure 135

Figure 136

(123)

HISTORIC PRESERVATION IN MINIATURE: UNIQUE EXAMPLES

Figure 137

dining-room. Several other rooms are similarly panelled, and arched doorways with keystones and random-width pegged floors may be found throughout. The house contains an unusually realistic floor plan in which three smaller rooms can be seen through the doorways of those across the front, and all the rooms open from each other and from hallways which extend the depth of the house. The Thorne rooms with their glimpses of rooms beyond were anticipated in this dolls' house.

There are such attractive architectural elements as French doors in the parlor, workable sliding doors between study and hall, a window seat in one bedroom, and a most unusual alcove containing a fireplace in another.

The handmade furniture is exquisite, and to do it any sort of justice would require a far lengthier summary than this one. There are poster beds (one with a tester) of great beauty and intricacy, and a Federal sofa with feet carved in what appears to be an acanthus pattern. Some of the furniture is commercially made, and one notes with interest the presence of the three-drawer iron chest and cradle, in a sort of iron filigree pattern, which are to be seen in the Stevens & Brown 1872 catalogue. In the same catalogue, and on the handsome chest in one bedroom, is a "toy patent mirror." On a duplicate of this mirror in the writer's collection, the mold is relatively unused and the patent date can be read: "February 5, 1867." *

Since the tool shed is the only dolls' house one known to me, it seems especially worthy of note. The baskets, lanterns, kettles, and crocks which supplement the tools speak for themselves, but I am grateful to Miss Barbara Luck, Registrar at the Abby Aldrich, for information about some of the tools.

"The large saw in the doorway," Miss Luck replied to a question, "appears to be a type of frame saw, used for ripping stock by hand." She added that "a similar example, although lacking the short bracing crosspiece," is illustrated in a Shelburne Museum pamphlet. "The smaller curved saw hanging on the wall is somewhat more of a puzzle, but I would guess that it represents a type of turning saw, used for cutting curves in the absence of a band saw. However, the usual turning saw had a narrower blade than would be indicated by the proportions of the little saw in the tool shed."

Miss Luck's information about the grindstone is especially informative:

The wheel, of course, does represent a grindstone, used for sharpening a wide variety of carpentry tools. A few items apparently were sharpened dry on grindstones, but as a rule, water was applied to the revolving disc, sometimes poured on by a second man, sometimes applied by means of various ingenious devices. The grindstone was turned by either a hand shaft or a treadle, and although our miniature example lacks either of these finishing touches, I think there can be no question that the tool represented is indeed a grindstone.

Even if eighteenth-century baby houses made in America were not in such short supply, this

---

* The same toy mirror may be found in Ellis, Britton & Eaton's August 1869 catalogue and in Stevens and Brown's 1872 (Fig. 373).

(124)

DOLLS' HOUSES FROM THE STATE OF NEW YORK

magnificent mid-nineteenth-century example would warrant a place in any museum. Few others could afford the space for the sizeable structure which the Abby Aldrich Rockefeller Folk Art Collection has been able to provide.

The builder demolishing the Long Island residence in which this astonishing miniature house (what German toy historian Karl Gröber would have called "a princely toy") was found, chose not to disclose the name of the original owners. His reticence is understandable, but one hopes that perhaps someone who recognizes the initials "H. A. B." will see these words, and take pity on history.

Figure 138

A PLEASURE DOME

DATE: MID-NINETEENTH CENTURY (?)
HEIGHT (TO TOP OF BATTLEMENT): 24″
      (TO TIP OF TALLEST TURRET): 37½″
WIDTH: 32″
DEPTH: 21″
OWNER: THE STRONG MUSEUM (ROCHESTER, NEW YORK)

Assuredly this is a confection to rival Brighton Pavilion, and one suspects that George IV could have entertained Mrs. Fitzherbert here and felt at home (so to speak). The onion-shaped domes of the Pavilion have been replaced by octagonal turrets, and the pistachio and macaroon flavor by gray stucco with gilded chocolate, but the effect is similarly delectable.

We long to know what flags once flew from those five turrets, and when they first flew. With the eclecticism of the Victorians, this pleasure dome might have been built in the United States as readily as anywhere. As to the date, a mid-nineteenth-century guess has been hazarded, based to some degree on the resemblance of this bit (bite?) of fantasy to the "Oriental villas" designed by Samuel Sloan and other mid-century architects who experimented with Greek, Gothic, Tuscan, Egyptian, and other styles. Only the onion-topped turrets with spires are lacking, but the octagonal substitutes make themselves felt. What nursery views did the eight windows in the central turret look out upon?

Behind the vaguely Moorish entrance, ornately frosted double doors lead to the interior. The façade itself swings open in two sections, and inside the elegance continues. A grand staircase with beautifully turned balusters curves to the second floor. Rooms are suggested not by walls but by ornamental columns supporting arches.

A MANSION FROM BUFFALO

DATE: 1868
HEIGHT: 55″
WIDTH: 44″
DEPTH: 27″
OWNER: MR. AND MRS. GEORGE EVANS STEINMETZ (OKLAHOMA)

A stately mansion once stood at 675 Delaware Avenue in Buffalo. The fact that an apartment

HISTORIC PRESERVATION IN MINIATURE: UNIQUE EXAMPLES

Figure 139

Figure 140

house now occupies the site is made more bearable for us by the survival of (1) a photograph of the mansion and (2) a dolls' mansion that was built as a copy of the actual one. Both are still in the possession of the original family.

Built in 1868 by a cabinetmaker employed by the Pierce Lumber Company of Buffalo, the dolls' house was commissioned by Charles Stewart Pierce, the great-great-grandfather of the present owner, who had it built for his two granddaughters, Annie and Mary Pierce. Mary, who was blind, lived only eight years, from 1864 to 1872, a fact which further places the house in time.

It is clear from the photograph, still in its original walnut frame, that the imposing residence the dolls' house imitated was a relatively restrained example of what Osbert Lancaster dubbed "Hudson River Bracketed." Lancaster pointed out that although in England the style, known as "Second Empire Renaissance," was a limited success, "its popularity in America, particularly in New York State, was phenomenal."

Although Buffalo is far from the Hudson, and the brackets so evident on the actual house are missing on the miniature version, Buffalo, after all, is in New York State, and the resemblance of the dolls' house to the original house, and to the style, is unmistakable.

Since dolls' houses reputed to be copies of actual houses often are vague approximations,* it is rewarding to see the clear resemblance of the Pierce dolls' house to the Pierce house. Although such features as the porch and the window in the belvedere have been omitted on the dolls' house, and much of the other detail simplified, there is no denying the family resemblance of the two houses. Most original is the builder's fanciful interpretation of the windows. His decision to merge the pairs may have been inspired by the dormers. He appears to have adapted the design of these by enlarging and glazing the spandrel that surmounts them, and omitting the two styles of lintels which

* Compare the Ramsey dolls' house in the Minnesota Historical Society. (Fig. 197)

DOLLS' HOUSES FROM THE STATE OF NEW YORK

crown windows elsewhere on the house. Even the foundation of the mansion appears to be an exact duplication in proportion and style, and one wonders if originally there might have been a porch section with stairs, or stairs alone, which lifted off, and were perhaps lost at some point in the lengthy history of the dolls' house.

(The upper slope of the mansard roof is not visible in the photograph of either the house or the dolls' house, and the chimneys placed at the rear are also out of view.)

The hand-painted brick exterior carefully imitates the original, as do the fish-scale shingles on the roof—10,000 of them, individually cut, according to Mrs. Steinmetz. It is fortunate, by the way, that the ancestral doll residence has fallen into such sympathetic hands. Mrs. Steinmetz has restored only when absolutely necessary. Because it was stored in the loft of the coach house for seventy years, the house was in amazingly good condition, she reports. Although, of the original contents, only the curtains and three pieces of filigree metal furniture (two sidechairs and a dresser) survived, everything about the house itself is original. The outside trim was touched up with paint to match the existing gray, and a pair of broken window frames in the attic replaced. Mrs. Steinmetz has assiduously collected suitable Victorian furnishings for the six rooms, two of which are wide stairhalls. (The attic is sealed.)

Oil paintings in ornate gold-leaf frames of the two little girls who first played with the house have been photographed, and these miniature family portraits hang in the parlor.

A house "very, very much like the Pierce home," says Mrs. Steinmetz, stands "kitty-corner across the street" from the apartment house which replaced "675." For those of us who have little faith in the amount of time that remains before this, too, will be gone, it is reassuring to have "675" in miniature, with its number painted on the glass above the front entrance door, in such appreciative hands.

KIMBALL HOUSE

DATE: CA. 1870'S
HEIGHT (TO TOP OF BELVEDERE): 46″
WIDTH: 44″
DEPTH: 18″
OWNER: THE STRONG MUSEUM (ROCHESTER, NEW YORK)

One confronts this mustard-painted edifice with its rust trim and charcoal-gray mansard with acute nostalgia. Surely one has been there. But where? At the seaside, surely: with all those windows placed to catch the view and the salt air? Even the very name, "Kimball House," painted on the rectangular light above the glazed doors, sounds familiar. Perhaps someone will recognize this airy structure and tell us where the original is. Or was.

The interior is as handsomely detailed as the front elevation suggests. The three-story bays on each side provide nice nooks with views of miniature furnishings for people looking in, as

Figure 141

HISTORIC PRESERVATION IN MINIATURE: UNIQUE EXAMPLES

well as ocean views, no doubt, for dolls looking out. As one might suspect from the balanced façade, the interior is "center hall plan." There is a curving stairway to the third floor, and built-in fireplaces which correspond logically to the chimneys.

One can picture the guests rocking on the veranda before a nine-course dinner.

A METAL HOUSE FROM UPSTATE NEW YORK

DATE: CA. 1870'S
HEIGHT (TO PEAK OF GABLE, NOT INCLUDING CHIMNEY): 33"
WIDTH: 50"
DEPTH: 14"
OWNER: THE STRONG MUSEUM (ROCHESTER, NEW YORK)

Victorian dolls' houses made of metal (usually tin) turn up from time to time. One which is a copy of an actual New York City house may be seen in Fig. 147. The Maryland house also appears to be one-of-a-kind, but metal dolls' houses were also commercially made. In 1869, reporting on Christmas toys, *Harper's Bazar* described large dolls' houses "of tin, painted to imitate brownstone, with real doors and glass windows, and furnished throughout." These were $40, not a small sum in 1869. (I have never seen one of these houses.) The metal house pictured, with many metal accoutrements, is the most elaborate I have encountered, and it, too, appears to be custom-made. Though its metal façade has been lost or, one hopes, only misplaced, mercifully its original furnishings and part of its history survive.

The white house with green trim was bought by Mrs. Homer Strong, reportedly in the early 1950's, from an eighty-eight-year-old woman in Watertown, New York, who was moving to Florida. Since this was her dolls' house when she

Figure 142

was a child, arithmetic would suggest a 'seventies origin, though most of the furnishings, dolls, and decor have a 'ninetyish look. It is possible that the owner supplemented the furnishings in later years, or lent the house temporarily to another generation. Unfortunately, a few facts have been mislaid along with the façade. (Windows on the back wall of the house, hung with their original lace curtains, make the loss of the façade less evident.)

Perhaps it can be assumed that a tinsmith built this house, and if this is true, we can also assume that he fitted up the kitchen which has such unusual features as tin shelves in a small pantry wing which may be seen at the right, and a hot-water heater at the left. There are also built-in laundry tubs and a painted tin table and chairs. The tinsmith's art also may be seen in the tall stovepipe which leads, accurately, to the chimney on the kitchen wing. The tinsmith, however, was not entirely carried away; the stove itself is iron, as it would have been in a full-sized kitchen. The bathroom is similarly realistic, with a dark varnished tank and seat, and a footed tub.

There's a good staircase with a metal balustrade and green stair carpet. On brass rods in the hall, green beaded portieres hung from brass rings contribute to the gemütlich feeling that infuses the house.

Figure 143

Figure 144

THE "JOHN HOWARD PAYNE" SALT BOX

DATE: CA. 1875
HEIGHT (TO ROOF PEAK): 14¾"
WIDTH: 13¾"
DEPTH: 15½"
OWNER: MRS. CHARLES G. SUNSTEIN (PENNSYLVANIA)

Although the connection of John Howard Payne with this Long Island salt box is tenuous, to say the least, the dolls' house is of considerable interest apart from such name-dropping.

To get the latter out of the way, the cottage of which this is a miniature copy was built at East Hampton in the 1730's,* but was bought over a century later by a family named Payne. Since the author of *Home, Sweet Home* lived in East Hampton, the title of his song, which he composed in 1823, was given to the dolls' house

* The house is very like "Ganset House," which may be seen in *The Treasury of Early American Homes* by Dorothy and Richard Pratt (Hawthorn Books, 1959), which was built at Amagansett, a few miles from East Hampton to which this salt box was moved.

HISTORIC PRESERVATION IN MINIATURE: UNIQUE EXAMPLES

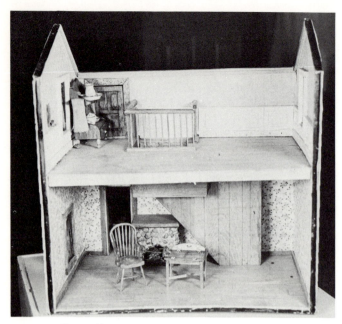

Figure 145

Figure 146

when it was built in the 1870's. (Since he had died in 1852, his fame had had two decades to mellow.)

Inasmuch as the original was washed away by a hurricane in 1890, it is especially satisfying to have a miniature version.

As the photographs illustrate, the house is a typical Long Island shingled salt box, of the mid-eighteenth-century style, with a boxed-in staircase inside, and an unusual arrangement of rooms: On one side there is a large room down and one up, and, on the other, two rooms down plus, on top, what the owner refers to as a "barn." One wonders if the latter is not, rather, an unfinished attic. In any case, with the exposed lath and mortar wall and the unfinished floor, This room is an informative addition to a dolls' house, whatever its purpose.

No furnishings came with the cottage (the few pictured are additions), but the wallpapers appear to be old, including a lovely pink and green-sprigged pattern on beige.

The exterior shingle is also beige, probably to simulate the weatherbeaten look such seaside houses attain, and the trim is green. The "1760" on the door is not original, but the owner feels that the metal bracket above the door must have had a sign of some kind. (One wonders if the metal downspout on the back of the house was part of a complete drainage system.) The windows are painted to simulate the diamond-paned variety once seen on casements of the earliest salt box cottages. (This detail cannot be seen in the pictures.) The type of window framing and the center chimney are typical of such Long Island houses.

A DYCKMAN STREET COPY IN TIN

DATE: CA. 1880'S
HEIGHT (TO TOP OF CHIMNEY): 19½"
WIDTH: 15"
DEPTH: 13"
OWNER: MRS. JAMES TIMPSON (NEW JERSEY)

Although tin brownstones with "real doors and glass windows" were, according to *Harper's*

DOLLS' HOUSES FROM THE STATE OF NEW YORK

Figure 147

Figure 148

Bazar in 1869 available for sale at Christmas (page 128), this house was clearly not one of them. It is believed to be one-of-a-kind, its owner having been told that it was a copy of a house on Dyckman Street in the Bronx, and it is

no brownstone but rather a "greenstone" with a crimson mansard and chimneys.

The house had been repainted in part before Mrs. Timpson bought it, and she doubts that the painted swags which dramatize the windows are all original. There is a one-piece floor between the first and second stories which is removable, and, as the detail picture shows, so is the roof.

Mrs. Timpson points out that the tin work is "very nicely done," and she wonders if it might not have been made as a showpiece rather than a toy. However, as we know, with dolls' houses, such a line must be finely drawn, and the fact that this house has a removable roof and floor suggests that it was made for play.

"1074" FROM NEW ROCHELLE

DATE: CA. 1885
HEIGHT (INCLUDING BASE): 54″
WIDTH: 60″
DEPTH: 20″
OWNER: MARIANNE VAN RENSSELAER WILSON (CONNECTICUT)

There is more than one impressive dolls' house in Mrs. Wilson's collection, but this imposing specimen from New Rochelle, New York, is especially choice. There are six rooms and an attic, halls upstairs and down, a "very good stairway," and, over the front doors, a bay window which contains a sewing machine. The seamstress had plenty of light, and the whole house appears to be very "livable."

There is even a clue as to who "lived" in it: The number "1074" is visible from the *back* of the glass over the door. The front, alas, has been painted over, but this is, at least, an inkling of past history. (New Rochelle residents, please note.)

Because kitchens and baths are rarely found in original condition, even in carefully restored, full-sized period houses where utility under-

(131)

HISTORIC PRESERVATION IN MINIATURE: UNIQUE EXAMPLES

Figure 149

Figure 150

Figure 151

standably replaces antique plumbing, it is in such rooms as these that dolls' houses are especially useful in revealing the past.

Here the bathroom and kitchen have their original dark varnished wainscoting, and both are as found, with a radiator and perhaps one or two oddments added by Mrs. Wilson to the bathroom, and an iron gas stove "for summer use" added to the kitchen. The latter also contains its original "regulator" stove set in the fireplace, an arrangement recalled by Mrs. Wilson as "almost exactly" like her grandmother's. She remembers it that way "as of 1914," and remembers that her mother lived in the house prior to her marriage in 1905. The hot-water heater, covered sink, and laundry tubs are other fixtures not found in every dolls' house kitchen.

In the bathroom, the tin tub and basin, framed in wood to match the wainscoting, and the early commode with its square lid set into an alcove, are also rare miniature additions to plumbing history. (The sash windows in both bath and kitchen are workable.)

It is of interest to note that the floors of the master bedroom, the dining-room, and both halls are laid in alternating stripes of light and dark wood, not unlike some of the inlaid floors in the "mystery" houses (page 216). There are other similarities to be found between this house and the "mystery" series: the sheer bulk of the house, the gambrel roof, and the latticework base (to be seen on some of the mystery houses) are among them. One wonders if this house might not have been a custom-made version by the "mystery" maker honoring a request for a simple clapboard rather than the ornamental

(132)

DOLLS' HOUSES FROM THE STATE OF NEW YORK

detailing customarily provided by the mysterious maker? Or possibly an early production by the latter?

It seems appropriate, since a separate photograph was unavailable, to add a postscript about the house that looms in the background of the New Rochelle. This marvelous mansion, with its tall belvedere, seems the essence of a "Tuscan villa," and it is fortuitous that an important bit of it, at least, is in view. Mrs. Wilson relates that this house came from Baltimore where it was bought at auction. The number "529," obviously part of its address, is to be found above the door, a proper companion piece to "1074."

A PHILIPPINE MAHOGANY MANSION

DATE: 1889
HEIGHT: 44"
WIDTH: 24"
DEPTH: 25"
OWNER: MICHAEL P. NOLAN (NEW YORK)

Unfortunately, the Rochester, New York, owner knows nothing of the history of this house, which he has been restoring with great care, except for the date, "1889," in gilded numerals on the cornice. Perhaps someone will recognize the photograph and furnish a clue to the identity of this Philippine mahogany mansion.

The sizeable belvedere (almost a penthouse in current terms), arched windows, window balconies, widow's walk, and coigning give the house much of its character. The fact that it *has* character is underlined by the fact that each of the two second-story bays is composed of forty-five pieces. This intricacy was discovered when Mr. Nolan had to reconstruct one of them. Much care, it is clear, also went into the making of the fish-scale shingle roof.

Of the original interior decoration, the only bits remaining when the house was found were

Figure 152

curtain rods (suspended by screw eyes) and white fringed shades at some of the windows.

BESSIE MITCHELL'S "XMAS," 1879

DATE: 1879
HEIGHT (TO PEAK): 51"
WIDTH: 35"
DEPTH: 19"
OWNER: LYME HISTORICAL SOCIETY (OLD LYME, CONNECTICUT)

The dolls' houses that offer a name and a date are few. When a name is found, sometimes on a small brass or silver door-plate, it is usually brief—"Estelle" or "Gertrude"—rarely with a surname. Here we are given a date (1879), along with a surname (Bessie Mitchell's), but we are greedy: we have the title, but not the book. We long to know who Bessie Mitchell was and, among other things, what color her hair was,

HISTORIC PRESERVATION IN MINIATURE: UNIQUE EXAMPLES

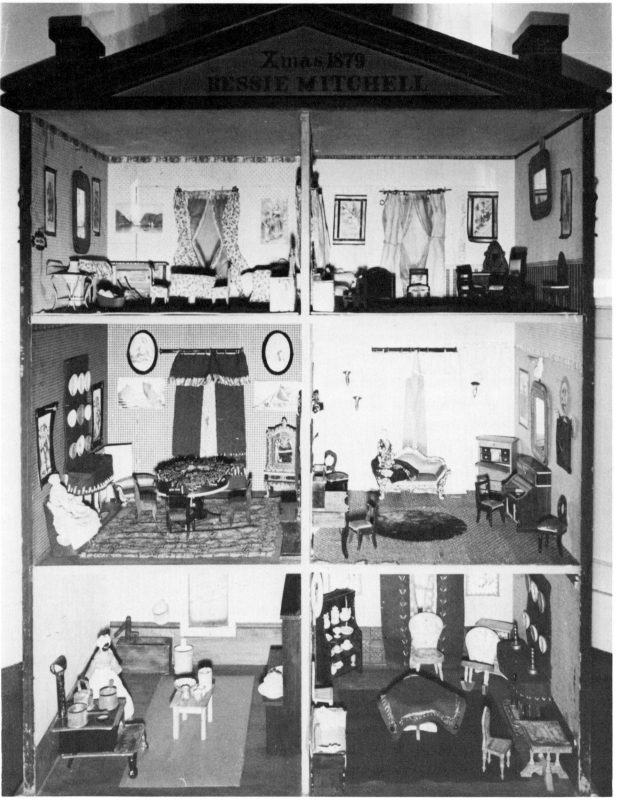

Figure 153

DOLLS' HOUSES FROM THE STATE OF NEW YORK

and what she said on December 25, 1879, when she confronted her six-room townhouse.

One thing is clear. She was a lucky girl. When she received her "Xmas" present, it was no mere store-bought house "fitted up" at a local toy shop. It must have been planned weeks or months ahead, built by a carpenter, doting father, or other relative. It was furnished, it is evident, by a doting mother (or other relative!). The six spacious rooms are filled with the sort of graceful details which can only be supplied with love as well as imagination.

The furniture is rather a mixture, ranging from imported (and early) Biedermeier to American (and late) Bliss. (A Bliss table and two chairs may be seen in the lower-right-hand room.) The furnishings are spotty, but what appears to be original is the decor, suffused by a mellow assortment of handmade curtains and draperies (hanging on small rings from proper rods), and a marvelously diversified (and very Victorian) assortment of pictures, in homemade frames, along with Japanese fans and other fancies, glued or otherwise fastened to the walls. Two fireplaces, one in the room above the kitchen, and the other in the room to its right, have lambrequins surmounted by most unusual over-mantel decorations in which a display of decorative plates is affixed to a panel of matching fabric. The colors of the wallpapers are muted, and the whole effect of the house is evocative of the year (and the era) so helpfully specified.

A Postscript: The day after the proofs of these pages were returned to the publisher, new information arrived about Bessie Mitchell and her dolls' house.

Bessie, born August 10th, 1871 in Flushing, Long Island, was given the house, which was built by a German carpenter employed by her grandfather, Dr. James Macdonald, at his sanitarium, for her seventh Christmas. A "doting mother" (as predicted above) supplied the "graceful details." Bessie's niece, Ethel Mitchell Danenhower, remembers that "clothes for dolls, curtains, tablecloths, mantel-covers, etc." were made by Bessie's mother, Margaret Macdonald Mitchell (Mrs. Ernest Mitchell). Although Bessie married, she had no children of her own, but three generations of Mitchells played with her house.*

A WEST 69TH STREET BROWNSTONE

DATE: 1892
HEIGHT (TO PEAK): 45"
DEPTH: 58½"
WIDTH: 18"
OWNER: MRS. ROBERT BANKS (MARYLAND)

The New York brownstone has been interpreted in miniature more than once, and in ways both abstract (Fig. 129) and specific (Fig. 127), but this 1892 copy of a house still standing in 1972 at 113 West 69th Street, is an excellent compromise.

* Mrs. Danenhower gave the dolls' house years ago to Mrs. Woodward H. Griswold whose collection of toys is exhibited at the Lyme Historical Society.

Figure 154

HISTORIC PRESERVATION IN MINIATURE: UNIQUE EXAMPLES

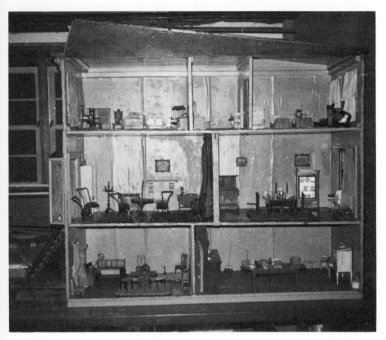

Figure 155

Very different in character from the writer's Tiffany house or the Museum of the City of New York's handsome Goelet, both of which are also of earlier make, this house is more specific in several ways. One is immediately struck by the balustraded flight of outside steps, eleven in all, which climb steeply to the double doors, leaving height enough beneath for an arched entrance to the basement door.* Adjoining this is a proper fenced "areaway."

The owner's grandfather had the house built in 1892 for her aunt, Miss Anna Brush, and in this miniature version, as in all proper brownstone mansions, depth is important. Unlike most dolls' houses, open at front or back, this one is open at the side, disclosing this depth, unusual in a dolls' house, seven rooms on three floors. In the original house, there are three stories between the attic and the basement, with the servants' sitting-room and the kitchen on the basement floor and servants' bedrooms on the attic floor. In the dolls' house, the attic is implied rather than present, with closed green shutters on the dormers, and no access to the space which slopes back from the top of the façade.

Although they are not to be seen on the miniature house, two other features of 113 West 69th, recalled by Mrs. Banks' father, must be mentioned. One of these is related to relations: "111," the house next door, belonged to his aunt and uncle, and a door was cut through the wall to the adjoining house (which might be news to the current tenants of each).*

The other was the presence, in the second-floor parlor, of a messenger box. When a telegram was to be sent, a handle on the box was pulled down and "someone showed up to take the telegram." There was also a hand-wind phone, and it is possible that a miniature one once hung on a wall of the dolls' house.† The fact that three generations have played with the house, and thoroughly, is reflected in the furnishings, and the fact that the early ones are largely departed. Among the late Victorian survivals are a pier mirror between the dining-room windows, and portieres between parlor and dining-room.

Whether there was ever a miniature messenger box is not known. Although I haven't yet come across one, I shouldn't be at all surprised to do so, possibly tomorrow.

---

* On the original row, there are alternating box stoops with landings. The eleven steps come within Webster's definition of the "seven to fourteen steps" a stoop (from the Dutch *stoep*) should have.

* It had been hoped to include a picture of the original house. When, in April 1972, the writer paid West 69th Street a visit, the once prestigious row was intact, but although it had clearly fared better than most, the original entrances, along with their tall stoops, had been removed from just these two houses, and only the basement entrances remained. Though the neighboring houses, obviously of the same style and vintage, had been spared, a picture of one of them seemed somewhat less to the point, and taking one was resisted.

† See Plate 185, *A Book of Dolls and Doll Houses*

DOLLS' HOUSES FROM THE STATE OF NEW YORK

A CHRISTMAS PRESENT, ALBANY, 1900

DATE: 1900
HEIGHT (INCLUDING CHIMNEY): 54″
WIDTH: 21½″
DEPTH: 18½″
OWNER: MRS. GORDON MAC LAREN (CALIFORNIA)

Although the three little Danaher girls of 446 Quail Street, Albany, New York, look quite solemn in their turn-of-the-century photograph, undoubtedly what we see is quiet pride. Neither the name of the older girl in the background, nor of the doll in the chair is known, but Mary, Eleanor, and Elsie are not the least bit anonymous, and it is clear that they had a marvelous Christmas in 1900.

It is sufficiently seldom that a dolls' house survives, as this one has, with its original furnishings and history. When it is accompanied by such a photograph as we gaze upon here, the miniature cup (see table) runneth over.

After she acquired the house in 1971, Mrs. MacLaren received a letter from Mrs. Frederick W. Pratt, the youngest sister (Elsie), which charmingly documents the house and that long-ago but unforgettable day:

446 was given to us on Christmas 1900. . . . The carpenter made it for us as a copy of our house—sort of a city brownstone house, only my father when it was building, ordered a dull yellow brick from Holland for the front. It was really quite handsome. We lived there about fifteen years, then moved to

Figure 156

HISTORIC PRESERVATION IN MINIATURE: UNIQUE EXAMPLES

the upper part of Albany where we could have lawns and garden. It was a great Christmas because among dolls and books, etc., we were given a canary named "Cherry" and our Irish cook taught him to walk through our silver napkin rings on the dining-room table! . . .

Quite a bit of furniture was gathered together by my mother when she gave [the house] to us. Of course my sister put in the partitions and went on collecting, but much later.

As this last reference indicates, this sister, Miss Mary Danaher, who is seen next to the house, became a dolls' house collector. Another of her houses, described in the "mystery" series discussed in pages 215–18, was acquired by Catherine MacLaren from her estate, along with this one, following her death in 1971. Miss Danaher had been head of the art department* in the Bronxville, New York, schools, and her art training was evident in her dolls' houses. Mrs. MacLaren comments on her conversion of the original three rooms to five in the 1900 house, accomplished without damage to the original wallpaper. One of her additions, a favorite of the present owner's, is the kitchen sink, "a converted church envelope container complete with a superimposed pump."

Caye MacLaren, who edits *Nutshell News*, wrote in the March 1971 issue that "cracks in the somber grey coat of paint on the outside show the original yellow of yesterday." There are over-sized bricks incised on the sides, and when they were their original yellow, they, and possibly the windows, were the features which made "446" a "copy" of the Danaher house in Albany.

Although it has not been possible to obtain an adequate picture of the house as it presently looks, given a choice of such a picture and the one shown here, a grateful antiquarian would not hesitate.

* There was art in the family. The sisters were nieces of the celebrated Bronxville artist Will Low.

A COTTAGE DATED DECEMBER 1901

DATE: 1901
HEIGHT: 19½"
WIDTH: 16½"
DEPTH: 19½"
OWNER: MRS. CLAUDE CALLICOTT (TENNESSEE)

This small house with its scalloped bargeboard is engaging per se, but this appeal is heightened by the presence, on its underside, of a date, "Dec. 1901," and an additional notation: "Willa Serre, Painter and Builder." One thing is missing—the name of the town in which Willa Serre built and painted this modest two-room cottage. Mrs. Callicott bought it in New York State, which may be a clue.

The period is thoroughly evoked by the late Victorian color scheme of the house, painted two shades of green, with a few embellishments in white. Since Willa Serre was clearly as proud of his abilities as a painter as well as a builder, it is not surprising that the nostalgic feeling that this cottage conveys is enhanced when it can be seen in color.

Figure 157

DOLLS' HOUSES
From the South

A RARE EIGHTEENTH CENTURY TIDEWATER HOUSE

DATE: MID-EIGHTEENTH CENTURY
HEIGHT (INCLUDING CHIMNEY): 22″
WIDTH (OVERALL): 14″
DEPTH: (OVERALL): 10½″
OWNER: MISS ELEANOR V. LAKIN (MARYLAND)

As so often happens, almost the moment the galley proofs for this volume were returned to the publisher, I learned of another eighteenth century house. Although it is a one-room house, with its façade missing, it is of such interest that it has been added, at the zero hour, to this compilation. By great luck, the small house, whose simplicity might have gone unappreciated by a less sophisticated collector, fell into the sympathetic hands of Eleanor Lakin, a Hagerstown architect, whose description is indicative of her knowledge.

Miss Lakin points out the "very steeply pitched roof and . . . interesting chimney form designed in the manner of (full-sized houses of the period) in Tidewater Maryland and Tidewater, Virginia." She notes that "many Southern Maryland houses constructed during the eighteenth century were built with exaggerated roof slopes and 'outside' chimneys; an architectural style brought from England."

Miss Lakin has dated the house from many clues and her own account is so illuminating that it is offered herewith:

The doll house form is that of a Transitional one-room deep house. This single space would have been called the 'Great Room.' Looking at the end elevation, one feels the suggestion of a first story and a loft space tucked away under the roof. . . . The roof, sidewalls and base are made of white pine, and the graduated chimney is made of light oak. American oak is light in color, while the English is dark. The back wall and side walls meet at butt-jointed corners secured by nails. These early 'rose head' nails are hand wrought, irregular in shape, angular and almost flatheaded. Thumbnail moulding runs completely around the base of the structure, adding a detail commonly found on early furniture of this period.

At one time, the missing frontwall of the house opened out as a single door—on two pairs of hinges, a leather hinge and a pin type hinge . . . The oak chimney has been painted or rubbed with red lead tinged with a pigment known as Spanish Brown.

The new owner was especially pleased with the clearly untouched condition of her find, and observes that "original pigments on the dolls' house match the gold ochres and ferrous reds historically documented as a part of the eighteenth century Williamsburg paint pallette." The interior of the house she believes is whitewashed, also in character for a full-sized house of its period and style.

Miss Lakin mentions that she "would like to believe that this little house is a Maryland piece.

HISTORIC PRESERVATION IN MINIATURE: UNIQUE EXAMPLES

Figure 158

THE GOVERNOR JOHNSON DOLL MANSION

DATE: MID-NINETEENTH CENTURY (?)
HEIGHT (INCLUDING 9½" BASE): 61½"
WIDTH: 40"
DEPTH: 17½"
OWNER: MARYLAND HISTORICAL SOCIETY (BALTIMORE, MARYLAND)

The accession card indicated that this extraordinary dolls' house was "said to have belonged to Governor Johnson's children." Since Thomas Johnson was the first governor of Maryland, holding office from 1777 to 1779, this was clearly a house of unusual historical interest.

When the house was viewed, it proved to be the only example with a summer kitchen that the writer has encountered in more than twenty-five years of studying miniature architecture.

Both of these facts, one historical and one architectural, seemingly point to an eighteenth-century origin for the house, but in attempting to assign a date, one hesitates. The heavy lintels over the windows and doors clearly are as Victorian as the four rectangular panes beneath them. It is not inconceivable that the panes might have been rearranged by a later generation, and even the lintels might have been added—along with the mid-nineteenth-century drawer handles on the base. To a house with a long history, whether it be miniature or full size, many "improvements" are likely. Meanwhile, it seems more moderate to write of a dolls' house "associated" with the family of Governor Johnson.*

It seems unlikely that someone would bother to move such a simple toy with the family belongings, if a long move were being made. It is more likely the sort of thing that was pushed into a dark corner of the attic and forgotten for several generations."

Needless to say, there were no furnishings found with the house, but this modest toy is an important addition to dolls' house history in the United States.

Miss Lakin has added such appropriate furnishings as an early hooded pine cradle, with a handwoven coverlet; a pine bench with its old blue paint, and a miniature crock which she feels may very well have been made as a test piece in her own (non-Tidewater) Hagerstown area. This small crock, of natural red clay, unglazed on the outside and glazed within, she thinks may be ca. 1830, but like the other furnishings, not as early as the house.

---

* It seemed possible that the house might have been a copy, or an approximation, of a house once occupied by Governor Johnson, and Mrs. Richard R. Kane, who went to great trouble to investigate this possibility, learned that the Johnson family occupied various residences, most prominently, "Rose Hill," a Georgian mansion bearing no resemblance to the dolls' house. No illustration has been found to compare "Richfield," another Johnson address.

DOLLS' HOUSES FROM THE SOUTH

There are characteristics other than the kitchen wing which might relate to a baby house earlier than Victorian. There are bail handles at the base and on the second story, often found on early dolls' houses and essential, of course, for lifting such a bulky specimen as this one. There is the keyhole on the front, suggesting that the furnishings were prized—though, it is true, such care was frequently taken of Victorian dolls' houses. And almost as remarkable as the summer kitchen is the attic story with the ceiling of the two rooms sloping back as they might in a "real" attic. The roof-line, too, is unusual, with a sort of variation on an egg and tongue molding beneath the raised cornice.

The attic section opens separately, giving the dolls' house the additional distinction, with the kitchen wing counted, of three entrances. The kitchen has its own chimney, another eighteenth-century aspect, corresponding as it does to the kitchen fireplace. There are fireplaces in all the rooms as well as fancy baseboards and cornices.

A side door in the dining-room is logically located opposite one to the kitchen wing, assuring only the briefest exposure to the elements on the part of doll cooks and others likely to move between the two buildings. One is impressed by the fact that the kitchen wing really works, and isn't just plunked down next to the house proper.

It is regrettable that layers of paint, the most recent a chalk white with dark green trim, have coarsened the details of the exterior woodwork. Within, the walls are painted and the house supplied with mostly Victorian furniture, including a rare bedroom set exquisitely upholstered in a rosebud stripe.

A TENNESSEE VILLA

DATE: SECOND HALF OF THE NINETEENTH CENTURY
HEIGHT: 40″
WIDTH: 40½″
DEPTH (NOT INCLUDING 7″ PROJECTING BAY): 19½″
OWNER: MRS. CLAUDE CALLICOTT (TENNESSEE)

Regional dolls' houses from the South are relatively rare, and it is pleasing indeed to include this singular example which Mrs. Callicott, one of the pioneer dolls' house collectors, found in the late 1940's in Smyrna, Tennessee, the birthplace of Tennessee's boy Confederate hero, Sam Davis.

Although the exterior of the house is relatively modest in architectural detail, it has the small projecting portico frequently found on mid-century houses in middle Tennessee. Usually these have a balcony above, and Sam Davis' own house in Smyrna has a pedimented portico with balcony. On the dolls' house, there is a second-floor bay rather than a balcony, but the imposing belvedere above it makes up for any deficiency. Catherine Callicott replaced the

Figure 159. From the collections of the Maryland Historical Society

HISTORIC PRESERVATION IN MINIATURE: UNIQUE EXAMPLES

Figure 160

Figure 162

Figure 161

downstairs porch which was missing when she bought the house, carefully following the marks which indicated the size of the two posts (though one wonders if there *was* originally a railing). She also added the steps, placing them at the side to conserve space.

What is most striking about this house is the exquisite interior woodwork. As the detail pictures indicate, the moldings over the windows and doors are embellished at each corner with the boxed "rosette" to be seen in so many ante-bellum houses. Mrs. Callicott points out that the woodwork at the Hermitage, which of course dates much earlier than the dolls' house,* has this style of trim. The delicately turned spindles, to be seen abundantly in the hall, both above the pole for the portieres, and as balusters for an unusually handsome staircase, are later. "There are no spindles in the Hermitage," Mrs. Callicott notes, "as it was built twenty-five or

* The reconstruction of the original earlier house dates from 1836.

DOLLS' HOUSES FROM THE SOUTH

thirty years earlier than the use of such in homes here."

In any case, the staircase, and a frosted green glass window which overlooks the columned landing, lend the downstairs hall an appealing degree of reality. Transoms at each side of the second-story bay (not visible in the illustration) contain red stained glass. The front transom obviously held a matching glass, not yet replaced.

As for the belvedere above the bay: There is a room behind it, and it seems worthy of mention that in *The Architecture of Country Houses*, A. J. Downing's plan for a "Southern Villa in the Romanesque style" included "an apartment in the upper part of the tower," which with "both dressing-room and belvedere attached to it" might be the "state bed-room." Who amongst us can say that the miniature version was not inspired by a house designed by Downing!

Mrs. Callicott bought this fascinating house for $6.50 in the late 1940's, which one records to show how little such treasures were esteemed in some areas in those days, and how grateful we must be that this, like many other antique dolls' houses, wasn't bought as a second-hand toy and doomed to playtime demolition.

SUDBROOK HOUSE: A MARYLAND VILLA

DATE: CA. 1865
HEIGHT (NOT INCLUDING 10″ BELVEDERE): 53″
WIDTH: 46½″
DEPTH: 33″
OWNER: HISTORICAL SOCIETY OF CARROLL COUNTY (WESTMINSTER, MARYLAND)

"What we mean by a villa, in the United States," wrote A. J. Downing, "is the country house of a person of competence or wealth sufficient to build and maintain it with some taste and elegance."

This formidable dolls' villa was built for dolls

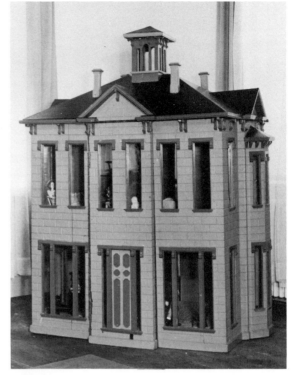

Figure 163

Figure 164. Photo by Frank D'Aquila, D.D.S.

well-qualified to represent this definition. More importantly, it is historic. It is a copy of "Sudbrook House," a mansion built, c. 1860, by James Howard McHenry, the grandson of James McHenry, George Washington's Secretary of War, after whom Fort McHenry was named. The dolls' house was Mr. McHenry's gift to his eldest daughter Julia about 1865.

Although the original Sudbrook House, west of Pikesville, Maryland, burned in 1913, somehow the dolls' house escaped and was found in recent years in the attic of the Carroll County Historical Society. Unfortunately its furniture was lost, but the dolls' house and its tradition as a copy of Sudbrook House remains.

The pictures appear to support this tradition, amply. Since the photograph of the original is of the "East façade," and the one of the dolls' house is of the front, the bases of comparison are not ideal. They might be improved by growing ivy on the dolls' house, but even without, there are striking resemblances. The bay to be seen on the original may be seen in miniature at the right of the dolls' house. This bay projects beneath a similar broken pediment on the roof. The prominent bracketing to be seen on the house and its belvedere may also be found on the dolls' house and *its* belvedere. The Sudbrook belvedere itself is virtually duplicated on the dolls' house, with openings of similarly narrow proportions. These appear to have been boarded up on the original, perhaps to discourage bats in the belfry! A metal hook inside the miniature one may have held a bell. Beneath the ivy on the original, the stone can be discerned which is imitated in sanded-gray blocks on the dolls' house. The trim is painted brown, including the deep lintels which closely resemble the ones to be seen amongst the ivy.

The central projection on the front of the dolls' house lifts off when it is unfastened, and the remaining portions of the façade swing open in two sections. There is no hallway, and the two big rooms with their bay windows to the right, as one faces the house, one above the other, go all the way through. And it is a long way: the 33″ depth of the house. The rooms on the left are divided front and back. The scale, needless to say, is for furniture larger than inch-to-the-foot. The back opens in two sections.

The original Sudbrook house was built about 1860. Sometimes, as with "Linwood" (page 155), a dolls' house was constructed by the builder of the full-sized house. That is a lovely thought which one will presume no more than to suggest.

A CIVIL WAR POW HOUSE

DATE: CA. 1864
HEIGHT (TO PEAK OF GABLE): 21″
WIDTH: 21″
DEPTH: 12″
OWNER: MRS. COURTENAY S. WELTON (VIRGINIA)

While Yankee soldiers were building a dolls' house (see Figs. 22–3) during their confinement in a Confederate prison, a Confederate soldier was building this small house while he was confined to a Yankee prison camp. One wonders (1) how many dolls' houses were built in prison camps during the Civil War and one muses (2) upon a lovely scene which might have ended the

Figure 165

DOLLS' HOUSES FROM THE SOUTH

war sooner: Yankee and Confederate builders of dolls' houses meeting and comparing notes about roof-lines, hinged fronts, and proper scale.

L. W. Caldwell of Warrenton, Virginia, could have taken a prominent role in such a meeting. A soldier from Virginia, Mr. Caldwell served under General Lee in the Civil War battles around Richmond. During his imprisonment, he clearly spent many hours carefully building to scale this small house for his daughter, Jessie. When the war ended, Mr. Caldwell, who in later years was editor of the *True Index*, Warrenton's weekly newspaper, came home, bringing her the dolls' house. It now belongs to Jessie's daughter, Mrs. Welton.

The original glass glistens from the side lights and top light of the nicely panelled front door. Behind the shuttered façade there are six rooms, if the handsome staircase halls may be counted. There is a door at the end of the downstairs hall, and rear windows in the other rooms. Mrs. Welton remembers that the staircase is like the one in the Warrenton house in which her grandfather was born. The curved bottom step is wider than the others to support the handsomely turned newel post. The same careful hand made the two fireplaces with their well-turned columns.

It is unfortunate that when the original furnishings were taken to a cabinetmaker to be repaired, they were lost. Termites had been eating the floors and staircase, and the house too had to be restored. Originally the exterior was a stained mahogany color, which has been painted white with green trim. Only fragments of the wallpaper were left, and the friend who restored the house for Mrs. Welton removed them and papered the rooms in white. (One regrets the paint on the exterior, but the white wallpaper seems an excellent solution for dolls' house restorers confronted with a problem about paint versus paper. Having a timeless quality, white wallpaper does not detract as modern papers do from the antiquity of an old house. And it can always be replaced if an old paper is found.)

"VILLA DE SALES"

DATE: CA. 1870
HEIGHT: 32"
WIDTH: 25"
DEPTH: 17"
OWNER: MRS. FORBES BOWLING (MARYLAND)

Vivien Greene* has mentioned how frequently the tradition that a dolls' house is a replica house has proved to be fable. A most understandable misconception of this sort existed with respect to the Villa de Sales, a country mansion in Aquasco, Prince George's County, Maryland, still in the possession of its original family.

When the photograph of the dolls' house arrived, it was clear that this boxlike structure with its curiously crenelated roof was pure fantasy, with no physical resemblance to the original villa (a structure with shutters and dormers and porches on three sides). However, two unusual facts, rarely available about dolls'

* *English Dolls' Houses of the 18th and 19th Centuries.*

Figure 166

houses, were undoubtedly responsible for the impression that this one was a replica: The dolls' house was built by the carpenters who built the big house, and it was built of the same white pine.

The hinged front gives access to the four rooms, whose varnished walls match the exterior. The curious nailhead trim on the door, on the pair of windows above it, and on the cornice heighten the impression of a Gothic stronghold. Since a castelated tower is sometimes found on a Victorian Gothic house, it was disappointing to learn that the indented parapet on the dolls' house was to be found nowhere on the original. Perhaps the carpenters who built this well-fortified doll residence for little Mary Eleanor Forbes more than a century ago preferred building a castle to building a dolls' house, and this was a compromise.

It is of interest to note that at one time "A license to crenellate was the equivalent of a permit to fortify a residence." *

Clearly the fortifications on the dolls' house were effective because only two or three of the original glass windows have had to be replaced.

BALTIMORE'S SELLERS MANSION

DATE: CA. 1870'S
HEIGHT (NOT INCLUDING CUPOLA): 37″
WIDTH (NOT INCLUDING CORNICE): 25″
DEPTH: 25″
OWNER: THE STRONG MUSEUM (ROCHESTER, NEW YORK)

Sometimes the history of a dolls' house is more arresting than the house itself. Although this four-square mansion with the often-seen mansard and cupola is not the most graceful example of the genre, its engaging history fortuitously has been preserved.

One January day in 1965, Elizabeth L. Davis

* *Illustrated Glossary of Architecture, 850–1830*, by John Harris and Jill Laver, Clarkson N. Potter, Inc., 1966.

of Linthicum Heights, Maryland, was looking at her Baltimore paper when she noticed a picture of an old Baltimore residence which looked "vaguely familiar." Then, to her surprise and pleasure, she realized that the house, known as the old Sellers mansion, was the original from which the dolls' house she had played with as a child had been copied.

In a letter to the editor which was printed a few weeks later, she wrote: "In checking with my father, I find that the Sellers mansion was built by my grandfather, Edward Davis, and that he had employed two carpenters to build a scale model of the mansion which he had given to his own daughters as a doll house. This house has come down through our family."

According to Miss Davis, the only difference between the picture of the original and the model was that "somewhere in moving from one family to another the front porch of the model was removed." Miss Davis felt that except for

Figure 167

DOLLS' HOUSES FROM THE SOUTH

this, the house looked "very like" the original.

As in the case of many dolls' houses said to resemble specific houses, a look at the photograph of the Sellers mansion requires a stretch of the imagination to detect a resemblance. There are, for instance, five windows across the second floor front of the original, and only three on the dolls' house, but, to dolls' house fanciers, stretching the imagination is an appealing exercise.

In any case, the original, built in 1869 at 801 North Arlington Avenue, and the first house built on the west side of Lafayette Square, was occupied for many years by Mathew Sellers, Jr., an aviation pioneer credited by some sources with having flown before the Wright brothers. The feature story about it was related to the unfortunate fact that in February 1965, the entire 800 block of North Arlington Avenue was threatened by demolition.

The dolls' house itself has a practical arrangement—the front and back are identical, permitting two little girls, sisters or friends, to play without colliding. Both are hinged, and downstairs two front rooms lead to an arched opening in the drawing-room (where such friends might meet). In the upstairs rooms, two built-in fireplaces are back to back.

The walls are tan with reddish brown trim and white window frames under a dark green roof. The cupola or belvedere, to be seen on so many Baltimore dolls' houses of the period, crowns the mansard roof.

THE JULIETTE GORDON LOW HOUSE

DATE: CA. 1870–75
HEIGHT: 33½"
WIDTH: 37"
OWNER: JULIETTE GORDON LOW BIRTHPLACE (SAVANNAH, GEORGIA)

This unassuming cottage from Savannah, Georgia, has two features that are of special interest. One is its history. It was built early in the 1870's for the founder of the Girl Scouts, Juliette (Daisy) Gordon Low, and her sisters.

The other feature is architectural, however unlikely this may seem at first glance. The closed shutters, which dominate the house front, substitute for windows, a highly regional reference to the Deep South where they served a practical rather than a decorative purpose. Although in the dolls' house the shutters actually replace the windows, and do not open, glazed windows, not visible in the photograph, on both sides of the house, give light to the rooms.

There is also a reference to weather of a different season within—a fireplace in each room, just as they are in the mansion where "Daisy" Low grew up, and where the dolls' house is now on permanent view. Since in the full-sized house these fireplaces burned coal, presumably the dolls' house fireplaces are also coal-burning.

Except for these fireplaces and the staircase with its plump newel post (Daisy Low, who was born in 1860, may be seen sliding down the banister), the interior is largely latter-day. The house was played with by three generations of the family and refurbished from time to time,

Figure 168

HISTORIC PRESERVATION IN MINIATURE: UNIQUE EXAMPLES

Figure 169

most recently by the Junior League after it was returned in 1957 by an elderly relative in whose possession it had been. Its furnishings are a mixture of antiques and reproductions. It is particularly sad that the original contents were lost inasmuch as the presence of a lock on the front door implies that they were of quality and that this house, despite its architectural simplicity, was highly prized.

In view of this "simplicity," it is gratifying to note that even if the history of the house had not been known, the simple panelled front doors with white porcelain knob, other than the shutters the only architectural element included by the "architect," would have placed the house firmly within the Victorian era.

Incidentally, the clapboard, painted cream with white trim, plus the green shutters and black roof, lend the house a charm in color which is perhaps not discernible in our black-and-white illustration.

In any case, it seems appropriate that a dolls' house, a symbol of girlhood, built for the founder of the Girl Scouts, exists.

DOLLS' HOUSES FROM THE SOUTH

ARCHITECTURE FROM FREDERICK, MARYLAND

DATE: CA. 1880'S
HEIGHT (TO GABLE TIP, NOT INCLUDING CHIMNEYS): 41"
WIDTH (INCLUDING EAVES): 39½"
DEPTH: 24¾"
OWNER: AUTHOR'S COLLECTION

In February of 1954, a letter arrived from Miss Constance Harding of Frederick, Maryland, which began, "I have been interested in doll houses all my life. . . ." Miss Harding mentioned that she'd been collecting dolls' house furnishings for years, as well as houses. "We owned a number," she wrote, "but the one I've kept is like the old houses in Frederick." She alluded to a dolls' house exhibition just concluded at the Baltimore Museum of Art, and the interest it created; and she mentioned the affinity of cats to dolls' houses.* She ended with an invitation: "If you ever come to Frederick, I wish you would drop in and see mine. I think you would like it."

When I thanked Miss Harding for her invitation, I invited her and her sister to see my collection, then quite small. Frederick was only forty miles away, but somehow the years passed without my visiting Miss Harding's dolls' house, or her visiting Chevy Chase.

However, as one often notes, the dolls' house world is small, figuratively as well as literally, and in 1969 Mrs. John H. Hanna of Frederick notified me of a Victorian dolls' house to be sold as part of an estate. It was, as may be guessed, Miss Harding's. Mrs. Hanna who, as executrix, had come across the few letters I'd exchanged with Miss Harding fourteen years before, hoped to have the Harding house remain in the Maryland area, and she liked the idea of its

Figure 170

eventual display in a museum where it would be seen by the public.* At long last I went to see the house and furnishings I'd been invited to see so many years before and, ultimately, acquired it.

The roof line of the house with its dormered central gable is certainly typical of rural houses built in the Frederick area, and in other parts of Maryland during the nineteenth century; the lovely old row houses which line the residential streets of Frederick are mostly narrow and deep. Many of them are Federal or earlier and most, happily, have survived. When Miss Harding referred to "the old houses of Frederick," perhaps she was picturing houses remembered from her youth, which eventually gave way to commercialization or demolition.

Without documentation, one is faced with the dilemma of when the dolls' house, obviously

---

* "I noticed in the article about your book," Miss Harding wrote, "about the Siamese cat's interest. Cats of ours always loved to play in the doll houses, and never broke anything." This charming footnote is included in deference to an association often observed by dolls' house owners.

* It is hoped. It is currently displayed in a private one.

HISTORIC PRESERVATION IN MINIATURE: UNIQUE EXAMPLES

Victorian, may have been copied or adapted from existing architecture. Its sheer bulk suggests a reasonably early date, a time when nurseries were still sufficiently sizeable to accommodate such Gargantuan toys. The care with which the house was built—the raised-panel double-doors; the clapboarding and coigning all around; the rows of shaped shingles under the side gables (a double-rowed variation embellishes the roof); even the rather shallow dentelated cornice *suggests* an origin no later than the 'eighties.

The style of the few bits of hardware on the house help to reinforce this dating, although some expertise on Victorian latches would be welcome.* A large flat hook fastens the façade, which swings open in one huge section. The double front doors may also be opened, and small hooks, one at the top of the right-hand door, and one at the center of the left-hand one, secure them. There is a neat porcelain knob inside as well as outside on these.

The interior, however, is disappointing. The only windows are on the façade, and there is a casual division into four rooms; the central partition may be seen through the central window on the second story, which it bisects. There is *no* interior embellishment.

Lovely old furnishings came with the house, and although they were a collection rather than pieces original to the house (and though many of them had been "restored" by Miss Harding in a manner not entirely acceptable to a fanatical antiquarian),† it is planned to place them in the house in toto.

---

* A dolls' house historian should, ideally, have information about every aspect of architecture and antiques. Willy-nilly, laborers in this miniature vineyard acquire a little knowledge about many things. As this one has remarked more than once: "If a little knowledge is a dangerous thing, I am a very dangerous person."

† A fanatical antiquarian has no right to complain. The double doors of this house were originally painted white, and one's blunder in having them restored to their "original" dark stain is disclosed in the section on restoration.

The late owner of the house, who was born in 1885, was a pioneer collector, and I regret not having met her.

A COTTAGE FROM NAG'S HEAD

DATE: CA. 1880
HEIGHT: 26″
WIDTH (BASE): 17¾″
DEPTH: 13½″
OWNER: AUTHOR'S COLLECTION

The dealer from whom this small house was acquired found it in Nag's Head, North Carolina, which does not, of course, guarantee that it originated in the seaside resort. It seems more a

Figure 171

(150)

DOLLS' HOUSES FROM THE SOUTH

townhouse: the bisque lady, somehow, appears more likely to be surveying a cityscape from her balcony rather than the ocean's waves. On the other hand, the widow's walk atop the deep mansard has its traditional seaside associations. Wilmington, located on a considerably more southerly segment of the North Carolina coastline, with an excellent supply of Victorian (and earlier) architecture, seems a plausible alternative.

The small house bears other seaside or, by extension, *nautical* clues to a coastal origin. With only the mildest stretch of the imagination, it is possible to construe small wooden mounts applied to the dormers as anchors; and the deep brackets which flank the entrance door also project an anchor-like image. Fish-scale shingle, on the roof, was not limited to seaside cottages, needless to say, but its presence here does nothing to dispel the tang of salt air.

A tool which had a busy revival beginning in the 1870's, the fret saw, has given the house much of its character: the cornice, balcony, dormers, and widow's walk, unmistakably part of this revival, help to suggest a date. (Since a dolls' house is often a copy of an earlier house, the architecture alone would be inadequate evidence.)

The gracefully arched windows have well-defined keystones and, on the inside, lace curtains tied back with crimson ribbons, which appear to be original. Matching net may be found, rather surprisingly, behind the red stained-glass lights above both the entrance and balcony doors. (The latter are a panelled pair; the lower single door contains a square frosted pane.)

Although the lemon-yellow house with its blue-gray trim has an open back and is, except for a division between the first and second floors, a shell, it is such an appealing shell * that a lack of interior detail is readily forgiven.

---

* Any further seaside connotation is unintended!

A HOUSE FROM SUFFOLK, VIRGINIA

DATE: CA. 1890'S
HEIGHT (FOUNDATION TO CHIMNEY TOP): 42"
WIDTH (WITH KITCHEN WING): 47"
DEPTH (INCLUDING DOUBLE FRONT PORCH): 26"
OWNER: THE VALENTINE MUSEUM (RICHMOND, VIRGINIA)

Even the plastic vine on the kitchen wing* cannot detract from the charm of this lovely house which was built in the early 1890's in Suffolk, Virginia, for young Bess Holland. When the young owner grew up and married,† she moved to New Orleans, taking her dolls' house with her. In recent years, she had it restored with a view to presenting it to a children's hospital, but luckily for the Valentine Museum, the hospital refused it, believing it "too fine to entrust to so many children." One commends the heart of the giver but the wisdom of the hospital: There have been too many tales of quick doom met by fine old dolls' houses presented to orphanages and similar establishments.

With the reeded columns of its double-decker porches, hairpin balustrade, and finely panelled front door, the house is said to be typical of many clapboard houses in the southeastern Virginia area. (The second-floor balcony is typical of Southern plantation building.) Thinking that it might be a "replica," the writer sent an inquiry to the New Orleans address of the elderly donor, but, sadly, it was returned unclaimed.

Although a refurnishing clearly had taken place in recent years, limiting our interest in the interior, two views of the latter are shown to demonstrate the ingenious plan of the dolls' house, which has high-ceilinged rooms on the

---

* On a photograph taken before the house was given to the museum, one hastens to add.

† Mrs. E. F. Creekmore, the donor of the house to the museum.

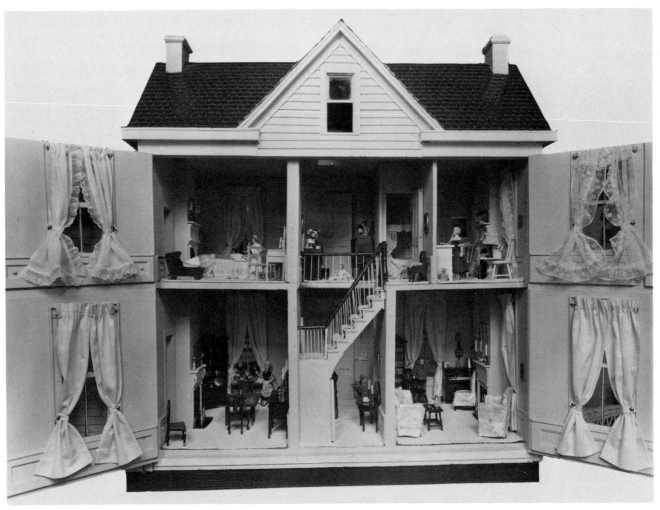

Figure 172

Figure 173

Figure 174

ground floor and a good winding staircase with a mahogany railing and a landing. This house looks very livable—there are five rooms, two halls, and an attic, all connecting logically, and there is even a broom closet under the stairs. It is regrettable that with a few final answers seemingly near, they have eluded their questioner.

A COLONIAL REVIVAL MANSION FROM BALTIMORE

DATE: CA. 1892
HEIGHT (INCLUDING WIDOW'S WALK): 34″
WIDTH: 33″
DEPTH: 10½″
OWNER: MISS GERTRUDE SAPPINGTON (CALIFORNIA)

Elsewhere, I have written of the eighteen-room "Gay Nineties" mansion created by Gertrude Sappington, formerly of Baltimore, who over a period of years collected for it antique furnishings meticulously true to period and scale. For these pages, it seems appropriate to consider just the center section of the mansion, a lovely late Victorian dolls' house to which Miss Sappington added two wings and a great measure of taste and style based on careful research and skill.

The original Baltimore dolls' house is well documented, having been built for the mother of Miss Ethel Howard, Gertrude Sappington's long-time friend and companion. Clearly Colonial Revival, the clapboard house with its fanlight over the door,* portico, Palladian window, and beautiful widow's walk (the latter one of the loveliest I've seen in miniature), was made in the early 1890's for Miss Howard's mother in her brothers' sash factory, the Tinley factory in Baltimore.

"She was rather the pet," Miss Sappington notes, "having been the youngest and the only American child of that English family . . . Ethel, as the oldest daughter, naturally inherited [the house] . . . she says that she doesn't remember ever having been without it."

The house looks so like a "real" house (if fellow collectors will pardon the expression) that this collector was delighted but not startled unduly when while working with material about this house, a sketch of the D.A.R. Chapter House on a note from a Baltimore friend suggested more than a casual resemblance!

A letter of inquiry was promptly dispatched to California, but though proof is unlikely, the reply left the door open: "Legend has it that there was another house, built just like it, in the Tinley brothers' factory, and evidently since . . . the lathes were cut [they thought] they might as well give it to their 'little sister.' . . ."

In any case, as the sketch of the Chapter House reveals, there are on both houses similar columns, placed in threes at the corners and twos between, as they are on the dolls' house.* The tall chimneys, which do not show, unfortunately, in this photograph of the dolls' house, are placed in the same position at the side of a similarly hipped roof. The panelled front doors with fanlight above (not visible in the photo) and sidelights may be found on both houses, and the paneless windows are similar on both. Most importantly, the beautiful and unusual balustrading on the widow's walks is similar.

Even one of the differences, the Palladian window on the dolls' house is not totally absent: On the Chapter House it has moved to the third floor in the form of a dormer. There are, of course, more important differences. The dolls' house lacks the upstairs porch and the turreted bay to be seen on the Chapter House, but many dolls' houses which are reportedly copies of actual houses are frequently no more "identical" than this. Simplifications are inevitable.

---

* This cannot be seen in the photograph. Unfortunately, the tall chimneys and a bit of the balustrade on the widow's walk are obliterated in the picture.

* It is true that this arrangement of columns is to be found on many porches of the period.

HISTORIC PRESERVATION IN MINIATURE: UNIQUE EXAMPLES

Figure 175

Figure 176

If the resemblance of the two houses, chapter and dolls', is purely coincidental (and inspired by some wishful thinking by the writer), at the very least the Tinley dolls' house must be a most specific reflection of Colonial Revival architecture in Baltimore.

DOLLS' HOUSES FROM THE SOUTH

"LINWOOD"

Figure 177

Date: 1900
Height: 41"
Width: 25"
Depth (including central projection): 18"
Owner: Maryland Historical Society (Baltimore, Maryland)

"Ground was broken for my house in the fall of 1884 and [the house was] completed in 1886 . . . built under the supervision of my father, who was his own architect and draftsman."

Ground did not have to be broken for the dolls' house which was built by Mrs. Clayton Englar's father, but he was also his own architect and draftsman in 1900 when he made a "copy" of the full-sized "Linwood" for his two small daughters. It is marvelously satisfying to have a firsthand account of these two houses, large and small (along with their pictures), from the daughter who was "born, reared and married" in the original "Linwood" in Carroll County, Maryland, and who played with the miniature version with her younger sister.

Like most dolls' houses which are copies of full-sized ones, this is an approximation. If one mentally removes the porch from the big one, the resemblance between the two becomes clear, and it is of interest to learn that Linwood's present owners literally have removed the porch which was a somewhat later addition. (Mr. Englar would not have the porch on the dolls' house, his daughter relates, because it was not on the original.)

It is pleasing to examine the numerous resemblances—the identical arrangement of windows on the front, the projecting central section, the arched lintels on the mansard's dormers. Unfortunately, the dolls' house has been rather too thoroughly restored to suit the more fanatical among us—with new brick paper for the exterior. However, the presence of brick paper, new or old, serves to point up the importance of the brick on the dolls' house

The house with its two wings, which was perfected over a period of many years of collecting and decorating, is the only one I know for which the owner actually taught herself to marbleize paper, a delicate craft which enabled her to choose the covering she considered appropriate for the walls of the bathroom. Miss Sappington, a retired Baltimore history teacher, also sought, and was lent, a blueprint by the Vermont Marble Company, for creating the only non-antique piece in the house, a marble mantel in the blue drawing-room, made from an old Belgian clock.

When Gertrude Sappington added the wings to the Tinley dolls' house, she took as her model, Readbourne, an eastern shore mansion dating back to the eighteenth century, and, therefore, there had to be a formal garden. French street lamps once lighted by wicks (see Fig. 84) illuminate this garden which is laid out with paved walks among which mingle marble statues, iron garden furniture, and topiary trees.

As a project fulfilled, the "Gay 'Nineties Mansion," a name inadequate for such a miniature residence, is a superior example.

HISTORIC PRESERVATION IN MINIATURE: UNIQUE EXAMPLES

Figure 178

inasmuch as the brick on the original was made by Mrs. Englar's maternal grandfather, Elhanan Englar, in New Windsor, about four miles away.

Even the flagpole is present to represent the one from which a flag flew on the Fourth of July and other national holidays "but not often as the roof was reached through a trap door." (Mrs. Englar remembers hearing her father tell how he went up on the roof to see Halley's Comet.)

After Mrs. Englar's father built the dolls' house, her mother furnished it completely. The lace curtains and Brussels carpet she provided still remain, and were made from scraps used in the full-sized "Linwood."

The three floors were not partitioned, but the two small sisters arranged their furniture to designate the rooms, undoubtedly keeping in mind that in the full-sized house there were a wide hall, parlor, library, dining-room, pantry, and kitchen on the first floor, four bedrooms and a bath on the second floor, and two bedrooms, a large playroom, and a storage room on the third.

Figure 179

DOLLS' HOUSES FROM THE SOUTH

"I can still smell the moth balls!" Mrs. Englar remembers.

One unusual change in the floor plans that the sisters recall, however, is that in the dolls' house the third floor "was arranged like a kitchen and we would have tea parties."

There were four red brick houses in the town of Linwood, Maryland, and it seems fitting that the Maryland Historical Society should contain a miniature interpretation of one of them.

"BOWLING HALL"

DATE: CA. 1900 (?)
HEIGHT (INCLUDING CHIMNEY): 2'7"
WIDTH: 2'
DEPTH: 14"
OWNER: MRS. RICHARD ROBBINS KANE (MARYLAND)

The owner's father inserted a newspaper advertisement for a dolls' house, and the family who sold him this one said it was old. That was in 1916. Anyone's guess will do to date this confection which if it were painted all white and provided with candles and smilax, would very much resemble a wedding cake.

When the writer first saw pictures of the dolls' house, the roof of Baltimore's Belvedere Hotel came vaguely to mind. Inasmuch as the dolls' house is from Baltimore, perhaps this reaction was under the influence of information, and seemingly the Belvedere roof required another look. Eleanora Bowling Kane, whose father had bought her the dolls' house for Christmas, did take a good look on behalf of this impression.

"While the Belvedere roof is pure French mansard," she decided, "there *is* something about the way its dormers are set in that is really reminiscent of 'Bowling Hall' or vice versa." "It may well be anyway," she added tactfully, "that the builder was thinking of a hotel when he put

Figure 180

Figure 181

(157)

in all those windows—*some* hotel anyway." *

Bowling Hall is indeed all windows. There are thirty-five of them and, as Mrs. Kane so aptly pointed out, they are arranged "to mislead the viewer completely as to the room and floor arrangements." The first two banks of windows below the second-story porch, however, are a fraud—they belong to one floor. The second floor is similarly supplied.

The house is white with green trim, and the numerous finials that sprout from dormers and roof have been restored to their original gilt, which Mrs. Kane remembers disliking as a child. She also disliked the front door which "is completely out of scale and never did admit the bisque dolls who lived in that house."

Mrs. Kane's father had removed the staircase which was in the dining-room because it took up too much space, and his daughter remembers propping it up against the second floor and pretending it was in a hall. The strange proportions of the house made it difficult to furnish, but it still contains most of the furniture Mrs. Bowling bought from the Schwarz toy store in Baltimore and from Putts', another Baltimore store which sold jewelry, china, and housewares —with toys added at Christmas.†

The interior of the house was not made with the same care and detail as the outside. This is true of more than one dolls' house, and one wonders if this relates to the fact that most dolls' house builders are men, who are likely to have a greater interest in exterior architecture than in interior decoration.

---

* Inasmuch as a belvedere is "a turret or lantern on a house, to afford a view," the hotel seems well named, and Bowling Hall logically related.

† In the writer's collection is a set of jackstraws with the label of "Henry Schwarz, 15 E. Baltimore Street, Baltimore" affixed to the wooden container. On page 316 reference is made to the frequently seen labels of G. A. Schwarz, the Philadelphia brother. Henry Schwarz appears to have been considerably more sparing of labels.

FIVE ROW HOUSES FROM EAST BALTIMORE

DATE: CA. 1900 (?)
HEIGHT (FRONT): 18¼"
    (BACK): 15"
WIDTH (OF ROW, AT CORNICE): 56"
DEPTH (INCLUDING CORNICE, NOT INCLUDING STEPS): 9⅞"
OWNER: AUTHOR'S COLLECTION

Urban renewal seemingly has claimed acres of Baltimore's brick row houses with their little white steps. More than a few remain, but still it was reassuring to come across this row of five, and to rescue them, sitting forlornly on a curb at a Pennsylvania flea market in 1971, at two o'clock in the afternoon.

Although this quintet was not made for use as dolls' houses, they might readily qualify. They await restoration, and though only a few partitions remain, it is evident from the remnants and the construction that each of the five contained two rooms, one up and one down, and that wallpaper lined the walls, a few shards of which linger. (Even though this interior decor would not have been visible in the setting in which they were originally maintained.)

The houses had come from a Christmas garden in a firehouse in east Baltimore. Years ago, one belatedly learned, many Baltimore firehouses had such displays, constructed by the firemen in their spare time, and displayed to the public at Christmas.

These carefully observed copies even have their street numbers—"10" through "18"—on the glass panes above the workable doors; and one wonders whether the street name was also specified. The brick paper is peeling, and the rundown row was apparently made many years ago to represent houses built in the 'eighties or 'nineties. With their hooded chimneys (covered in brick paper of a smaller scale), and their seamed and sloping roof-tops, they appear to lack, beneath the white shades still neatly drawn

DOLLS' HOUSES FROM THE SOUTH

Figure 182

half-way at their windows, only an aspidistra or a fern behind the glass.

SEMI-DETACHED HOUSES FROM WASHINGTON, D. C.

DATE: CA. 1900
HEIGHT (NOT INCLUDING CHIMNEY): 34″
WIDTH (AT BASE): 24″
DEPTH (INCLUDING STAIRS): 21″
OWNER: AUTHOR'S COLLECTION

Every city has its proper share of semi-detached houses, and Washington, D. C. is no exception. This pair came to its present owner with the information that its builder had emigrated from Germany to the District of Columbia and had built this disarming duplex at the turn of the century.

Certainly it is atypical of D. C. semi-detached houses, most of which, with small front porches marching monotonously across them, bear no relation to the red-white-and-green piece of ingenuity to be seen here. Black and white cannot do justice to this irresistibly colorful piece of gingerbread in which arched windows, coigning, and miscellaneous rustication mingle in giddy profusion, clearly in tribute to the builder's Teutonic origin.

A theory was advanced by a perspicacious visitor in recent years that the pair of semi-detached houses might well be a pair of semi-detached shops. He based this theory on the presence of the narrow but deeply projecting windows at the side of each of the front doors, which lock with an ornamental key. This opinion may be reinforced by the room arrangement on the right-hand side which includes a small front vestibule with its own door into the rear room. (The "house" on the left contains a single chamber.) However, it is possible that this division was made in order to conceal the

HISTORIC PRESERVATION IN MINIATURE: UNIQUE EXAMPLES

Figure 183

early transformer behind the inner wall, which once served to illuminate the plump, old-fashioned light bulbs.

There is a second entrance to this room on the side, where a hinged section of the wall, containing a sizeable arched window, may be opened; again perhaps with relation to the lighting arrangements and their accessibility. The rest of the house opens from the front, also in segments. Like those on the ground floor, two sections on the second floor, each containing a deep room, also are hinged for access. The single room on the third floor opens in the same manner, and on both floors a hinged section of the wire railing lowers to allow this.

A large supply of hinges was required by the builder. One of the many ingenious features of his remarkable piece of work relates to the left-hand section of the roof. When this is lifted off, and part of its hinged side lowered, a wooden swing, suspended from chains, moves into place when its wooden framework is raised.

Inasmuch as a black stove pipe runs from the ceiling of the ground floor to the chimney, it is evident that a stove with additional pipe once fitted into the opening (which is finished off with a circular metal rim). It is unfortunate that the stove and the other furnishings were lost. Marvelous paper wall and floor coverings remain in all rooms, and most of the lace curtains, in various patterns, are at the assortment of windows. These include several appealing pairs of pointed Gothic windows on the back, for this house is presentable at any angle. Only interior stairs were omitted, owing undoubtedly to the exigencies of space, for, seemingly, no other detail has been overlooked.

A "QUEEN ANNE" COTTAGE

DATE: CA. 1910
HEIGHT (TO CREST OF VERGEBOARD): 26″
WIDTH (NOT INCLUDING BAY): 16¾″
DEPTH (INCLUDING PORCHES): 26″
OWNER: MRS. CECIL ST. C. KING (VIRGINIA)

The "Queen Anne" style, which began to take over the architectural scene in the 'eighties, was a melange of Jacobean and Elizabethan, and not Queen Anne at all.

This winsome example of the genre, in miniature, is believed to be from the Washington, D. C. area; it puts one in mind of numerous turn-of-the-century specimens in the capital's Cleveland Park, and in the Maryland and Virginia suburbs. Innumerable close relations may be encountered in New England and in late Victorian villages and suburbs throughout the country.

As on the full-sized originals, scarcely a bit of wood has been left unturned or uncarved by the

DOLLS' HOUSES FROM THE SOUTH

Figure 184

architect. An assortment of windows (single, triple, bay, diamond, and dormer), a trio of porches (front and back, and up and down, with nicely turned posts and spindled cornices), and imposing vergeboards—all are provided with a generous but delicate hand. Above the porch, the clapboard siding yields to scalloped strips, and on the third story to shaped shingles—a partial expression of the shingle style to which Queen Anne lent itself in many a late Victorian seaside mansion and inland residence. The shaped shingles are decoratively repeated in triple rows on the steep roof.

The architect clearly spent himself before he got to the interior. There is one large room each on the first and second floors, plus an attic. But even this is in character inasmuch as the Queen Anne style was "characterized by large open interior spaces"! *

Originally, most of these houses "were painted in somber, artistic tones, in browns and reds; now many of them have been 'vulgarized,' as it would have seemed to their builders, by

* *The American Heritage History of Notable American Houses.*

white paint." * Mrs. King's house is, as she found it, white with green trim, and the substantial chimneys, as well as the foundation, are of red brick paper. (An interior concession to these chimneys is a tiny brick fireplace on the first floor.)

The house is deep, and opens in back with a relatively narrow panel, the only part of the exterior which has not been treated architecturally.

Unquestionably, this engaging domicile is a replica of a house which exists, or once existed, in some suburb, and one is convinced that, at any turn, one will come upon it.

ELEANORA'S HOUSE

DATE: CA. 1917–18
HEIGHT: 14½"
WIDTH: 13"
DEPTH: 8½"
OWNER: MRS. RICHARD ROBBINS KANE (MARYLAND)

This small house was made by Alexander Worthington Bowling II, ca. 1917, for his daughter Eleanora. Since Mr. Bowling was born on a tobacco plantation in Charles County, Maryland, it is of interest to note, as his daughter points out, that the chimney on the dolls' house is the type with "steps" frequently seen in southern Maryland.

Another unusual feature of the house can be seen on the side opposite the chimney—a porte-cochère, a convenience often found on full-sized houses at the turn of the century (and earlier), but rarely noticed by dolls' house builders. On this one, Mr. Bowling provided the same modified hipped roof that he built for the roof of the house itself, and for the small porch at the front.

The back swings open on hinges, and inside there are two rooms, now furnished in the

* *The Tastemakers* by Russell Lynes, Grosset and Dunlap.

HISTORIC PRESERVATION IN MINIATURE: UNIQUE EXAMPLES

Figure 185

Tootsietoy furniture of the 'twenties. Its owner remembers that the original was of the "silver" filigree type. Variations of such metal furniture have, of course, been made both in the United States and in Europe for generations (Figs. 393–7).

Mrs. Kane's lawyer father enjoyed making small buildings in a basement workshop for what his daughter remembers as "an enormous, exciting Christmas garden." She said after he built her this house, "It always reigned over the 'garden' as a sort of manor house."

A "TEXAS STUCCO" OF THE 1920's

DATE: CA. 1920'S
HEIGHT (NOT INCLUDING CHIMNEYS): 29"
WIDTH: 37"
DEPTH: 24½"
OWNER: MRS. DELANNE LOPEMAN DUBOIS (TEXAS)

To represent the Southwest, the only dolls' house which has so far surfaced is from the

Figure 186

(162)

DOLLS' HOUSES FROM THE SOUTH

1920's, but it is typical of many full-sized houses in its region, and unusual in its construction.

The white stucco house has "French doors all around the entire exterior," as its owner points out; and these doors, all containing their original curtains, open in pairs to reveal the high-ceilinged interior, constructed to relieve the "intense Texas heat in pre-air conditioning years." Inside, there are three rooms, kitchen and bath, all containing their original wallpapers, curtains, furnishings and lighting. The furnishings include "built-ins," among them such a standard feature of the 'twenties as the breakfast nook (built-in benches and table). The floors are of hardwood except for linoleum in the kitchen "much worn from scrubbing by small people." A small terrace leading to the front door is linoleum-covered to resemble stone.

Mrs. DuBois observes that Texas stuccos are referred to these days as "Spanish." This miniature version of the genre came with its own stand, painted green to match the trim.

A 1735 REPRODUCTION FROM VIRGINIA

DATE: 1969
HEIGHT: 29"
WIDTH: 24"
DEPTH (NOT INCLUDING PORCH): 15"
OWNER: MRS. JOSEPH ANDREWS (VIRGINIA)

If even a selection of the gifted artists and hobbyists who are working in miniature were to be assembled, they would command a sizeable volume of their own. I hope someone will write that book; it would be diversified and informative, and history for the future. It is impossible to offer in these pages of primarily antiquarian interest more than a brief selection to represent this vast group. One's choices must be arbitrary.

One of these is a replica of a general store and post office which was built in Rockett Mill, Virginia, in 1735, and I am in awe of the manner

Figure 187

in which Mrs. Andrews of Ashland, Virginia, went about reconstructing her inch-to-the-foot model. Intrigued by the history of the house which is just a few miles from Patrick Henry's birthplace and which was occupied by Lafayette's retreating troops in 1781, Mrs. Andrews has, literally, left no stone unturned: The rocks which form the basement foundation came, with the owner's permission, from the original house, and had to be taken to a quarry and crushed for use in the miniature one.

Mrs. Andrews used other materials from the original building: the exterior siding, floors, and

HISTORIC PRESERVATION IN MINIATURE: UNIQUE EXAMPLES

Figure 189

Figure 188

porch were made from wood in the decaying original. Especially impressive is the manner in which she and her young son John built the chimney. Using a hammer and sieve, John pulverized two bricks, one light and one dark, from the full-sized chimney. Then his mother molded the miniature bricks from the pulverized originals. "The darker bricks were baked next to the heat and the light ones were in the middle of the oven."

Even the topographical setting of the original building, situated on a hill, was re-created with the aid of papier-mâché. Ten-inch bin beams in the original floor in which Mrs. Andrews believes grain may have been stored and an assortment of windows with varying arrangements of panes, were also duplicated, and the indefatigable Mrs. Andrews even "collected and grew" a cobweb for the attic!

The four rooms inside have cardboard walls painted to resemble whitewash. "After all, this was the miller's house on a very large Plantation," Mrs. Andrews notes. "There was no color paint at this time for farm houses." The architect also made most of the furniture, from pine taken from an old house ca. 1650.

DOLLS' HOUSES
From the Mid-West

A HOUSE FROM NORWALK, OHIO

DATE: CA. 1840
HEIGHT (TO PEAK OF ROOF): 46″
WIDTH: 30″
DEPTH: 15″
OWNER: MILAN HISTORICAL MUSEUM (MILAN, OHIO)

Years ago, through the courtesy of an Ohio collector, the writer learned of the existence of this attractive dolls' house, which had been sold at the auction of an old mansion on the main street of Norwalk, Ohio. Extraordinarily, the house and many of its furnishings were donated by a generous antique dealer to the Milan Historical Museum.

Although I have not seen this house in person, I have seen it in color, and it is most appealing with its handsomely painted red brick exterior and its exuberantly wallpapered interior. The windows and door on the façade of this cupboard-type structure are painted rather than actual; the window panes are strikingly painted black with white mullions, and both the door and the coigning are a chocolate brown. Glazed windows on the sides admit additional light to the seven rooms which are surmounted by an attic with an arched opening under a pitched roof.

Mrs. Richard Fairchild, the collector who told me of the house, bought some of its furnishings and dolls from a second dealer who attended the auction, including a rare parian doll with a snood and two pink bows in her hair. Considering how many dolls are still in the house (a casual count reveals a dozen), this must have been a thoroughly populated household. In the

Figure 190

(165)

Figure 191

Figure 192

photograph, it is possible to identify a Stevens & Brown black iron table and two chairs* in the lower-right-hand room, Biedermeier chairs with upholstered seats in the room above, and fretwork furniture in the center room above that, on the third floor.

In the hope of learning the name of the family to whom the dolls' house had belonged, I wrote to Mr. B. A. Decker, the antique dealer who presented it to the museum. Months later a reply came from Mr. Decker who had belatedly received the letter. His "only knowledge" of the dolls' house, he wrote, was that it belonged to the "Cunninghams of New York State."

* See Figs. 370–1.

(166)

DOLLS' HOUSES FROM THE MID-WEST

With the passage of years, facts are often mislaid or misapplied, and it is difficult to sort the conflicting information here. Both are offered, with the hope that a clarification will be forthcoming, perhaps by a reader of these words.

THE KUEFFNER CIVIL WAR COTTAGE

DATE: CA. 1860
HEIGHT (NOT INCLUDING CHIMNEY): 25″
WIDTH: 23″
DEPTH: 15″
OWNER: RAMSEY COUNTY HISTORICAL SOCIETY (ST. PAUL, MINNESOTA)

Built about 1860 for the two daughters of a Civil War general, this modest "masonry" cottage with its hand-shingled roof has been given, in recent years, by the General's nephew, Mr. Walter Kueffner, to the Ramsey County Historical Society for their Gibbs Farm Museum in St. Paul.

Brigadier General William C. Kueffner practiced law in Belleville, Illinois, and the house, built by a client, is believed to be a replica of the General's house there. In 1894, when he died, the dolls' house was shipped up the Mississippi River to St. Paul, where a younger brother's five daughters played with it. In all, five generations played with the house which was refurnished, with care for history, by Mr. and Mrs. Walter Kueffner in the early 1940's. A family of dolls, inherited with their residence, were dressed in costumes reproduced from ones in Godey prints and old photographs. These include the General, "field hat in hand," in his blue uniform of the Union troops. (His civilian clothes hang suspended from pegs on the wall in the attic.)

There are no bedrooms in the cottage, but the attic with its unfinished rafters is well filled with "discarded furniture and china, spinning wheel and yarn, a mouse browsing along the mop board behind the old cat's back, and a painted

Figure 193

bride's trunk of very early days." Downstairs, the parlor and sitting-room in the front and the kitchen at the rear are also thoroughly furnished. (Two large doors in the rear of the house give access to these.)

At the Minnesota State Fair in 1944—during a different war—Mrs. Kueffner once wrote, "A Civil War veteran examined the house carefully, his face wreathed in smiles, and said, 'It is all there, just as it used to be, even to the shell on the floor for a doorstop.'"

THE HILL-GRAY HOUSE

DATE: CA. 1880
HEIGHT: 54″
WIDTH: 49″
DEPTH: 20½″
OWNER: MRS. WILLIAM HYLAND (CONNECTICUT)

In about 1900, this enormous dolls' house was moved by railroad from Minnesota to Connecticut. It seems more than a footnote to dolls' house history that the house belonged to a little girl named Helen Gray, and that the railroad belonged to her grandfather, James J. Hill.

HISTORIC PRESERVATION IN MINIATURE: UNIQUE EXAMPLES

Figure 194

When the Grays moved to Stamford, their only child was in her teens. After Helen Gray married and became Mrs. Edwards, the dolls' house remained with her mother till her death in 1935. It was in storage till 1955 when Mrs. Edwards, who had no children, presented it to Mrs. Hyland, the present owner, complete with its furnishings and dolls.

It is the contents and the interior of the house they thoroughly furnish* that are of particular interest. There is a proper staircase, notable in the dolls' house world of illogical staircases, that

* The photograph fails to do justice to these, understandably, because it was taken for a newspaper shortly after the new owner had received the house, and before much of the furniture was unpacked or accurately arranged.

leads realistically both to the second floor and the attic, and has two nicely turned newel posts besides. Although the kitchen door with its workable brass knob is the only door in the house, the double-framed doorways between the rooms have portières. These are red velvet downstairs and faded cretonne in a diminutive floral pattern upstairs, hung with tiny brass rings from solid brass rods, and lending considerable atmosphere.

The decor is further enhanced by the presence of the original carpeting, of various fine pieces of tapestry or upholstery fabric, and the original curtains, also on brass rods.

It was Mrs. Gray's pleasure, according to her daughter, to let visiting children play with the house, and some furnishings were destroyed. However, except for additions in the 1920's, the contents include a virtual catalogue of commercially made dolls' house furnishings before the turn of the century, and are so complete that it is hard to believe that many are missing.

Of particular interest is the "Cozy Corner," at the back of the sewing-room. A commercially made example is pictured elsewhere,* but it is delightful to come upon a homemade version in a dolls' house. Tiny silk-covered pillows are heaped upon an elaborately upholstered divan. A lighting fixture I have not seen before is an electric wall sconce in the hall which contains the pointed glass bulb of the 'nineties and, by means of a brass ball held by the curving leaves of the fixture, can be adjusted to any angle chosen by the resident dolls.

There are many other wonders: a brass bed with curving footboard, custom-made for the house when it was new. There is a platform rocker manufactured by the Fairy Toy Works. Even the attic is crowded, with cast-offs which would be the making of another house. Two pieces are of particular note because they have documentation possibilities. One is a sturdy cardboard washstand with cupboard and towel rack, circa 1910, bearing the label of "D. M. Read, Bridgeport, Conn.," the well-known department store still in existence. The other is a metal bed with an embossed headboard and wooden posts. This is labeled "Bed of Roses Sachet," and as a knowing collector* has pointed out, "This might well be mistaken for commercially-made dolls' house furniture."

THE CARNAHAN SISTERS' CHRISTMAS PRESENT

DATE: 1886
HEIGHT (NOT INCLUDING STAND): 50"
WIDTH: 53"
OWNER: ALLEN COUNTY—FORT WAYNE HISTORICAL MUSEUM (FORT WAYNE, INDIANA)

Christmas 1886 started out as usual for Clara and Virginia Carnahan of Fort Wayne, Indiana:

Mina . . . called us at 5:30 a.m. It was still dark. We dressed, had a glass of milk in her clean kitchen. Then she took us by the hand and led us through the dark winter morning streets to her church, St. Paul's Lutheran. . . . The service began at six a.m. with soft organ music. We could smell the pine trees on either side of the altar [but] . . . the special thing about this morning was yet to come as we walked home.

After breakfast the sisters went "eagerly" to their nursery on the third floor:

Standing higher than [their] heads was the dolls' house, a beautiful new house with six rooms, a winding staircase rising from the center hall to the second story, a kitchen and dining-room downstairs, a bedroom and a sitting-room upstairs, all completely furnished in doll size furniture, even to the pins in the pincushion out of tiny bolts of ribbon.

* Fig. 398.

* Mrs. John H. Grossman, who supplied the excellent inventory.

HISTORIC PRESERVATION IN MINIATURE: UNIQUE EXAMPLES

Figure 195

Never has a dolls' house been better documented. Not only is its complete history known, but a nostalgic recollection (of which the above is an excerpt) was recorded in their old age by the sisters who had played with it in their youth. Therefore, when the museum secretary, Mrs. Perry, wrote later to tell me that a picture of the dolls' house in its original nursery had come to light, the documentation seemed almost dazzling.*

This rare photograph, taken early in the history of the dolls' house, shows at a glance why the small sisters immediately saw the corner with the dolls' house when they walked into their huge nursery on Christmas morning. Even without the four-legged stand which was added later, it was formidable. Apart from the gable with its bull's-eye window* in the steeply pitched roof, and the delicately scroll-cut brackets which embellish the upper corners of the

---

* Since the position of the dolls' house in the museum makes it difficult to photograph as a whole, this was especially welcome.

* Similar windows are also beneath the gables in the clapboarded sides, with rectangular windows below them.

(170)

DOLLS' HOUSES FROM THE MID-WEST

rooms, there is no façade, but the interior is spacious and luxurious.

Even in the aging photograph, the winding staircase with the grandfather's clock on the landing is readily discernible. And so is the father in his top hat in the room above. The whole house is furnished with the loving detail to be seen in the parlor (shown here), and all have their original wallpapers (note the deep paper border), curtains, and carpets. It is reassuring to learn that the handsome Biedermeier upright can still "play;" the fine wire strings inside these pianos are usually silent. One longs to move the bristol-globed lamp perching uneasily upon the top to the more secure marble-topped center table upon which the family Bible reposes.

The coin silver tea set on the tea table near the fireplace is one frequently discovered in Victorian dolls' houses, and many must have been made. These are usually found with an ornately embossed tray which seems to bear no relationship to the austere pattern of the service itself. An embossed brass music rack—with embossed bird in flight—a brass screen with a pastoral portrait of a very young shepherd and shepherdess, and a pedestal which holds a most important-looking jardinière are included in a parlor which is a veritable compendium of the bric-a-brac to be seen in dolls' houses of the

Figure 196

'eighties. It is known that most of the furnishings came from wherever else, Schwarz in New York or Schwarz in Boston. The sisters discovered on that Christmas morning in 1886 "what had happened on those trips east mother and father had made. Father had to go four times a year to buy shoes for the W. L. Carnahan Boot and Shoe Company on Clinton Street between Wayne and Berry. So mother had taken little floor plans with her to New York and Boston on these trips with father. . . ."

Louise, an older sister, "had sewed and hemstitched all the towels, napkins, tablecloths and doilies." She undoubtedly was responsible, too, for the antimacassars to be seen on the flowered chairs and sofa, and for the highly essential scarf on the piano.

The dining-room is not shown, but beneath its dark rose wallpaper there is wainscoting so realistic that it was described in a Fort Wayne newspaper story as "ornately carved." I inquired and learned that it is "a long piece of tooled leather attached to the wall with pins."* A bristol tea set in this dining-room is only the second I have seen in this pattern. The other may be found in Fig. 404.

The kitchen contains such accoutrements as a hand-turned ice cream freezer and a bucket of drinking water with ladle on the oak table, a common accessory before the advent of tap water.

Even the activities of the dolls' house family, whom the sisters named the Aldrich family, are documented: "Mr. and Mrs. Aldrich are always standing in the upper hall to greet guests, their son in the lower hall with his cat and dog beside him." There were also a baby, a cook, and a nurse, and they are still in residence with the wonderful agelessness of fortunate dolls' house families. (We shall not speak of the evicted ones.)

It is of special interest to note that the dolls' house, built by Charles Muchlenbruck, a Fort Wayne cabinetmaker, on the premises of the Carnahan shoe company, has a twin,* and the curious circumstances establishing this fact appear to warrant more than a footnote.

In the 1965 edition of *A History of Dolls' Houses*, I referred to a dolls' house in the collection of Mrs. William Redd Mahoney of Oak Park, Illinois, which was reportedly from the well-known Hanna family of Fort Wayne. After this information was published, I received, in November 1966, a letter from Mrs. Herb Harnish of Fort Wayne, who had recently cleaned the Carnahan house for the museum and suspected from my description that the maker of the Carnahan house and the Hanna house "were one and the same," especially since the Carnahans and Hannas were related.

Mrs. Harnish wrote: "For years, I am told by local residents, a doll house was on exhibit at the Fort Wayne Public Library. Where it went, or when, I have been unable to find out for certain. From your description of the 'Hanna' house, I have a sneaky suspicion they were one and the same. For this reason I should like to correspond with Mrs. Mahoney. . . ." Mrs. Harnish was sent forthwith the address of Mrs. Mahoney who, to my regret, has not supplied pictures of *her* house which I saw in her apartment a number of years ago. But the resemblance is more than a family one: There is the same arrangement of rooms on each side of a wide stairhall, the same open front with a gable in the roof, and similar scroll cut brackets on the beams.

---

* Similar wainscoting in a full-sized house may be seen in the Physick mansion in Cape May, New Jersey, built in 1881, where pressed leather may be seen on the lower part of the staircase wall.

* It is of interest that another pair of twin dolls' houses may be found in museums in the midwest—in Milwaukee (see Fig. 202). Another house belonging to Mrs. Mahoney, the Watkins baby house, also evidently was made not only in duplicate but in triplicate for related children. There must have been many others, of course.

DOLLS' HOUSES FROM THE MID-WEST

This is not surprising in view of the fact that the Carnahan sisters were the daughters of William L. Carnahan who married Clara L. Hanna, the daughter of James Bayless Hanna, in 1864. It is believed that James Hanna's daughter Mary Margaret was the original owner of the Hanna dolls' house. Since the Carnahan sisters and Mary Margaret Hanna were first cousins, their having twin dolls' houses is charmingly plausible, and one wonders what Mary Margaret Hanna received for Christmas in 1886! (She would have been seven years old, a satisfactory age in such a chronology.)

As for what happened to the Hanna dolls' house in between its mysterious departure from the Fort Wayne Public Library and its purchase by Mrs. Mahoney, the writer has participated in two coincidences which are literally related to this dolls' house, and which shed light on (1) where it was during part of 1942, and (2) how Mrs. Mahoney happened to acquire it:

When I saw the Hanna house in her apartment, "there was nothing about it," as I reported in the 1965 edition of *A History of Dolls' Houses*, "that jogged a memory or rang a bell." Later on, however, looking through some old clippings, I came across one about a Victorian dolls' house, a feature story written years ago when I was a cub reporter on a Washington paper and knew nothing of dolls' houses. I hadn't even remembered writing such a thing. There was one picture with the story—of one room in the dolls' house. Somehow it looked familiar, and, as things turned out, it *was*. Examination proved it to be one room in the Hanna house! In 1942, the dolls' house had been on view in a Washington, D. C. department store in connection with a promotion relating to the showing of the Orson Welles film "The Magnificent Ambersons," in which Indiana, 1885, happened to be the setting. A print of the very photograph in the story was in Mrs. Mahoney's possession, one of a set she was given when she bought the house!

And how had she happened to buy the house?

I've alluded elsewhere to the fact that Gertrude Mahoney and the writer seem always to be related to the same dolls' houses—and Mrs. Mahoney's purchase of this one resulted from the purchase (from an Ohio antique dealer) of another to which I'd referred her.

THE GOVERNOR RAMSEY DOLL MANSION

DATE: 1887
HEIGHT: 40"
WIDTH: 48"
DEPTH: 17½"
OWNER: MINNESOTA HISTORICAL SOCIETY (ST. PAUL, MINNESOTA)

This most historic plaything was built in 1887 as a Christmas present for Miss Laura Furness, the younger granddaughter of Governor Alexander Ramsey, Minnesota's first territorial governor, and it is on view today in the Ramsey mansion in St. Paul. Although it has been referred to as "an approximate replica" of the mansion itself, and that may be stretching a point, a comparison by the late Elsa Mannheimer* does suggest that any resemblance is not purely coincidental.

This is not surprising inasmuch as the dolls' house was built by Matthew Taylor, the master carpenter who built the mansion itself, the latter completed in 1872.† Mr. Taylor's original bill for the dolls' house is still extant. It was for $25. It seems unfortunate that a picture with the façade in place is not available. "When the front is put on the house (it is removable and not hinged)," Miss Mannheimer once wrote, "there

---

* Miss Mannheimer (see pages 246 and 247) restored the dolls' house for the Society in 1965.

† "Hon. Alexander Ramsey's elegant residence on Exchange Street is approaching completion," according to a November 1872 news story. "Mrs. Ramsey gave a very fine entertainment and banquet to the workmen on the building on Thursday last." (From a brochure about the Ramsey house.)

HISTORIC PRESERVATION IN MINIATURE: UNIQUE EXAMPLES

Figure 197

is a marked resemblance to its prototype, and they would make an engaging pair of pictures."

"The mansion," she added, "is of gray limestone and has several porches, but the doll house is innocent of both. However, the carpenter undoubtedly meant to suggest his larger effort, as the doll house is painted stone gray (though, of course, made of wood), and has the roof, dormer windows and general look of the house façade." No effort had been made to reproduce the interior, she wrote, but as the picture indicates, there is a handsomely detailed staircase with a window lighting it, and a landing, and there are other interior details of interest, especially the arches, one in the parlor and another in the upstairs sitting-room.

Much of the furniture in the dolls' house is original, although some was evidently lost during years in which this historic piece was lent to settlement houses and other St. Paul institu-

DOLLS' HOUSES FROM THE MID-WEST

tions. Although the house was repapered years ago,* the carpets and curtains are original, as are all the parlor furnishings (except for the brass étagère in the corner). This includes the astonishing metal fireplace in which two caryatids in classical drapery support amphorae which in turn, presumably, supported the mantel—a mid-Victorian reference to the earlier classical revival.

The dolls are also original to the house, although the only one really visible in the photograph is the gentleman in the lower hall who carries a silk hat and—most unusual and appropriate—a house key. Although it has been suggested that this black-mustachioed dolls' house man "might be the governor himself," the latter was cleanshaven. Governor Ramsey, incidentally, who was a United States Senator from Minnesota for twelve years, was recalled to Washington in 1879 by President Hayes to be his Secretary of War. Mrs. Ramsey during these years as a cabinet wife undoubtedly had many opportunities to view the two splendid dolls' houses belonging to Fanny Hayes, and it is of interest to compare the Ramsey dolls' house with Hayes House II (Fig. 90).

A MANSARD IN MISSOURI

DATE: CA. 1880–90
HEIGHT: 42″
WIDTH: 21″
DEPTH: 16″
OWNER: MISSOURI HISTORICAL SOCIETY (ST. LOUIS, MISSOURI)

"The French Roof is in great request," wrote Samuel Sloan. "Public and private dwellings and even stables are covered with it and no man who wants a fashionable house will be without it."

* The house was restored in 1949 for a territorial centennial celebration. It was evidently at that time that it was repapered, and therefore, Miss Mannheimer wrote to a fanatical dolls' house historian in 1965, "It wouldn't hurt to do it again."

The Victorian architect was, of course, writing about the United States where the mansard roof was so enthusiastically adopted that such roofs outdid, in multiplicity, the number to be found in their native France.

The unknown builder of this bewitching miniature residence was clearly inspired by an actual house, one with a mansard which had to be formidable indeed to be noticeable beneath such an overbearing cornice, chimneys, and belvedere, and above the thoroughly embellished tops of the pair of two-story bays. (See Fig. 199.)

Although it is lamentable that the history of this confection is unknown, it is marvelous that it has been preserved, along with its fenced garden which further dramatizes this very vertical extravaganza. The deep shaped base, with barred cellar windows, is another pleasing detail,

Figure 198

HISTORIC PRESERVATION IN MINIATURE: UNIQUE EXAMPLES

Figure 199

along with the casement windows, placed between sash windows, on the second floor, by an architect who plainly left no possibility unexplored. The finial on the belvedere is the final exuberance. Regarding it, one can almost hear the architect grinding, reluctantly, to a stop.

Perfectionist though he was, however, he evidently knew where to stop, if not *when*. The floors are not divided into rooms and in order to play with the house, it was necessary for the young owner to remove the floors in sections.

This seems the only unsatisfactory feature of a most satisfying dolls' house.

The furnishings have been added from the Missouri Historical Society's considerable collection of furniture.

The Society also has in its possession other dolls' houses, in storage as these words are written. These include several Bliss houses and one, built in 1880, in the style of 1710!

Shown in Fig. 198 is a surprisingly similar house in the Baltimore Museum of Art.

DOLLS' HOUSES FROM THE MID-WEST

THE BINGHAM DOLLS' HOUSE

Date: ca. 1890
Height: 3′1″
Width: 3′4″
Depth: 5′8″
Owner: western reserve historical society (cleveland, ohio)

The essence of the Colonial Revival house, this imposing residence is of interest from several points of view. It was a Christmas present, in about 1890, to two sisters, one of whom later became the Hon. Frances P. Bolton, for years a congresswoman from Ohio. When Representative Bolton and her sister (Mrs. Dudley S. Blossom) came across the dilapidated house in a cellar of the old Perry residence in Cleveland many years later, they decided to have it restored.

Since they decided to "make it an outstanding example of a fine Georgian Colonial home," and they employed an interior designer and a Cleveland company of craftsmen to do the restoration, the result is more related to the Thorne miniature rooms than it is to dolls' houses. Nevertheless, because it originated as a dolls' house, it belongs to dolls' house history as well.

The interior furnishings, most of them built for the restoration, are outside our province. A booklet available at the museum describes and pictures the drawing-room, dining-room, "early American kitchen" (which seems misplaced in such an elegant city mansion), colonial bedroom, etc. Some antiques are among the furnishings, including a grandfather clock that runs, and a collection of miniature books. The scale is 1¼″ to 1′.

In reply to a question, an official of the Historical Society wrote, "At this distance in time it would be difficult to say whether any changes had been made to the exterior." There is a carriage entrance at the side and a kitchen door in the rear, and one longs to know what

Figure 200

the house looked like when it was presented to the two little girls so many Christmases ago.

A VICTORIAN GOTHIC FROM ILLINOIS

Date: 1893
Measurements unavailable: the stand is 33″ × 25″
Owner: mrs. a. m. ray (minnesota)

In 1893, just forty-three years after Andrew Jackson Downing wrote *The Architecture of Country Houses*, a Mr. Swan of Moline, Illinois, built this dolls' house for his children. The latter told Mrs. Ray that it was "their father's dreamhouse as they had never owned a home." The rare bit of miniature architecture which resulted, has the gabled windows to be seen on several of Downing's "small Gothic cottages," as well as a variation on the turret to be found on an imposing "villa in the Norman style" shown

(177)

HISTORIC PRESERVATION IN MINIATURE: UNIQUE EXAMPLES

Figure 201

the *Ladies' Home Journal*. Elsewhere* I have briefly summarized an article in the December 1901 issue entitled, "How I Made a Dolls' House for $3," and although this seems late for a dolls' house built in 1893, the ladies' magazines, in their Christmas issues, frequently included such instruction.

In an 1893 issue of *The Girls' Own Paper*, an English periodical, complete details were given for constructing and furnishing a dolls' drawing-room. This contained such modest furnishings as "a writing-cabinet from three match boxes" and—most astonishing—"an American wicker chair . . . made from a coarse blue and white sailor hat." † Mrs. Ray copied many of the old pieces which were too battered to use.

in Downing's influential work. With true Victorian eclecticism, the dream house also has a few variations Mr. Downing never dreamed of.

When the hinged front of the cottage is open, the parlor, sitting-room, and upstairs music room are in view. The room plan is realistic: off the parlor, for instance, is the small sitting-room with a fireplace, and there is a bay window with a velvet window seat. The stairway mounts from the parlor to a small upstairs hall which leads to the three rooms. (These can be seen from the back of the house, which is open, as well as through a glass skylight in the roof.)

Unfortunately, when Mrs. Ray bought the house many years ago, it was in poor condition, and some walls had to be replaced, and all of them repapered. The furniture was also nearly all in unusable condition, but it is engaging to learn that it was created of cardboard, paper, wire, plush, and other scraps and, Mrs. Ray thinks, must have been made "by an ingenious mother who no doubt received her ideas from

CHRISTMAS 1893 IN MILWAUKEE

DATE: 1893
HEIGHT (INCLUDING BASE): 5'6"
WIDTH: 49½"
DEPTH: 25½"
OWNER: MILWAUKEE PUBLIC MUSEUM (MILWAUKEE, WISCONSIN)

It may not be altogether surprising that this marvelous dolls' house should have been made in Milwaukee, and that it bears more than one resemblance to the great seventeenth- and eighteenth-century dolls' houses to be seen in museums in Nuremberg and Munich and other German cities.

With the enormous proportion of Milwaukee residents of German background,‡ it is not unlikely that the unknown cabinetmaker who

* *A History of Dolls' Houses.*

† Thanks to doll historian Clara Fawcett, this was reproduced in its entirety in *Hobbies* in August 1963.

‡ In 1900, 72 per cent of the population was either German by birth or of the "first generation."

(178)

Figure 202

gave this house its highly ornamented cupboard-like façade, and its majestic and vertical proportions, was working in a tradition which came naturally to him. The careful workmanship and degree of embellishment seem also to relate to such a background.

Although his name is not known, the history of the house is otherwise complete. Its 1893 date is emblazoned on the stained glass panel over the front door. That was the year that Mr. and Mrs. Fred Vogel had the house built for their seven-year-old daughter who "found it under the Christmas tree," according to a *Milwaukee Journal* reporter who clearly got carried away in writing about a house which only a Giant Redwood might accommodate; but one can't blame her. The recipient was a lucky girl—later Mrs. Joseph E. Uihlein, Sr. (of the Schlitz brewery Uihleins), who gave the dolls' house to the museum when it became clear that none of her grandchildren's homes was of sufficient size to accommodate such a monumental heirloom.

Although the general aspect of the dolls' house reminds one of its tall German ancestors, there is, as the illustration suggests, a great deal of originality in its plan, and in many details. There is a most ingenious—and immediate—blend of the rooms themselves with architectural implication—architecture *implied* by the elaborately embellished roof, the three-story staircase hall with its ornately balustraded staircase open to view,* its frosted glass exterior doors, and a delectable display of gingerbread ornament—moldings, headings, carvings, and fret-sawings with every conceivable loop, medallion, and curlicue. The catalogue is long. There is a substantial bay window on the second story lighted by the same lovely stained glass which is also placed, in varying colors and patterns, throughout the house.

One of the most arresting adornments, all of which are heightened by the pale olive and coral with which the fanciful frame is painted, consists of the Muses' heads which surmount the exterior cornice of each of the four principal rooms. "The woman's head generally represented a Muse and was very common in the decoration of Milwaukee architecture at the time the house was built," the curator of the museum once wrote in response to a question, adding that one of the houses which contained the dolls' house for many years "had a large pottery head of the same type built into a side wall." Undoubtedly the house was one of the "series of imposing houses" built for members of the Uihlein family "in an affluent neighborhood that came to be known as 'Uihlein Hill.'" The Alfred Uihlein house, pictured in *Lost America*,* a tragic compendium of architectural treasures which have been demolished or otherwise destroyed and lost forever, has the same flavor of solid and delectable gingerbread (with a whiff of hops) which may be savored in the dolls' house. "The house survived in remarkably good condition until it was razed in the course of an urban renewal project." †

The use of such decorations as the Muse's head was, of course, widespread. In the handsome *American Heritage History of Notable American Houses*, there is a two-page spread of such "sculpture," which according to the editors, "exemplifies the ornamental brownstone trim that was applied to single family dwellings in New York during the late 1800s." ‡

Although the dolls' house was played with by several generations of children and "remained in fairly continual use up to the 1930's, with additional furnishings which "reflect the changes

---

* Whether by accident or recollection, this is a variation on the balustraded open fronts which are a trademark of its South German predecessors. Unfortunately, this cannot be seen in this picture.

* The Pyne Press, Princeton, 1971.

† *Ibid.*

‡ "Using brownstone imported from quarries in New Jersey, journeyman craftsmen produced moldings, entablatures and brackets by the gross . . . designs included acanthus leaves, garlands, masks, and mythological figures."

DOLLS' HOUSES FROM THE MID-WEST

in taste," as the curator pointed out, "the newer pieces are generally more spotty than the original ones." This may be a tribute to the sturdy yellow cherry German furniture (Figs. 388–90) which can be discerned in the principal rooms. The old dolls are also present, including a staff of servants and even a pair of twins who were added when a pair of infant Uihleins joined the family.

Originally there was a set of stairs which hooked into the unusual latticed base, but except for this small loss, urban renewal has not reached this dolls' house, and it has been lovingly preserved.

The same cabinetmaker who built this towering edifice is said to have made "at least one similar house," to be seen in the Milwaukee County Historical Museum, but an effort to obtain a picture of this twin has been fruitless. The curator wrote: "The Uihlein dolls' house in our collection is similar to the one owned by the Public Museum, although I believe theirs is more complete." The reference to a second Uihlein dolls' house is arresting, and it is frustrating not to be able to compare the two.

Figure 203

A MICHIGAN COTTAGE

DATE: 1896
HEIGHT: 32¼"
WIDTH: 26¾"
DEPTH (INCLUDING PORCH): 19"
OWNER: MRS. JOHN H. GROSSMAN (CONNECTICUT)

Though this cottage is unusually simple and unembellished for one built in 1896, it has a personality all its own, and no one would mistake it for anything made in recent decades.

Built in Detroit by Allen Price Ford for his two-year-old daughter Laura,* the house moved

* A surprising number of dolls' houses—literally baby houses—have been made for infants. Perhaps the rule-of-thumb which, when an exact date is unknown, may supply an age between six and nine for the original recipient, is a poor rule-of-thumb to apply to dolls' houses which frequently are built for the pleasure of their builders.

with the family to Bridgeport, Connecticut, in 1906. When Laura Ford Sturges died in 1966, Mrs. Grossman bought the house, but unfortunately much of the furniture had been disposed of before she knew it was for sale. She gave the house the name "Laureston," painted above the door, in honor of the original owner. (The number "1708" is a reference to its present address.) "Cottage" seems a suitable noun for a small building with upstairs and downstairs porches and a pair of bays. One can picture it near a lake with a view of a postcard sunset.

The rugs and the dolls are original, as are the wallpapers in the parlor and the right-hand bedroom. (The others were in poor condition and have been replaced.) The marvelously deep

HISTORIC PRESERVATION IN MINIATURE: UNIQUE EXAMPLES

Figure 204

alcoves formed by the bays lend an appealing reality to the interior.

A MINNESOTA FARMHOUSE

DATE: CA. 1900 (?)
HEIGHT: 26″
WIDTH: 15″
DEPTH: 27″
OWNER: MISS MARGUERITE MUMM (MINNESOTA)

A previous owner of this sturdy farmhouse arranged the auction scene which the present owner does not find especially appealing. However, it is, to say the least, Americana, and so is the farmhouse itself which Miss Mumm considers typical of farmhouses, and even of many city houses, in the St. Paul area.

There are two main rooms, one up and one down, plus the lean-to visible at the rear, which has a door opening into the downstairs room

(182)

Figure 205

Figure 206 *Figure 207*

and one onto the back steps. The house itself opens at the side to reveal the two large rooms and stairs against the back wall. These stairs have a balustrade made of a strip of the picture molding which, ingeniously sliced, forms the lower porch railing. The painted tin balcony on the upstairs porch is pierced in an attractive pattern, and the front door is oak with a glazed panel at the top and a white china knob.

Miss Mumm knows nothing of the history of her house, but says that one amusing feature are the screens which take the place of glass in all the windows. "If anything is more necessary than screens in this climate," she wrote, "certainly window glass is it." As collectors can attest, the idiosyncrasies of dolls' houses are often as appealing as their diminutive imitations of reality.

(In the detail picture, the handsome black stove to the left of the pot-bellied example, identical to the one in Fig. 359, is rare indeed.)

(183)

HISTORIC PRESERVATION IN MINIATURE: UNIQUE EXAMPLES

A SCHOOLHOUSE FROM OHIO

DATE: CA. 1900 (?)
HEIGHT (INCLUDING BELFRY): 38½"
WIDTH (INCLUDING EAVES): 27¼"
DEPTH (INCLUDING EAVES): 23"
OWNER: AUTHOR'S COLLECTION

This schoolhouse came via a Cincinnati dealer, who believes it may have originated in southern Ohio. Whatever its origin, it authoritatively represents that American institution, the one-room schoolhouse, and it represents it with style.

The bell in the imposing belfry may be rung by a "rope" suspended in the classroom. The casement windows may be opened or closed. The blackboard, which extends the width of the room, may be written on. Two clock faces surmount the belfry, one on the front and one on the side, in perpetual disagreement (quarter to twelve and ten to one), but it is always satisfying to see time suspended, no matter how.

Except for the blackboard and bell, the schoolhouse was empty when found. An opportunity which came soon after to acquire the contents of a French schoolroom, in perfect scale for this one, was not resisted. Included were desks, maps, a terrestrial globe, an abacus, four school girls, and one teacher. Visually, at least, the combination appears logical.

The Hotchkiss patent clock (Pat. 1876) has been added. At the right, a tall and most architectural flight of steps, which is portable, fits alongside the door. (Only the back of this flight is visible in the photograph.) An arch beneath the landing duplicates well-designed repetitive arches which ornament the base of the small building. This degree of architectural detail suggests that the schoolhouse may be a copy of an actual one, and one with some architectural pretensions.

Figure 208

A MISSOURI HOUSE IN INDIANA

DATE: CA. 1900
HEIGHT: 49½"
WIDTH: 43⅝"
DEPTH (OVERALL): 19⅛"
OWNER: CHILDREN'S MUSEUM OF INDIANAPOLIS (INDIANA)

Even full-sized houses are sometimes moved and rebuilt elsewhere. (A most impressive example is "The Lindens," an elegant colonial from

DOLLS' HOUSES FROM THE MID-WEST

Massachusetts which for many years has been an antiquarian landmark in Washington, D. C.) Since dolls' houses are considerably more portable, it is surprising that so many are discovered in their original neighborhoods.

While delving into boxes of papers and old letters for the present volume, I came across a 1961 clipping from an Indianapolis newspaper showing an antique dolls' house on exhibit at the Children's Museum which had been "made by an Indianapolis cabinetmaker." Since the house was the attractive specimen pictured, I "inquired."

The Children's Museum also inquired. When the Director, Mrs. Mildred Compton, reached Mrs. Garvin Brown, who had been given the dolls' house for Christmas when she was eight-year-old Nina Gilbert (at the turn of the century), she learned that the house had been built not by a cabinetmaker in Indianapolis, but by one in St. Louis, where the Gilbert family had been living at the time. The cabinetmaker had copied it exactly from a dolls' house belonging to a close childhood friend of Mrs. Brown's. (One wonders where this twin house may be!) Later her dolls' house was put in storage in St. Louis, and, alas, when she retrieved it for her daughter in 1928–30, all the boxes of furniture had been stolen.

Mrs. Brown remembers that the original furniture came from F. A. O. Schwarz* and that her house had been "beautifully furnished." Her description of the parlor furniture as "white with small painted flowers, and upholstered in American beauty satin" suggests the French furniture illustrated in Figs. 289–92. Hers was undoubtedly similar if not identical.

The original wallpaper and lace curtains are gone, but the seven rooms have been provided

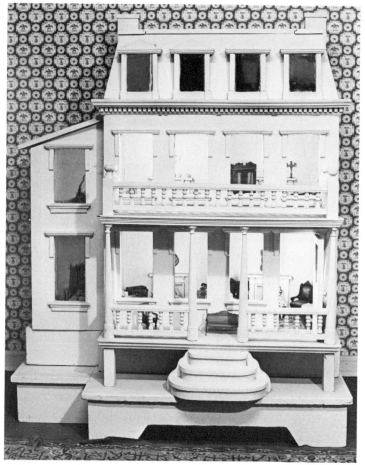

Figure 209

with antique pieces of the correct period, and a family of eight bisque dolls' house dolls. The latter includes a gentleman with the curious name (on the museum records) of "Mr. Xmas." who is wearing a Prince Albert-type suit.

The front of the house swings open in two sections, the larger revealing the four main rooms, which have pleasing built-in mantels. The smaller leads to the kitchen and bath wing, which was added during the 1928–30 refurbishing. The windows in the top of the attic (which lifts off) contain mirrors rather than glass, and Mrs. Brown remembers that she used the attic area to store games and other toys.

---

* The number of Victorian dolls' houses from all parts of the country which were furnished by Schwarz is impressive indeed.

DOLLS' HOUSES
From the West

THE MACLISE HOUSE IN OAKLAND

DATE: CA. 1880'S
HEIGHT (TO CUPOLA): 22"
WIDTH: 22"
OWNER: THE OAKLAND MUSEUM (OAKLAND, CALIFORNIA)

There are two extraordinary dolls' houses in the Oakland Museum. Both clearly are models of actual houses, and with respect to the Maclise house, pictured herewith, the history is complete except for the name of the architect. The second house (Fig. 211) is known to have been built by a Bay Area architect in San Francisco for his children, but all else about the house is a complete mystery.

There are several curious relationships between the two houses apart from their Bay origins and their present location in the Oakland Museum. Although both are built with the verisimilitude of models, both were unmistakably playthings. This we know from the manner in which they were made. Both are divided into rooms, and both are assembled in sections, each having three floors, one above the other. Window bays and cupolas are detachable. Although this type of dolls' house is occasionally found, it is relatively rare, possibly because it is less convenient than the customary hinged front or open back. These similarities are sufficient to make one wonder if the same anonymous San Francisco architect might not have built the two.

However, we must be content with what is known about the Maclise house which was a copy of a mansion which once stood at 544 Hobart Street, Oakland. The house was owned by James Maclise, a druggist who had a pharmacy at the corner of San Pablo Avenue and 17th Street. It is unfortunate that the photograph of the miniature house was taken without the miniature fence, inasmuch as an advertisement for the pharmacy is painted on it. In response to a request, the most cooperative curatorial staff at the museum attempted to locate a picture of the original house, but several efforts lead only to a Maclise family reference in an 1892 history,* with no illustration.

Although the relationship of dolls' houses to full-sized houses is usually a mass of modifications, especially with respect to their interiors, the room plan of the Maclise is of an elaboration which suggests that it may be, like its marvelously detailed exterior, to scale. Fireplaces, stairs, and hallways are all logically present, and even without the hallways, there are more than a dozen rooms on the three floors. There are no bathrooms.

As the photograph illustrates, there are curtains and window shades in the rooms, but carpets, if there ever were any, have been removed.

The small mansion is painted a moss green

* *Bay of San Francisco.*

DOLLS' HOUSES FROM THE WEST

Figure 210

Figure 211

with a darker trim, and its condition, the museum believes, indicates that it has not been repainted. The flag which flies from the cupola above the mansard roof has thirteen stars, and was made for one of the commemorative expositions.

SAN FRANCISCO BAY ARCHITECTURE

DATE: CA. 1880'S
HEIGHT: 31½"
WIDTH: 24"
OWNER: THE OAKLAND MUSEUM (OAKLAND, CALIFORNIA)

Perhaps it is unfair to the relatively modest San Francisco Bay front house in Fig. 212 to compare it with this magnificent Victorian mansion in the Oakland Museum, but both dolls' houses were reportedly built by San Francisco architects* for their children, both are distinctively Bay Area houses, and both date from the 'eighties.

Since this handsome plaything (of the munificent ilk the German toy historian Karl Gröber called "a princely toy") also is related in other ways to the Maclise house in the Oakland museum (Fig. 210), it is a dolls' house of unusual interest as well as beauty.

Like the Maclise, this has the perfection of a model, but it is also unmistakably a toy, being assembled, again like the Maclise, in sections for play. Three floors, one above the other, may be

* Unfortunately, the name of neither architect is known.

(187)

lifted off, and window bays and cupolas are similarly detachable. There are six rooms on the ground floor and five on the two upper floors.

The exterior is a "dark olive drab," sanded to resemble stone.

This is unmistakably a mansion, built possibly for a family of newly rich dolls, whereas Mrs. Harrell's house is in the modest Carpenter Gothic tradition that lined the hills of San Francisco with an assortment of ornamentation, much of which remains to fascinate us.

A GOLDEN GATE RESIDENCE

DATE: 1886
HEIGHT: 44½"
WIDTH: 25"
DEPTH (INCLUDING PORCHES): 43"
OWNER: MRS. JOHN HARRELL (MARYLAND)

When the owner bought her house in a San Francisco antique shop in 1940, she was told it had been built by an architect whose name she would have known immediately (and she has suspected the best!). Lamentably, as is so often the case with families giving up their treasures, this one wanted to remain anonymous, thereby obscuring still another page in dolls' house history.

Since most Golden Gate houses of this period (and dolls' houses, too, undoubtedly) were destroyed by the earthquake and fire, we must be grateful that this corner row dolls' house with its sizeable bay windows has survived.

One longs to remove the awkward balustrade around the eaves, which appears to be a replacement, and once perhaps matched the nicely turned balcony balustrade above the front entrance. An almost identical balcony may be seen on the San Francisco doll mansion in Oakland (Fig. 211). The front opens in two hinged sections revealing a staircase hall, two sizeable rooms, and the two thoroughly furnished bays. The back opens similarly upon four more, including a relatively rare Victorian dolls' house bathroom.

Mrs. Harrell declares that she bought the house because of the zinc tub, but it was also almost completely furnished in what many antiquarians thought of in 1940 as "The Ugly Period," including a large assortment of the German marble-topped furniture which has now come into its own. Mrs. Harrell was told that the anonymous architect had a friend "in the toy game" who bet him the furniture that he'd never finish the house. When he won the bet, the furniture was moved in, marble-tops and much else.

Figure 212

DOLLS' HOUSES FROM THE WEST

A more homespun item of furniture is a bed with a mattress of corn shucks. Among the residents of the house is a Chinese cook, most appropriate to the California scene, who has for some years been overcooking a tin turkey for a family that includes a maiden lady named Etta. *Her* distinction is that she wears a gown copied from her First Lady, Mrs. Grover Cleveland.

There is dusty Brussels carpet on the parlor floor, and engravings of "The Dying Child," "Babes in the Wood," and other lachrymose subjects on the bedroom wall. Mrs. Harrell has embellished the original decor with imagination and verve, furnishing the back porch, for instance, with gray dish rags, mops, and pails. In a bedroom, there was once a hair receiver made from a very small shell, but this has disappeared.

The house color is a "deep, dirty cream" with the original dark red roof, chimney, window trim, and base.

remarkable versatility, this "torch" has been similarly celebrated for her magnificent dolls' house, a castle which toured widely for charity during the 'thirties, and which has since been seen by millions more at the Museum of Science and Industry in Chicago where it is on permanent view.*

That castle, *Colleen Moore's Dolls' House*, has been so thoroughly described elsewhere† that its presence in these pages seemed redundant, but to write about dolls' houses in America, and to omit Colleen Moore, seemed unimaginable. The famed castle was the seventh of a series of dolls' houses which were made for her beginning when she was two. During the pleasure of a visit from this fellow collector while these pages were

---

* In 1966, over one-and-a-half million people, more than four thousand a day, visited the dolls' house there. Colleen Moore Hargrave has willed it to the museum.

† Colleen Moore did a handsome book herself on the subject in 1970, illustrated in full color (Doubleday), and earlier this writer included a chapter about the castle in *A History of Dolls' Houses*.

THE SEVEN DOLLS' HOUSES OF COLLEEN MOORE

DATE: 1924
HEIGHT: 25″
OWNER: MISS KATHLEEN MOORE COLEMAN (ILLINOIS)

To one who has been delving into the subject of dolls' houses for what begins to seem a lifetime, the name of one collector, when the subject has been introduced, has echoed down the years.

The name is an illustrious one; the collector, a star of the silent screen, is Colleen Moore, the number-one box office attraction in 1926, and the original "flapper" of whom F. Scott Fitzgerald wrote: "I was the spark that lit up Flaming Youth; Colleen Moore was the torch." * With

---

* It seems pertinent to note here that this oft-quoted line was written by Fitzgerald in a miniature version of *This Side of Paradise* for the library of *the* dolls' house.

Figure 213

HISTORIC PRESERVATION IN MINIATURE: UNIQUE EXAMPLES

Figure 214

Figure 215

DOLLS' HOUSES FROM THE WEST

Figure 216

in progress, I asked about the possibility of including her first dolls' house. As it turned out, that house was long gone, and she had no picture of it. Her mother and father had made it for her out of cigar boxes and, as she mentioned in her autobiography, *Silent Star*, "I know now they didn't make it for me so much as for the fun of doing it." She remembers that they also made the furniture, some of which she had for years, and some of which may be seen in the picture of dolls' house number two.

During her childhood, her father made "four more doll houses, each more elaborate than the last." He was, in her words, "an imaginative man, no stranger to the leprechaun. He shared with me all my life the love of little things." *
She describes a miniature Bible her father gave her when she was five which she considers the "touchstone" which led to her lifelong love of miniatures.

Pictures of houses number two and six were

* *Colleen Moore's Doll House.*

available. "Two" was also built for her by her father. "As you can see," she wrote when she sent the photograph, "I had not tidied it up. You can probably cut off my brother and cousin who are standing by the house in case you decide to use the picture." Although it would have been even more delightful if the little girl in the picture had been Colleen, her two stand-ins serve to show the scale of the house and to give it a sort of period flavor. (The house was built in 1909 or 1910; the picture taken ca. 1913.) Dolls' house buffs can even recognize a few of the pieces; for one, a kitchen shelf hanging a bit askew at the left. The nostalgic owner remembers that this house was made by her father when she was about eight.

"I remember he asked me if I wanted an elevator, and I chose a staircase which, by the time I was ten, I regretted. I remember that [the house] had running water and electricity. The bulbs were completely out of scale and must have been flash light bulbs." She also recalls that this house had a small set of purple drinking glasses, two of which, along with a Delft tea set, may be seen in the celebrated castle.

The rest of the chronology, in Colleen Moore's own words, is this:

No. 3 was a store-bought house which went to pieces. As I look back, it must have been made of cardboard. An aunt sent this one to me about 1914.

No. 4 was made about 1920 and was really a series of four rooms which we papered and used as a sort of vitrine to hold some of the silver furniture, etc.

The latter included "tiny, exquisite silver cabinets and chests, Battersea enamel tables and chairs and a Sèvres china tea set," sent to small Kathleen Morrison when she was a child (and before she was re-named for the movies), by her mother's six sisters who had no children of their own—and clearly doted on their niece. Most of this, too elegant to play with, and displayed in a cabinet, was known as Kathleen's collection, and eventually inspired, and helped to furnish, the splendid castle.

Doll House No. 5 was given to Adela Rogers St. Johns' daughter and was a very unpretentious five-room house with a roof and staircase. I tried to trace this and it has been lost.

Which brings us to house number six, the elegant "Spanish" mansion which is illustrated. This one, now in the possession of Colleen's granddaughter, Kathleen Moore Coleman, in Chicago, was built for her by her father and mother, and Colleen recalls that she worked on it too, and that her father and his friends "used to gather in the garage in Los Angeles and, after golf, play with making the house."

Although the owner was "a grown-up movie star" when this house was built for her in 1924, much of the furniture it contains, except some of the silver things, have been kept since she was a child, but part of the furniture was bought for her granddaughter a few years ago. (The recently made but already collected "Petite Princess" furniture, plastic but realistically and well designed, can be recognized in several of the rooms.)

It is the house itself which is of most interest. This was described neither in Colleen Moore's autobiography, nor in her dolls' house book; when the picture arrived, I was delighted to discover that number six was everything a Hollywood mansion should be. Not only was this the indigenous Hollywood architecture which the movie colony helped to popularize throughout the country in the 'twenties following the Spanish colonial revival in California (see page 217–18), but it bore resemblances to two Colleen Moore full-sized houses which were important during her film years. The first, Miss Moore's studio bungalow, which the studio bosses built for her after she became a star, was "Spanish . . . built around a small patio containing a fountain. . . ." Inside, there was a high-beamed ceiling and a fireplace.

Her Bel Air mansion was more monumental, to say the least, with two acres of gardens, an Olympic-sized swimming pool, and a theater, among other luxurious odds and ends, but it had the same sort of red-tiled roof and "adobe" walls to be seen both on the studio bungalow and on dolls' house number six and, like the latter, the mansion had a patio and a winding staircase with a metal balustrade. Even the step-down living-room in the Bel Air house had its counterpart in the dolls' house—"a step down to what we called the music room."

The seventh dolls' house—the castle—outdid them all and, along with the previous six, it established the vital (still full-of-vim-and-vigor) personality who inspired them as the most celebrated dolls' house collector in the United States. (If not the "torch," she was at least the spark who, with her fabulous castle, ignited the interest of many a future collector . . .)

DOLLS' HOUSES FROM THE WEST

A SPANISH CASA IN LOS ANGELES

DATE: CA. 1930 (?)
HEIGHT (TOWER SIDE): 19″
WIDTH: 24″
DEPTH (MAIN WING): 18″
BASE: 27″ × 19″
OWNER: MRS. ARTHUR LA VOVE (CALIFORNIA)

The Spanish colonial revival style has been described as "at its best . . . featured by flat, red-tiled roofs, relatively plain plastered walls, grilled windows, occasional patios and other reminiscences of the indigenous provincial houses. . . ."* Mrs. LaVove suspects that her house, which she found in a Los Angeles antique shop in 1971, is a late example, perhaps as late as the 1930's, but it contains a number of the "reminiscences" alluded to above.

The house, which is cream color with a red-tile roof and an off-white interior, has windows with proper metal balustrades, and there is a patio. There are two arched windows on each side of the house, and the front swings open in two sections. Curiously, there is a noticeable resemblance to the Tootsietoy Spanish Mansion (Fig. 336) in style and proportion, in the manner of opening, and even in the measurements, which are almost identical. This coincidence makes me wonder if both houses might have been adapted from a California residence or other building well known (but not to me).

These resemblances, however, between Mrs. LaVove's house and Mr. Dowst's mansion, are superficial. In spirit, they are worlds apart, the Tootsietoy mansion tacky with 'twentyish lithography, and this structure modest with a purity and simplicity which *would* do credit to a Mission where silence and order are carefully observed.

It seems entirely possible that both were adapted from a mission church or similar

Figure 217

Figure 218

building. "Most mission churches were based on either a simple basilican or cruciform plan, with twin towers (one or the other often left unbuilt) planned to flank the façade, and a pierced belfry above it."* On Mrs. LaVove's *casa,* the twin

* The American Heritage History of Notable American Houses.

* Images of American Living by Allan Gowans, Lippincott, 1964.

HISTORIC PRESERVATION IN MINIATURE: UNIQUE EXAMPLES

towers (with one unbuilt!) flank the façade, and perhaps the oriel window beneath the gable can pass for "a pierced belfry"!

A HOUSE BY #30780: SAN QUENTIN

DATE: 1926
HEIGHT: 22″
ROOF, INCLUDING OVERHANG: 45″ × 32½″
OWNER: WILLIAM BRINER (CALIFORNIA)

"Stone walls do not a prison make," but a prisoner really did make this dolls' house; and the so-called prison houses (Figs. 243–5) have another bonafide competitor. Like Mrs. Whitton's handsome Pittsburgh house (Figs. 98–9), there is no doubt of prison origin; and here we have not only the name of the prison—San Quentin—and the name of the prisoner—Joe Mert—but even his number—"30780"! The ranch-type house is also dated—September 20, 1926—and the only fact that appears to be unknown is why the house was made. It is in the collection of Mr. William Briner of San Francisco, who believes it to be a copy of an actual house. "Even the bedroom has a clothes closet," he notes. "Between the living and dining-rooms are half bookcases with square columns above, which are typical of the house style." The stone work of the foundation, and the chimney are hand-carved. The hinged roof, which lifts, is of tar paper.

THE FARNSWORTHS' CA. 1860 REPRODUCTION

DATE: RECENT
HEIGHT: 42″
WIDTH: 59″
DEPTH: 51″
OWNER: JUDGE AND MRS. W. FRANKLIN FARNSWORTH (CALIFORNIA)

Among miniature houses built "today," this one seems outstanding because Judge and Mrs. Farnsworth adapted and scaled down plans of an actual house, ca. 1860, which they found in the state library in Sacramento.* The thirteen-room, inch-to-the-foot clapboard residence was made with some modifications: rooms were "opened-up" for viewing purposes, for instance, and a bathroom was added. Notable exterior details include sixty-two workable sash windows (a stained-glass bay among them), and brick cut down from full-sized brick and laid with mortar. The thoroughly furnished interior is a blend of

Figure 219

---

* Originally, it had been hoped to include these plans, or at least to identify them, but the Farnsworths consulted many books in the state library when the house was begun, and an effort, in recent years, to locate these proved unsuccessful.

DOLLS' HOUSES FROM THE WEST

Figure 220

Figure 220a

old pieces and of reproductions which are the work of many hours and hands. These include a marvelous roll-top desk with numerous and infinitesimal pigeon-holes (of old pine) by Judge Farnsworth, and draperies, curtains, samplers, and other pieces of gossamer needlework from the gifted hands of Mrs. Farnsworth. (One of her exquisite samplers is shown in Fig. 220a.) Other well-known laborers and artists in the miniature vineyard are represented, including John Blauer of San Francisco who presented, as a housewarming present, a box of chocolates, one of many engaging accessories which give the house a generous degree of warmth and reality.

DOLLS' HOUSES
From Canada

A CHURCH FROM ILE D'ORLEANS

Date: SECOND HALF OF NINETEENTH CENTURY
Height (INCLUDING SPIRE): 31½"
Width: 21½"
Depth: 22"
Owner: ELIZABETH BENNET-PERCIVAL COLLECTION (CANADA)

This church was made in the small French village of Ste. Petronille on the island of Orléans in Quebec, and was brought there by a Montreal antique dealer who sold it to the present owners in the early 1960's.

It bears a striking resemblance, even within the range of variations usually to be seen on so-called replicas, to the Church of St. Laurent, a historic parish church on the Ile d'Orléans built in 1695 and destroyed in 1864. According to Allan Gowans,* "the first distinctively Canadian architectural form . . . [began] in the parish churches . . . on the Island of Orleans," and it is likely that these churches bore a regional resemblance to one another. Therefore, this may not be a copy of the Church of St. Laurent, but the resemblance of the nave with its strikingly similar steeple set in exactly the same manner upon the roof gable, and with an identical oeil-de-boeuf window beneath it, and similarly arched windows on the sides, seems more than coincidental, or even regional.

* *Images of American Living*, Lippincott, 1964.

It is true that the miniature church has a second smaller steeple above the chancel not to be seen on the Church of St. Laurent. Mr. Gowans refers to this church as "a combination of craft and Baroque elements."

The miniature "replica" is all original including the interior. As the illustration indicates, the whole building lifts off, exposing the original

Figure 221

DOLLS' HOUSES FROM CANADA

Figure 222

Figure 223

U" has been cut out of silver paper and stuck on the front of the main altar. The other two altars have (M) and (JF). "Fretwork letters," Elizabeth Bennet Lewis writes, "have been cut out of the wood around the bell in the main steeple: J U M J F." I assume these stand for (J)es(U), (M)ary, (J)ose(F).

Miss Lillian Percival points out that the back of the church is round, forming the chancel, and there is a bell in the belfry.

The Percival sisters were told by the Montreal dealer from whom they bought the church that small boats were built by the inhabitants of Ste. Petronille. And, it seems, at least one small church as well.

THE SAILORS' CHURCH IN MONTREAL

DATE: SECOND HALF OF THE NINETEENTH CENTURY (?)
HEIGHT (INCLUDING STEEPLE): 46½"
WIDTH: 20"
DEPTH: 28"
OWNER: ELIZABETH BENNET-PERCIVAL COLLECTION (CANADA)

This old copy of an ancient church—the celebrated Notre Dame de Bon Secours—was found in recent years in an antique shop on St. Paul Street in old Montreal a few blocks west of the church itself, both church and replica one street away from the river and docks. With its proximity to the St. Lawrence, it is not surprising that it is known as the Sailors' Church. High up, above the chancel, is the statue of Marie, with outstretched arms facing the river and blessing the sailors.

Like the nuns' residence belonging to the same owners (Fig. 225), the church was a shell when it was found, and most dilapidated. Because the original was so old and historic (it was begun in 1678 and restored in 1885), the Bennets and Percivals felt the months of hard work they put into it were worthwhile.

fittings: wooden pews, choir stalls, the priest, members of the congregation, and the choir made up of nuns, the figures, carved, painted, and dressed. There are three altars, with busts of Jesus, Mary, and Joseph, and these, along with the walls and ceiling, are decorated with blue, silver, and gold papers and paper flowers. "J H

HISTORIC PRESERVATION IN MINIATURE: UNIQUE EXAMPLES

With many collectors seeking advice about restoration (see page 351), it seems of interest to quote Mrs. Lewis' account of the elaborate restoration (and additions) which were undertaken:

The shell is original and the gray paint representing stone is untouched. The silver roof and decorative elements are touched up. The metal galleries around the steeples, etc., and the metal crosses in filigree on top of the steeples are made and replaced by us. The statues of Mary ("Our Lady of Good Help") with her hands out over the port blessing the sailors, and the surrounding angels, as well as the Virgin and Child over the front door, were made by my mother from modeling plaster and painted green to resemble bronze. (There were no statues when received.)

The interior is now only to be reached by the front door. (The base was sawn off the church to enable us to furnish the interior.) Wooden pews, congregation, altar with candles, flowers, etc., and the famous hanging lamps in the shape of boats are reproduced.

There are, among the most dedicated antiquarians, those of us who may prefer to restore such treasures of the past as this one, and to omit such additions which, with care and effort, have been supplied here. However, the hands of the dedicated quartet who renewed the decaying antique described here are skillful and artistic—and considerate of history.

"LA MAISON MÈRE"

DATE: SECOND HALF OF THE NINETEENTH CENTURY
HEIGHT: 31½"
WIDTH: 25½"
DEPTH: 12"
OWNER: ELIZABETH BENNET-PERCIVAL COLLECTION (CANADA)

Although this charming residence for elderly (and miniature) nuns was probably made as a model rather than a toy, it is part of a comprehensive collection of old dolls' houses and toys in Montreal, and is included here, like the architects' model in Fig. 86, out of deference to the fine line which exists between models and playthings.

When "La Maison Mère" was found in a Montreal antique shop in the early 1960's, the interior was unpainted and "contained no second floor, no staircase and in fact only a wasps' nest." The interior stairs, railings, floors, partitions, and furniture were handmade by the Misses

Figure 224

DOLLS' HOUSES FROM CANADA

Figure 225

Figure 226

Muriel and Lillian Percival, their niece, Elizabeth Bennet Lewis, and the latter's mother, Gertrude Bennet. The iron beds were ingeniously made from one-and-a-half-inch nails painted white.

"There is a crucifix on a stand, coloured gold and silver, and made of a superior lead, in France"; Mrs. Lewis writes, "this is in the attic chapel next to where the novices sleep. The figure looking down on the first floor is a bisque figure of St. Anne with a child and a book, and could have been made at any time within the last hundred years."

This ecclesiastical confection is dark gray with white trim beneath an apple-green roof.

DOMVILLE HOUSE, 1899

DATE: 1899
HEIGHT (OVERALL): 45¾"
WIDTH (OPEN): 70¼"
DEPTH: 27¾"
OWNER: DUNDAS HISTORICAL SOCIETY MUSEUM (DUNDAS, ONTARIO)

This twelve-room town house is remarkable from several points of view: It is a relatively rare Canadian dolls' house, and an approximate copy of an actual house still standing (at 285 Park St. South) in Hamilton, Ontario.* Not only is its external architecture related to an actual house, but its unusual hinged construction was probably inspired by actual plans for a dolls' house in an 1883 publication.

Best of all, it is thoroughly documented by the original owner, who was three when her father built her cherished toy for Christmas 1899. Mrs. Philip Ross-Ross, then little Mary Domville, has in her possession a letter written

* Unfortunately, the picture of this house arrived too late to permit a detailed comparison, but it can readily be seen that, except for the porch (which Mrs. Ross-Ross believes was added in relatively recent years), there is a remarkable resemblance to the dolls' house.

by her mother to her grandfather on December 17 of that year, which tells all:

> My dear Papa, Many thanks for your letter and the enclosed Post Office Order. A year goes by so quickly. I, as usual, can hardly persuade myself to believe Christmas is again actually upon us. But Mary will not let us forget the fact, for she seems to think and dream of nothing else. Of course she firmly believes in Santa Claus, and this year has set her heart upon his bringing her a dolls' house—which of course she will get, as Percy has been employing his spare time in building one for her. It is so pretty and complete in every way, I think it almost too good for so young a child. However, nothing else would satisfy him for if he attempts work of any sort, it has got to be thoroughly well done or else not at all. . . .

Mrs. Ross-Ross declares that she of course remembers none of this, but that she is sure her father wanted to build a small house and *he* put the idea into her head. She adds, "My mother has told me that I was too young to appreciate my good fortune, and that I would amuse myself by taking all the furniture out of the house and making a procession of it on the floor where it was inevitably stepped upon and broken."

What remained disappeared in later years. Mrs. Ross-Ross writes that she nearly lost her house in 1914 when, "in an excess of patriotism," she refurbished it and donated it to be raffled at a bazaar organized by the "Imperial Order of the Daughters of the Empire," to raise money for "comforts for soldiers." The teenaged owner was lucky: "$60 was raised, but no one came forward to claim their prize, so it was returned to me." Over the years it was lent to several children, and when it was retrieved in the 1940's, the only original piece of furniture which remained was a Morris chair.

"Mrs. Ross-Ross, who obviously inherited some of her father's talent, has built several dolls' houses of her own including a store, "Hall's Hardware," from her memories of such

Figure 227

Figure 228

DOLLS' HOUSES FROM CANADA

Figure 229

an establishment, very old, destroyed by fire in 1963.* She decided to refurnish Domville house "as it might look today if we were still living there." She added stairs to the attic, a continuation of the grand staircase in the front hall, "as it was very tiring for the family to have to fly up there all the time," and she also made all the doors with knobs converted from corsage pins. Then, in 1968, she gave her house to the Dundas Museum where it has been impressively

*To be seen in the Stormont, Dundas and Glengarry Historical Society Museum in Cornwall, Ontario.

fitted with machinery which permits it to open and close slowly—and automatically.

The English publication *Amateur Work* described the making of a house of this plan in 1883 in three installments of such complexity that (as I have written elsewhere) "Anyone who gives the instructions even the most casual perusal knows that building this house is not work for amateurs." Mrs. Ross-Ross believes the article which, among other things, showed the "carcase" of the house in "isometrical perspective," inspired her father. (See Fig. 230.)

A sample sentence gives the flavor and

HISTORIC PRESERVATION IN MINIATURE: UNIQUE EXAMPLES

Figure 230

A FRENCH-CANADIAN COTTAGE

DATE: CA. 1900
HEIGHT: 13″
WIDTH: 10″
DEPTH: 10½″
OWNER: ELIZABETH BENNET-PERCIVAL COLLECTION (CANADA)

Architect's models, mouse houses, the small buildings to be found in Christmas gardens . . . there was sufficient confusion in the small world of miniature architecture before the winsome portrait of this tiny cottage arrived from Montreal with a description of still another miniature building category.

The Percivals and Bennets think it "the kind of model which was sometimes glued to the top of a post and placed in the front garden of the house of which the model was a replica." If many such houses survive, those of us who find Lilliputian buildings irresistible should pack

perhaps suggests how the house, basically two boxes hinged together, opens and closes: "As the boxes are drawn apart, and turn on the hinges, the point A travels along the dotted circle, in the direction of the arrow, to A′, F to F′, C to C′, and D to D′, the points B and E describing semicircles, which it is unnecessary, on account of the space that would be taken up, to show in the diagram."

The small illustration of the dolls' house closed certainly demonstrates a constructional kinship to the one built by Lt. Col. Domville. Another house, in the possession of Mrs. William Mason Smith of New York City in 1961, when it was shown at a Craft Center exhibit in Worcester, Massachusetts, was obviously inspired by the 1883 article, and appears to be identical not only in construction but in almost every architectural detail.

Over the front door of her house is what Mrs. Ross-Ross describes as an "historic site" plaque, a silver shield inscribed:

DOMVILLE HOUSE
BUILT IN 1899 by
PERCY DOMVILLE
for his daughter
MARY PERCY

Figure 231

some luggage and a camera and head promptly for the province of Quebec.

This petite French-Canadian cottage, which is all mansard roof, was found in a Montreal antique shop. Miss N. Lillian Percival specifies that it cannot be called an old habitant house but is rather of the type often seen on country village roads. It was sealed when found but the collectors opened the back which they hinged, and they supplied stairs, wallpaper, and furniture. The exterior, which is all original, is painted white and green. The roof is gray and the door of varnished oak.

A CURRIER AND IVES COUNTRY HOUSE

DATE: TWENTIETH CENTURY
HEIGHT (TO TOP OF CHIMNEYS): 38"
DEPTH (WITH FAÇADE IN PLACE): 28"
WIDTH: 50"
OWNER: BLACK CREEK PIONEER VILLAGE (TORONTO, CANADA)

Although this house was built in the twentieth century by a Canadian who was himself a collector of "Canadiana," it is the ultimate in Americana, a dolls' house meticulously copied from a country house in a Currier and Ives print.

The house was built by the late Percy Band, who became a toy collector in 1931 when he went to see "some early furniture belonging to a friend" on Ontario's Niagara Peninsula, and returned home with an antique doll. A slender book* was published in 1963 about the Band "Collection of Nineteenth Century Toys, Played with by Canadian Children."

Mr. Band built the house as a copy of an 1855 N. Currier print, Large Folio, of the "American Country Life" series. Entitled "October Afternoon," a detail of the print, showing the house,

Figure 232

Figure 233

is nearby. The original drawing was by Fanny Palmer, one of the leading Currier and Ives artists, who did the set of four prints. "Its documentary value," Colin Simkin* points out, "is enhanced by the fact that she chose four different houses rather than one house at four different seasons. We may be sure that each was drawn 'from life.'"

Mrs. Band recalls that her husband took

---

* *Playthings of Yesterday*, Ryerson Press, Toronto.

* *Currier and Ives' America*, edited by Colin Simkin, Crown, 1952.

Figure 234

about a year and a half to construct the house. (Mrs. Band herself nailed on all 1,500 shingles with two nails per shingle.)

The length of time that was required by Mr. Band to build the house is not surprising. Comparing the pictures of the original and his copy, one can see that although he has faithfully reproduced the plan of the house, he has elaborated on many of the details, adding an elaborate frieze to the cornice, and an assortment of finials to the posts of the two balustrades. The plain louvered shutters in the Currier and Ives house are capped with decorative panels in Mr. Band's version.

In addition, he has omitted no realistic detail to be found in the house of the print. The four chimneys (two of them are not visible in the photograph) are present, and even the drainpipes and lightning rods have been carefully copied, the only dolls' house lightning rods known to me. The clapboard, by the way, is painted the same lemony yellow as the clapboard in the print. (In the print, the side of the house visible is of red brick. Mr. Band continued the "lap siding.")

"The house obviously belonged on a well-to-do estate," according to the Band book. "It has the luxury of French doors, and a romanticized Greek façade in the pillars and portico."

In going beyond the print, Mr. Band has entered this country residence and imagined an equally detailed interior with a central staircase. The furnishings are eclectic, some of them are old, and most are reproductions. Baxter prints are alluded to in a brief summary of the contents in the book—the writer has seen photographs only—and can only hope there is at least one Currier and Ives print on the walls.

PART 2

HISTORIC PRESERVATION IN MINIATURE: Factory-Made Buildings

"Commercial Property"

DOLL MANSIONS BY STIRN & LYON

Date: patented 1881
Height (not including 3¼" chimneys): 24"
Width: 26"
Depth (not including 4¾" steps): 10⅛"
Owner: author's collection

One can picture a father on Christmas Eve of 1882 struggling to assemble this "Combination Doll Mansion," just as fathers of recent years struggled with the notoriously strange instructions for Japanese toys. Or perhaps it lay unassembled, wrapped in its wooden box under the tree, and on Christmas morning father and child coped with it together.

It is to be hoped that the young recipient wasn't expected to set up the house herself; if she was, she may have suffered from a frustration syndrome the rest of her life. Mansard roof, dormers, balcony and all, this toy house came "knocked-down," in a sizeable wooden box (24" × 10½"), and with its thin wooden siding and tongue-and-groove (and dowel-and-peg) construction, putting it together (one speaks from experience)* is an exercise in patience and dexterity. The relatively flimsy result may not have been worthwhile for a family of dolls in 1882, but it is an intriguing piece of miniature architecture for a collector some nine decades later.

Unfortunately, because the box becomes the ground floor of the house, it has had hard usage, and bits are missing of the handsomely lithographed label, an idealized rendering of the mansion, a stable, and an elegantly turned out Victorian lady, but most of it is intact, including what every collector most longs to know: "Combination Doll Mansion, Stirn & Lyon, NY." And though the date was lacking, this information is intact on the smaller "Combination Doll House," and on the "Combination Grocery Store" (Fig. 239). The first says "Patented 1881 by Stirn & Lyon, N. Y." The date on the lid of the store is even more specific: "Patented April 11, 1882." Presumably the mansion also was protected by the 1881 patent. How many years these were made is unknown to me, but with all of the pieces there are to lose, and the fragility of many of them, the fact that even a few* have survived suggests that they were manufactured for several years at least.

The mansion, the smaller house, and the grocery store all have a family resemblance, both in their patented construction and in their

---

* The mansion, it must be confessed, was set up and glued into position before it was acquired, by a prior owner. Our experience was with the smaller "Combination Doll House" shown here, and with the "Combination Grocery Store" (Fig. 239).

* The late Genevieve Angione described a duplicate of the smaller "Combination Doll House" in the December 1967 issue of *The Spinning Wheel*. (Part of the manufacturer's name was missing on the label of her house.)

HISTORIC PRESERVATION IN MINIATURE: FACTORY-MADE BUILDINGS

Figure 235

Figure 236

appearance. The framework is composed of corner and interior beams which peg into the foundation and connect the top with the lid. The second floors of the two houses rest on ledges glued to the inside walls. The windows, pres-sure-printed on the light wood to resemble shutters on the mansion, and four-light sash on the small house, were cut out and then partially re-fastened with adhesive tape so that they may be opened in pairs, in the manner of a casement. (One was opened by a two-month-old kitten who went inside and made himself at home.)

In appearance, both houses and the store are heightened by a lovely reddish stain which is applied to parts of each structure; the four pilasters across the front of the mansion, the dormers, cornice, balcony, and chimneys, all of this hue, are an effective contrast to the similarly pleasing deep cream shade to which the unpainted wood, printed to imitate bricks on the mansion, and possibly brownstone on the smaller house,* has turned with age. On the latter, the reddish stain is used mostly on the curious embellishments (two of them missing) that peg into the house along with the balconies themselves. The cornice, which attaches to the top of this house and shields the flat roof, is not unlike the false fronts often seen on small, late-nineteenth-century buildings. (Mercifully beyond the reach of restorers and "modernizers," these upper sections usually survive intact, often with a date to let us know when each was built.)

A very different sort of Stirn & Lyon "patent" dolls' house may be seen in Fig. 237. This pretty toy is, as its picture reveals, rich in lithographic color, and it appears to be related to the other Stirn & Lyon houses mostly with respect to their colorful labels as well as, almost unnoticeably, to the low fence which surrounds the garden, and is of the same painted, unfinished wood to be seen in the other buildings.

The lid of this house, which folds down to become the garden, contains a great deal of information about other Stirn & Lyon toys. Referring to themselves as a "Manufacturer of Patent Combination Toys," they proceed to

* The measurements of this house are: height: $22\frac{1}{4}''$; width: $18''$; depth: $9\frac{3}{4}''$, not including $4\frac{1}{4}''$ steps.

"COMMERCIAL PROPERTY"

document this claim, listing "doll house mansion, bridge, grocery store" on one side, and "menagerie, stable, circus, game of Rinaldo" on the other. Unfortunately, when the house was made, the patent had only been applied for, and no date is given. It seems possible that the "doll house," "mansion," and "grocery store" may be the ones shown in these pages, and that this folding house may be a somewhat later toy.

The interior is given short shrift. Between the elaborately lithographed-on-wood façade and the plain back, which hook together,* there is a wooden floor that can be lowered into place, but the plain white walls of the single room this forms are pale literally and figuratively, compared to the garden. There's an accordion fold at their center, and a few fancy windows printed in black ink on their exterior, and that's it.

The garden, on the other hand, is overstuffed, and the fact that the stuffing (the positioning of the figures) was evidently left to the discretion of the young owner has not helped this one. The fountain and the trees and children are mounted on small wooden blocks with a wire brad at each side, and these figures can be folded down readily when the house is closed. The brads fit under metal staples which resemble wickets—and surely croquet would have been a more suitable game for this lawn! As the picture indicates, the fountain has been properly located, but the badminton players are crowded by strangely placed trees, and the small girl emerging from the tasseled tent looks lonely. These figures are placed between the house façade and the garden and, when the toy is closed, they are ingeniously protected by the low wooden fence.

This is a strange and fascinating toy.

STIRN & LYON: GROCERIES

DATE: PATENTED 1882
HEIGHT: 21¾"
WIDTH: 18"
DEPTH (NOT INCLUDING 5¼" STEPS): 10"
OWNER: AUTHOR'S COLLECTION

If the two Stirn & Lyon "Combination" dolls' houses shown in Figs. 235–6 are charming and

Figure 237

Figure 238

* When closed, the façade of the house fits between the garden and this rear section, like a sandwich.

HISTORIC PRESERVATION IN MINIATURE: FACTORY-MADE BUILDINGS

Figure 239

unassuming, perhaps it is fair to say that this Stirn & Lyon "Combination Grocery Store" is comely and imposing. It is assembled in very much the same tongue-and-groove, peg-and-dowel manner as the two houses, and is of the same unpainted wood with pressure-printed lettering and decorations. It has beams and other accents in the bittersweet red which adds so much decorative warmth to the houses, but it has considerably more personality and beauty.

Like the two houses, its parts fit into a wooden box which becomes the foundation when beams, walls, and other segments are "combined." Like them, its lid is covered with a lithographed label bearing an idealized and ornamental portrait of a Victorian grocery plus some basic information: "Manufactured by Stirn & Lyon N. Y. Patented April 11, 1882." The label also offers the names of groceries one might expect to find in such a store at the time, and even some trade names which may very well be useful to future food historians—who are unlikely to find a more vivid or concise memo on the subject. It is of interest that these products pictured on the box label differ almost entirely from the ones inside; a discrepancy which suggests that the toy was made by Stirn & Lyon, but that the lithography may have been done elsewhere.

Some of the products sold are still available—Royal Baking Powder, for instance. A specialist might write a monograph about these "classics," and those no longer familiar—"Warrington Mills" on a barrel, "Morgan's Hand Sapolio" on a case. And was Sudsine H. B. & F., as it sounds, a laundering agent? What about "S. K. Mumm Extra Dry 12450"—we wonder if this was the delectable vintage its name evokes?

There are many others; none of them the same as the stock inside. The stock on the shelves consists of the same wood to be found in the store itself, unpainted or stained with that marvelous shade of red, but made in blocks, rectangular or square, embossed with the names (though not the shapes) of the products they represent. We'd suspect, even if the manufacturer's name were not available, where he was located, from such labels as "N. Y. State All Cream Factory Cheese" and "Pride of Jersey Tomatoes." There are also such exotic imports as "Jamaica Allspice," but the implication is clear.

The clock over the counter ungraciously states "No Time Here," but even if "Cash & Co" did not give credit, it undoubtedly gave pleasure to the young shopkeeper who played with this engaging establishment.

The steps across the front of the store, made with treads which fit into grooves (as are the narrower flights on the Stirn & Lyon houses), resemble the wide steps one used to see in front of old country stores. One can envision two gentlemen in wide-brimmed hats and droopy moustaches lounging on these, perhaps till a moment before the picture was taken.

"COMMERCIAL PROPERTY"

AN AMERICAN GROCERY IN SCOTLAND

DATE: CA. 1882
HEIGHT: 7¾"
WIDTH: 16½"
DEPTH: 3"
OWNER: THE MUSEUM OF CHILDHOOD (EDINBURGH, SCOTLAND)

Figure 240

In a compilation entitled, with due deliberation, *Dolls' Houses in America* (to allow for the presence of certain imports which have reached our shores), this charming toy is an exception: an *American* grocery store which may be seen in Scotland.

It is of interest to compare this to the Stirn & Lyon "Combination Grocery Store" shown in Fig. 239 inasmuch as it is made of wood similarly pressure-printed and unpainted, and there is printed embellishment on the counter very like that to be seen on the main arch in the Stirn & Lyon. Part of the stock in this store, like all in the Stirn & Lyon, is made from labeled (again printed directly on the wood) blocks.

Here the labeling is more fanciful. There are, as in the Stirn & Lyon, some actual trade names (Baker's Cocoa, for instance), but others are more playful: "Family Salt," "David's Soap," and "Best T Japan" are among them. Other products, entirely different in style, have lithographed paper labels which appear to be facsimiles of actual ones (canned goods, for instance, with "W. K. Lewis & Bros." labels, a brand unknown to me).

It was intriguing to discover what appears to be a larger model of this store in Ehrich Bros. toy price list of 1882. Since this was available in the same year that the Stirn & Lyon "Combination Grocery Store" was patented, it may have helped to inspire the latter which had patentable features not to be seen in this straightforward model, which seems to be little more than a wooden box with dual-purpose built-in shelves and a counter. The Stirn & Lyon grocery, which had to be assembled, offered a challenge to a child (and his parents!) which appears to be lacking here.

In the Ehrich Bros. illustration, a sign between the two chimneys says "Groceries & Provisions" rather than "Choice Family Groceries" as shown in the photograph from Edinburgh, but a similar wooden lid, dimly glimpsed in the background of the latter, appears to be embossed with similar windows and the identical words across the top: "Wholesale Department." The catalogue refers to this as a "Country Store: Wholesale and Retail," and further notes that this is "an exact representation of a complete grocery-store." Among the accessories listed are "tea, coffee, spices, flour, molasses, canned fruits, patent medicines, toy money, delivery wagon, etc." Toy money may also be seen on the counter of the example in Edinburgh. The delivery wagon and a scale to be seen in the illustration may have been lost over the years, or they may have accompanied only the larger models.

Ehrich Bros. describes only one size, thirty-four inches in length, almost twice as big as the one in Curator Patrick Murray's museum, and it sold in 1882 for ninety-five cents (by mail, fifty-eight cents extra—it obviously paid to go to the big city to shop). Ehrich Bros., from whose

Winter Fashion Quarterly the toy price list was extracted, was at 285 to 295 Eighth Avenue, New York, in 1882.

In the Ehrich catalogue, "The Country Store" was advertised on a page of toys which included several by the well-known Leominster, Massachusetts, firm of W. S. Reed. Since Reed specialized in wooden toys, with and without lithographed papers, and the style of manufacture is similar to Reed's (as well as to Stirn & Lyon's), I had, in a previous draft of these comments, included a suspicion that Reed may have manufactured this store. Some weeks before, hoping to have further details about his American grocery, I'd written Mr. Murray, who had generously sent me its photograph, following a visit to Chevy Chase in the 1960's. Just before these words were due at the printers', I received Mr. Murray's reply in which he reinforced my theory, asserting that the small grocery was "almost certainly made by Reed about 1880." He also alluded to Reed's Church Building Blocks, a partial set of which are pictured in his paperback about toys.* These blocks, "The Gothic Church," are also among the toys shown in Ehrich's 1882 list, and the style of the printing bears more than a casual resemblance to the store—especially to the "Gothic" chimneys which supply much of its character.

DUNHAM'S COCOANUT DOLL HOUSE

DATE: CA. 1890'S
HEIGHT: 29"
WIDTH: 11¾"
DEPTH: 7¼"
OWNER: AUTHOR'S COLLECTION

The above heading is incised in red and black on the top of the wooden house. Typical Victorian four-light windows with arched tops and fancy lintels are incised on the "brick" sides.* And that is all there is to indicate that one is in the presence of a dolls' house unless the engagingly lithographed papers applied to the interior walls and floors remain in the four rooms.

In the three examples known to me, only shreds linger in one, the colors are faded in another, and a crack down the back (which seems common to all) is severe in the third, but they still beguile.

At first glance, the dolls' house appears to be merely a crate, and that is not surprising because, clearly, such was its original purpose, with boxes of shredded cocoanut packed into the kitchen, dining-room, parlor, and bedroom so explicitly indicated by their lithographed decor. So far, I have not learned how the houses were assigned once they were emptied: A present to the children of a favored customer? The grocer's own children? A raffle? A premium?

One's heart beat faster when an "1892 Premium Catalogue of Toys and Fancy Goods and Articles of Use and Value Given Away to Consumers of Dunham's Cocoanut" was discovered in an antique shop. A tin kitchen was shown, and a doll "tastefully dressed," but, alas, there was no mention of a dolls' house. At that time, a New York Box number was the address given for Dunham's—or at least for their Premium Department. In an 1885 Dunham's leaflet,† two addresses were offered; one on Reade Street in New York, and one on Locust Street in St. Louis.

The Ashburnham (Massachusetts) Historical Society Museum has one of these houses with the original cardboard furniture. Through the

---

* *Toys* by Patrick Murray, Studio Vista/Dutton, 1968.

* On one of two specimens, the detail appears to be lithographed paper on wood. "Trade Mark Registered" is printed under the sill of this one, but not on the other, which may be older.

† Found by Mrs. Donald J. Marion.

"COMMERCIAL PROPERTY"

Figure 241

courtesy of the curator, Mrs. Hazel F. Morse, who went to the trouble of listing all the pieces, still another address is provided. On the underside of the kitchen table this may be found, at the end of a most rewarding sentence:

If you want another piece of furniture like this, send us the Cake Trade Mark from a half pound package of Dunham's Cocoanut (or Cake Trade-Mark from two quarter pound packages), and ask for piece of Furniture No. 4.

Address: Premium Department
Dunham Manufacturing Company
377 Pearl St.
New York, N. Y.

On the top of the table, to no one's surprise, is a cocoanut cake.

There is additional advertising of the maker's product on the bottom shelf of the cabinet lithographed on the kitchen wall. Behind a crimson curtain, neatly drawn back, four shelves of crockery are shown. The dolls in this house were plainly meant to subsist on Dunham's Cocoanut; there are three boxes on the bottom shelf, the only provisions to be seen in the kitchen.

There is a sink with a *batterie de cuisine* hanging above it, surmounted by a stained glass window. At the other two walls, windows with shades half drawn and a shelf with a clock and an hourglass are provided by the artist. The rest is to be placed by the young owner on the red-and-white checked floor.

Obviously bright and cheery, the dining-room has three single windows at the side walls and a triple one at the back in which four plants bloom exuberantly. There is a curtained dish cupboard at one wall and a still life hanging on another, but the room is completely dominated by a huge aquarium on a substantial four-legged base and a mammoth moose head mounted on the wall. (A red and green Oriental rug is also provided, along with crimson wallpaper beneath the chair rail and, as a border, above the vivid blue which is between.)

On the next level, there is nothing quite so dramatic in the parlor, with the possible exception of a most imposing fern. "Love Song" is the title of the sheet music which rests on the upright piano. Three bases (two containing bouquets) and three photographs mingle on the top. The inevitable aspidistra sprouts from a red and black floral porcelain jardinière on a matching base. A small tripod table with an embroidered cover holds another bouquet. Half a dozen framed pictures on the walls include a lady in a high collar and a large flowered hat.

There are more pictures hanging on the walls of the blue-and-cream striped bedroom, which is

(213)

HISTORIC PRESERVATION IN MINIATURE: FACTORY-MADE BUILDINGS

dominated by a triple stained-glass window partially obscured by net curtains. Floral rugs are on the floors of the two upper rooms.

The better of the two Dunham houses in the author's collection has two identical layers of the lithographed papers (both, alas, chipped in the same places!) offering a sudden theory: Might the lithographed interiors, like the cardboard furniture, have been available as a premium, to be added to the wooden house when it was emptied of its cocoanut burden?

Whatever the means, such a house is peculiarly satisfying to those of us who are antiquarian dolls' house collectors; and it offers most specific guidelines to the furnishing of other old dolls' houses whose interiors may be more spacious but are less specific than Dunham's about the manner in which they, and the full-sized houses which they imitated, were furnished.

IMPORTED AND LITHO-GRAPHED: THE ULTIMATE IN GINGERBREAD

DATE: CA. 1890
HEIGHT (NOT INCLUDING CENTRAL PROJECTION): 42"
WIDTH (OF BASE): 44"
DEPTH (OF BASE): 34"
OWNER: THE STRONG MUSEUM (ROCHESTER, NEW YORK)

For those of us who are addicted to Victorian dolls' houses, Victorian houses, Victoriana in general, or all of these, this imported mansion is unquestionably the ultimate. Lithographed paper-on-wood dolls' houses were made in the United States by Bliss, Converse, Whitney-Reed, and other manufacturers, but when this wondrous concoction of gables, turrets, spires, spindles, brackets, balconies, bays, and balustrades crossed the ocean, there could have been nothing on this side to rival it.

Elsewhere, when the writer was younger and more foolish, she characterized as German a

Figure 242

lesser model of the same species as this gingerbread residence, basing the attribution upon a patent warning: "Gesetzlich geschützt!" on the underside. This admonition was undoubtedly added when the four-room model (see illustration) was exported to Germany, but I am now persuaded by many details, including the French blue roof and some documentary evidence, that these houses are French.

A black-and-white photograph fails to do full justice to the multi-colored façade with its yellow "stone" below, its pink brick above, its cream windows with apple green and rust trim, and its pairs of tan panelled doors. The choice assortment of windows is evident—casements which open with the same metal handles found on the front doors of lesser houses in the series, sash windows which can be raised and lowered, even bull's eyes on the third story (which perhaps with reference to a French house may be

"COMMERCIAL PROPERTY"

referred to as oeil-de-boeuf). The doors are also unusual—three pairs, glazed above and panelled below, are capped like the casement windows, by fanlights. There is even a workable door beneath the balustraded turret in the roof. There are so many metal spires, including a surprising pair at the front entrance, that a television aerial would be less noticeable on this roof than on most. An unusual accessory is the pair of moveable urns on standards from which spill now limp but evocative aspidistras. These have been placed at the foot of the stairs for the picture, but there were obviously others: When the Strong collection was visited, a third urn lacked a perceptible opening for its pegged base.

Inside the house, the front of which opens in the usual hinged sections, there is similar grandeur. This is the only commercially made house I've seen with a vestibule "tiled" with the same paper pattern as that to be found in a French milliners' shop.* From this vestibule, a doll steps grandly down two steps to the hall. There is a central staircase and the original wallpapers and draperies—always colorful and beguiling in even the more modest houses in this elegant series.†

A FORMIDABLE SERIES OF "MYSTERY" HOUSES

DATE: CA. 1895
HEIGHT: 44½"
WIDTH: 54½"
DEPTH: 17½"
OWNER: MRS. HERBERT HAWKINS (CONNECTICUT)

In recent years, a series of remarkable dolls' houses, clearly produced by the same maker, has been emerging one by one from attics, mostly in the Northeastern United States.

Sizeable, and handmade with great care, these

* *A Book of Dolls and Doll Houses.*

† See also Fig. 287.

Figure 243

imposing toys have an unmistakable personality. All have distinctive exteriors in which strips of wood, deeply chamfered to resemble stonework, are applied in what appears to be a fanciful interpretation of rustication.* Employed for coigning, cornices, and miscellaneous trim, this detail, on which a coating of glitter sometimes remains, is always painted in sharp contrast to the rest, charcoal gray on the numerous examples we have encountered, and is present in varying degrees of elaboration. The effect is curiously charming and a trifle clumsy, naïve as folk art; and if the resulting style relates to any full-size architecture, one has yet to come upon it.

Other hallmarks of these extraordinary houses include handsomely panelled doors, inside and

* Shortly before these pages went to press, Mrs. Cecil St. C. King of Virginia acquired from a Connecticut source a house with similar measurements and plan to that of Mrs. Hawkins, but with half-timbering on the façade in lieu of rustication. The inlaid floors are striped rather than patterned. It is clear that the house is one of the series, and it is helpful indeed to be aware of this variation. See also Mrs. Wilson's "1074" from New Rochelle Fig. 149.

HISTORIC PRESERVATION IN MINIATURE: FACTORY-MADE BUILDINGS

Figure 244

out, parquetry floors inlaid in intricate and colorful patterns, and windows with lintels that may be found in either of two styles: with keystones (as in the Hawkins house), or with a scroll-cut embellishment (per the McKennon house and the catalogue illustration).

Combined with the sizeable proportions of even the smaller houses of this genre (someone referred to one specimen as "A great ark of a house"),* these characteristics imply great effort spent in their construction, and considerable time. It is perhaps owing to this obvious time requirement that a theory evolved relating the houses to prison manufacture, possibly a prison in Massachusetts. It is true that many specimens have been found in Massachusetts or elsewhere in New England.

There has been speculation about their date as well as about their manufacture. Mrs. J. W. McKennon of North Carolina was told by the Delaware dealer from whom she acquired her excellent example that it was "about 1860." The proprietress of a doll shop in Vermont, Mrs. Jean Schramm, who has pictured hers on the front of a brochure, has labeled it "our 1870 house."

* Mrs. John Grossman of Connecticut, who generously provided the photographs of the Hawkins house.

Therefore, it was with a sense of discovery that the writer came upon the illustration of one of these houses in an F. A. O. Schwarz 1897 *Christmas Review* soon after it was reproduced early in 1971. Although its presence in the Schwarz catalogue does not solve the mystery of where the houses were made, the illustration does offer a date, and of course it indicates that these toys were manufactured in numbers that even the numerous examples which have been appearing may not have implied. It also offers a possible clue to their origin.

As Mrs. Ashby Giles of Schwarz's Antique Toy Department pointed out when the writer with some excitement came upon the catalogue illustration, Schwarz had a store in Boston as well as in New York, and the house might well have been made in Massachusetts. It has not been possible to learn whether or not Schwarz contracted for them with a prison in Massachusetts or anywhere else. Any bills of sale are long gone, and a letter of inquiry to the celebrated toy firm has proved fruitless.

Figure 245

"COMMERCIAL PROPERTY"

However, prisons are not necessarily the only source of supply for craftsmen with time on their hands. We respectfully submit the suggestion that firemen have a great deal of spare time, too. (In Baltimore, Christmas gardens of considerable intricacy used to be an important part of the holiday scene. The writer recently acquired a block of five East Baltimore row houses of this origin. See Fig. 217 and Plate 1.)

There are variations in details as well as in size of all the houses. Some have dormers, staircases, and wings, and some have none of these, but all have rooms which invite furnishings somewhat larger than the popular "inch-to-a-foot." The most sizeable models contain seven rooms, plus an attic room and staircase halls. The smallest contain four.

One of the latter, in the collection of Mr. and Mrs. Raymond Knapp of Rhode Island, appears to be identical to the one shown in the Schwarz catalogue.* This house is 45″ high, on a base 24″ by 35″, and it is surprising to note that even in 1897 the price for this small size was $33, a not inconsiderable sum for those days. It would be of interest to know what the larger versions with wings were bringing. Although under the illustration of the smaller house, "Dolls' Houses in many styles and sizes" are listed—from $2 to $80, with nine prices between, these obviously include houses of other manufacture as well as those in our "mystery" series.

In the enormous collection of the late Mrs. Homer Strong in Rochester, there are four of these tantalizing behemoths. (Mrs. Strong gave another to a Massachusetts collector who has since disposed of it.) These may be reduced in number by the time the Strong Museum is open to public view, but two are of the mammoth variety (the built-in base is nearly five feet long) shown in the accompanying photographs.

One illustrated belongs to Mrs. Herbert Hawkins of Connecticut, and it is shown because, like the two biggest in the Strong collection, it has a wing, staircase, and dormers, and it also has the most detail to offer.* Of two of these houses which belong to the Knapps, the larger appears to be identical to these till one studies it closely; then one discovers that it was built without the "stonework" above and beneath the windows. (This is also true of Mrs. MacLaren's four-room specimen.)

Mrs. McKennon's house, especially desirable with its original paint, wallpapers, and curtains, appears to be identical to these elephantine models, but there is no staircase. Studying the façade carefully, one suddenly realizes that an additional window to the left of the main door, and an extra one above, to be found in the largest houses, are lacking here. In the biggest models, the door opens into a proper stairhall, forming an additional narrow room upstairs and down.

A more minor variation in the McKennon house is the presence of scroll-cut openings in a strip coated with a substance resembling the Christmas sparkle on Victorian cardboard ornaments. A strip of this material also underlines an exterior cornice on the same house (Strong collection).

Perhaps the most astonishing feature of all of these houses are the parquetry floors, with each room in a house inlaid in a different pattern. Some are relatively simple geometric designs; others are composed of decorative wooden shapes stained in red, black, and, sometimes, green. They are pure fantasy (though I have recently been told that there are such floors, in full-sized houses, in Cambridge, Massachusetts).

---

* Mrs. Gordon MacLaren of California and Mrs. George Steinmetz of Oklahoma also have this four-room version, as did the late Mrs. Verdelle Flynn Coddington of Illinois, but theirs have pitched roofs rather than the usual gambrel, and no "rustication" under and above the windows. The late Elsa Mannheimer had a four-room example (Fig. 247) which obviously never had a façade!

* Only these big ones have windows in the rear wall, as in a real house.

HISTORIC PRESERVATION IN MINIATURE: FACTORY-MADE BUILDINGS

All of these variations in detail may relate to the date of the particular house rather than to the size or price. One longs to know how many years these small mansions were made before, in 1897, they turned up in Schwarz's catalogue. And one also longs to know who made them. Perhaps some kindly octogenarian with a long memory will come up with a clue. Possibly one who was given one of these unbelievable playthings as a child . . .

Or, possibly, an ex-convict . . .

MISS MANNHEIMER'S MERCANTILE ESTABLISHMENT

DATE: CA. 1895
HEIGHT: 21"
WIDTH: 47"
DEPTH: 18"
OWNER: MRS. JOAN L. THAYER (MINNESOTA)

In the 1965 edition of *A History of Dolls' Houses,* this enormous and handsome establishment was shown as a toy shop. It is a tribute to the versatility of the late Elsa Mannheimer of St. Paul, Minnesota (page 219), that it was completely believable and appealing in that trade, and that it is also entirely believable returned, with its late owner's inimitable embellishments, to its original business of dispensing miniature food.

By far the largest and most impressive I have encountered, the store is one of a late Victorian series which was clearly imported in great numbers and variety* possibly from France. Miss Mannheimer found it empty in a Goodwill store many years ago, bought it for a trifling sum, and made it into a well-stocked toy store. A few years before her death, she wrote, "My toy shop has reverted to its original purpose. It was meant to be, and now is, a food shop, and ten times better than before. A friend has just presented me with a beguiling dispenser of wrapping paper, blue tin—German—." She put back the twenty spice drawers, with their painted tin labels, which she

* *A Book of Dolls and Doll Houses*

Figure 246

had removed but carefully stored away, and restored the long counter.

The shop is painted cream with red trim. The panelled door at the rear can be opened, the showcases are glazed, and the entrepreneur was proud of such additions as the fish table at the right, in which she placed fish on a realistic bed of unmeltable ice (rock candy), and the fruit display stand at the left which was once "a cheap container for dime store perfume bottles," and which she bought empty, at a Goodwill store, for ten cents.

As somebody once wrote of Elsa Mannheimer, "The unimaginative and uninspired look at a bead and see a bead, look at a watch spring and see a watch spring. Elsa Mannheimer looks at a bead and sees a dolls' house world globe—or a lamp—or a vase. She looks at a watch spring and sees a very very miniature gramophone record, complete with grooves." Although the writer is an antiquarian not usually caught up in such improvisations, Elsa Mannheimer practiced her art with a skill which finds admirers in all collecting circles.

AN ELSA MANNHEIMER HOUSE

DATE: CA. 1895
HEIGHT: 41″
WIDTH: 31″
DEPTH: 16″
OWNER: FROM THE COLLECTION OF THE LATE ELSA MANNHEIMER

On February 3, 1972, Elsa Mannheimer of St. Paul, Minnesota, sent this picture (at my request), along with two others. "I realize I am putting you to extra trouble," she wrote with her usual spirit, "since I want them *all* returned." Five days later, at the age of ninety-one, she "went to bed and died peacefully in her sleep." The small world of miniaturia of which she was a pioneer, and which she inhabited with such taste, style, wit, and warmth for so many years,* had lost one of its most illustrious practitioners.

Every house or room she dealt with bore her stamp, and perhaps this house, which came discarded and empty from a garage, will serve, along with the "food shop" in Fig. 246, as examples of her range.

The house itself is the simplest of the "mystery houses," and the only example without a façade known to me. When I questioned this unusual fact, Elsa Mannheimer defended her treasure with customary gusto: "I beg to differ with you as to a façade. It has none and could never possibly have had one. Not only are there no holes to indicate dead-and-gone hinges, but the saw-tooth molding decorating the front edges would definitely prevent a front being used." Her house, however, was "blessed [like its cousins] with very nice panelled, ornamented doors and baseboards in every room, also good window moldings, white inside, brown carved outside. . . ." Unlike the floors in most houses in the series, these contain no inlay.

She was once describing the "lovely old pieces" in this house: "one room about 1875, another about 1850, etc.," and, to an insistent antiquarian, added characteristically, "eked out, shame on me? with bits I have made such as a papier-mâché and pearl tip-top oval table, crystal chandelier and other things you wouldn't approve of . . ."

She was also proud of the Baxter prints she had framed in the drawing-room, the Blackamoor vase with feathers in it, and the Greek statues in front of the windows: "The Greek Slave" and "Androcles and the Lion." Her specialty was the lived-in look accomplished with artfully created homey details—spectacles she'd fashioned from a bit of wire resting on a piece of partially finished needlepoint, or a

---

* "Making something out of nothing," a St. Paul feature writer wrote in 1964, "has been Miss Mannheimer's hobby, she says, 'for about 200 years, or possibly 198.' "

HISTORIC PRESERVATION IN MINIATURE: FACTORY-MADE BUILDINGS

Figure 247

(220)

"COMMERCIAL PROPERTY"

tureen filled with, of all things, chicken noodle soup.

Resourceful as well as creative, when she first realized the need of a bell pull (she later made others), Elsa Mannheimer got herself a needlework pattern for a full-sized model, and reproduced it, stitch for stitch, in a suitable five-inch length.

Her wit was verbal as well as visual. In a letter written shortly before her death, she mentioned her disappointment when, for "The Pied Piper," one of the numerous shadow box scenes she created, she ordered from a Milwaukee shop a flock of mice which she specified should be running. "They came, and every damn one was sitting up!" she wrote. "Imagine being chased by a horde of sedentary mice—the rats!!"

THE VANISHED HOUSES OF WHITNEY-REED

Catalogue pages through the courtesy of Mrs. William S. Maunder and Mr. William H. Green, both of Leominster, Mass.

It may be something of a presumption to refer to Whitney-Reed's dolls' houses as vanished. It is possible and even likely that examples exist, and flourish, in the hands of unknowing collectors, though Mr. William H. Green, head of the Whitney-Reed Chair Co. in 1957, when what remained of it was sold, is aware of no existing specimens.

The word "unknowing" is used advisedly. There is no evidence that Whitney-Reed dolls' houses were marked, as were some, at least, by Bliss, Converse and other makers; and this can make them difficult to trace. It was through the courtesy of Mrs. William S. Maunder, a doll collector and a resident of Leominster, Massachusetts, the home of Whitney-Reed, and of its celebrated predecessor, the W. S. Reed Toy Co., that the catalogue illustrations shown were made available, and that I had the pleasure of meeting Mr. Green.

It is informative to compare the illustrations, all taken from a 1902-3 catalogue in Mrs. Maunder's possession, with dolls' houses and other toys illustrated in an earlier, 1897-98 edition belonging to Mr. Green. It is not surprising to discover that in the five-year interval, Whitney-Reed had developed a new line of dolls' houses, not shown in the earlier listing. This "New Practical Doll House" is shown here; three smaller models were also illustrated. These, "constructed of wood on an entirely new plan," represented "a modern brick dwelling." However, just in case this house, with an open back, a hinged roof, and windows of mica instead of glass, proved to be *too* practical, part of the 1897-98 line was still available.

In that year, houses in eight sizes had been described, though the two largest were not illustrated,* and all were Bliss-like structures "lithographed in handsome colors," with hinged fronts, glass windows, and curtains. In 1897-98, the heading on three of these was "Up-to-date in Style and Finish." In 1902-03 this was amended to read "Fronts and Doors Hinged," and the two largest models, as well as the smallest, were no longer listed. The houses in both lines were "neatly papered inside."

Similarly, a new line of stores was to be found in 1902-03, which had not been available five years before: "Original in design, large, strongly built, well painted in four colors and varnished." The largest came with a counter with money desk and metal scales, shelves and twelve drawers, but the big new "feature . . . is that we do not enclose the back, thus making it possible for the boy or girl who is keeping store to serve over the counter." This was indeed a *moderne* concept for 1902.

In 1897, there was a lithographed "well

---

* The most sizeable, 10" deep, 22" high, and on a base 15" by 18", was three stories high, with five rooms, a front door, and eight glass windows draped with lace curtains, "a mansard roof and piazza across the front, with balcony on second and third stories."

HISTORIC PRESERVATION IN MINIATURE: FACTORY-MADE BUILDINGS

Figure 248

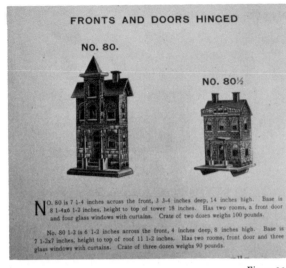

Figure 251

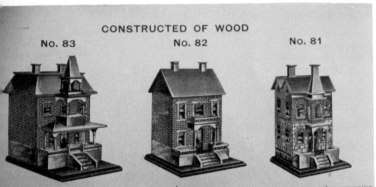

Figure 249

Figure 250

furnished" meat market (not shown here) "with the proprietor ready to wait upon you." There was a supply of blocks to represent meat and fowl, and a cloth awning which could be raised and lowered by using the knob at the side. This was twelve inches wide and twelve inches tall. More remarkable still was the "Wholesale Grocery." This, too, came in a smaller size, but also with a "horse and cart," in a different style from the "horse and delivery wagon" in the de luxe model, and with, presumably, a smaller selection of "barrels and blocks." The smaller version had two doors on the outside instead of the "three sets of double ones" the big one featured, and a hoisting apparatus in lieu of the "elevator running from bottom to top, operated by a crank at the side" to be seen on the twenty-three-inch tall, and obviously flourishing, "Wholesale Grocery."

The Coal Yard, the only one this collector has ever heard of, was illustrated in both catalogues, and seems to epitomize an era gone forever. There was also a lithographed United States Armory (not illustrated here), 36" wide and 13½" high, with each of its four towers "surmounted by an American flag." Twenty-four soldiers mounted on bases, plus a cannon and ammunition, came packed in a "strawboard box" and all of this was "very easily set up."

(222)

"COMMERCIAL PROPERTY"

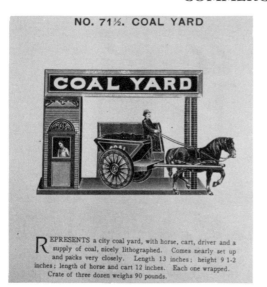

Figure 252

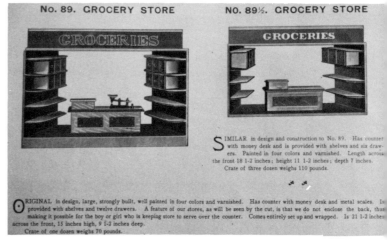

Figure 253

Whitney-Reed also made a smaller military toy, a fort with "a disappearing gun." This gun was "so arranged that it [could] be loaded behind the fort, raised and fired, disappearing immediately."

All of these lithographed toys must have been very colorful and appealing, but the furniture made "in imitation of mahogany and varnished" for the houses is disappointing. It will be noted that the parlor set pictured appears to have been made in two sizes. Unfortunately, the box sizes are given rather than the furniture sizes, and it is impossible to know whether the "nice covered box, 15x10½x3" was larger than the set "arranged and fastened in a box 12x11x3" because there were more pieces, or because they were also a larger size. Dining-room and "chamber" furniture was also shown, similar in style to the parlor pieces, and also in two "sets."

Mr. Green furnished a brief and informal history of his firm which is offered herewith:

The Whitney-Reed Chair Company was formed in 1893. About 1895, the W. S. Reed Toy Company that started in Leominster in 1875 was merged with the Chair Co. Mr. W. S. Reed was really a genius. Some of his toys are extant.* The Whitney Reed

* The "American Grocery" (Fig. 240) is believed to be by Reed. Many Reed toys are marked with the company name.

Figure 254

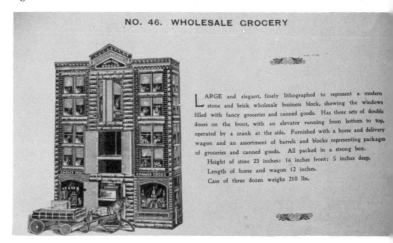

Chair Company was located in a group of buildings with sort of a Rube Goldberg set-up. We made reed and rattan chairs, three dimensional wooden rocking horses and swinging horses, children's furniture, baby and doll carriages and a large line of wooden toys.

In 1907, a "combine" of toy factories was formed for the purpose of cornering the market. They went under the name of the Hardware and Woodenware Corp., and were in business for about six years*

* This is generous. The McClintocks relate that the corporation went into receivership in 1909 "but continued to operate with fifteen companies as associates for about two more years."

before going into receivership. My father at that time was manager of the Whitney Reed Chair Co., and together with some friends bought the Leominster business in 1912. It ran successfully until 1929.

My father died in 1925, and I was made manager, but the toy and furniture business became slow, and then ground to a stop in the depression, so in 1933 we had to close. An auction of the buildings and contents was held for several days in March, 1933. Prices were lower than the stock market, buyers few, and the whole kit and caboodle went for junk prices or less. I salvaged enough funds by selling my home to buy the essential patterns and machinery for the manufacture of hobby horses, starting with $600. In April of that year, I moved into a vacant building that had been the Steinert Piano Company case factory, and set up and shipped horses by hook or crook, in time for the holiday season, as things were beginning to improve. . . . But it was touch and go for a long time, operating without adequate funds. We were always worried about . . . the weekly payroll . . . and things were difficult for several years.

Later, in 1957, the plastic horses, injection-molded in one operation (as against the hundreds of hand operations of the wooden horses) came onto the market. I was getting near retirement age, and decided that the time had come to sell, which I did.

Because there had been an impression that some of the lithographed papers used on the houses had been imported, I asked Mr. Green about their origins. It was his "guess" that they all came from the Forbes Lithograf Company of Boston, Massachusetts. Others may have come from Europe, he said, but there did not "seem to be any records to prove this."

In *Yankee*, December 1971, there was a feature story about Whitney-Reed and Mr. Green, one especially relating to the hobby horses turned out by the firm during his tenure.

Because to a large degree the illustrations from the Whitney-Reed catalogue speak for themselves, perhaps reproducing them will enable collectors to identify specimens in their own collections, and will allow the word "vanished" to be stricken from this summary.

THE SMALL WORLD OF R. BLISS

The R. Bliss Manufacturing Company of Pawtucket, Rhode Island, was established in 1832 and incorporated in 1873, and these illustrations from a rare 1901 company catalogue* may serve to introduce the sequence (on succeeding pages) of houses,† stables, stores, firehouses, armories, churches, and other buildings which constitute their small and appealing lithographed-on-wood world.

With the exception of Schoenhut, whose dolls' houses came later, and possibly of Converse, perhaps no maker of American dolls' houses is better known, and though the houses are also sturdy, realistic, and charming, and warrant their fame for these reasons alone, the name of Bliss is best known for a very simple reason: it was lithographed, along with the bricks, doorways, window frames, and gingerbread ornamentation onto the papers applied to the buildings themselves. Frequently the name is on the front door, sometimes on a pediment, occasionally elsewhere. On some houses it is missing entirely. In any case, in a field where so much material has been destroyed, and relatively little information is available, dolls' house collectors have long been grateful to the firm in Pawtucket.

Numerous toy manufacturers, both in the United States and abroad, made houses and related toys of lithographed paper-over-wood, but it seems unlikely that any outsold those

---

* Catalogue No. 15, courtesy of Louis H. Hertz.

† And furniture. See Figs. 382–5.

"COMMERCIAL PROPERTY"

Figure 255

Figure 256

made by Bliss. Judging by the quantity that have survived, it is clear that many were built, in an enormous variety of sizes and styles. A street of houses (see above), found one by one over the years (and more than once compared by visitors who frequent Martha's Vineyard to the gingerbread houses at Oak Bluffs), helps to illustrate this fact.

In 1907, Bliss took a full page in *Playthings* to advertise the line of dolls' houses which had been launched "about twelve years" before, and which the firm declared had been "an emphatic success from the very start."

"Not many years ago," they asserted, "every doll house sold in this country was imported. These goods were unsatisfactory in every way, but nothing else was to be had." Then Bliss introduced "A large line . . . including Stables, Stores, Cabins, and so forth, as well as houses. All were made in American designs to suit the tastes of American children . . . of well-seasoned lumber . . . [which] not being subject to climatic changes . . . eliminated the greatest objection to these goods." Previously, it seemed, "many dealers" were discontinuing the line which, when carried over from one season to another, often led to "a serious loss, owing to the warping and cracking of the wood. . . ."*

Bliss had gone "underground" briefly for a few years beginning in 1903 when the National Novelty Corporation, a "toy trust" composed of

---

* In a 1904 editorial which may relate to Bliss, *Playthings* referred to the substitution of nails for the once inevitable glue in dolls' house construction. Imported dolls' houses made with glue instead of nails "slowly but surely began to fall apart," said the editorial, after they had stood on store counters for a while.

(225)

thirty-seven American toy manufacturers, was formed, with Bliss among them. Despite high-flown goals (one was to obtain a greater share of the toy business for American-made wares), the short-lived monopoly was out of business by 1907.

But many Bliss houses and other toys were advertised under the National Novelty Corporation banner during the four years in which it was extant. The familiar three-room Bliss (Plate 2), a popular model to judge by the number which survive, was shown in a National Novelty Corporation advertisement in *Playthings*, both in 1904 and 1905 issues.* The two rare Adirondack cottages (Fig. 271-3) have no lithographed name on the premises for positive identification, but they are most probably Bliss, with the larger one illustrated in a National Novelty Corporation 1904 advertisement. The stable with National Novelty Corporation as an almost unnoticeable part of its lithographed decor (Figs. 275, 277) is undoubtedly Bliss. The smaller stables (Fig. 276) with the Bliss name lithographed above the narrower stall (on each) demonstrates this relationship in reverse—the left-hand one was shown (but not identified) in a National Novelty Corporation advertisement in 1904.

Playthings, in its early years at least, maintained a policy, often followed by news media, of keeping its editorial content rigidly separated from its advertising. This was maintained to a degree which eliminated the names of all manufacturers in its editorial columns. This may have been partially owing to the restrictions imposed by the corporation itself, but it was in 1905, during the reign of the Trust, that *Playthings* wrote about a factory "located at Pawtucket, Rhode Island, for many years famous for its wooden toys." There was no doubt about who was meant, especially when reference was made to recent "improvements" in dolls' houses and stables.

"Formerly," said the editorial, "dolls' houses seemed to have a peculiar architecture of their own. Like nothing else on the earth or the waters thereof." Now "actual reproductions of the standard designs" were available, "correct to the smallest details."

This is not surprising inasmuch as according to the 1901 catalogue from which the illustrations of these two houses were taken,* Bliss dolls' houses were "designed and modeled by a practical architect." The houses pictured and described range from the smallest Bliss house (5" by 7" by 11") with one chimney to the "Modern City Residence" illustrated here—the $5 size. This "doll mansion unequaled," with a stylish turret, is also shown in John Wanamaker's 1903-4 "Holiday catalogue." The Philadelphia department store also illustrated one of the smaller Bliss houses.

"An Elegant Suburban Home," the $4 size shown, may be seen on Bliss Street (the end house on the right, Fig. 255), and surprisingly, it contains only two rooms, one up and one down. The third story is sham, forming what might be described these days as a "cathedral ceiling" to the second floor. On the other hand, another Bliss Street residence (extreme left), not shown in the catalogue and presumably later than 1901, is very little larger in base dimensions and height, but this one contains four rooms and a rare Bliss staircase. The staircase has a simple metal rail downstairs and a metal balustrade upstairs which matches the railings on the exterior. On the smaller house, the balustrades are of lithographed paper on wood, and one theorizes that such railings may have been used on the earlier houses. It is observable that the houses with metal balustrades usually have squared posts covered with lithographed paper, while the paper-on-wood balustrades are to be found on houses with turned wooden posts.

The 1901 catalogue alludes to "the splendid

---

* This model was still advertised in *Plaything* in 1920.

* Four models advertised by Butler Bros. in 1910 are also shown. (Fig. 260)

"COMMERCIAL PROPERTY"

Figure 257

Figure 258

interior decorations" of the houses, the lace curtains, and "clear mica windows." Although a reference is made to hinged fronts and doors, the four-room house with the staircase may be opened on each side, and the three-room "Seaside Residence" (to the left of the small stable on Bliss Street) on one side, to give access to the kitchen on the left. The front may be swung open as well. The houses are to be found both with lithographed foundations and painted wooden ones.

In 1905, the *Playthings* editorial quoted above referred tantalizingly to a "fine dolls' house . . . made up with its front representing the end of the Congressional Library. It might take a vivid imagination to notice the similarity but the general outline is there." One has attempted to train a willing if not vivid imagination on various Bliss houses with this end (no pun intended) in view, but without success. Any theories or discoveries would be welcome.

Since not all Bliss buildings are marked, it might be useful to call attention to three described and shown in Figs. 265–7.

Another unmarked Bliss house, the "Fairy Doll-House," is shown herewith. This was illustrated with the anonymity customarily accorded manufacturers in jobbers' catalogues, but, in the nick of time for the purposes of these pages, the *Antique Toy Collectors of America* reprinted a rare 1889 Bliss catalogue which contained this one small house. Since previously I had been able to find no actual reference to Bliss dolls' houses before 1895, this was a happy discovery. As the catalogue illustration indicates, all three sections of this house have a packable

HISTORIC PRESERVATION IN MINIATURE: FACTORY-MADE BUILDINGS

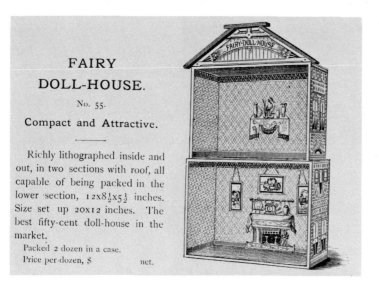

Figure 259

Figure 260

Figure 261

principle not unlike that of the McLoughlin house and the writer's "knock-down" Bliss house, and all three have the lithographed interior decoration which gave way to wallpapers in the later, marked Bliss houses. Here, as the catalogue text discloses, the upper and roof sections pack into the lower section of the small house.

Composed of blocks, the Bliss church shown is toy architecture rather than doll architecture, but with its lithographed paper-on-wood construction and architectural aspect, it bears a distinct kinship to other Bliss buildings. (AUTHOR'S COLLECTION).

In 1907, Bliss proudly asserted that the prices of its houses ranged as high as $25. I cannot imagine the size and style of such a Bliss house (none is over $5 in the 1901 catalogue), and I've

"COMMERCIAL PROPERTY"

never seen one, but I'd like to! * The small world of R. Bliss reflects the world of late Victorian architecture with a fidelity that beguiles, and it is not surprising that small-scale reproductions of these houses have been made in recent years, with more on the way.

A GROCERY STORE BY BLISS

DATE: CA. 1895
HEIGHT (NOT INCLUDING CHIMNEY): 9½″
WIDTH (INCLUDING EAVES): 9¼″
DEPTH (INCLUDING ROOF PROJECTION): 8″
OWNER: AUTHOR'S COLLECTION

Instead of "R. Bliss" on the door of this small grocery, there is a sign saying "Fresh Dried Beef."

There is no Bliss name elsewhere either, but because the grocery store was a peculiarly American establishment, it has always been clear that this miniature example was made in the United States. The presence of an American flag in the hand of the small boy in an upper window only underlined this realization, but it was not till the store was discovered in a 1901 Bliss catalogue that its maker could be identified.

The grocery had been patented in 1895 (it was the only miniature building in the catalogue for which a patent date was indicated) and had been "materially improved for the year 1901." Perhaps the patentable features were the awning, braced by a movable wooden bracket on one side, and the double cardboard dormer which fits an opening beneath the folding roof (exactly as it does on the unmarked Bliss house in Fig. 270).†

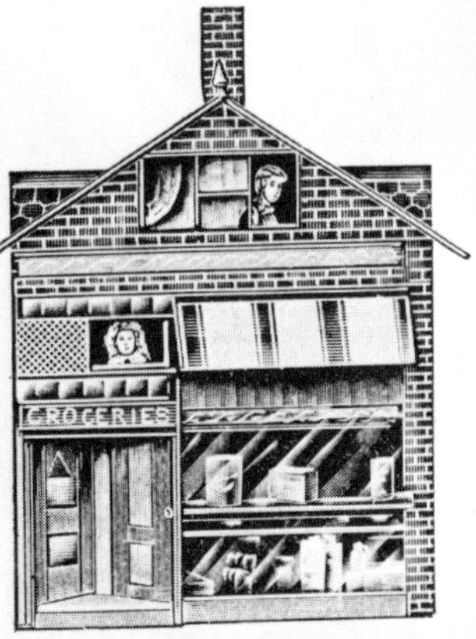

---

* Variations continue to appear. In the Spring of 1973, Margaret Whitton found a large Bliss house in the form of a semi-detached pair.

† Many patents were ordered and paid for while this book was in progress. Most of the cards were returned (though payment was not) marked "Cancelled." It has not been possible to learn what this means.

Figure 262

Figure 263

The Bliss lithography is, as usual, imaginative, and it is also—to students of inflation—informative. In a window showing numerous cuts of meat, there is a barrel of apples with a sign: "15¢ a peck." Pickles are "10¢ a doz." Along with sacks of flour and tubs of butter and lard, there are several items which were staples then which are no longer to be found on grocery shelves: stove polish and bottles of blueing.

A cake of lithographed paper-on-wood soap glued to the counter, and several wooden bottles and barrels appear to be original.

(229)

HISTORIC PRESERVATION IN MINIATURE: FACTORY-MADE BUILDINGS

It is of interest that in 1898, in *The Hustler* (W. A. Cissna & Co., Importers and Jobbers, Chicago), this is described as a "country store." According to Cissna, the stores were made to retail for fifty cents apiece "and at our price, they are going like hot cakes." (This jobbers' price was $2.10 per dozen!)

There may be a point to mentioning here a trio of buildings in the 1896 *Youth's Companion*, "a combination toy" marketed under the 1896ish name of "Dollyville." The three buildings which came "knocked down," but made a thirty-inch-wide row when set up, consisted of (1) an opera house and bank, (2) a drugstore and bakery, and (3) a market and grocery. The buildings, according to the advertisement, could be used together or separately, and the "market and grocery" is so similar in style to the one which has been described that "Dollyville" was clearly marketed by Bliss—and one wonders if the other buildings were also marketed separately.

Another Bliss grocery store (in the writer's collection), too incomplete to warrant photographing, must at least be described. This is clearly the lower half of a grocery larger than the one pictured, and this one is marked. The Bliss name, placed where the store proprietor's might have been, but in an understated manner as usual, is above the door, part of a ten-inch lithographed strip across the top, which features the words "Grocery Store" in sizeable letters. Even larger is the "address" of the store—"396" beneath the "Bliss," which corresponds to a model number in the lower-right-hand corner.*

The door and the sides offer more information for inflation buffs: The door, which is lithographed on wood rather than on the flimsy cardboard of the store pictured, has a sign hanging in the window which says "WE SELL HOME MADE BREAD 5¢ each." In a side window, another sign of those times says "MILK 6¢ Qt."

Both the front of the store, which contains a large window (glass or mica missing), and the hinged door, swing open. Upstairs, it is evident, there were living quarters once upon a time. It is clear that wooden strips at each side of a red-and-white paper carpet once guided the upper section into place on what is now the top of the store. A wooden counter with a cardboard front also survives.

Undoubtedly lithographed people were looking out of upper windows on this missing section. Bliss never left a window unoccupied or, probably, a stone unturned.

A BLISS WAREHOUSE

DATE: CA. 1898
HEIGHT: 15"
WIDTH: 12"
DEPTH: 6¼"
OWNER: AUTHOR'S COLLECTION

It is necessary to go out on a limb only a little way to identify this warehouse positively as a Bliss. Although there is no absolute proof, it has all the earmarks of the Rhode Island maker's style—the familiar lithographed paper-on-wood, the Bliss-type cardboard dormer, the same sort of wooden barrels—and even the typical, obscurely placed model number.

Two models of warehouses are advertised in the 1901 Bliss catalogue, but they have numbers which differ from the "293" at the bottom of a door of this one. It is also possible to offer the date of one year in which the warehouse was sold: Cissna of Chicago, that faithful buyer of Bliss products, advertised the identical warehouse in 1898. The advertisement indicated: "It has four double doors, large platform and office, pulley and ropes for hoisting cases from one floor to the other. A large wagon 12 inches long goes with every warehouse." (The price to the retailer for all this was $4.75 per dozen.)

---

* The model number "347" is on the roof of the model in the photograph—and this corresponds to the number in the catalogue.

"COMMERCIAL PROPERTY"

Figure 264

Figure 265

The "Modern Warehouses" (Nos. 466 and 467), advertised in fifty cent and dollar sizes in the Bliss 1901 catalogue, also included a horse and wagon, along with "the usual hoisting apparatus for boxes, barrels or other articles."

"The modern warehouse is thoroughly represented in the construction of this toy," Bliss asserted.

UNMARKED BLISS HOUSES

DATE: CA. 1898
HEIGHT (INCLUDING CHIMNEY): 24″
WIDTH: 19″
DEPTH (INCLUDING FRONT PORCHES): 12″
OWNER: AUTHOR'S COLLECTION

When this house with its lithographed interior was acquired in October 1971, I'd never seen another. It was obvious that four posts were missing across the front porch (not shown), but the lithographed interior, to be seen through the open back, was in pristine condition. With one of those curious coincidences of timing so often encountered, a week or two later, during a visit to the Strong collection in Rochester, I saw two

Figure 266

similar houses. In early December, Mrs. Betty Chart of California sent me a picture of another!

Mrs. Chart felt that her house had many characteristics of a Bliss, and wondered if any Bliss houses were unmarked. Before my Rochester visit, I could not have answered her question,

(231)

but one of the dolls' houses there, unmarked on the outside, had the familiar marked Bliss doors connecting the four rooms (two up and two down) inside.

One of these houses was exactly like Mrs. Chart's, with two mica curtained windows downstairs at each side of a lithographed door and another one upstairs between two lithographed windows with drawn shades. The porches had the metal rails (possibly a later addition to the Bliss line), rather than the wooden railings upstairs and down, and the wooden posts on the front porch (missing on mine).

However, as we learn, variations in Bliss houses are infinite. The other Strong house, similar to mine, with wooden railings and posts, was conventionally made, with the customary papered interior. The house illustrated here comes apart for packing, and as the illustration suggests, the walls are elaborately lithographed. All exterior detail on the house is also lithographed, with no mica windows or operable doors on the front to interrupt the interior decoration.

The latter is of the distinctive blues, reds, and gilt, highly glossed, that one associates with much of the Bliss furniture. Exuberant floral patterns paper the walls, surmounted by an alphabet border—cupids gambol upon the letters that surround the three walls from "A" to "Y." (Somebody flubbed that one.) Dolls and/or children traverse the halls of the upstairs border.

Children, as they well might, dominate the decor—in pictures on the wall, as mantel ornaments. A pair flank an enormous clock on the mantelpiece, and two more surmount the clock itself. There is a fire roaring summer and winter in the fireplace, and elaborate crimson draperies are at the windows—through which views may be observed. Four elaborately draped windows are upstairs, but the rest of the bedroom furnishing is left to the imagination of the young owner.

Figure 267

The few pieces of Bliss furniture shown in the house did not come with it, but may very well have been made for this type of house.

A "playhouse" with the identical wooden pillars and railings was advertised in *The Hustler* in 1898 by W. A. Cissna & Co., Importers and Jobbers, Chicago.* It is described as "very large,"† and the seller proudly added: "This house would make a good window attraction, and you would have no trouble selling it when you get through with it." The price for this "very large" house was $1.75—presumably to retailers.

There is nothing in the Cissna advertisement to indicate whether the house contained the lithographed interior and the "knock-down" feature‡ of the one in the writer's collection, or

* Through the courtesy of Mrs. Dorothy Cook of Malibu, California, who most helpfully compiled, reprinted, and marketed rare doll material in the 1960's.

† Mrs. Chart's house measures: height (to the top of chimney): 22″, width: 17″, and depth: 11″.

‡ The porches, front steps, side window sills, and gable ends are attachable to the house with metal pegs. The double dormer, which fits snugly into the roof, and the roof itself are of heavy lithographed cardboard, but all other parts are of lithographed-paper-on-wood, including the removable second floor. When the latter is removed (despite its age, it still slides with ease), all the other parts can be packed inside the body of the house.

"COMMERCIAL PROPERTY"

whether it was a conventional-type Bliss house with paper walls like the one in Rochester.

Also from the Strong collection, the unusual Bliss house with the lithographed stone on the first story of the façade and the pair of bays above is also believed to be an unmarked Bliss—unless the interior Bliss door, similar to the ones which have been described, were left-overs bought from the Bliss factory. Despite the parts-swapping theory concerning Converse-Cass and others, this seems unlikely. The measurements of the stone house are: height: 23½″, width: 18¾″, and depth: 8¾″. (It is difficult to standardize measurements; one would have first to standardize measurers.)

BLISS FIRE STATION NO. 2

DATE: 1901
HEIGHT (TO TIP OF GABLE): 19½″
BASE: 10½″ by 8″
OWNER: AUTHOR'S COLLECTION

Bliss advertised three firehouses in 1901, in twenty-five, fifty, and seventy-five cent sizes, and the glory of late Victorian firehouse architecture is to be seen in all of them.

Both belfry and bell have been replaced in the model pictured, but there is so much to see elsewhere that such minor substitutions are quite unnoticeable. There are partial views of pumpers lithographed on the side windows of the lower half, and there are pieces of firemen's paraphernalia to be seen through the windows of the front bay upstairs: lithographed firemen's hats, a coat, boots, and even a speaking trumpet, ready for action. (These are set back two inches behind the window openings and, with the mica which once concealed them entirely in place, they are as good an example as any of Bliss thoroughness.) Young firemen viewing all this exterior realism may have been somewhat taken aback when the double doors (or the whole

Figure 268

front—there is a choice) were flung open and two wallpapered rooms, exactly like those in their sisters' dolls' houses, proved to be all there was inside.

On the other hand, a pumper, "Niagara," with horse and driver, was sold with Bliss Fire Station No. 2, and probably there was a lot of clanging around the parlor before this barren interior scene was disclosed.

The original pumper was missing when the firehouse pictured was acquired. The one shown was borrowed from a smaller version of No. 2 Fire Station (also in the writer's collection). The smaller fire station, approximately 17″ tall on a base 9¼″ by 7″, has its original belfry* with gilded wooden bell, and its original mica windows in the second floor bay. Peeking behind the mica, one discovers that even in this smaller

* This is detachable, helping to account for the loss of the original on the firehouse pictured.

HISTORIC PRESERVATION IN MINIATURE: FACTORY-MADE BUILDINGS

model, the firemen's equipment is present. Everything to be seen on the larger model is there, but reduced in scale, and the colors of the smaller version are more garish—with bright greens and reds on doors and trim, and only one wallpapered room inside. (The number "509 B" is on the lower-right-hand side of this small firehouse; undoubtedly a smaller version of "509" in the 1901 Bliss catalogue.)

With these different sizes available, presumably conflagrations both small and large could be dealt with.

"MODERN JACK'S HOUSE"

DATE: CA. 1898
HEIGHT (NOT INCLUDING CHIMNEY): 13"
WIDTH (INCLUDING EAVES): 18¼"
DEPTH (INCLUDING EAVES): 10¼"
OWNER: AUTHOR'S COLLECTION

When this lavishly lithographed structure was first encountered, in almost mint condition at a Maryland antique show, it looked vaguely English, and it seemed—as indeed it still does—more stable than house.

It did not take long to discover that it wasn't made in Britain: stamped beneath the gabled roof is some precise documentation: "Pat'd. March 12, 1895. Manufactured in U. S. A." Later it was found in the 1898 catalogue of a Chicago importer and jobber, W. A. Cissna & Co., where it was identified as "Modern Jack's House," along with another, smaller model labeled "House that Jack Built."

It is only an educated guess that the house is a Bliss, but the circumstantial evidence is strong. On the same page of the Cissna catalogue may be found other Bliss toys, including the unmarked house shown in Fig. 267, a small unmarked house with awning (Fig. 270),* and the small store with awning (Fig. 262). Inasmuch as the store was also patented in 1895 (the only patent date indicated in the 1901 Bliss

* From the collection of Mrs. W. Graham Claytor.

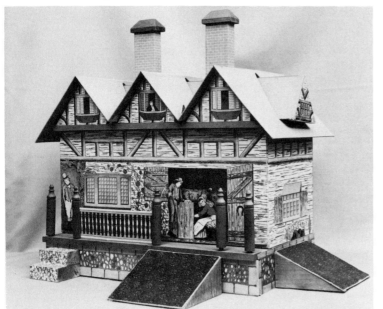

Figure 269

Figure 270

(234)

catalogue), and manufacturers frequently took out patents in batches, this seems highly admissible evidence of Bliss ownership.

What is mysterious is why this curious building is referred to as a house. The decor is similarly enigmatic. Although inside there is a spacious room (reached through the open back), with blue-and-white printed walls and red-and-white printed floor, the exterior, as the illustration suggests, is strictly barn-like in aspect. Both this model and the smaller "House that Jack Built" appear to have identically lithographed façades, with a milkmaid milking a cow while a farmer (or hired hand) stands by, scythe in hand. The gentleman in the top hat at the left-hand entrance looks like a country squire in his blue jacket and red weskit. A small rotund figure in the upstairs window (repeated on the back) is totally unidentifiable, and there seems very little to relate to "the farmer sowing the corn, that kept the cock that crowed in the morn, that waked the priest all shaven and shorn, etc. etc. . . . in the house that Jack built" (a house described by the catalogue itself, by the way, as "made to imitate a stone and brick house with porch and windows").

The smaller house is shown with only two gables, rather than the three in Jack's house, and one chimney rather than two. The cardboard balustrade between wooden posts is absent on the lesser model, and so is the wooden frame, lithographed to represent colored stone, upon which "Modern Jack's House" is steadied by two wooden pegs. The catalogue mentions a box of furniture provided with the smaller house, and the fact that it comes "knocked down, but is easily constructed, as it fits with wooden pegs." (This type of peg construction also relates these two houses to Bliss. Small shaped pegs identical to these may be found on the unmarked Bliss house and the Bliss warehouse.)

While the price, to retailers, of the smaller house was $4.25 per dozen, the cost of the larger model was more than double: $8.75. The suggested retail price of this model was $1, and no box of furniture was mentioned.

The wooden ramps and steps shown in the photograph are not to be found in the ad. All in all, this most barn-like house, or elegant barn, with its climbing red roses, dormered bay windows, and mystifying cast of characters, is an intriguing addition to the Bliss microcosm.

AN ADIRONDACK COTTAGE

DATE: 1904
HEIGHT (TO PEAK OF ROOF): 17½"
WIDTH (OF BASE): 17½"
DEPTH (OF BASE): 10¾"
OWNER: AUTHOR'S COLLECTION

In the late 1960's, in a New York State antique shop, this collector saw the apparition pictured here. The lithographed paper-on-wood log house seemed almost surrealistic with its lithographed paper-on-wood Indian head (which in metal might have served creditably as the radiator cap on a 1926 Pontiac!), coasting eternally in profile down the second-story dormer. With the deer head on the uppermost gable (repeated on the rear), the effect was of a dolls' house seen in a dream.

The purchase of this house was resisted at the time, and one never expected to see its like again, but it was remembered when the small log version was acquired. Then, some months before these pages went to press, the files of a 1904 issue of *Playthings* yielded up the apparition, lithographed logs, deer head, Indian head, and all! The National Novelty Corporation, a toy trust founded in 1903, and one which would certainly require antitrust counsel today, displayed, in a double-page spread of miscellaneous toys, and in all its rustic glory, the dolls' house from the New York State antique shop with (as the illustration indicates) the label: "Adirondack Cottage. Novel Doll House."

HISTORIC PRESERVATION IN MINIATURE: FACTORY-MADE BUILDINGS

Figure 271

ADIRONDACK COTTAGE. NOVEL DOLL HOUSE

Figure 272

Figure 273

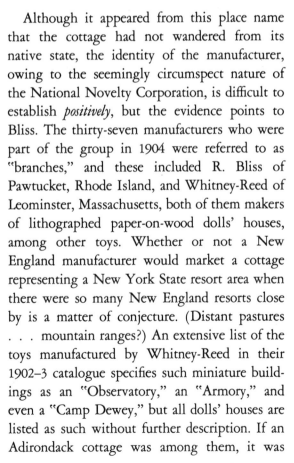

Although it appeared from this place name that the cottage had not wandered from its native state, the identity of the manufacturer, owing to the seemingly circumspect nature of the National Novelty Corporation, is difficult to establish *positively*, but the evidence points to Bliss. The thirty-seven manufacturers who were part of the group in 1904 were referred to as "branches," and these included R. Bliss of Pawtucket, Rhode Island, and Whitney-Reed of Leominster, Massachusetts, both of them makers of lithographed paper-on-wood dolls' houses, among other toys. Whether or not a New England manufacturer would market a cottage representing a New York State resort area when there were so many New England resorts close by is a matter of conjecture. (Distant pastures . . . mountain ranges?) An extensive list of the toys manufactured by Whitney-Reed in their 1902–3 catalogue specifies such miniature buildings as an "Observatory," an "Armory," and even a "Camp Dewey," but all dolls' houses are listed as such without further description. If an Adirondack cottage was among them, it was neither illustrated nor described. A Bliss 1901 catalogue throws no light on the subject, but since the cottage was not advertised by the National Novelty Corporation till 1904, it may

(236)

"COMMERCIAL PROPERTY"

not have been in 1901 even a gleam in its maker's eye.*

Of the remaining manufacturers in the group, I have at present no clue to relate one of them to the Adirondack cottage, but it is peculiarly satisfying to have found the illustration and the Adirondack identity of the log house even if the identity of the maker is presently relatable only to the National Novelty Corporation, a group defunct by 1907.

By some miracle, the Adirondack cottage in the New York State antique shop in the late 1960's was still there in the summer of 1972—and its purchase was not resisted this time around. It contains three rooms plus a small attic room formed by the dormer; access to the latter is gained by the Indian head which serves as a sort of handle to the section! With the meticulous detail one associates with Bliss, even this tiny room is papered, as are the other three, with papers on walls and floors suitable for a cottage in the Adirondacks—"knotty pine" or some other rustic finish in perfect scale on walls and floors. Both front doors, like the dormer-with-Indian, are hinged and workable. The back of the house is open, and lithographed segments identical to ones on the front (i.e. one on the pediment above the two-story section and one beneath the dormer section of the roof) are duplicated on the back, along with the Indian and his dormer.

To judge by the small two-room house, which has glazed windows, glass was also originally in the windows of the larger model, which is otherwise in remarkable condition. The smaller house, also in excellent condition, has two rooms and an open back, and is presumably a more modest Adirondack cottage. It is 17½" tall, 9¼" wide not including eaves, and 7" deep not including balcony. (The horse is a candybox with a removable head.)

* In a 1907 advertisement, Bliss referred to the line of "stables, stores, *cabins* and so forth" they'd introduced.

FIVE BLISS STABLES

DATE: CA. 1905
HEIGHT (OF LARGE STABLE INCLUDING FINIALS): 20"
WIDTH (OF BASE): 23¾"
DEPTH (OF BASE): 9"
OWNER: AUTHOR'S COLLECTION

In 1965, I wondered in print if this large stable might not be a Bliss.

The gate to each hinged stall fastens with a metal catch similar to the ones on Bliss houses. . . . The metal railings on the stalls, balconies and hayloft are identical to those used on (many) Bliss houses. The lithographed paper-on-wood columns are almost identical in design to smaller ones on (various) Bliss houses. But amongst the lithographed profusion of scrolls and orange and blue embellishment, the Bliss name is nowhere to be seen. The only printed clues are numbers (624K or 624E, etc.).*

* The "624" was, of course, the model number, with the letters (such as "E" and "K") to guide the proper lithographed segment to its location on the wooden foundation.

Figure 274

HISTORIC PRESERVATION IN MINIATURE: FACTORY-MADE BUILDINGS

With egg on my face, I herewith amend this. The egg is owing to the considerable clue on each side of the stable which, with a want of imagination (and information), I had dismissed as decoration. As the illustration shows, on the side of the stable (duplicated at the other end) and above the stall a bit of lithographed embellishment contains an "N" at the left, another in the center, and a "Co" at the right, if one looks at it with the proper spirit—and a degree of information. The Library of Congress does not possess the first four years of the files of *Playthings*, the toy trade publication, and the National Novelty Corporation, until recently, had eluded this researcher. In any case, Bliss was a member of the "toy trust" which flourished for a few years (ca. 1903-7), and this stable unquestionably is a Bliss. Unfortunately, the missing cupola must have been a handsome addition and

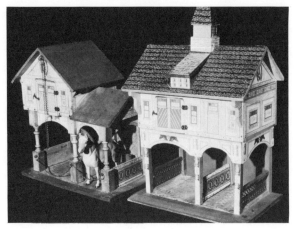

Figure 276

Figure 277

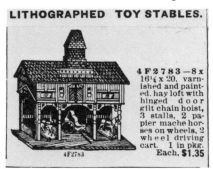

Figure 275

sizeable, to judge by the two holes in which it obviously fitted. The feeding rack is of pierced metal. The wood-and-metal gates to each stall have hinges and hooks.

Two smaller Bliss stables, each with the Bliss name, may be seen in Fig. 276. The example with the wooden posts, thought to be earlier than the one with the lithographed paper-on-wood posts, is 13½" tall to the gable tip, on a base 7¼" by 12¾". Its cupola is missing, but its hoist and railing chains have managed to survive. The other stable, including cupola, is 16¼" tall on a base 7¾" by 12".

Two of the illustrations* are from the 1901

---

* One other, from Butler Bros., 1910 (above), is nearly identical, and nearly as sizeable, as the large Bliss which leads off this summary.

"COMMERCIAL PROPERTY"

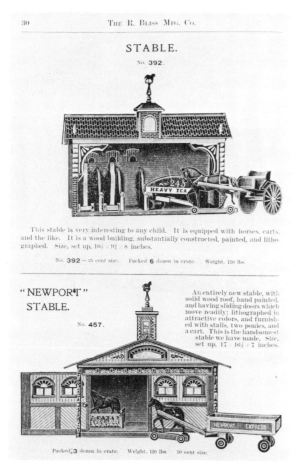

Figure 278

Bliss catalogue. Because it is printed in modest type, it seems pertinent to call to the casual reader's notice the fact that the more expensive "Newport stable" was the "50 cent size."

A BLISS "FORTRESS"

DATE: CA. 1905
HEIGHT: 14"
BASE: 8½" BY 14½"
OWNER: AUTHOR'S COLLECTION

In 1905, *Youth's Companion* advertised this small stronghold as a fortress. Since it resembles the armories still to be found in considerable numbers throughout the United States, it may be considered authentic American "architecture" despite its somewhat misleading label. Undoubtedly "fortress" was a more comprehensible and glamorous term to soldiers under ten.

Although the example pictured and the one illustrated in *Youth's Companion* are the only two I've seen, many must have been made and sold—and given away. Given away almost literally, because in 1905 *Youth's Companion* was offering the fortress *plus* a small Bliss stable shown in Plate 4 for one new subscription.

It is true that the *Companion*'s fortress was advertised as eleven inches tall, and if this figure is not in error, theirs was a smaller model than the one pictured above. (The stable was also a small size.) Even so, the offer was impressive—the fortress came complete with soldiers, cannon, and flag.*

Two small lithographed medallions, the size of a nickel, above the entrance serve to identify the maker of the fortress as well as the country in which it was made. The Bliss name, in minuscule letters, is inset in the one at the right,

---

* Since the picture was taken, a flag has been added to the proper turret!

Figure 279

and the American eagle is modestly encircled by the one at the left.

The lower section of the front swings open to reveal a small room inside, presumably large enough to accommodate the soldiers when they are not on parade, and possibly the cannon.

A CASA FROM SPAIN

DATE: CA. 1900
HEIGHT (NOT INCLUDING CHIMNEY): 28"
WIDTH (NOT INCLUDING BAYS): 27½"
DEPTH (NOT INCLUDING BAYS): 14"
OWNER: AUTHOR'S COLLECTION

The preposition "from" is used after some soul-searching; it seems more likely that this house, which appears to be commercially made, might have been manufactured in Germany or France for the Spanish market. Whatever its origin, it is rare.*

It is also exuberant, both inside and out, as its pictures suggest. A confection of pink brick with green frosted glass glittering behind Moorish-styled window frames painted cream (as in whipped), the only solemn notes in color or style are the dark brown double entrance doors and the matching cornice beneath a roof of dark gray "tile," with a curious balustrade in a sort of grape pattern (and a grape color).† Those doors,

Figure 280

Figure 281

which would do credit to a moated castle, are set into a foundation with spattered dark gray rustication which matches the coigning. Dormer windows at each side of the roof contain the same frosted green glass to be found below, and the front dormer has been converted into a sort of clock tower with more frosted green glass

---

* On behalf of *A History of Dolls' Houses*, this writer began to search for Spanish examples in 1945. The only one which surfaced was (to judge from a photograph unsuitable for reproduction) an imposing specimen in Vigo, Pontevedra, in the possession of a Count who did not reply to an inquiry. In recent years, the writer acquired a "Mediterranean Seaside Villa," undoubtedly commercially made, and again probably in Germany or France. (This needs to be restored before it can be photographed.) An elaborate house in the possession of Mrs. Helene A. Mitchell of New York, found in Madrid in 1960, has painted inside: "en 24 Dicibe—1888, R. Liern. lo hizo, Pintor Rafael.

† Parts of the house, unfortunately, have been repainted, including the pink brick. An attempt will be made to match a paler pink which was the original and can be glimpsed near edges.

"COMMERCIAL PROPERTY"

subtly decorating the pierced ornament surrounding the clock's face.

The hinged front divides to reveal four rooms of a similarly motley aspect, and unusual architectural elements of their own. As the photograph indicates, the decorative arches which overhang the two lower rooms are supported by columns, and the two upper ones, balustraded in the manner of the early German houses, have a decorative wooden crosspiece (with wooden tassels!) which has no counterpart known to me in miniature or full size. The bays on the sides of the house are sham and do not open into the rooms, but the ones on the façade are open to the interior, and the nooks they form hold several small pieces of furniture.

The exterior would not suggest a commercial origin; it is largely the wallpapers in the four rooms, and the W. C.* tucked into a small cubicle in the kitchen, one step up, with a workable door, which most imply a manufactured piece. A floral-patterned paper in the bedroom competes horticulturally with the floral-patterned furniture (which came with the house), but the most remarkable paper is to be found in the adjoining room. In luscious colors, above a papered dado, there are lushly lithographed murals, on the three walls, of children attending what appears to be a very elegant birthday party—in a velvet-curtained room of considerable opulence. It would be possible to go on at length about these murals, if space permitted; but one detail must be noted: the three kegs of wine on a stand, which may also be found in actuality in the dolls' house. One which may be seen in this room came with the house; the one in the kitchen has been added. This accessory, peculiarly Spanish, suggests that both the wallpaper and the house may be, after all, of Spanish manufacture. It was said, by the way, that the house had "been in the Franco family," which is name-dropping of a not especially informative order, offering no real clue to its history.

More research is needed, to say the least, before this unusual house and its architecture can be properly documented. Friends* took pictures, in northern Andalusia, in Ubeda, a "National Monument city," of a townhouse with hanging bays similar to these on the dolls' house, but containing windows less Moorish in style. On another house, they photographed a

---

* It is the overhead tank of this fixture, as well as the style of the wallpapers, which suggest a turn-of-the-century date for the house.

* Doll historians Dorothy S., Elizabeth A., and Evelyn J. Coleman, who took a slide of the dolls' house along on a journey to Spain in the autumn of 1972.

Figure 282

HISTORIC PRESERVATION IN MINIATURE: FACTORY-MADE BUILDINGS

turreted chimney not unlike the one (unfortunately rather washed-out in the print) to be seen on the dolls' house. One suspects that this is meant to be a fairy castle, very small, to be occupied by a very small knight, but the fantasy assuredly mingles with actuality.

A brief postscript must be added to these paragraphs. Shortly before they went to press, a snapshot of the elaborate twelve-room mansion which is also pictured, arrived from California. The mansion, said to be a copy of a townhouse "recently" torn down in Seville, Spain, was in the process of changing hands, but at the time of this writing was in the possession of Mrs. Elyse Law. It is dated above the door "1889," and grandly and thoroughly furnished; and it puts to shame the modest fairy tale "castle" which has been described above.

(The mansion from Seville is 45 inches tall [not including the 25-inch turrets], 56 inches wide, and 27½ inches deep.)

Figure 283

Figure 284

A HOUSE WITH A COINCIDENCE

DATE: CA. 1900
HEIGHT (TO ROOF PEAK): 41½"
WIDTH (NOT INCLUDING PORCHES): 34"
DEPTH: 20½"
OWNER: MRS. HOWARD WILLARD (CONNECTICUT)

When Mrs. Willard bought the unusual house pictured, she was told that it had been "built for the children of the Kayser underwear people in 1900 in New York." The house was in poor condition with some parts missing, including whatever had filled the "oblong openings" over the windows and doors.

"My big question," she wrote, "is what was in the oblong openings? . . . The window in the center front just under the roof is of a pale green ribbed or mottled glass . . . Do you think this could have been what was over the other windows and doors?" Mrs. Willard's reason for thinking it was not was that all the other door and window glass was intact.

The writer, who had never seen another house like it, and who sometimes feels well qualified as a Sherlock "Homes," wrote back: I think those *were* transoms over the windows and doors, and I think your guess that they were of

(242)

"COMMERCIAL PROPERTY"

Figure 285

the same pale green glass is a good one . . . But it should be relatively easy to come by some old glass of the right color and have it cut to fit." It seemed possible that the same "restorer" who had done some repainting had removed the transoms temporarily and had never got them back in.

In the same letter Detective "Homes" fell flat on her face: "The staircase has a carpentered look," I ventured, "and I suspect the house is one-of-a-kind."

It did not seem necessary to eat these words till the spring 1972 issue of *Nutshell News* arrived with an illustration of "The House with the Green Windows," a recent addition to Editor MacLaren's own collection. Needless to say, the "Tiffany glass windows" she described were similar in size and shape to the missing transoms on Mrs. Willard's house! And with the architectural variations to be seen in the two, a new series of "mystery" houses appeared to be launched.

It is difficult to decide which is the front and which the side of the Willard house. Two views are shown, and looking at the long side head on, with the single door and the window boxes, it seems a reasonably conventional model with front and back porches. Looking at it, however, with the double porches in view, one also sees double doors, both upstairs and down, and a "duplex," as such apartments used to be called, or a semi-detached house, is suggested. The interior, of course, is no clue, since one rarely expects or finds logic in dolls' house interiors.

The MacLaren house, on the other hand, is a conventional front porch model with a mansard roof (unlike the overenthusiastic gable on the Willard) and a single door. However, the upstairs and downstairs porches also resemble those on the Willard house, and the half-glazed doors are similar.

Under the castered base of her house, Mrs. MacLaren found written in bold pink and green script (matching the final colors she reached upon removing innumerable coats of paint), "Merry Christmas, 1903," and therefore even the date Mrs. Willard had been given is another clue that fits.

Both the front and the back (the non-porch "sides") open in three hinged sections, and there is a central hall with a winding staircase. Apprised of one's apartment house theory, Mrs. Willard thought it might be "a good idea . . . although with the exception of the halls, they would be one-room apartments." The second floor hall also contains a large closet. All the rooms have doors and these are numerous. As the small illustration indicates, the MacLaren house is smaller, with three rooms, and the spindles of the porch railing are simpler in their turnings.

Inasmuch as both of these houses were found in the New York area, it seems possible that one of the large New York department stores might have commissioned them at Christmas time from a small factory or individual. More are likely to turn up, and one hopes to hear of them.

HISTORIC PRESERVATION IN MINIATURE: FACTORY-MADE BUILDINGS

AN IMPORTED HOUSE WITH A WALLED GARDEN

DATE: CA. 1900
HEIGHT (NOT INCLUDING FINIAL ON TURRET): 32½"
WIDTH (INTERIOR): 21½"
DEPTH (INTERIOR): 12"
BASE: 20" by 30"
OWNER: MRS. LUTHER SCULL (PENNSYLVANIA)

Although this pleasing imported house may appear to be unrelated to the ones in Fig. 242, it bears sufficient resemblances to suggest that it was made by the same, presumably French, manufacturer.

There is the identical and inevitable lithographed yellow stone on the bottom story and pink brick on the top. The brick paper used is itself of a predictable style with thick "mortar" between the bricks. It is true that more than one manufacturer must have used these papers, but there are other resemblances—the chimneys, which, as Mrs. Scull suggests, may originally

Figure 287

Figure 288

Figure 286

(244)

have been spools, and, more than anything, the diversified and appealing architectural detail to be found in each of these houses.

Mrs. Scull's includes the charming addition of a flocked lawn enclosed by a brick wall, and even the wall is of architectural interest with posts and a pattern. This walled lawn, on its own small base (6½" deep), is part of the hinged façade which swings open in one section. Although Mrs. Scull thought the plaster embellishments might be additions, decorations of this type are to be seen on other houses of this make.

Since the wallpapers had been replaced in the house when she acquired it, Mrs. Scull felt justified in "replacing the replacements." Happily, the "parquet" floor papers were not disturbed. Best of all, some of the furniture came with the house, including the dining-room furniture.

A most unusual piece in the dining-room is a pewter water cooler on its own footed pewter stand. Mrs. Scull's description of this treasure is appealing: "It has a bouquet of roses, etc., on the front and, so there will be no mistake, says 'Ice Water' above this, all in low relief. A cup hangs from a hook on the stand, and there is a faucet."

Other rare pieces in the dining-room include the brass candleholders which Mrs. Scull has described as "a pair of ill-tempered knights." Each of these gentlemen in brass armor upholds a candleholder (in lieu of a sword), and Mrs. Scull has placed them on brass tripods which are suitable not only because of their size. Their design also was inspired by chivalric motifs stemming from the earlier Gothic revival; the top of each bears in relief a knight of its own, referred to by their owner, in her own inimitable style, as "the twins, Peevish Parsifal and Sulky Siegfried." Their manufacturer obviously was carried away with this subject matter, and Mrs. Scull seems to gravitate toward their products. "Later," she wrote, "I found two hanging plaques, one with an identical knight, the other with his lady, looking equally cross." *

The dining-room furniture is the German "yellow cherry" with "cane" seats and backs on the chairs. This is from Gebrüder Schneegass (see Figs. 387–8), and chairs, with curving "cane" backs between elaborately turned posts, were still to be found, though undoubtedly made in earlier years as well, in their 1914 catalogue.

A FRENCH HOUSE WITH SEWN-IN FURNITURE!

DATE: CA. 1900
HEIGHT (NOT INCLUDING 4½" SPIRE): 34"
WIDTH (BASE): 19⅝"
DEPTH (BASE, NOT INCLUDING STEPS): 10⅛"
OWNER: AUTHOR'S COLLECTION

When it first loomed on the miniature horizon, the house alone was sufficiently captivating, a French seaside villa which recalled, to admirers of Jacques Tati, *M. Hulot's Holiday*. Appealingly absurd with its outsize but windowless turret,† crowning a steeply gabled roof; and haphazardly punctuated by two rather foolish chimneys and a gilt spire, the only thing missing appeared to be the seaside itself.

It was true that the small house had everything else—even its original furniture—*still sewn*

---

* Mrs. Scull made a most interesting point with respect to these tripod tops and matching plaques. She also found a gilt metal table some years ago, and about six years later, a mirror with a frame exactly the same size and pattern as the table top. "I'm sure you've found these thrifty makeshifts many times," she writes. "I think they're fun and I always look for them." The most notable example of this type of economy, which I've mentioned elsewhere, relates to the much sought brass chandeliers with "bristol" fittings. It is clear upon examining the nineties-type electric fixtures with their pointy bulbs that the earlier gas type with their globes facing ceilingward was reversed and the strands hung upside down to contain the electric bulbs pointing to the floor.

† This is removable, evidently for packing.

HISTORIC PRESERVATION IN MINIATURE: FACTORY-MADE BUILDINGS

Figure 289

Figure 290

in. Such a thing had been unheard of, at least to this collector.

Until our present graceless era, packaging, like many other possible minor arts, was, as we know, usually accomplished with charm, and not with plastic. Even after the turn of the century, candy boxes usually were beautiful *per se*, with lace linings and gilt trimmings (in the United States as well as abroad); and dolls' house furniture, like other small objects, often was artfully arranged in paper lace-edged boxes and sewn into place. Occasionally today one makes a lucky find, and comes across old dolls' house furniture or accessories still fastened into their original boxes (Figs. 406 and 408). But this collector had never before heard of furniture so fastened into a *dolls' house*. To learn of such a delight might have seemed sufficiently rewarding; to see it (and to acquire it) seemed almost miraculous. One often speaks of finding a house with its original furniture. This was the ultimate of such a halcyon possibility.

Beneath the French blue roof, and within the pale yellow exterior walls on which lavender and aquamarine panels are engagingly lithographed, the sides of the slender house swing open to reveal four rooms containing a total of seventeen pieces of furniture. This is the white-painted French furniture so often seen, in various grades and vintages, in French doll rooms (which still appear to be more readily found than complete French houses). The customary gilt-paper edging outlines the pieces, and the usual and beguiling embossed floral scraps are affixed to

(246)

table tops, headboards, and other straight surfaces.

The furniture in these four rooms is set off by wallpapers and cardboard "tiled" floors in surprising color combinations which, with customary French panache, seem charmingly right. Pink upholstered chairs and bedding in the bedroom somehow are delightful against a green-and-yellow floral pattern and a red, white, and blue "tiled" floor. The bedroom furniture, incidentally, is so complete that two rooms are required to contain it: the upper-left-hand room with bed, armchair, side chair, round pedestal table, and wardrobe, and the downstairs entrance hall with two more chairs and a dressing table.

With this one exception, the furniture is logically placed, even though it was not expected to remain as, with more luck, it may, till the end of time. A mirrored fireplace, two armchairs, two side chairs (red-upholstered), and a shaped oval table are in the parlor which is papered in a perfectly scaled pattern of lilacs and green leaves; in an upstairs sitting-room are a sofa and chair upholstered in pale green with a four-legged plant stand. Red flowers sprout from the mossy vegetation always found in these "ferneries," although sometimes only shreds remain. (The chairs are 3¼" high.)

As the 1897 catalogue illustration indicates,* this type of furniture was referred to as "Louis XVI." The chairs and sofas in the house are of the identical shape and style, but the two tables in the house, one round and one oval (with "turtle" turnings) have more interesting pedestal bases than those shown in the catalogue. A French bedroom with a similar type of table, again with the familiar chairs, is also shown. This is somewhat larger in scale and of better quality than the furniture in the house.† Such a bedroom is referred to in the advertisement.

The rooms are connected by interior doors on each of the two floors which are of lithographed paper on wood of a simpler graining than the panelled front door. The latter has, as its picture shows, an ornate metal knob. Identical lace curtains are stretched across the upper halves of the glass windows.

* Through the kindness of Mrs. Dorothy S. Coleman, who found this in the catalogue of the Parisian department store, *Au Paradis des Enfants*.

† Author's collection.

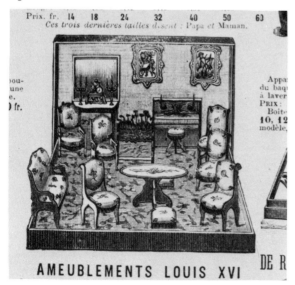

Figure 291

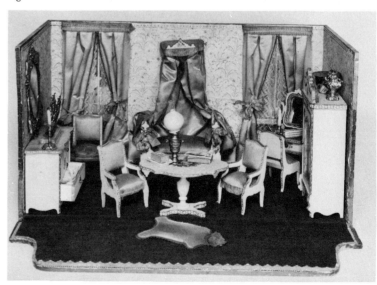

Figure 292

HISTORIC PRESERVATION IN MINIATURE: FACTORY-MADE BUILDINGS

"DOLLY'S PLAYHOUSE" BY McLOUGHLIN

DATE: CA. 1884–1903
HEIGHT: 18"
WIDTH: 12"
DEPTH: 9½"
OWNER: AUTHOR'S COLLECTION

In May 1905, *Playthings* printed an obituary of John McLoughlin, the celebrated New York manufacturer of games, blocks, books, and various paper toys. According to the article, McLoughlin, in 1855, had taken his brother Edmund into partnership, establishing the McLoughlin firm. This was a successor to R. H. Elton & Co., of which John McLoughlin had become a member when he was twenty-one.

The McClintocks have observed that John McLoughlin, "being an engraver by trade, was interested in good printing, with emphasis on color, which appealed so strongly to children."

They might have added that such printing "with emphasis on color" also appeals strongly to latter-day collectors. Three of his dolls' houses, illustrated in these pages, are prime examples of his work.

When Montgomery Ward, in 1903, advertised "Dolly's Playhouse," they really failed to do it justice. With a dimly printed illustration not much more than an inch tall (McLoughlin should have helped with Ward's catalogues), they described under "folding doll houses" a specimen "two stories high, made of strawboard and wood, lined outside and in with paper printed to represent carpets, wall paper, brick walls and windows."

"This is a very fine residence for any family of small dolls," they asserted, and they might well have added, "even a royal family." Although the rooms are only two, they are so palatial that even a princess, of the proper size, would feel quite at home.

Figure 293

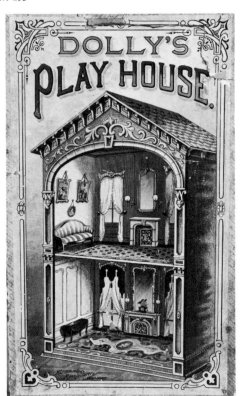

Figure 294

"COMMERCIAL PROPERTY"

Unfortunately, these gorgeous rooms are difficult to photograph, but the lower one, the drawing-room (it is too sumptuous to be called a parlor), with its elegantly panelled walls hung with paintings in gold-leaf frames, and its ornately carved white marble mantel with ormolu clock and "garniture," surmounted by a ceiling-high "looking-glass," is the Victorian drawing-room incarnate. If, as Frances Lichten* has written, "Lavish outlay on window draperies was a particular stamp of worldly success," the head of this dolls' house must have been extremely successful. (After all, he paid 75 cents for his house in 1903.) Lace curtains which are clearly Brussels are accompanied by gold-leaf cornices from which hang tasseled lambrequins of mauve (of course). But the decoration that gives the room much of its opulence is the green carpet which is centered with a multi-colored floral medallion of astonishing elaboration, and surrounded by a floral harmonizing border. And horticulture is overhead as well as underfoot: The fact that the ceiling is of the identical pattern, with somewhat more subdued coloring, may well have been overpowering to all but the sturdiest dolls.

The second floor, with striped wallpaper and a blue, gold, and white figured Brussels carpet, is almost prim by comparison, but it is suitably fashionable nevertheless.

In its construction the house is ingenious. The principal section consists of hinged walls and floors which swing into position and are then firmly slotted by the lithographed paper-on-wood cornice which fits over a wooden strip at each side of the front. The shingled roof, which then is placed over the pediment formed at front and back, miraculously stays in place. The chimney fits snugly into an opening in the roof.

Marian Howard, whose careful research in the fields of paper dolls and their houses is well known among collectors, included one of these in a privately printed booklet in 1953.* She also referred to McLoughlin dolls' houses of considerably earlier vintage in an 1875–76 catalogue in her possession. These were not illustrated but were described as "two-story wooden houses eighteen inches high, and eleven inches wide, made in imitation of brick, with slanting tiled roof, chimney, etc. The floor of each story is furnished with a patterned carpet, and the walls are handsomely papered. . . . The separate parts of the house are compactly put up in a neat box, with full directions for putting together." †

These were $24 per dozen (presumably wholesale), and if one exists, it is rare indeed.

The earliest McLoughlin house known to me‡ is still "No. 544," the handsome four-room folding house which was invented by a Baltimore woman in 1894. Her house—"a series of partitions radiating from a common hinging point"—was clearly popular, to judge by the number which have survived. It was also the most portable of dolls' houses, folding into a book 13" square and an inch thick. An 1896 McLoughlin Bros. catalogue in which it was advertised is shown, and the house itself may be

---

* *Decorative Arts of Victoria's Era*, Scribners, 1950.

* *Homes for Paper Dolls and Kindred Paper Toys*. The box lid for Marian Howard's "Dolly's Playhouse" suggests that this toy was made over a period of time. At least it is evident that the box was re-designed at some point. The houses appear to be identical, but on the Howard's lid there is additional wording on the brick side: "An Elegant Toy to Accompany Paper Dolls, Paper Furniture, etc.," as well as a head of a child in each corner of the lid.

† Shortly after these pages went to press, a friend, Mrs. Donald Moe, gave the writer the back cover of a McLoughlin Bros. ABC book illustrating and advertising this very house. Since the book was published in 1884, the theory in the preceding footnote has been proved. The wording of Marian Howard's 1875–76 catalogue refers to a wooden house, and the 1884 ad refers to a "Paper doll house," but the descriptions are identical. The measurements are also identical, as they are to the house pictured. (The extra inch of the house illustrated in the photograph includes the roof gable.) These houses sold in 1884 for $1.25 each.

‡ The two preceding footnotes, added after these words were written, may alter the latter.

HISTORIC PRESERVATION IN MINIATURE: FACTORY-MADE BUILDINGS

Figure 295

seen in all the glory of its glorious color in Plate 5. (The type of cloth hinge used on "Dolly's Playhouse" seems to be identical, and may derive from the 1894 patent.)

The lid of a later McLoughlin folding house may be seen in Fig. 314.

A "DANDY TOY HOUSE" BY GRIMM & LEEDS

DATE: 1903
HEIGHT (INCLUDING CHIMNEY): 20½"
WIDTH: 19"
DEPTH: 12½"
OWNER: AUTHOR'S COLLECTION

"Your collapsible toy house is a winner." No less a merchandising authority than John Wanamaker is quoted in an advertisement by the Grimm & Leeds Company of Camden, New Jersey, in a 1905 issue of *Playthings*, the toy trade journal.

Probably there were assembling instructions inside the missing box lid of the example pictured, but the butter-fingered owner managed to construct this cardboard gem in two or three hours of triumphal engineering. Talent only was required; no glue. The structure is an ingenious arrangement of folding cardboard with only the porch and roof sections reinforced by blocks.

Figure 296

Figure 297

Junctions are formed by heavy cardboard pockets in walls into which floor and roof sections are inserted. There are four rooms, two up and two down, a beguiling sprigged wallpaper, and lace-edged dark blue window shades behind mica windows. Only one floor strip was sheared off in assembling; a tribute to the strength of the aging cardboard.

On the bottom of the box, the foundation of the house, was the name "Leeds Toy House,"

"COMMERCIAL PROPERTY"

the manufacturer's name and town, and the patent date of September 22, 1903. It is clear that the company lost no time putting these into production.

As the 1905 advertisement reveals, the firm made a large, four-room model as well as a two-room version 10″ by 14″ by 20½″ tall.* There were four models: "One Dandy Toy House" in two sizes and "One Colonial Toy House" in two sizes. In the same 1905 advertisement in which J. Wanamaker is quoted, a photograph of a substantial sheaf of orders dominates a tiny cut of a two-room specimen and we read: "Sales one store 500 houses." With such a success, it is not altogether surprising that at least this one example of a toy so fragile has survived.

BUCK'S FOLDING DOLL TENT

DATE: 1905 +
SIZE (SET UP): 14″ by 18″ by 21″
MAKER: GEORGE H. BUCK (BROOKLYN, N. Y.)

Although the tepee, that earliest of American shelters, is not represented in these pages (inasmuch as a miniature example of suitable vintage seems not to have been discovered), we content ourselves here with a different tent-like structure—a folding tent manufactured in relatively recent years for a different order of native.

George H. Buck of Brooklyn, the enterprising maker of "trimmed metallic beds," and then, astonishingly, of Oriental Cozy Corners (Fig. 398), ingeniously found another use for his metal and his fabrics in 1905 when the need for Cozy Corners apparently declined.

He introduced "Buck's Folding Doll Tent," furnished complete with "2 Chairs, 1 Table and 1 Settee." Although no reference was made to full-size inspiration, as it inevitably was with Mr. Buck's Cozy Corners, one cannot help but note the prevalence of tents in full size at the turn of the century, the result of the Chautauqua movement and the tent communities that resulted. "By 1900," writes Russell Lynes,* "there were two hundred such centers of culture and propriety. . . ." These were "other Chautauquas . . . on the shores of lakes all over the country. . . ."

Whatever Mr. Buck's inspiration, his tents came "packed one each in paper box" and featured: "New folding device, wire frame, white cover, red striped furniture set; no tacks, no glue, no paper, no center pole." The tent was "strong and desirable for outdoor use," and what was more, the cover could be detached and washed.

Mr. Buck also mentioned, in bold type: "This Toy is Good for Summer and Winter." With equal emphasis on seasonal versatility as well as

* *The Tastemakers.*

Figure 298

---

* As the advertisement indicates, the measurements given for the four-room house are not exactly the same as those of the one in the photograph. Allowance must always be made for inclusion or exclusion of chimneys, porches, etc., and measurements must, to some degree, be approximate.

HISTORIC PRESERVATION IN MINIATURE: FACTORY-MADE BUILDINGS

on outdoor use, it is not surprising that, however strong they were, none of Buck's Folding Doll Tents has, to the knowledge of this collector, been found. It is possible that more than one piece of the red-striped furniture has wandered from its original tent to repose grandly in the parlor, or on the lawn, of a less ephemeral structure. Vigilant collectors one day may be rewarded by finding one of the tents pitched by Mr. Buck, or at least one of his settees or chairs.

A LITHOGRAPHED APARTMENT HOUSE?

DATE: CA. 1905
HEIGHT (NOT INCLUDING 3½" BASE): 23¼"
WIDTH: 20"
DEPTH: 17"
OWNER: MRS. CLAUDE CALLICOTT (TENNESSEE)

Perhaps it is high-handed to refer to this small building as an apartment house, but with its three-decker porches and multitudinous windows, such a designation is tempting. It is also tempting to assume that it is American. Although Mrs. Callicott bought it from a Nashville attic (for five dollars!—her exclamation point) in the early 1950's, she is inclined to think of it as German. She remembers that it came from a family "who were very wealthy and traveled abroad a good bit." However, American makers such as Bliss and Whitney-Reed, who imported some of the lithographed papers they applied to American woods (page 224), made buildings of such variety that an apartment house might well have been among them.

Perhaps the strongest reason to infer an American origin for this intriguing toy is that, with its triple porches, it bears a striking resemblance to the modest, three-story, three-family apartments with narrow porches on each floor which, though considerably run down, are still to be seen in large numbers in New England states, especially Massachusetts and

Figure 299

Rhode Island, where so many American dolls' houses were manufactured.

There are two entrances (the second can be seen between the windows of the first-floor porch) and two rooms on each floor.

CONVERSE OF WINCHENDON

DATE: CA. 1905 (?)
HEIGHT (NOT INCLUDING 3" CHIMNEY): 19¾"
WIDTH: 12"
DEPTH (NOT INCLUDING 3" STEPS): 7⅞"
OWNER: AUTHOR'S COLLECTION

In 1878, Morton E. Converse who, with a partner named Mason,* had begun to manufac-

---

* The firm was Mason and Converse from 1878 to 1883 when it became the Converse Toy and Woodware Co. The name underwent several minor mutations in 1885 and 1889 before it became, in 1905, Morton E. Converse & Son.

"COMMERCIAL PROPERTY"

ture strawberry and fig boxes, accidentally got into the toy business. When his daughter was ill in bed, he whittled a few doll dishes, made a tea table from a round wooden collar box, added legs and—not long after, found himself in a business described in later years as "the largest toy manufacturing firm in the world." * Its headquarters, Winchendon, Massachusetts, was known as "the Nuremberg of America."

An 1885–86 Converse catalogue shows dolls' house furniture. Much later, in a 1913 Converse catalogue,† a bungalow is shown very similar to the one reproduced (with telephone pole) in the photograph, but I believe the three-story house with the balcony (measurements above) to be earlier, though both houses have identically printed yellow and green interiors. (The windows and "wallpaper" printed on the wood inside the bungalow are exactly like those in the lower room of the house.)

The 1913 catalogue refers to the bungalows as "perfect models printed directly on wood by our new three-color process" and these were obtainable in five sizes, ranging from a model approximately nine inches in height, width, and depth, to one 17″ by 17″ by 15½″.

With the exception of one small marked lithographed paper-on-wood two-room house,‡ similar to a two-room Bliss, all of the houses known to me which are marked Converse, or are believed to be Converse, are of the printed-directly-on-wood process. For comparative purposes, I lined up five of these, suspecting kinship. All have the same basic construction, with hinged fronts, two columns, "verandas," and printed interiors. Three are bungalows and

Figure 300

Figure 301

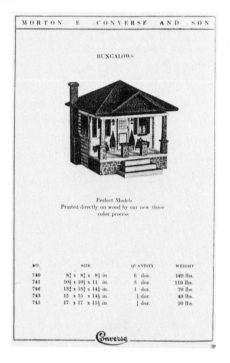

two are "three-story" * residences. The marked Converse bungalow and the marked three-story house have been mentioned; in each, the name is printed on the front border of the orange-and-green rug (which I take to be a Navajo). The other houses are unmarked, but if they are not Converse, they are probably Cass, of Athol, Massachusetts, a town about fifteen miles from

---

* I am indebted to the McClintocks' fascinating and extensive account of this beginning in *Toys in America*.

† The catalogue illustration is reproduced through the courtesy of Louis H. Hertz.

‡ Shown through the courtesy of Mrs. Blair Whitton. The house, with a first story of stone, and an upper one of brick, has its name (à la Bliss) on the door, along with a model number.

* The third or attic story is sham.

(253)

HISTORIC PRESERVATION IN MINIATURE: FACTORY-MADE BUILDINGS

Winchendon. There appears to have been a great deal of exchange (swapping parts, etc.) between the neighboring firms, and in the later catalogues, identical toys were, in a few cases at least, marketed by both.

Two of the houses I believe to be Converse or Cass are printed in red and blue (in contrast to the red-and-brown of the three-story Converse, and the red-and-green with brown pillars of the marked bungalow). One is the small bungalow with the Model T parked in front. The door with its printed oval "glass" bears a close resemblance to the door on the tall house. (The bungalow, 10″ tall to its peak, and on a base 7¾″ by 1″, has red-stained pillars.)*

The unmarked "three-story" house, also printed in red and blue, is clearly related to the red-and-blue bungalow, but is also a tiny version of the marked three-story (10¾″, not including chimney). The proportions and plan are very like. In the marked Converse, identical bespectacled matrons gaze from side windows, clearly minding someone else's business, and a cat peers from the attic. In the small house, a bird in a

Figure 302

* This red-stained wood, used on all three houses, resembles in texture and color the red-stained wood on the Cass grocery. (See Fig. 320)

Figure 303

cage hangs in one front window, and a potted plant blooms in another. The front windows on the marked house are glass, and the door is hinged. The other houses have printed windows and doors, without such luxuries as glass or hinges.

Four models in the "red-and-blue" series were advertised by Butler Brothers in 1912, the largest with "extension roof, veranda, front and side porch, steps [to both porches], and pillars with attic." Since the 1912 catalogue had a number of Cass and Converse toys, this seems further evidence of Converse or Cass manufacture.

It was in the 'twenties and 'thirties that this relationship became most evident. In a 1926 Converse catalogue, there were "Toy Town Bungalows" ("attractively painted in white with green and red trim") very similar to the model in the 1913 catalogue (with white turned pillars rather than squared ones). The identical bungalows were shown in 1929 by Cass! This was also true of the "Stucco doll house" advertised by Converse in 1926.

Among the five houses in our miniature survey, there appeared to be one possible inter-

"COMMERCIAL PROPERTY"

Figure 304

loper. This, which can best be described as an ugly house, has a rather rustic appearance, owing to its brown base color, one which even the red printed "brick," solid green window shades, and door fail to enliven. This is very similar in style and proportions to the marked Converse bungalow. Though it fastens at the side, rather than the front, and has no printed interior, it has a printed brown stone base identical to the base on the red-and-blue bungalow, plus the general styling and proportions of all the bungalows. A "stone" chimney on the side which pierces the roof is similar to the one on the marked Converse. Although the windows on the "brown" house are slightly arched, they have similar latticing and curtains and, of all things, identical shade pulls. After recording these Sherlock Holmesian observations, it was gratifying to look more closely at a vague snapshot from the 1931 Converse catalogue and discover that this was a bungalow in the "Toy Town" series. Ugly though they be, they were evidently popular; a new size was offered in 1931—one of six.

In 1931, Converse brought out "The Realy (sic) Truly Doll House," a toy with a name almost as revolting as Tootsietoy, and one calculated to destroy any child's faith in proper spelling. This house was of fiberboard reinforced with wood (21″ by 12″ by 15″), with four rooms meant to hold "Realy Truly Doll Furniture." The furniture, made of "beautiful mahogany woods, gum and walnut," was of the style known as "over-stuffed." The living-room included a "davenport" and a radio. The house, according to Converse, was "the largest, strongest and most practical doll house ever put out to retail for a dollar."

Converse went out of business in the 'thirties. On a post card one can buy today in the vicinity of Winchendon, "the world's largest rocking horse" is pictured. "Built in 1914," says the legend on the back with strict inaccuracy, "to commemorate the 150th anniversary of M. E. Converse & Son Co., at the time the world's largest toy factory." If this had been true, Converse would also have been America's oldest toy factory! Actually, the horse was built by Converse, manufacturer of many rocking horses, to commemorate the 150th anniversary of the town of Winchendon itself.

Figure 305

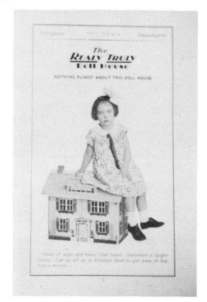

(255)

HISTORIC PRESERVATION IN MINIATURE: FACTORY-MADE BUILDINGS

As recently as 1931, James S. Tippet, writing about "Toys and Toy Makers," referred to Winchendon, Massachusetts, "which has three large factories" as the "Toy Town of the U. S." "In Winchendon," he wrote, "more toys are made than in any other town or city in the whole world. More even than in Nuremberg or Sonneberg in Germany."

By contrast, a wistful sentence in the McClintocks' book* can serve as an epitaph to Converse: "It seems incredible that the largest toy-manufacturing firm in the world could disappear with scarcely a trace in the course of only twenty years, but nothing remains of it except Toy Town Tavern and the heroic rocking horse."

THE RAMSHACKEL† INN OF ZASU PITTS

DATE: CA. 1905
HEIGHT: 38″
WIDTH: 30¾″
DEPTH: 16½″
OWNER: SHELBURNE MUSEUM (SHELBURNE, VERMONT)

Although "refurbished" dolls' houses‡ are outside the scope of this book, "Ramshackel Inn" has such an unusual history, as well as a permanent and important setting (in the Shelburne Museum), that it is offered herewith, accompanied by the few bits of available information.

It is also a footnote to footlight history. The late ZaSu Pitts,* the fluttery comedienne whose helpless expression was familiar to the viewers of more than four hundred films of the 'thirties and 'forties, played with the dolls' house as a child. Since she was born in 1900, perhaps it is fair to assume that the house was given to her between 1905 and 1910. There are two clues to identify the house itself (otherwise thoroughly altered) as one of the commercially made series, believed to be French, available then and into the 'twenties. The first clue, to be found on the sides, consists of the familiar pressed cardboard mullions to be found on the windows of such houses. The second is the steep roof containing the large dormer—of the same proportions of a model in the series. (Figs. 309–10.)

In any case, ZaSu Pitts (née Elza Susan Pitts), was born in Parsons, Kansas, and the house found its way there. In relatively recent years, she gave it to her friend, Electra Havemeyer Webb, Shelburne's founder, who had it "refurbished" in the spirit of "Ramshackle Inn," a Broadway play in which ZaSu Pitts made her theatrical debut in 1944. The tale of a haunted Massachusetts inn became a hit, and ZaSu toured in it in 1944–45.

It is impossible to learn which furniture was original to the house and which was added. Even the obviously antique pieces, the numerous marble-topped tables, washstands, and so forth, may very well have been borrowed from the extensive miniature holdings at Shelburne. The artist at work in the attic, and the bar on the first floor are obvious additions, and the hall is known to be a miniature version of the Ramshackle Inn stage set. There are Pitts memorabilia on the walls of the parlor and bedroom—daguerreotypes of ZaSu Pitts as she appeared in various roles during her long career.

---

* *Toys in America.*

† It is clearly purposeful that "Ramshackel" is spelled in a ramshackle manner on the mammoth dormer, though it was spelled correctly in the title of the play it commemorates.

‡ See "Restoration," pages 351–9.

* ZaSu Pitts died in 1963 and it is no longer possible to learn what the original façade, apparently discarded, was like. The wide edge on the right side of the house suggests that the façade was attached there, and maybe a strip added to cover the hinge marks.

"COMMERCIAL PROPERTY"

Figure 306

HISTORIC PRESERVATION IN MINIATURE: FACTORY-MADE BUILDINGS

SOME FLATS IN PARIS?

DATE: CA. 1910
HEIGHT: 43″
WIDTH: 35″
DEPTH (OF ROOMS): 13½″
OWNERS: MR. AND MRS. ALFRED H. STILES (ILLINOIS)

This fetching house is perhaps the largest and most deluxe model in a commercially made series,* probably from France. It assuredly resembles apartment houses in Paris with flowers blooming from the upper balconies. In the summer of 1971, the writer stayed in such an apartment in the rue de Grenelle with friends who were proud that their flowers had won first prize in a competition in their arrondissement.

Like its full-sized counterpart, the dolls' house has four stories and an elevator to carry the resident dolls to each of them. The elevator, open like the numerous "cages" one still sees frequently in Europe, has a workable door, a seat inside, and a crank to operate it on the wall alongside. The house was purchased, fully furnished, in 1952 from "a little girl who wanted to use the money for a bicycle!" Mr. and Mrs. Stiles were the third owners, and they have made efforts to learn its exact age. Since there was a Marshall Field stamp on the back, they wrote to Field, but learned that the firm's catalogues did not go back far enough to include their treasure. (On the bottom, a number, "T 5508," is separated by a line from the price: "$55.")

It is of interest to compare this dolls' house with one in the collection of Mr. and Mrs. Raymond Knapp which, except for a few minor variations, is identical. The Knapp specimen contains in multiplicity the pressed cardboard panes which, unglazed, are common to the windows of these houses, and may be seen here in a diamond pattern on the doors and on the balcony balustrades. The windows on the Stiles house are of glass and are not divided into panes. Since the doors are not glazed, one wonders if the fragile pressed cardboard gave way at some point, with glass substituted.

On the other hand, the balcony railings are intact and identical to the ones on the Knapp house. On the latter, the front door panes are square, and there are two chimneys, somewhat smaller than the single one here. Both houses have window boxes (as alluded to) across their second- and third-story balconies, well filled with the pretty fabric flowers that invariably bloom on these houses. It seems likely that these two were manufactured in different years, with the variations in commercially made doll buildings which so intrigue laborers in miniature vineyards.

The furniture which came with the Stiles house, most of it German, includes the pressed cardboard variety, white or dark red, that is frequently seen in pre-World War I doll residences. But two items, considerably older than the house, and of unusual interest, were added

Figure 307

Figure 308

* See Fig. 339 for other models.

Figure 309

Figure 310

(259)

HISTORIC PRESERVATION IN MINIATURE: FACTORY-MADE BUILDINGS

Figure 311

A McLOUGHLIN HOUSE WITH A GARDEN

DATE: CA. 1911
HEIGHT: 15″
WIDTH: 15″
DEPTH: 10″
OWNER: THE STRONG MUSEUM (ROCHESTER, NEW YORK)

In July 1971, Miss Catherine Cook, a Massachusetts collector, sent snapshots of a folding McLoughlin house of heavy cardboard. Along with the customary vivid and appealing McLoughlin lithography, this bears a number of other similarities to the folding house described in Fig. 293, but there are also many differences.

The most obvious addition is the architectural exterior on all four sides, and a garden which materializes when the front façade is lowered. To judge by its interior decoration, the house is of later vintage than the other folding houses, with great emphasis on windows—and window seats. Miss Cook's specimen has "McLoughlin, New York" over the door, along with a small company seal, but unfortunately the roof is missing.

by Mrs. Stiles. These, illustrated separately, are the three-inch highchair, which converts into a two-inch rocker,* and the baby carriage, both of die-cast white metal. These are not unusual pieces, but they are documented, having been given to Mrs. Stiles by a ninety-year-old friend of her mother's, whose father ran the Chicago variety store from which they came.

The rare photograph of the store, at 824 Milwaukee Avenue (a practiced eye can detect two Noah's arks in the left-hand window), shows the owner, Mr. Peterson, and his wife, who is holding in her arms Mrs. Stiles' nonagenarian friend—as she looked about 1885—which is also the approximate date of the highchair and carriage. Of course both items may have been manufactured over a period of years, but it is helpful to have this information.

Figure 312

---

* This highchair was no figment of a toymaker's imagination. A similar highchair in full size was found in an antique shop in recent years for the writer's daughter. Of walnut, with cane seat and back, this has a mechanism which raises it to several levels, and it can also be lowered and made to rock like the toy one. It was patented in 1876.

"COMMERCIAL PROPERTY"

Figure 313

Figure 314

appealing invention, by the way, similar to that of an imported wooden cottage related to Fig. 309). The back of Miss Cook's house is also shown, along with an illustration from a Christmas catalogue of "Toys and Games" issued by Woodward & Lothrop, the Washington department store, in 1911—a year which helps to date the house.*

FARM PROPERTY BY CONVERSE

DATE (OF ROOSEVELT): CA. 1907
HEIGHT (OF BOTH BARNS, NOT INCLUDING 3½" CUPOLA, AND 3" FOUNDATION ON ROOSEVELT): 13"
WIDTH (OF BOTH BARNS, INCLUDING EAVES): 19½"
DEPTH (OF BOTH BARNS, INCLUDING EAVES): 10¼"
OWNER: AUTHOR'S COLLECTION

President Teddy Roosevelt seemed to inspire toys. The Teddy Bear, commemorating an incident during a 1902 visit to Mississippi, created a vogue, during the years of his presidency, which has been having an overwhelming revival more than six decades later. One representing his African safari, reproduced by Schoenhut, is the epitome of the toy as a work of art. The "Roosevelt Stock Farm" is a more modest example.

From the manner in which the two barns pictured are printed, their colorings as well as their decoration, one might not suspect that both were manufactured by one maker. It is only when they are examined carefully that it becomes apparent that the "Roosevelt Stock

A few months later, during a visit to the Strong collection, I saw an identical folding house with the roof intact. This is illustrated, with the front open to reveal the garden (an

---

* Since only the box lid of this folding house is shown, it is not possible to know whether the $1 model advertised is identical. The façade of Miss Cook's house is different in only one detail from the one on the lid; there are single rather than double windows at each side of a triple window on the second story. The house was evidently made in more than one size and/or model: Mrs. Henry Erath has a small McLoughlin house of this architectural style which has no garden and is open at the front rather like the earlier one shown in Fig. 293.

HISTORIC PRESERVATION IN MINIATURE: FACTORY-MADE BUILDINGS

Figure 315

Figure 316

Figure 317

Farm," which is not marked, as well as "Red Robin Farm," which is, were both by Converse. Although both were made in several sizes, the two models shown have the identical measurements.* And, as the illustrations suggest, the "Roosevelt" barn shown in the photograph is the same as the one labeled "Red Robin Farm" in the 1913 Converse catalogue illustration.† The windows are of the same latticed design; and there is the same arch, near the roof line, with sliding doors.

Both barns include features advertised by Sears, a year earlier, in 1912, under "Stock Farms," also illustrated by the "Roosevelt" model: "Six stalls with mangers [and] cut-out windows." (These, not visible in the illustrations, are small circular openings, the size of a half dollar, across the back.) There was also the usual "assortment of farm animals and poultry." Although both the 1912 Sears catalogue and the 1913 Converse showed the model with sliding doors, Sears described "swinging" ones. An old

---

* A three-inch foundation printed with windows and stone, on the Roosevelt, is pegged on and came with the "deluxe" model only, as later described.

† The page reproduced through the courtesy of Louis H. Hertz may be compared with barns from Butler Bros., 1910. (Fig. 315)

"COMMERCIAL PROPERTY"

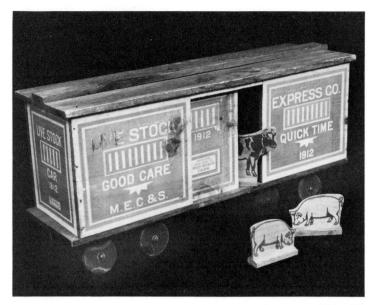

Figure 318

cut, as we know, is not always promptly replaced, and when Converse, in 1913, refers to "New Construction and Colorings on No. 752," and labels the model pictured "752," the illustration clearly lags behind the information.

A catalogue issued by the John M. Smyth Company of Chicago, ca. 1907, shows Roosevelt Stock Farms in two sizes (at 44 cents and 88 cents), and the identical toy is represented.* Only the "metal rooster weather vane" which accompanied the barns a few years later was not to be seen. Since, in 1912, President Teddy Roosevelt had been out of office for a few years, perhaps it was decided to discontinue the "Roosevelt Stock Farm" name, which had been printed in red across the roof, and to make a few alterations in the model.

The 1912 Sears advertisement referred to the "burnt wood effect" in which "all pieces" were finished, a reference to one of the popular minor arts of the period, and there is a subtlety to the shadings in the Roosevelt model which corresponds to this, along with soft colorings, yellows

Figure 319

* The "larger" 88-cent size in the Smyth catalogue appears to be the same as the one in the photograph, although seven stalls (rather than six) are described. The advertisement also mentions "Main building stands over a cellar," rather curious since the barn is the *only* building.

HISTORIC PRESERVATION IN MINIATURE: FACTORY-MADE BUILDINGS

and rusts. The later typical Converse red and dark blue, which is to be found on Converse houses and barns on into the 'twenties, is to be seen on the "Red Robin Farm" barn pictured. In 1920, Sears advertised a stock farm very similar to the latter, in a page of toys frankly labeled Converse. (One wishes all retailers had so identified toy makers, and earlier!) There is no cupola, but there are sliding doors with "Red Robin Farm" printed on the surmounting arch, both doors and arch as in the Roosevelt. There seems to have been some ambivalence, through the years, about hinged versus sliding doors.

Stock farms were also made in several sizes in various years, and it is obvious that, with their innumerable variations, they were popular toys indeed.

So, too, evidently, was the Stock Car, marketed in 1912, as well as later. The 1912 printed on the side is presumably the date of its origin. With "M. E. C. & S" on both front and back, and "Converse" on both ends, no magnifying glass is needed to track down the maker.

A CASS GROCERY

DATE: CA. 1912
HEIGHT (INCLUDING SIGN): 9½"
WIDTH: 7¼"
DEPTH (NOT INCLUDING 3⅛" EXTENSION): 2½"
OWNER: AUTHOR'S COLLECTION

American toy makers of the nineteenth and early twentieth centuries were almost pathologically modest and, except for Bliss, Converse, Schoenhut, and a very few others, did not trouble to put their names on their toys. Therefore, it was gratifying when this Cass grocery loomed on the miniature horizon, offering a name known to collectors, but a toy previously unencountered, at least by this one.

It was also of particular interest to discover that the N. D. Cass Co. of Athol, Massachusetts,

Figure 320

was still in business and, having been established in 1897, celebrated its 75th anniversary in 1972 * (in which year I happened to visit the company).

Unfortunately, of the few catalogues remaining in the firm's files, the earliest is from 1922, and no grocery stores or dolls' houses are shown. Curiously, a lone photograph filed with the lot was of this very grocery—undated and, indeed, unblemished by any identifying word of any kind. The finish of the photograph is of the sheen one sees on some of the old post cards from the second decade of the twentieth century. Armed with this impression, plus information suggested by the vintage of the groceries among the store stock,† I was about to settle for "ca. 1915" as an approximate dating for the store when a muddily printed inch in a Butler Bros.

---

* It is through the great kindness of Mrs. George Glasson of Massachusetts, who also did some preliminary research on my behalf, that I learned of the active status of the factory.

† Old magazines, needless to say, are an excellent source for the dating of such products.

"COMMERCIAL PROPERTY"

reproduction catalogue caught my eye. There, listed under "Toy Grocery Stores," was the very model: and since the catalogue was from 1912, a dating of "ca. 1915" seemed a trifle conservative.*

The small store, which is of heavy cardboard with wooden shelves (a quarter inch thick), includes a counter mounted on a solid block of wood, with a cardboard counter top lithographed to represent graining. The counter is attached to a red-and-black checked floor which may be folded flush with the lower shelf (the counter fits inside), undoubtedly to save space in packaging.

According to the 1912 Butler Bros. catalogue, the stock of the Cass store included "10 facsimile pkgs. staple groceries, some filled." The groceries in this store, and in a larger and more costly "Little Toy Town Grocery Store," † also illustrated in the Butler advertisement, contained "real groceries guaranteed under pure food law." (The pure food law had been passed only six years before, and this was a prompt reference.) "Some" of the packages in the Cass store were filled, according to the advertisement, but the eight surviving staples to be seen in the photograph appear to be dummies, including the square of Fleishmann's Yeast, which is filled with wood, and with the possible exception of the outsize tin of Royal Baking Powder, marked "Free Sample" and still sealed. Empty cardboard containers include Lifebuoy Soap (also marked "Free Sample"), Minute Gelatine, Minute Tapioca, Drake's Cake, and two kinds of Educator crackers—chocolate and oatmeal. (Although I had never heard of this brand, a 1910 periodical lists twenty varieties.)

The fragility of the stores may account for their rarity, but it is also possible that they were manufactured for a relatively short period, although there is a recollection at the factory that these were made from about 1900 to 1920.* In later years, grocery stores were made by Cass in a somewhat different style. In the 1930 catalogue, a line of "Junior National Stores" was advertised. These were made in three sizes, the smallest 13" high and 9" wide, and the largest 17" by 12". All came equipped with a counter, shelves, cash register, scales, canisters, packages, and food platters. "Colored background makes real-looking store," the catalogue boasted, and the largest had an awning.

As for Cass dolls' houses, the close relationship between this firm and neighboring Converse is described in more detail in pages 253–4, in which are cited two instances in which dolls' houses exactly like those advertised by Converse in 1926 were advertised by Cass in 1929. The reverse may also be discovered. In 1930, Cass advertised "Wood houses—stucco exterior, glass windows enclosed in real window casings. Doors are hinged and can be opened and closed." A year later Converse described "solid wood houses" in almost the exact words.

If Cass made dolls' houses earlier than these, they would be among those described in pages 253–4. It seems very possible that the "red-and-blue" series, which bear many resemblances to Converse houses, were made by Cass. The red-stained wood used on this small store is of the exact texture and color of columns and other trim to be found on the houses in the series.

---

* This toy was made for at least three years; it was later discovered in a 1914 Butler Bros. catalogue.

† This contained "16 assorted articles in packages and cans," and was undoubtedly made by Converse of "Toy Town, U.S.A." As has been mentioned, Athol and Winchendon were only a dozen or so miles apart, and Cass and Converse (like other New England toy factories) obviously had a close relationship with parts "swapped," and so forth.

* In a *1918: American Made Toys Trade-Book*, Cass advertised "grocery stores, doll furniture, kitchen cabinets and doll trunks." The kitchen cabinets—a similar line was made by Converse—contained related groceries.

HISTORIC PRESERVATION IN MINIATURE: FACTORY-MADE BUILDINGS

DOROTHY COLEMAN'S DOLLS' HOUSE

DATE: CA. 1914
HEIGHT (INCLUDING "CAPTAIN'S WALK"): 31"
WIDTH (NOT INCLUDING BASE): 21"
DEPTH: 17½"
OWNER: MRS. DOROTHY SMITH COLEMAN (DISTRICT OF COLUMBIA)

Figure 321

When the owner's father bought her this dolls' house in 1914 or '15, undoubtedly he'd have been astonished to know that his daughter (*and* his two granddaughters) would, many years later, be among the great authorities and scholars on the inhabitants of such houses.*

Dorothy Smith Coleman remembers asking her father, a Washington, D. C., builder, for a dolls' house for Christmas, reminding him that he built houses for other people, and would he please build one for her. Mr. Smith didn't build a dolls' house, but he went down to Woodward & Lothrop and bought one of the engaging imported houses that is clearly one of a series (Fig. 287). These were made with infinite variations, but had certain features in common—an unmistakable type of brick paper, doorknob, turned embellishment, etc. This double-decker porch version had not been encountered by me before.

Unfortunately, the brick paper on this house was removed and paint substituted at some point, and two of the rooms have lost their charming dolls' house wallpapers, but the printed paper "parquet" floors are still intact and in almost mint condition along with pretty wallpapers in the two lower rooms.

The furnishings have survived, and it is not surprising that in *this* house the dolls have, too. There is a complete dolls' house family, including twins with glass eyes. The other members of the family have painted eyes, but all are related by bisque, the most customary persuasion of

Figure 322

---
* *The Collector's Encyclopedia of Dolls*, by Dorothy S., Elizabeth A., and Evelyn J. Coleman, Crown, 1968.

"COMMERCIAL PROPERTY"

dolls' house dolls from the 'nineties and on into the 'twenties. One accepts the authoritative statement of the original owner that the girls have Rembrandt hairdos—bangs in front and flowing locks behind. The warmth of the household of which these dolls were a part is suggested by the fact that they have all been carefully re-dressed in Pilgrim costume. Their owner recalls that this was done for a Thanksgiving celebration.

The original furnishings, plus some relatively recent additions provided for Anne and Jane Coleman, are what one might expect at the time, but it is of interest to have them dated so precisely. There is a settee and chairs of light unvarnished wood with dark red "leather" upholstery. Such furniture was advertised by Gebrüder Schneegass in Thuringia in 1914—in a catalogue well timed for this dolls' house. There is an "heirloom" Biedermeier sofa handed down by a friend perhaps four years older who also presented the dining-room furniture. This set must have been made over a span of years inasmuch as it is advertised by Montgomery Ward in 1900. ("Finished in choicest natural oak," says the advertisement, though this is always varnished to a fare-thee-well. This set sold, in 1900, for 75 cents.)

Unusual, because it is relatively recent, but not encountered previously by me, is a bentwood rocker, pure Thonet, in the German pressed maroon cardboard which filled so many dolls' houses of the period with "suites of furniture." Many chairs are to be seen in this material but the rocker is rare. Also uncommon is a glorious metal mantel clock with an Art Nouveau lady swathed in drapery on top, and a gilded urn at each side. (Figs. 321–2)

One "rolled a little ball" and got a prize, Dorothy Coleman recalls, on the Atlantic City boardwalk where she spent Easter holidays with her parents. An inlaid Japanese desk, and a few other wooden pieces from old Japan, were among the prizes. And prized they are still . . .

ALBERT SCHOENHUT'S BUNGALOWS (AND SUCH)

DATE: 1917+
HEIGHT (NOT INCLUDING CHIMNEY): 21"
WIDTH (INCLUDING EAVES): 25"
DEPTH (OVERALL): 26"
OWNER: AUTHOR'S COLLECTION

When, early in the twentieth century, a Mr. Gustav Stickley, "who was largely responsible for the bungalow," * was followed by a Mr. Henry L. Wilson, who called himself "the Bungalow Man," and bungalows burgeoned all over the United States, could Albert Schoenhut be far behind?

The answer, of course, is no. The Philadelphia toy firm, well known for its toy pianos, dolls, and Humpty-Dumpty circuses, had been founded in 1872 by Albert Schoenhut, who had come from Germany after the Civil War. In 1917, a new line was launched, "of Very Artistic, High-Class Doll Houses and Bungalows." It was clearly the bungalows which caught the public fancy in miniature as they had in full size; they are the Schoenhut houses most often found today.

They were made in various sizes in a combination of wood and "strong, heavy fibre board." The 1917 catalogue promised dolls' houses "less expensive than the fine imported doll houses, but at the same time much stronger, more durable and beautiful." Judging by the condition of the example pictured, this promise of durability was kept. As for beauty, it remains in the eye of the beholder.

And inside the small houses, there was much for the beholder to behold. Instead of having

---

* *The Tastemakers* by Russell Lynes, Harper, 1949. Mr. Stickley was editor of *The Craftsman* and in 1909 wrote disparagingly, to say the least, of the American home. "When luxury enters in . . . and a thousand artificial requirements come to be regarded as real needs, the nation is on the brink of degeneration." Mr. Stickley recommended "craftsman homes" which were, in effect, bungalows.

HISTORIC PRESERVATION IN MINIATURE: FACTORY-MADE BUILDINGS

Figure 323

Figure 324

Figure 325

doors from room to room, there was a novel device: "doorways lithographed on the wall, showing a perspective view of another room inside . . . producing the illusion of a house full of fine rooms." In addition to exuberant wallpapers with Christmas-all-year-round borders (the reddest of poinsettias with the greenest of foliage lushly bloom beneath the dining-room ceiling, and a less identifiable floral border of crimson, green, and brown encircles the upper reaches of the parlor), there are alluring glimpses into other chambers we long to enter. Through lithographed portieres on the dining-room wall, we see a lithographed staircase which, in the parlor, is not lithographed at all, but meticulously built of dark varnished wood, and, complete with a well-turned balustrade and a landing, mounts to the second floor. A lithographed fire roars in the fireplace in July as well as December. Also real are the net curtains edged with lace, still crisp at each window.

From a tiled kitchen, there is a glimpse of a butler's pantry with brightly patterned glass in the cabinet doors, and from the bedroom, a view of the bath, doubtless by Crane, with a footed tub, towels neatly hung, and even a bathmat.

The small bungalow shown in the catalogue had just two rooms; the "big" one in the photograph has two at each side, and two upstairs. On both houses the roof with its dormer lifts in the manner of an old phonograph; a metal brace holds it in place. The upstairs ceilings are low—these are indeed bungalows.

If this summary sounds critical, it is not meant to: A bedroom with blue-striped yellow wallpaper bordered with huge red cabbage roses is somehow, in miniature, irresistible.

In the 1917 Schoenhut catalogue,* bungalows

---

* The Schoenhut catalogues were most helpfully made available by Mrs. Blair Whitton.

"COMMERCIAL PROPERTY"

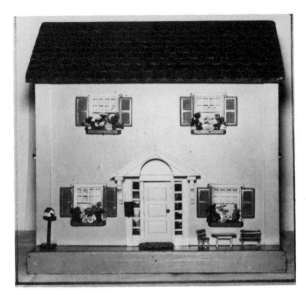

Figure 326

were shown in four sizes, and two-story houses in three. The bungalows consisted of one-, two-, three-, and four-room models. The two-story houses were obtainable with two rooms or five, a jumbo mansion with eight. In 1922, the identical styles were shown, and the success of the line was clearly indicated by the presence of two additional sizes both in bungalows and two-story houses. These, however, were smaller and presumably cheaper than the others.

By 1927, the character of the Schoenhut dolls' house had been considerably modified. The front porches were gone on the two-story houses, although they necessarily remained on the bungalows. Departed from both houses and bungalows was the "fibre board embossed to represent stone wall," and doors and windows were updated to "colonial" by the arrangement of glazing bars in the latter, and by panels surrounded by top and side lights in the former. Shutters were provided for all windows, and window boxes with flowers for most.

A most noticeable addition was the option of "garden, shrubbery, trees and garage with automobile" at an additional cost on both two-story models and bungalows. The most noticeable subtraction were the lithographed perspective views on the interior walls which were replaced by "tinted wall paper." The small colonial shown in the photograph, from the collection of Mrs. Delanne Lopeman Dubois of Texas, is 18″ tall, 17″ wide, and 13″ deep, and contains four rooms.

In 1928, Schoenhut began to manufacture dolls' house furniture. Except for the bathroom pieces, which include a most realistic shower with a curtain on a round rod, and a lavatory with a well-turned pedestal, the furniture is not distinctive. The houses were available furnished and unfurnished, as were the "toy apartment house rooms" which "folded" on hinges and which were added in 1930.

Needless to say, Schoenhut made small buildings other than dolls' houses. A railroad station is shown in Fig. 328. Considerably earlier than the house is the U. S. Armory which came complete with soldiers in 1903. From the advertisement in *Playthings*, it appears to be a more elaborate representation of the species than the Bliss Armory shown in Fig. 279.

Figure 327

(269)

HISTORIC PRESERVATION IN MINIATURE: FACTORY-MADE BUILDINGS

A SCHOENHUT RAILROAD STATION

DATE: CA. 1917
HEIGHT: 13″
WIDTH: 17″
DEPTH: 12″
OWNER: MRS. CHESTER WOMACK (TENNESSEE)

At a Maryland antiques show in late 1971, there was for sale a small building, obviously incomplete. It resembled, with its red pressed cardboard roof and simulated brick walls, the Schoenhut houses in the series introduced in 1917, and it had the metal Schoenhut label on its base. The dealer was hoping for further information about it, and by a coincidence the writer had seen several of these in the Strong collection in Rochester just a few weeks before. There had been so much to see in the vast collection that I hadn't taken notes on these, but recollection made it possible to identify the building for the dealer.

All of the signs were missing on the station for sale, but it was possible to discern on the isinglass windows the fading frosted pattern which suggested ticket "cages." A week or so later I saw the dealer again and she had had "a brainstorm." Since Schoenhut made circuses, she had decided, quite logically, that this was a circus ticket office. (I had not remembered specifically the metal "Ticket Office" and "Telegraph Office" signs over the windows, or I might have mentioned that circuses were unlikely to have had the latter.)*

Another good theory went out the window when, a few days later, a letter arrived from Mrs. Womack in Tennessee describing her Schoenhut station. One loves coincidences, and this one was timely.

Figure 328

These Schoenhut railroad stations had been introduced in 1917 (along with the firm's new line of dolls' houses) for the "many boys" who had "longed to have a good Railroad Station and not a tin contrivance of foreign style."

In the 1917 Schoenhut catalogue, the size was indicated; the station illustrated was of the dimensions of Mrs. Womack's model. By 1922,* there were two smaller sizes available—the celebrated Philadelphia firm had once again correctly gauged a "long-felt want."

GROCERIES AT NUMBERS "6" AND "8"

DATE: CA. 1918
HEIGHT: 17″
WIDTH: 22″
DEPTH: 14″
OWNER: THE STRONG MUSEUM (ROCHESTER, NEW YORK)

During a visit to the Strong collection late in 1971, I was pleased to come upon this grocery and several other shops, clearly of a series, and one not encountered by me before.†

---

* The front and back of the small building are identical, both having the panelled door with brass knob between the ticket windows. There is also a double-size window of isinglass at each end of the station. A bit of the one chimney may be seen at the left.

* We are in the debt of Mrs. Blair Whitton who lent her valuable collection of Schoenhut catalogues.

† One of the small groceries has since been discovered in the Walker Museum (Fairlee, Vermont). This has a flat roof and one entrance door.

"COMMERCIAL PROPERTY"

Figure 329

Unlike most of the imported shops with their open fronts and tops, these have removable roofs, and doll customers may be admitted in the unorthodox manner this convenience permits, as well as through the two glazed doors. It is of interest to observe that the "addresses" on these doors, gilt numerals outlined in black, consist of "6" and "8" on the grocery store illustrated, while a toy shop bears the numeral "5." Probably these numbers afforded the manufacturer a means of identifying the shops in the series, and also provided a touch of realism. (Two similar but smaller grocery stores in the Strong collection were evidently not considered sufficiently important by the maker to warrant numbers.)

The groceries inside the stores are unmistakably American: such staples as Graham Crackers, Kelloggs' Krumbles, ZuZu Ginger Snaps, and Uneeda Biscuits are included in the stock. Therefore one jumps—cautiously—to the conclusion that the stores themselves were made in the United States, especially since both ZuZu Ginger Snaps and Uneeda Biscuits are closely related to dolls from these shores.

In their definitive *Collectors' Encyclopedia of Dolls*, the Colemans† describe the Uneeda Bis-

† Dorothy S., Elizabeth A., and Evelyn J.

cuit Boy (alias the Uneeda Kid) and the ZuZu Kid, two dolls copyrighted and made by the Ideal Toy and Novelty Company of Brooklyn, N. Y. The Uneeda Kid (1916–17), in his yellow sateen coat and hat (representing oilskin) and high black boots, represented (by special arrangement with the National Biscuit Co.) the figure on the Uneeda Biscuit box, and he carried under his arm a miniature box of Uneeda Biscuits. The ZuZu Kid of the same date, dressed as a clown, carried, needless to say, a package of ZuZu Ginger Snaps.

The two packages carried by the "kids" may very well have been identical to the ones in these stores, but it was not at first clear whether the groceries (and the stores) were made earlier than the dolls, nor whether they, like the dolls, were made by the Idèal Toy and Novelty Company (founded in 1902). An inquiry to the Executive Secretary of the company (now the Ideal Toy Corporation), whose catalogues showed no stores, served only to establish the fact that these were not made by Ideal.

However, in the summer of 1972, several months after this summary was (I thought) completed, while browsing in some old F. A. O. Schwarz catalogues, I had the pleasure of coming upon these very stores, in a 1918 issue, somewhat later than I had judged them to be, but logically relating in date to the Uneeda Biscuit Boy and the ZuZu Kid. As usual in shop catalogues, no maker was indicated, but there was size and price information, along with the date.

Two kinds of stores, grocer and toy shops, as in the Strong collection, were available, with one door or two, in various sizes and price ranges. A photograph, somewhat murky but entirely recognizable, is shown of "6" and "8"; a barrel and another object not entirely distinguishable may be seen outside, and groceries are vaguely visible in the window.

Grocery stores "furnished with one door" were advertised in four sizes, beginning at $6.50 for a model 12" by 14" by 10" and ending with a sizeable two-door model, 30″ by 20″ by 17″, for $22.50.

The toy stores, "filled with small toys," were available in two one-door sizes, beginning with a 14″ by 16″ by 12″ at $8.50, and one two-door version, 23″ by 17″ by 15″, at $15.

The shops were also shown in the 1919 catalogue at slightly higher prices. No 1920 catalogue was available, but the shops were not in the 1917, and it seems logical to assume that the rarity of these stores, despite their relatively recently manufacture, may be owing to the likelihood that they were made for only a few years—which if true may relate to their relatively high cost.

An attractive bit of nostalgia may be seen (though not as clearly as might be wished) in the decoration of the glazed upper section of the shop front. A type of decorative translucent paper applied to glass, this once was made as an inexpensive alternative to stained glass, and is to be seen in varying patterns of gold and red on each of these shops. A Baltimore friend remembers hearing this referred to as "window-faning," a term not discoverable in Webster, but I recently came upon the trade name "window-phanie" in a 1910 *Ladies' Home Journal*. There it was described as "a thin translucent material which makes stained glass out of plain glass" and "appropriate for doors, transoms, windows in houses, churches, hotels, etc." Such paper was often used in bathroom windows, and variations may be found for sale today.*

"STOCKBROKERS TUDOR" FROM BEACON, NEW YORK

DATE: LATE 1920'S
HEIGHT: 30″
WIDTH: 56″
DEPTH: 29″
OWNER: MRS. B. R. CAMPBELL (OHIO)

This solid bit of miniature real estate looks straight out of Summit or Scarsdale; if this very

* For such a use in a dolls' house, see page 56–7.

Figure 330

photograph were run in the *Times* on a Sunday, the house undoubtedly would be sold by the following Thursday. Only one thing might give it away: Where is the path to the front door?

Dolls are less demanding than people; no path is needed, especially when a dolls' house is as comfortable as this one appears to be. A classic example of what Osbert Lancaster dubbed "Stockbrokers Tudor," * this dolls' house was learned of when an enterprising reporter for the *Dayton Journal-Herald* phoned from Ohio. Assigned to reply to readers' questions in an "Action Line" column, the reporter was looking for an answer to the following query:

The family of the late S. C. Allyn, former NCR [National Cash Register] president,† donated an elaborate English Tudor dolls' house to the Children's Medical Center which raffled it off this [1971] Christmas. We'd like to know a little of the history of this superb toy. A label says "Toy Crofters, Beacon, N. Y." but we can't locate such a firm. Can you help us?

Word of the "Toy Crofters" was news to me, to put it journalistically, and the reporter thereby added to my sum of knowledge, but unfortu-

* *Here, of All Places*, Houghton Mifflin, 1958.

† One wonders if the Allyn family ever saw the miniature National Cash Register pictured in *A Book of Dolls and Dolls' Houses*).

"COMMERCIAL PROPERTY"

Figure 331

nately, at the time, I was able to add very little to hers. Her quest led to Arizona where a daughter of Mr. Allyn, Mrs. Thomas Sunderland, remembered her pleasure when she received the dolls' house for Christmas in the late 1920's. She thought it might have been ordered from F. A. O. Schwarz in New York, and checking there the *Journal-Herald* reporter learned that "Toy Crofters probably was a small custom manufacturing firm for the store." Since Beacon is not many miles north of New York City, this would have been a convenient source.

Mrs. Sunderland's recollection proved to be accurate. This account had been written when, in August 1972, it became appropriate to re-write it. During a visit to New York, I re-examined the small collection of old Schwarz toy catalogues in the firm's possession.* There, in one of them, unfortunately undated (its cover and several other pages were missing), was the exact duplicate of the Allyn dolls' house! The catalogue was obviously from the late 'twenties,

* Through the courtesy of Mrs. Ashby Giles, manager of the Antique Toy Department.

Figure 332

judging by the children's clothes, other toys, and similar clues.

The description was of an "English half timber design doll house. Very strongly built, stucco effect, 50 inches long, 23 inches deep, 29 inches high.* Rear of house is open to enable a

* These measurements vary slightly from Mrs. Campbell's, but measuring dolls' houses has many pitfalls, and the inclusion or exclusion of eaves, chimneys, and such is at the discretion of the measurer.

(273)

child to play comfortably in each room. House has space for dining-room, living-room, kitchen, 2 bedrooms, bathroom. Each room is electrically illuminated. House is mounted on a table, with metal legs, which are detachable. Unfurnished, $200. Very elaborately furnished, $275."

The new owner of the dolls' house, Mrs. Campbell, has lent color snapshots which show even more vividly the degree of reality the firm achieved. The chimney is built of actual stone set with mortar, or a reasonable facsimile, and the upper section with miniature "bricks." Inasmuch as Mrs. Campbell had referred to the walls inside and out as "of the stucco type" which "feels like the real thing," before I sent her the catalogue description, it is clear that the "Toy Crofters" had succeeded well with their "stucco effect."

As the catalogue indicates, the back of the house is open, and the staircase is the only other unrealistic aspect.* Although upstairs it opens properly to two of the rooms, on the ground floor it is open only to the elements.

Even so, "It is the nearest thing to an actual house I have ever seen!" Mrs. Campbell writes; and a picture of the front door with a miniature *New York Times* furled outside it (in the manner of front-door newspapers everywhere) is the ultimate touch of actuality.

It is of interest to find this additional maker of "custom" dolls' houses from the affluent 'twenties. (The $200 price was not unusual before the crash.) The Tynietoy line of houses and furniture, discussed in pages 324–6, is the best known. During the depression, Delano & Aldrich, a well-known New York architectural firm, put unemployed draftsmen and designers to work building dolls' houses so handsome that even *Art News* applauded them. A decade or so later, in Washington, the late James W. Butcher was building imposing dolls' houses for children of local "notables" which contained much of the careful detail he included in the scale models he built for architects.

Other firms and individual craftsmen were obviously turning out houses in the 'twenties and 'thirties which are still in use, or will be emerging, one by one, from attics in the late 'seventies and 'eighties.

AN ARCADE LAUNDRY ROOM, ETC.

DATE: CA. 1926–1934
HEIGHT (OF ROOM): 10¼"
WIDTH (OF ROOM): 14"
DEPTH: 11"
OWNER: LAWRENCE L. BELLES (ILLINOIS)

In the twenty-first century, one can picture an antique dealer referring to the Thor Washer which is pictured in this miniature laundry room and saying, in all innocence: "Salesman's sample."

He could not much be blamed. Today a great deal of confusion exists about toys which so closely resemble full-sized models that they are often incorrectly so identified. In this laundry room, to add fuel to possible confusion, are

Figure 333

---

* Visible to the sympathetic eye. Allowances are always made by collectors and, presumably, by dolls.

miniature pieces which not only are patterned after full-sized objects, but which bear the actual trade names of the products.

They were, of course, made as toys, by the Arcade Manufacturing Co. of Freeport, Illinois, which, beginning in 1926, made, for perhaps a decade,* cast-iron furniture for all the rooms in a dolls' house, along with houses and/or cardboard backgrounds to contain them, all of which will serve future historians of the household scene with remarkable accuracy. Every room to be found in a substantial residence of the second quarter of the twentieth century was represented: The bathroom set, with fixtures by the ubiquitous Crane, included a *moderne* corner bathtub, and was available in green or white. "The toy living-room," says a 1928 Arcade flyer,† "is so realistic in appearance that it gives one the urge to sit in [sic] the davenport while a musician plays the piano." The piano is a "Cable." No trade name is specified for the secretary, reading table, end table, or other furniture. (The ladderback chair may be seen in Plate 8.) The dining-room set contained a "finely carved Berkey & Gay sideboard and china closet, as well as a table and six chairs. The set is finished in Spanish red trimmed with gold." (Even the name of the color is evocative of the period, during which Hollywood, aflame with Spanish decor, was helping to popularize the style.)

The bedroom furniture was equally specific; all of it, bed, dresser, chair, rocker, and writing desk were by "Simmons," and were available in blue or rose.

In the kitchen, a doll had a choice of gas or electric—*le dernier cri*. The documentation offered to the future is comprehensive: Every

Figure 334

great appliance name, some still in business, was represented. In the electric kitchen, Arcade provided a Hotpoint Stove, Frigidaire, Kohler Electric Sink, Boone Kitchen Cabinet, Boone Table and Chair, and Curtis Dining Alcove. These were finished in ivory. The variants in the gas kitchen were a stove by Roper, a sink by Crane, and a refrigerator by Leonard.*

Because laundry rooms in miniature are not frequently found, Arcade's is illustrated. In addition to the Thor washer—and ironer—there was a "Standard Laundry Tray, Hotpoint Heater and copper-plated boiler." Arcade did not reproduce the gas meter in metal, but this household fixture is commemorated for posterity on the cardboard background, along with the basement windows.

As "exact models," they must have been mutually helpful advertisements both for the full-sized products they imitated and for the toys they were. Presumably the young owner, upon hearing that a new refrigerator was imminent for her family kitchen, would insist that it be the same model as the one in her dolls' house.

---

* Lawrence L. Belles, Director of the Evanston Historical Society, who has generously shared much Arcade information, found the furniture in Arcade catalogues beginning in 1926, and continuing till the mid-'thirties.

† This flyer is undated, but among the wheel toys advertised is Arcade's "new 1928 Ford coupe with rumble seat."

* The Hubley Manufacturing Co., of Lancaster, Pennsylvania, in a 1928 catalogue of Iron and Steel Toys, shows "Eagle" gas ranges and "Alaska" refrigerators almost identical in style to the Arcade models. The ranges were manufactured under patents taken out in 1926 and 1927. Patents had been applied for on the refrigerators and on kitchen "cabinettes." The stoves were made in seven sizes, ranging from (the smallest) $4\frac{1}{2}''$ tall to a model $12\frac{1}{2}''$ tall.

Conversely, the presence of a Frigidaire in her mother's kitchen would guarantee her interest in an identical specimen for her dolls.

Arcade not only supplied cardboard backgrounds for entire sets, but added a line of dolls' houses to contain their furniture. In a 1929 issue of *Child Life*, a proud owner is shown with an Arcade house with six rooms, including a laundry wing. To no one's surprise, other models were available with garages, the better to contain the maker's celebrated cast-iron autos which, like the furniture, are highly "collectable" today.

All of the houses known to me have open fronts with little exterior architectural detail. In a 1932 catalogue, two different models were shown. One, No. 892, described as a "small doll house," sounds rather large, as, of course, it had to be to hold the sizeable pieces of furniture. (The chair shown in Plate 8, maroon with gold trim, is $4\frac{7}{16}$" tall.)* The house is two-and-one-half feet tall, five-and-a-half feet wide, and nineteen-and-a-half inches deep. This six-room house is described as a "stuccoed building, trimmed in brown with a real shingle roof . . . lighted throughout by carefully wired 110-volt lamps." It came with a removable glass front. The house was apparently designed to receive the cardboard backgrounds which accompanied the sets of furniture. (At least at the beginning, these retailed at $7.50 per set. Today individual pieces, sold as "antiques," bring several times that amount. It was also possible to buy pieces of furniture individually.)

Through the kindness of Mr. Belles, Director of the Evanston Historical Society and a toy collector himself, a brief summary of the history of Arcade (in neighboring Freeport, Illinois) was made available. Based on his own research, Mr. Belles found that a "forerunner" of "the Novelty Iron Works was founded in Chicago as early as 1868," but this date is of less interest than 1885 when it went out of business and the Arcade Manufacturing Company was organized. After several moves and vicissitudes, including an 1892 fire in which the firm's building "burned to the ground," a new factory site was purchased and the company began manufacturing products which included "coffee mills . . . hinges, stove pipe dampers, lid lifters, cork extractors . . . and numerous notions and novelties. A large number of children's toys were also made, such as toy coffee mills, miniature trains, swings, doll carriages, etc. Cast iron wheel toys were thought not to have been manufactured before 1920, although other toys were made earlier.

"In 1946, the Arcade business and buildings were bought by the Rockwell Manufacturing Company of Buffalo, New York, and Arcade became a division of this business. Rockwell continued to operate at this location until 1954. . . ."

A SPANISH MANSION BY TOOTSIETOY

DATE: 1930
HEIGHT: 19″
WIDTH: 26″
DEPTH: 19″
OWNER: BERNARD J. MURPHY (ILLINOIS)

Although the Dowst Manufacturing Company of Chicago chose an unnerving name for their line of metal vehicles and dolls' house furniture, nothing could stop Tootsietoys: They were a great success when they were launched in the early 1920's and they are, as the current phrase is, highly "collectable" today.

The furniture became so popular that the next step was obvious—houses to contain it. Dowst brought out various models, beginning in 1925

---

* In addition to the small paper label under the seat, firmly applied and often intact, the name is embossed again on the back of one slat, along with a model number: "741."

"COMMERCIAL PROPERTY"

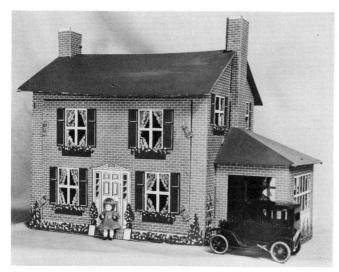

Figure 335

with "a fine brick Colonial home."* In 1930, they introduced a Spanish mansion. The latter undoubtedly was related to the Spanish Colonial revival in California and also, somewhat later, to the rise of Hollywood, where the revival flourished. What went on in Hollywood was noticed throughout the country: Patios appeared in Pennsylvania; stucco haciendas turned up in South Dakota. Northern gales swept iron grille-work balconies intended originally for Southern breezes.

The Tootsietoy mansion "designed by one of America's greatest architects who specializes in the Spanish type of architecture," was made of "heavy book-board and colored in oil colors (washable) in nine colors. . . ." The maker considered its product "the finest house five dollars can buy."

Mr. Murphy's example lacks the tile roof-caps which belong on the pair of belvederes. His house came unfurnished, but "it now abounds with Tootsietoy furniture."

* A similar "containerboard" house, in the writer's collection, with the same four rooms plus kitchen and bath, has the addition of a sunroom wing. It also has lace curtains instead of the "painted ones" of the 1925 house. The overall measurements (including eaves) are: height (including chimneys): 18"; width: 25"; depth: 15". (Fig. 335.)

In 1930, the Spanish mansion was obtainable both furnished and unfurnished.* The catalogue showed the five rooms of furniture "all packed in an attractive shipping carton." (The bathroom and kitchen fittings were fastened to lithographed cardboard linoleum; the other three sets of room furnishings were attached to lithographed Orientals.) The furniture was by no means the same as the line which Tootsietoy had launched seven years earlier. Dowst kept in step with the times and the painted metal manner was there, but the styles were updated; the old-fashioned round dining-room table was gone, the 1930 beds were provided with tin removable spreads, and even the kitchen chairs were re-tooled—a vaguely Windsorish style replacing the 1923 (also vaguely) Queen Anneish one.†

* The floor plan of the mansion was illustrated. A doll might enter the vestibule (3" by 4"), proceed to the hall and turn left to the living-room (9" by 12") in the wing; or right to the dining-room (9" by 14") and go through to the kitchen. Two bedrooms and a bath were upstairs.

† A 1923 ad is illustrated.

Figure 336

HISTORIC PRESERVATION IN MINIATURE: FACTORY-MADE BUILDINGS

Figure 337

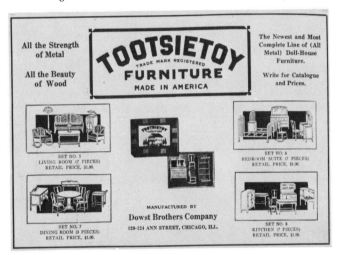

Figure 338

The intriguing story of how Dowst, a firm which began in 1878 as the publishers of a laundrymen's trade journal, got into metal toy-making, has been told more than once, but seems worthy of a brief summary here. When someone suggested that a tiny iron be made as a premium, Sam Dowst adapted the principle of the linotype machine, casting the iron from molten lead instead of type. The miniature irons were a big success, and so were the cuff-links and collar buttons which followed. "But there weren't enough collars in the whole country," the McClintocks wrote.* Dowst began to make Crackerjack prizes (also made in pewter by Peter Pia)† and one thing, as they say, led to another.

Tootsietoy was at its realistic best in kitchens and baths. In 1928, the firm advertised bathrooms "in the new orchid and green finishes" and kitchens in "two new colors, red and green, just like the colorful kitchens so in vogue." As described in toy catalogues of the 'twenties and early 'thirties, as I've noted elsewhere, the line offers enough information about the period to supply a standard essay upon its furnishing and decorating.

The "over-stuffed" living-room suite pictured, probably meant to represent cut velour, is vivid in bright orange and bright green. The grand piano is fitted with a workable top, music rack, and keyboard cover.

"THE INTERNATIONAL STYLE"

DATE: CA. 1930
HEIGHT (NOT INCLUDING CHIMNEY): 21¾"
WIDTH (OF BASE): 32"
DEPTH (OF BASE): 15½"
OWNER: AUTHOR'S COLLECTION

In his beguiling book *The Gingerbread Age* (a must for all collectors of Victorian dolls'

---

* *Toys in America* by Inez and Marshall McClintock, Public Affairs Press, 1961.

† See pages 318–19.

(278)

Figure 339

Figure 340

houses),* John Maass quotes Oscar Wilde: "Nothing is so dangerous as being too modern. One is apt to grow old-fashioned quite suddenly."

The house pictured is a dramatic illustration. With its angular lines and austere practicalities, it is the essence of what T. H. Robsjohn-Gibbings† termed "Machine-for-Living 'Modern,' " and a miniature example, seemingly, of the "International Style." It is also international in the sense that it is European in origin, but crossed the ocean to the United States where an American child stuck pictures cut from 1920's Christmas cards, and even a Campbell Soup kid, to the walls, possibly to render them less austere.

The box-like proportions, stucco walls, and metal railings of this commercially made house do not disguise the fact that it must have been made by the same ingenious manufacturer who turned out the houses in that earlier and more elaborate series which may be seen, for example, in Fig. 309. The curious architectural style of this model, with two front doors on each wing of the projecting central section (the one at left is screened by the angle at which the picture was taken), does not disguise the recognizable pressed cardboard mullions in the glassless windows and doors, nor the familiar embossed metal "butterfly" handles, both inside and out, on doors which may be fastened when the handles are turned. And, still to be found are the lithographed paper floors in the familiar parquet patterns and the attention to detail which was ever the hallmark of this maker (who is believed to be French).

Inside, though the wallpapers are simpler, the International Style ceases—there is no flow of space, no "living area," but only the conventional number of dolls' house rooms, connected to one another by narrow doors. The "attention to detail" has provided a closet under the staircase, a proper one with a landing and a

* Rinehart, 1957.

† *Homes of the Brave* Knopf, 1954.

(279)

HISTORIC PRESERVATION IN MINIATURE: FACTORY-MADE BUILDINGS

"functional" balustrade of solid wood (no balusters to gather dust). But this staircase has a glory of its own, which may be clearly seen on the exterior, as well as inside. This is a "large" stained-glass window (11" by 4⅝"), which illuminates the stairwell with the light which filters through its red and white geometric pattern.* (A friend learned in the ways of Frank Lloyd Wright, whose noble houses perhaps should not be mentioned in the same sentence with this modest effort, tells us that the master often included a stained-glass window even in his most austerely designed structures.)

Curiously, this glass window, and one next to it in the upper hall, are the only two glazed windows in the house which relate to it in style. The others, of the pressed-cardboard variety already alluded to, are, along with their lace curtains, clearly leftovers from the dolls' houses of the past, possibly included as a concession to economy.

The uses of the six conventionally arranged rooms are designated by their wallpapers as well as by the floor coverings. The back of the house has been left open; on the left, the staircase occupies two rooms (up and down) spacious enough to furnish. On the right, tile papers on the walls and tile papers on the floors clearly define the kitchen and bath. In the middle of the house are its two biggest rooms, connected by doors to the others. Along with the pictures stuck to the walls, a green wooden one-piece sink with two drainboards and a gilded faucet, probably by Schoenhut,† lingers in the kitchen; and, by the same maker, a lavatory with a mirrored medicine chest remains in the bathroom.

* This painted pattern was alluringly applied with a stencil.

† Several years ago the writer had the opportunity of acquiring sets of Schoenhut furniture in their original boxes. However, these turned out to be quite undistinguished (rather similar to Strombecker), without the charm of the earlier Schoenhut houses (Fig. 324), and the purchase was resisted. However, this was a matter of personal taste, needless to say, and one is well aware that such furniture is now being collected.

A COMMERCIALLY MADE COLLEEN MOORE CASTLE

DATE: 1934
HEIGHT: 20½"
WIDTH: 29"
DEPTH: 16"
OWNER: BERNARD J. MURPHY (ILLINOIS)

The vast popularity of Colleen Moore's magnificent dolls' castle (p. 189), inspired, in the 1930's, almost a toy industry of its own. There were many Colleen Moore toys manufactured—such items as dolls' house food and dishes and baking sets.

As in all fields of antiques, prices have so mounted in recent years, that such late, commercially made items have become, to use a term of relatively recent vintage, "collectable." This "Colleen Moore Doll House," manufactured by the Rich Toy Company of Clinton, Iowa, and sold by Marshall Field in Chicago in 1934 with Tootsietoy furniture, is an example. The eight-room house is of masonite, brightly painted.

The Colleen Moore dolls' house dolls in their original box are not in scale with the house but were purchased at the same time.

Figure 341

"COMMERCIAL PROPERTY"

Figure 342

Figure 343

(281)

HISTORIC PRESERVATION IN MINIATURE: FACTORY-MADE BUILDINGS

A SERIES OF ENGLISH HOUSES IN AMERICA

Date: mid-nineteenth century
Height (overall): 30½"
Width: 38¼"
Depth (not including 3⅓" base): 14"
Owner: Lady Samuelson (England)

It should be said at once that although the Palladian-windowed house illustrated is in England, its twin resides in Chevy Chase, Maryland. A surprising number of related houses, in what is clearly a series, are to be found in the United States.

This house and its nearly identical twin represent what is perhaps the most splendid model in the series, an assortment of relatively modest dolls' houses made over a period of many years, in many sizes, and with innumerable variations, most probably by a craftsman working at home assisted by members of his family. In *The Cricket on the Hearth*, Dickens described such a home operation: "Caleb and his daughter . . . at work . . . Caleb painting and glazing the four-pair front of a desirable family mansion." Writing in 1960, G. Bernard Hughes* referred to a report by the Jury of the Great Exhibition of 1851 which mentioned "the large number of well-designed and constructed dolls' houses made by English chamber masters," as such home artisans were called. Their productions were sold through jobbers and toy shops, and undoubtedly, over the years, similar houses were built by a succession of such craftsmen.

In a slim 1964 pamphlet, Herbert Hosmer compared four of these houses, including one of his own,† Queen Victoria's large two-room model (at Kensington Palace), a small four-room example in the possession of a Worcester, Massachusetts, collector, and another, the Salisbury dolls' house, which belongs to the Worcester Art Museum and which according to tradition was made, ca. 1810, in New Hampshire! (So much for tradition.) A notable idiosyncrasy, which most of the houses appear to possess in common, is a sort of false front covering a boxlike interior and rising several inches above it (a bit of architectural dishonesty sometimes found on full-sized buildings as well). This hinged façade, opening in one section or two, appears in varying styles with considerable elaboration, often with a balcony of pierced painted tin* or wood, dividing a first story painted to represent brick. Lintels, quoins, and other details are usually painted on, though three-dimensional elements—sills, porches, steps and cornices—are also to be found, in varying combinations, along with the balconies. On the three upper windows of a small house in the writer's collection (18 inches tall behind a façade 4½ inches taller), there are scalloped green awnings, seemingly of cardboard, supported by wooden brackets. (Fig. 348)

The house rests on a flat projecting base found with surprising frequency in its obviously original coat of faded green. Inside, the number of rooms varies with the size of the model; a projecting chimney-piece in each is likely to surround its original black-and-gilt tin grate.

When an illustration of the writer's Palladian-windowed house was published in *International Dolls' House News*, Lady Samuelson wrote Editor Felicity Locke expressing her surprise. Neither she nor the owner of the similar house had ever expected to see another. An exchange of letters followed, and later I was privileged to see the house and the rest of her collection in Sussex. There are only minor variations between the two houses; Lady Samuelson's lower story lacks the marked-off blocks to be found on the "twin"

---

* *Country Life.*

† Very similar to the Henderson house (shown in *English Dolls' Houses of the 18th and 19th Centuries*), to which a third floor was added by a later generation.

* Although a student of these houses questioned the originality of a similar railing on the balcony of another house, I know of several with such railings.

"COMMERCIAL PROPERTY"

Figure 344

Figure 345

house, as well as the applied wooden keystones above the toplight over the door and the windows of the lower floor. (It is possible that the base of her house was repainted at some point in its history, and the keystones, for some reason, removed, but it is also possible that the house was made without them and is possibly a somewhat later model.)

The panes, into which, with white paint, the windows in these houses are invariably divided, have also been obliterated on Lady Samuelson's, but it is miraculous when they survive, as they do on "the twin"; window washing is likely to remove them along with the grime, and achieving clean windows without effacing the panes is a tedious process.

Inside, the only variations between the two houses appear to be in the kitchen and the downstairs hall. In Lady Samuelson's house, there is a small closet at the back of this hall which contains a "W. C.," wedged in, she says, by the small hands of a granddaughter; where, in the "twin," there is only a sham door. There is no projecting chimney-breast on the kitchen in Sussex, as there is on the one in Chevy Chase, and in most of the kitchens in these houses. The fireplace itself differs. The kitchen in Chevy Chase contains the original built-in range with hot water tap, the usual "copper" and wooden sink; and there is also a shelf, and even a roller towel, though unfortunately the dresser is missing.

However, all the important features in the two houses are identical, such as the lovely, curving staircase with its stylishly turned newel posts, the interior doors, and that elegant Palladian exterior. It is interesting to see in a dolls' house of this late date a reappearance of the eighteenth-century classic revival style.

Although Mr. Hughes refers to this type of house as in production by the end of the eighteenth century, it is difficult to date these specifically. Certainly they were made over a period of many years, beginning in the early

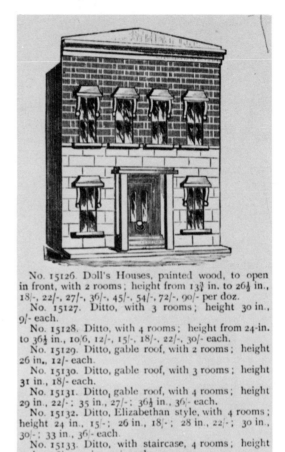

Figure 346

nineteenth century, at latest, and continuing almost to the twentieth. Silber and Fleming, London "Manufacturers, Importers, Warehousemen and Agents," show in their 1876–77, 1879–80, and 1889 catalogues* houses unmistakably of this make. There is the same imitation stonework lower story with imitation brickwork upper story, on a façade projecting well above the boxlike interior. In the 1876–77 model pictured, there is a pierced tin balcony, and on the model illustrated in the two later catalogues, there is a small columned porch framing the

---

* Shown through the kindness of Dorothy Coleman, who furnished the photostats.

"COMMERCIAL PROPERTY"

Figure 347

have a façade identical to Miss Gray's house, ca. 1864, which was also illustrated in the ubiquitous *International Dolls' House News*, and which is in the possession of Mrs. Moira Garland of Surrey, whose aunt's plaything it originally was. Mrs. Garland and I corresponded, but until I saw her house for myself, it was difficult to believe the gable hadn't been a later addition. There was another important variation: although other dimensions were the same, the depth of my house is 9½ inches; the depth of hers is 17 inches.* These additional inches are present with

---

* The height of Mrs. Garland's house is 3 feet and the width 16 inches. "Aunt Mary" was born in 1860, and it is assumed that the house was given her when she was about four.

Figure 348

door. The windows of the latter have the four panes to be found during much of the later Victorian era, rather than the small panes to be seen on earlier models. (These, presumably, are of the same precarious paint which has been mentioned.) The 1879 description was of houses of "Painted wood, to open in front," and there were nine models beginning at twelve pounds and going up to seventy-two pounds (per dozen!), with "plain villas" in five styles, beginning at four pounds six shillings and going up to twenty-two pounds each.

There was a gabled roof model at forty pounds each, and this is of special interest with respect to the three-story house shown nearby. This version (writer's collection) appeared to

(285)

HISTORIC PRESERVATION IN MINIATURE: FACTORY-MADE BUILDINGS

good reason; there are rooms behind those visible in front; doors open to a back staircase, and to a bathroom (most unusual in a house of this age, Mrs. Garland points out). The original tin bath is still nailed to the floor.

The 1879 illustration Silber and Fleming were still reproducing in 1889 was accompanied by a detailed description (here reproduced with the cut). One longs to know what the houses in "Elizabethan style" were like . . .

PART 3

RELATED MATTERS

Furnishings

THE GRADDON FAMILY'S PARLOR SET

DATE: 1850
HEIGHT (OF SIDE CHAIR): 3⅝"
OWNER: AUTHOR'S COLLECTION

Years ago, the parlor set shown in this Victorian doll room came from an antique dealer in Littleton, New Hampshire. It was that rarest of treasures, a set of very old furniture in its original paper-covered wooden box. But if that weren't "paradise enow," a perceptive someone had attached a label inside the lid: "TOY FURNITURE 100 YEARS OLD—1850" was carefully printed. Then, handwritten, perhaps as an afterthought: "In the Graddon family. Please take care of it."

Sufficiently rare without the embellishment of historical data, the "Empire" set is one of two in the writer's collection.* The minuscule "ormolu" mounts on the reddish, polished wood, and the matching gilt metal legs on table, desk, and console are the distinguishing features. (There are also embossed metal shelves on the desk, obscured by the plant in the photograph. These flank a circular mirror the size of a quarter.) The mounts are not "pretend," being applied with infinitesimal brads, and it is a tribute to the respect the set was accorded, as well as to its workmanship, that virtually all of this is intact.

---

* There is a similar set in the first Fanny Hayes dolls' house; found by Mrs. Webb C. Hayes III when she refurnished the empty house.

The set shown in the parlor is upholstered in blue silk, which has worn away in a few spots to reveal a darker blue lining beneath—another instance of the care with which toys of the past were often made. The second set is exquisitely upholstered in a fabric obviously designed especially for miniature chairs and sofas. Birds and bouquets are centered in a formal arrangement on the back and seat of the sofa, with a modified version on the chair-seats. One can recognize the rusty rose, the golden chrysanthemum, and the blue forget-me-not; and a European birdwatcher most probably can identify the birds. (Fig. 349)

The only structural difference in the two sets is a pull-out leaf in the center of the Graddon desk. There is also a green "baize" panel on its writing surface. Neither of these two refinements is to be seen on the more elaborately upholstered set, and perhaps this one is earlier. A three-drawer chest, which came with this second set, and is not duplicated in the Graddon pieces, is illustrated. With its metal knobs and pretend escutcheons, it is an especially engaging piece of miniature fantasy.

The second set was acquired many long years ago, even before the Graddon furniture, from a dealer who logically described it as "Empire," and it was till recently always thought of as French, and so was, of course, the Graddon. However, one was given pause in this thinking in recent years when a chair of the most frequently found "Biedermeier" style was discovered with the same flower-and-bird upholstery. It is possible that the fabric was made in France

RELATED MATTERS

and imported by the maker in Saxony, or even sent to France to be upholstered.*

Two other pieces bearing metal "mounts," in the writer's collection, are mentioned for comparative purposes. One, a chiffonier, and the other, a pier table with mirror,† are of a dark finish with a dark wash over the applied metal. This appears to be glued on rather than mounted and it is possible, since dolls' house furniture was often manufactured in different grades as well as scales, that this type was of a somewhat more modest make, but it is very likely of the same vintage.

The small room in which the Graddon furniture is displayed is 14⅝″ wide, 8¼″ tall, and 9″ deep, and contains its original wallpaper,

*Since these words were written, I have had the pleasure, during a visit to the United States by Vivien Greene, of showing her this furniture, and of having her establish its German origin. The noted English dolls' house historian has found, as has been mentioned elsewhere, early catalogues of the "beautiful Waltershausen" furniture, of which this style with metal mounts is one of innumerable varieties shown.

† If one accepts the nomenclature of full-sized pieces illustrated in 1853 by Blackie and Sons (*The Victorian Cabinet-Maker's Assistant*, Dover Publications, 1970).

Figure 349

Figure 350

with a forceful border of mauve and blue above a pattern featuring dotted stripes and floral sprigs. The net curtains beneath the gilt-paper-over-wood cornices are also original. The carpet is not, having been laid by a tackless, glueless method (see Restoration, page 357) over the original wooden floor, one printed to represent a simple tile pattern. The doll and accessories are considerably later than the furniture.

SAMUEL HERSEY OF HINGHAM

DATE: MID-NINETEENTH CENTURY
HEIGHT: 3¾"
OWNER: AUTHOR'S COLLECTION

It is rare, needless to say, to find full-sized pieces of mid-nineteenth-century furniture with their original makers' labels.* It may be even rarer to find dolls' house furniture of this vintage with labels intact. A label is, after all, more accessible on a table a few inches tall; acrobatics may be necessary to remove one on a full-sized piece. Moreover, the owners of diminutive pieces are young and inquisitive; their penchant for removing, disarranging, and even breaking is well known.

Indeed, it is not easy to find mid-century dolls' house furniture with or without labels. In many long years of collecting, this small card table is perhaps the only piece by Samuel Hersey or any member of the celebrated Hingham group that this collector has found. It is remarkable that its label is still firmly affixed. It was one of the few pieces of early furniture which came with the dolls' house from Somerville, Massachusetts (Fig. 25). It had not travelled far from its South Shore origin in South Hingham.

Inez and Marshall McClintock, who visited the sites of many old toy factories for their book *Toys in America*,† doing invaluable pioneer research, have written in detail of the Tower Toy Guild, which they refer to as "perhaps the earliest toy manufacturing business in the country." They explain that the Guild was "a

* Shop labels, especially such as those of G. A. Schwarz of Philadelphia, are more readily found.

† Public Affairs Press, Washington, D. C., 1961.

Figure 351

Figure 352

business organization of some size rather than an individual producing toys either part or full time."

According to their summary, "The Tower Shop, later the Tower Toy Co., of South Hingham, Massachusetts, was originally a kind of guild, an association of craftsmen in different fields who, by pooling their efforts and products, could offer a more varied and extensive line of toys than any single craftsman."

The man who started this Guild, "probably in the late 1830's," was William S. Tower, "a carpenter who also made wooden toys," and who was once referred to by *Toys and Novelties*, the trade publication, as "the founder of the toy industry in America." Among Tower's associates and successors was a boat builder who made toy boats and, more to the point here, "cabinet-makers who produced dolls' furniture."

There were a number of Herseys making toys in Hingham in the 1850's; Samuel Hersey, a founding member of the Guild, was active from ca. 1855–1880's* as a maker of wooden toys. In the late 1860's, Caleb and Samuel Hersey "also ran a retail toy store."

In any case, to handle this small unpainted card table is a tactile experience. Its concave sides, including the perfectly inset joints, are delicately smooth to the touch. It is unfortunate that half of the once hinged top is missing, but the remaining half still swivels perfectly. The tabletop is 5⅜" wide, and is, like much of the furniture, apparently somewhat larger than an inch-to-a-foot. The McClintocks illustrate a rectangular stool with a Hersey label on the bottom which bears the same words as the one on the table, though in a bolder type. They also illustrate cradles, a washstand, and a rocker made by Samuel Hersey, as well as another group by an unidentified member of the Guild. This includes a round table which has a pedestal base identical in style to the one shown here. These pieces are from an exhibit of the Guild's products at the Old Ordinary in South Hingham.

Figure 353

A SET OF "EARLY AMERICAN" TIN

DATE: MID-NINETEENTH CENTURY
HEIGHT (OF TABLE): 3⅞"
HEIGHT (OF ROOM): 17¾"
WIDTH (OF ROOM): 18¼"
DEPTH (OF ROOM): 18"
OWNER: AUTHOR'S COLLECTION

Because it is Victorian, the japanned tin furniture in this bedroom may not be "early American" by the usual antiquarian standards, but by toy furniture standards, it is early—and rare—indeed.

Hull & Stafford of Clinton, Connecticut, illustrated in one of their early catalogues a bed quite similar to the model to be seen in the photograph. The wire tester is of the same style, but where an elegant gilt finial at the juncture of the tester and post is present on the example in the photograph, the Hull & Stafford post is unadorned.

Another maker of early tin toys, Francis, Field & Francis of Philadelphia,* showed in one of their early catalogues a pedestal table which appears to be similar to the one to be seen in the bedroom,† and it is difficult to know which of the firms made the three tin pieces in this room. As Lawrence B. Romaine commented in *Antiques* more than thirty years ago, "Even the

---

* This does not seem to relate to the McClintocks' statement that Tower started the Guild "probably in the 1830's." Future study may serve to clarify this discrepancy.

* Also known as the Philadelphia Tin Toy Mfg. Co. These three bedroom pieces and the house and furnishings which accompanied them were found in the Philadelphia area; if this company was the maker, the pieces did not travel far.

† And also, more clearly, in the detail picture.

FURNISHINGS

Figure 354

Figure 355

Figure 356

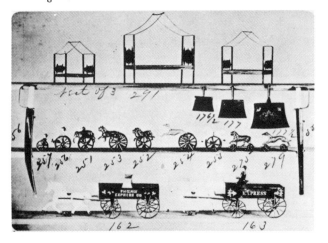

patent laws have not changed the general rule that the product of one man's inventiveness becomes the property of his contemporaries." Mr. Romaine, in an article about American toys after 1850, pointed out that "the best of American toys were patterned after European models." He might have added that American makers also copied one another.

The illustration he reproduced, to be seen herewith, was taken from a rare Hull & Stafford "Photographic Catalogue" which Mr. Romaine dated as ca. 1850–70. The McClintocks, in their invaluable checklist of toy manufacturers,* list Hull & Stafford (originally Hull & Wright) as in business from 1866 until the 1880's. Edith Barenholtz, in an excellent introduction to her superb *The George Brown Toy Sketchbook*, offers a later beginning, referring to the Union Manufacturing Company of Clinton as a predecessor, 1854 to 1869, with Hull & Stafford succeeding Union three years later. Mrs. Barenholtz, who offers a scholarly summary of the American tin toy business during the nineteenth century, suggests another hazard with respect to identifying a maker with any certainty:†

It was a common practice for the larger tin manufacturers to provide parts for toys. Entries in the ledger book of the Union Manufacturing Co. disclose that eighteen shipments, consisting of large quantities of "Large and small horses in parts, Men in parts and Ladies in parts," were made to George Brown (of Stevens & Brown) between the years 1851 and 1861.

She adds that Brown may have in turn supplied clockwork mechanisms, etc. (A late Victorian example of such parts' swapping is referred to on page 254.) Mrs. Barenholtz disclosed a further hazard with respect to identifying such toys as miniature covered pails and toy waiters. Often found in dolls' kitchens, the pail (as well as cups) "were available in every toy line," she

---

* *Toys in America*, Public Affairs Press, 1961.

† The Pyne Press, 1971.

(293)

notes, but adds that they may have been made exclusively by two or three companies. The waiters, miniature stencilled trays which appear now and then in old dolls' houses, "were available from *every* toy manufacturer" (italics mine).

The McClintocks offer 1847 through the 1850's as the dates of Francis, Field & Francis. More recently, Louis H. Hertz* has suggested an even earlier origin for the firm: ". . . the earliest accurate records that have come to light so far show that an extensive tin-toy factory was being operated in Philadelphia by 1838." It seems possible that the furniture, including similar tester beds, may have been manufactured by Francis, Field & Francis, and copied (or adapted) considerably later by Hull & Stafford. Whenever they were made, and whomever they were made by, the three pieces shown, elaborately embossed, and japanned in black and gold, are rare indeed.

Perhaps one day, someone will decipher some old letters and numerals inscribed, with antique flourishes, on the bottom of the bureau and the bed. The ones on the bureau are "E" and "O" and "7" and "5," and they are set down twice, side by side. Beneath the bed, "B E" and "5 0" are inscribed. It is possible that these symbols are the seller's code and markings, but they appear to be applied in black ink or paint, and the owner of the set prefers to think they are the maker's symbols.

The top of the pedestal table, painted to resemble marble, is hinged. When this lift-top was opened, shortly after its purchase many long years ago, the miniature linens were found inside which still, needless to say, remain. The fact that the bureau drawers were also supplied—with "drawers"—and other underclothing, and the bed with bedding, provides, along with the linens, an additional dimension of reality as well as delight.

* *The Toy Collector*, Funk & Wagnalls, 1967.

All the furnishings in this room came with the house,* with the exception of the lamp and ring tree on the bureau, and the floor covering. The scatter rugs, the wallpaper, the draperies, the chandelier with its workable wicks, the Biedermeier chair, the doll (whose undergarments have been mentioned), the cradle,† the chamber set, and all the pictures hanging from "cords" are original.‡ (The "bronze" clock under its glass bell came with the house, but it does not, of course, belong on the bureau, and has been moved since the photograph was made!) A cheval glass standing on the floor at left which cannot be seen clearly, but must be mentioned, is painted black and gold like the three tin pieces, but over a foundation of lead or pewter. Even though it is of a different material, and may have been made elsewhere, it is possible that it was sold with the bed, bureau, and table.

TIN PARLOR FURNITURE FROM NEW ENGLAND

DATE: CA. 1860'S AND LATER
HEIGHT (SIDECHAIR): 4¼"
(ARMCHAIR): 4¾"
OWNER: THE MUSEUM OF THE CITY OF NEW YORK

In its 1872 "Illustrated Price List of Tin, Mechanical and Iron Toys manufactured by the

---

* The Pennsylvania Cupboard House (author's collection) having been described fully in several previous books by the author, is not, except for this bedroom, included in this volume.

† This includes a bisque baby as well as bedding. The latter may furnish a clue to the original ownership of the house and its furnishing; the tiny lace-edged sheet is marked "Bethel," a good Welsh name, but reasonably uncommon. More important, the same name is on the top sheet on the tester bed.

‡ The word "original" has undergone much abuse. Here it is used to suggest that the furniture was in the house when it was found, and was presumably acquired by an early owner. It is a rare dolls' house, however, to which later generations have not made additions.

FURNISHINGS

Figure 358 *Figure 357*

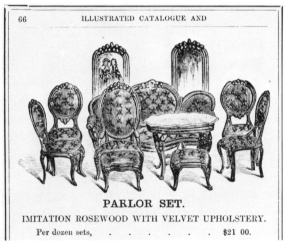

Stevens & Brown Manufacturing Company of Cromwell, Conn. U.S.A.," * The American Toy Company (the firm's warehouse and outlet in New York) included this sentence: "To meet a want long felt we have added to our list a number of Tin Toys expressly for girls, and as samples of this class, would call your attention to the Parlor and Chamber Sets."

Shown here are the "tufted" pressed tin parlor set (with flocked upholstery) as illustrated in the catalogue, and an actual set in the toy collection at the Museum of the City of New York. What is curious is that the "want long felt," it was clear, had been at least partially met by a sofa, table, and armchair identical to the ones illustrated by Stevens & Brown, and it had been met at least three years earlier.* It was in an 1869

* Reprinted for the Antique Toy Collectors of America.

* The Museum of the City of New York dates *its* set in the 1850's.

(295)

RELATED MATTERS

Illustrated Price List that Ellis, Britton & Eaton, at the Vermont Novelty Works, Springfield, Vermont, had pictured these three pieces, and had alluded to such others as sofas, "sitting chairs," "easy chairs," "centre tables, marble top," and "centre tables, plain," all of which appear to correspond to the "imitation rosewood with velvet upholstery" so handsomely depicted by Stevens & Brown.

Who actually manufactured this furniture? One who pounced with delight upon the illustration in Stevens & Brown's 1872 catalogue as "proof" of origin before encountering a similar set, a year later, in Ellis, Britton & Eaton's 1869 list, can only confess that the answer is elusive. The scholarly Colemans, whose *Collector's Encyclopaedia of Dolls** is truly encyclopedic, believe that some of the dolls shown in the same 1869 Ellis, Britton & Eaton catalogue may not have been made in the United States, much less in Vermont.

Even when a toy apparently has been manufactured in the United States, identification may be complicated by the fact that it may be composed partially of parts or material ordered from abroad. In the same way, when it is clearly of American manufacture, one cannot always be positive of the factory, since factories sometimes traded parts, or bought them from each other.† Dating toys is similarly confusing. Apart from the fact that a toy may have been made over a period of years, it is not always possible to count even on a catalogue illustration as evidence inasmuch as sometimes a "cut" was used for years to illustrate an item which may have been modified more than once.

Since Stevens & Brown speak, in 1872, of "adding" the line of tin toys for girls, and since Ellis, Britton & Eaton refer, in 1869, to "a quarrel among the manufacturers of tin toys last season," which resulted in their selling at less than cost (with prices advanced "considerably" this season, though not changing "hereafter"), it seems possible that Ellis, Britton & Eaton was not speaking of itself, and was not the manufacturer,* and it is possible that neither was Stevens & Brown.

Whoever the maker, the marvelous set from the Museum of the City of New York is not only extremely rare, but it has an attractive history, having been played with by "the Quackenbush children, probably in the old farm on Murray Hill." (The vision of a farm on Murray Hill is in itself entrancing.) As the illustrations indicate, the Stevens & Brown and Quackenbush sets have sofas, chairs, ottomans, and oval tables with marble-painted tops in common, but though the Quackenbush set lacks the matching framed mirror and picture to be seen in the catalogue, the Murray Hill children had a four-tiered whatnot and two Gothic clocks. These are also of pressed tin, but may, of course, have been acquired separately. (In the writer's collection is a similar Gothic clock, with imitation wood graining, and this does not appear to be part of the set.)

Sets were somewhat erratically assembled, to judge from the catalogues, and the pieces included must have varied considerably from year to year. It is startling, for instance, to note in "Set No. 501," Stevens & Brown, among "Toy *Parlor* Furniture," a "Toy Duck Iron and Stand" and "Stove No. 116." It is possible that the stove is a parlor type, for heating, but it is difficult to picture a duck iron in the same box with the parlor furniture.

---

* Crown, 1968.

† Mr. William H. Green, head of the Whitney-Reed Chair Co. (see Fig. page 224), believes that most of the printed papers used on the firm's dolls' houses came from the Forbes Lithograf Co. of Boston, and that possibly some came from abroad.

* The Vermont Novelty Works also had offices in New York, and it seems likely that some of the toys may have arrived there from other factories, but that some of the wooden toys were made in Vermont. However, not even all the wooden toys were made there. Hill's Alphabet Blocks and Crandall's Patent Building Blocks were also advertised in Ellis, Britton & Eaton's catalogue, by name.

FURNISHINGS

A quite complete set of this furniture may also be seen in Connecticut, in the extensive Griswold collection in the Lyme Historical Society. Mrs. James Timpson of New Jersey also has two chairs and an ottoman in the "velvet finish," as Ellis, Britton & Eaton refer to it. Her pieces are of a soft rose color, possibly faded from something brighter, she thinks. An ottoman in the writer's collection (the only piece of this parlor set found in more than twenty-five years of collecting) is green-tufted.

It also seems worth noting here that beneath the illustration of the parlor set in the Stevens & Brown catalogue is the office set shown in Fig. 359, and that in both the chamber set and the office set the chairs are identical.

Figure 359

ELLIS, BRITTON & EATON: A TIN "OFFICE SET"

DATE: CA. 1860'S
HEIGHT (OF CHAIR): 4⅛"
OWNER: THE WENHAM MUSEUM (WENHAM, MASSACHUSETTS)

The late Mrs. Frank C. Doble referred to this rare miniature room as a lawyer's office, and I so referred to it in 1965,* pointing out that, as caricatured by such satirists as Daumier and Spy, lawyers usually have their foibles—and their furnishings—magnified rather than diminished.

Mrs. Doble had bought her marvelous "set-piece" intact, and knew nothing of its origin. One pondered the possibility that the furniture, painted to resemble yellow-grained wood, was made in Bavaria, never suspecting that not only the painted desk, stool, table, and chairs were to turn up much closer to home, but that even the iron safe (largely hidden by the desk) was part of a set advertised in 1869 by Ellis, Britton & Eaton, at the Vermont Novelty Works, Springfield, Vermont. The company referred to

* A History of Dolls' Houses.

Figure 360

it as an "office set," and listed the price per set as "$1.38."

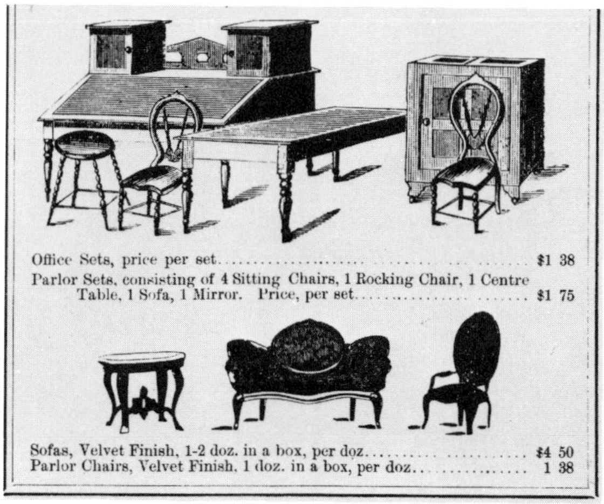

In Figs. 357–8 the parlor furniture shown on the same page of the catalogue may be seen, and in Fig. 361, the chamber set illustrated in the 1872 Stevens & Brown Manufacturing Company's illustrated price list is pictured. The fact that the identical chairs shown in this law office were also part of the chamber set makes the origin of these painted tin pieces less clear-cut than one might suppose.

(297)

RELATED MATTERS

A "CHAMBER SET" FROM CROMWELL, CONNECTICUT

DATE: CA. 1860's
HEIGHT (OF CHAIR): 4⅛"
OWNER: AUTHOR'S COLLECTION

When this rare, painted tin "chamber set," as the maker referred to it in 1872, was bought from a Connecticut doll dealer in relatively recent years, there was no towel rail, and it was real bit of collector's luck to find this missing item at an antique show a year or two later.

It was similarly exciting to discover the chamber set itself pictured in the 1872 illustrated catalogue and price list of the Stevens & Brown Manufacturing Company of Cromwell, Connecticut. The somewhat puzzling fact that identical chairs may be seen as part of an "office set" in the 1869 catalogue of Ellis, Britton & Eaton "at the Vermont Novelty Works, Springfield, Vt." is discussed elsewhere.

The tin is skillfully painted to resemble yellow-grained wood, the top of the lift-top commode is hinged and may be "lifted," and in 1872 it was possible to purchase a dozen sets for $22.50 (wholesale).

FURNITURE FROM MATTHEW VASSAR

DATE: CA. 1861
HEIGHT (OF CHAIR): 2¾"
OWNER: LITCHFIELD HISTORICAL SOCIETY (LITCHFIELD, CONNECTICUT)

Not only does this set of imported furniture have its original box, but it is accompanied by a most illustrious history. It was "brought from Paris about 1861 to Miss Elsworth's mother by Matthew Vassar, the founder of Vassar College." Although it was purchased in France, it is, of course, a set of the celebrated furniture from Waltershausen.

The only fact one might question in the accession book entry is the date. Since 1861 is the year in which "Vassar Female college" was incorporated, it seems a year in which its founder might well have stayed on this side of the ocean.*

The wooden box with its marbled paper covering is almost as intriguing as the name of the purchaser. Pasted to the lid, as the photograph shows, is the label marked "Moebelment B No. 1." Although the sofa illustrated is of a

Figure 361

CHAMBER SET.
OAK GRAINED.
Per dozen sets, ... $22 50.

Figure 362

---

* Since writing these words, I have been informed by a Vassar alumna that Mr. Vassar was a brewer whose contribution to the college was primarily money, and that he traveled a great deal. A jingle much quoted on campus before repeal was: "He made his wealth in beer. But we dare not drink it here."

Figure 363

different style,* and the mirror and low chest are missing, this set is a treasure from several points of view, and one is grateful to the donor who gave it to the Litchfield Historical Society approximately a century after it crossed the ocean.

Also in the Society's possession is a dolls' house which sounds formidable indeed. Although this is not on view, it is a reproduction of a house in Berkeley Square, London, and was made in England in 1929. What is extraordinary about it is that it was built by the cabinetmaker who made Queen Mary's dolls' house.† It was designed by Mrs. Saxbam E. Drury, who gave it as a Christmas present in 1929 to Katryna Hoffman Ray, daughter of the Reverend Randolph Ray, rector of New York's celebrated Little Church around the Corner. The furniture was collected by Mrs. Drury over a two-year period, and those must have been two busy years because the house, which is eight feet by five, contains fourteen rooms.

The Rays had a house in Litchfield, which accounts for the presence of the dolls' house there. The Society also has in its possession a guest book containing the signatures of visitors to Katryna's dolls' house—a thing in the tradition of the great dolls' houses. And it must be hoped that some day this one will be on view again.

DOCUMENTED FURNITURE FROM "THE CAPE"

DATE: 1862
HEIGHT (OF CUPBOARD): 8¾"
OWNER: MRS. JOHN H. GROSSMAN (CONNECTICUT)

The owner bought these five Biedermeier pieces at the auction of the Cobb estate in Cape Cod in June 1970. Each was marked at the bottom, in faded ink, "W. F. C., 1862" or "W. F. Cobb, 1862." Under this, in more recent ink, was "M. F. A. from E. C. A., 1936." A friend of the purchaser's, who lives on the Cape at Dennis, and knows several members of the family, was able to fill in the remarkable history of these much traveled toys.

It is so rarely that even the history of a dolls' house is known, that it is marvelous to have the genealogy of this handsome quintet.

Elizah Cobb, who was born in Brewster, Massachusetts, was a sea captain who sailed

---

* The sofa and chairs are upholstered, in the words of the Director of the Litchfield Historical Society, William L. Warren, "in a white cotton with a moss-like meander of blue."

† *The Book of the Queen's Dolls' House* (Methuen & Co. Ltd., 1924) records that the structure was built by Parnell & Son, Rugby, under the supervision of Robert Hudson. Perhaps the reference is to the Parnell firm.

Figure 364

clipper ships to Europe and around Cape Horn to the East. In 1862 he brought home this furniture for W. F. C.—perhaps a daughter? Somewhat later, Elizah and his family moved to Australia where he established the first overland coach company. The five little pieces of furniture went along. After a number of years, the family became homesick for the Cape, and returned. Elizabeth Cobb Allen, Elizah's granddaughter, gave the furniture to Mildred F. Allen, as marked, in 1936.

There never was a dolls' house, the present owner was told, but there was other similar furniture—chairs, beds, washstands, etc. The sofa is covered in faded rose china silk, but unfortunately the bolsters are missing.

A glass-doored cabinet identical to this one is in the writer's collection,* and it is, of course, of great interest to have a precise date to relate to it. Unfortunately, it is also necessary to remind oneself that similar pieces of Biedermeier furniture† were made over a period of many years, and therefore it is not possible to assign such a positive date even to an identical specimen.

However, there are signs to suggest which of the "rosewood" pieces, with their realistic gold stenciling, are earlier than others. There are indications that those with greater detail, such as the bone embellishment at each side of the drawer on cupboard and console, are earlier than similar pieces which lack such ornament.

On the other hand, as the writer has pointed out elsewhere,* sets have been made at the same time in different qualities. An old catalogue described different finishes in miniature sets of furniture, according to price: "red polished, fine polished, extra fine polished, etc."

Even without a date, one might have judged these "early" for their Gothic styling as well as their superior ornamentation. In any case, these beautiful German pieces were made in at least four scales, of which the Cobb examples are large but not the largest.

A RARE "BIEDERMEIER" PATTERN

DATE: MID-NINETEENTH CENTURY
HEIGHT (OF SIDE CHAIR): APPROXIMATELY 4¼″
OWNER: THE STRONG MUSEUM (ROCHESTER, NEW YORK)

The Bogers† describe Biedermeier as "a potpourri of some of the features, but not the best ones, of Sheraton, Regency, Directoire and especially French Empire," and they define it as "an incongruous assortment of several styles."

In miniature such a potpourri can look marvelous, and it is perhaps for this reason that Vivien Greene‡ chose the term "the dolls' Duncan Phyfe" to indicate the imitation rosewood dolls' house furniture with its gilt stenciling which felicitously furnished so many baby houses of the nineteenth century. Though this term has caught on in numerous dolls' house

---

* *A History of Dolls' Houses*, 1965, p. 129.

† Vivien Greene invented the term "Dolls' Duncan Phyfe" for this furniture, when she wrote about it in *English Dolls' Houses*, and it has received some currency. However, she has been completing a book about this furniture which she sometimes refers to as Waltershausen—the name of the town in which it was manufactured during a period of at least sixty years.

* *A Book of Dolls and Doll Houses*, p. 98.

† *The Dictionary of Antiques and the Decorative Arts*, Scribners, 1957.

‡ *English Dolls' Houses of the 18th and 19th Centuries*.

FURNISHINGS

Figure 365

circles, it has seemed a bit cumbersome, and because the wonderfully diversified furniture it describes came from Germany, Biedermeier seems a term perhaps both more apt as well as terse.

Many of the popular styles in which this furniture is still to be found are to be seen in our illustrations of chairs, but the beautiful parlor set illustrated above is unquestionably rare. Certainly the writer has never seen even a single chair resembling those in this set, although a simple chair with a cane seat in the earlier Biedermeier style may be seen in Plate 9. Mrs. Greene has discovered the origins of this "beautiful Waltershausen" furniture* and has promised a book on the subject, one eagerly awaited by collectors.

The catalogue illustration, taken from an 1886 issue of *The Youth's Companion*, shows us a more conventional "Dolls' Toy Parlor Set" of nine pieces. This includes a sofa, six chairs, a bureau, and "a real marble top table." What is of special interest is the contemporary description: "It is *imitation ebony and gold* upholstered in figured cretonne and is much handsomer than cut shows," (italics mine). Frances Lichten† has

pointed out that rosewood was the most favored of the exotic new types of lumber which replaced "Good old English Oak" and imported mahogany, and that "in mid-Victorian days no well-to-do home was without its parlor suite and piano of this dark red-brown wood" from which pianos and their keys were also made.

Whether one refers to "imitation ebony" or to "imitation rosewood," the gilt patterns, in infinite variations, are to be found both hand-painted (on some of the earlier pieces) and lithographed. The lithography was on "ebony" paper which miraculously adheres.

It seems of particular interest that such designs as the ones to be seen on this exquisite set from the Strong Museum were not pure fantasy, to be found only on dolls' house furniture. Alice Winchester, in *The Antiques Book*, shows a Greek Revival center table made, ca. 1830, in New York, and observes: "The fine stenciled decoration as a substitute for ormolu mounts is an American invention."

AN IRON PARLOR SET: VERMONT, CONNECTICUT, OR OHIO?

DATE (OF PATENT): 1867
HEIGHT (OF CHAIR): 3¾"
    (OF TABLE): 2¾"
    (OF PARLOR): 14½"
OWNER: AUTHOR'S COLLECTION

The iron furniture, photographed in the double drawing-room of the writer's mid-nineteenth-century house from Somerville, Massachusetts, (Fig. 25) has a curious history. It is collector's luck incarnate.

Many years ago, one sofa, three "parlor chairs," one "easy chair," * and one ottoman

---

* See Introduction.

† *Decorative Arts of Victoria's Era*, Scribners, New York, 1950.

* These terms are those given in the price list. Similar ones ("easy chair" for what we call today a gentleman's chair, for instance) are also applied to full-sized furniture illustrated in *The Victorian Cabinet-Maker's Assistant*, op. cit.

Figure 366

were found in an antique shop in upstate New York. They had the familiar "velvet finish," in a faded mauve.

More than a few years later, in New England, the fourth "parlor" chair (these sets were sold with four), a second "easy chair," a second sofa (perfect for such a double drawing-room as this one), a second ottoman, the "center table," and the cheval "mirror" miraculously appeared, exactly as though this set had always been together. Actually, the "velvet" upholstery was more of a bittersweet red, but except for this scarcely noticeable variation, the set dwells harmoniously in the Somerville house.

Most remarkable of all the coincidences associated with the combination is the cheval glass. Years before any of the furniture was found, I bought in Pennsylvania with a group of odd bits, the identical iron-framed mirror without the cheval stand. Although I did not know that the stand was missing, the glass was cracked, and I might have left it there except for the presence of the patent date impressed in the back of the frame: "Feb. 5, 1867." In a field of collecting where patent dates are infrequently found, this was seemingly worth having, if only as a reference. When the second batch of furniture was discovered, the patent date was illegible, this second group having evidently been made years later when the mold had become worn; and the date would have been undecipherable without the assistance of the partial frame found so many years before.

The set of toy parlor furniture in the Stevens & Brown Price List of 1872 was obtainable in "satin finish" as well as in "velvet," and it consisted of a "center table, four parlor chairs, two ottomans, a sofa, and an easy chair." However, Ellis, Britton & Eaton, in Springfield, Vermont, had, in 1869, shown identical furniture, with identical factory numbers—"No. 506" was "velvet finish" and "No. 507" was "satin

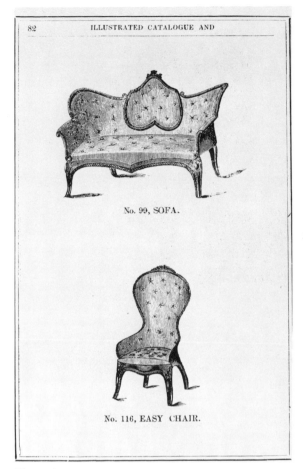

Figure 367

Figure 368

finish." The sets in both finishes were $1.25 each, but the Ellis, Britton & Eaton set included the cheval mirror, and also a rocking chair, both shown separately by Stevens & Brown.

All of this is confusing enough, in terms of identifying the manufacturer, but in the winter of 1972, Margaret Whitton, the astute Connecticut doll dealer, in all innocence compounded this small dilemma when she advertised an iron parlor set, clearly from the same molds, in its original box. To the utter consternation of those of us who keep score, although the style of the lettering was clearly antique, and the box old, the paper label did not read "Stevens & Brown," and it did not read "Ellis, Britton & Eaton." Instead, as the illustration reveals, it read "Toledo Brand Durable Iron and Steel Toys" and "Furniture Set of Five Pieces" and "Patented 1891."

One possible explanation is that the molds had been sold to the Toledo company, who took out a new patent and marketed the five-piece set shown. This, incidentally, is painted green with gilt trim, a combination not previously seen by me. Since such furniture seems reasonably indestructible, one wonders what has become of it all, and one suspects that a relatively small amount was made.* Judging from what little remains, the furniture appears to have had more manufacturers than customers!

The McClintocks' book† lists the Toledo

---

* It may be well to mention that a great deal of it is being made today, evidently from the original molds. Caveat emptor!

† *Toys in America*.

(303)

RELATED MATTERS

Figure 369

Figure 370

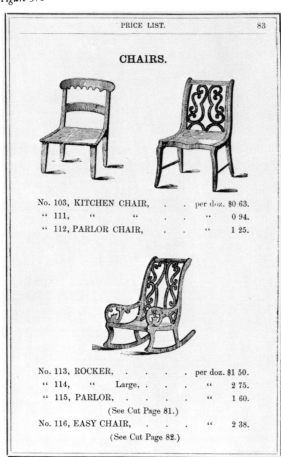

Figure 371

Figure 372

Figure 373

Metal Wheel Co., Toledo, Ohio, as a manufacturer of "wheel goods," having succeeded S. O. Barnum & Co. ("toys, vehicles, also retail shop") in 1885. The Whittons, along with the iron furniture in its original box, also acquired an iron wheel toy in a larger box, and one wonders if these two Toledos are one.

"SHELL PARLOR SUIT"–1876

DATE: 1876
HEIGHT (OF PIANO): 3″
WIDTH (OF PIANO): 6″
OWNER: MRS. M. A. SIMONELLI (NEW JERSEY)

For those of us who find it difficult to identify the numerous kinds of wood to be found in old furniture, the miniature set pictured is likely to be enormously satisfying. It is black walnut; that is to say, it is made of sliced walnuts—not the wood of the tree, but the nuts themselves.

But this astonishing "suit" (sic) has attractions beyond the material of which it is made. Furniture fashioned from walnut shells is not uncommon; similar chairs and tables (though without the red-velvet upholstery to be seen on these) are in this writer's collection. However, until Mrs. Simonelli sent pictures of her extraordinary set, still tied into its original box, I'd always assumed such furniture homemade, to be classed with such hand-crafted fancies as parlor sets of beads or feathers.

It is quite true that the possibility of encountering a square pianoforte made of shells,

RELATED MATTERS

Figure 374

Figure 375

complete with its own paper keyboard and sheet music, had not been dreamed of—and certainly not in its original box with its original label! The label indicates that the set was patented in 1876, so perhaps this was made as a Centennial item. There are eleven pieces tied with twine to a cardboard base which lifts out of the box.

Mrs. Simonelli relates that her son tried playing the music on his violin, but that it did not seem to be identifiable. The title of each of the two pages is illegible, and possibly is meant to be.

AN ALTHOF, BERGMANN BEDROOM

DATE: 1870's +
HEIGHT (OF CHAIR): 3½"
    (OF CHEST): 3½"
OWNER: MRS. JAMES TIMPSON (NEW JERSEY)

More than twenty-five years ago, in the dusty stacks of the Library of Congress, when the writer came upon the 1874 catalogue from which the illustration was taken, old toy catalogues were still being used, presumably, to stoke furnaces; and, for years, finding others proved to be almost an impossibility. The furniture illustrated was, for different reasons, also elusive.

These many years later, it is satisfying to place Mrs. Timpson's rare tin bedroom set in juxtaposition to this illustration, from the 1874 catalogue of Althof, Bergmann & Co. of "30, 32, 34, 36 Park Place at the corner of Church Street in New York City." Although the firm, which according to the McClintocks,* began in 1867, referred to themselves as "importers of toys and fancy goods, china and Bohemian glassware," they also alluded with some pride to "toys of our own manufacture." These included tin toys in the making of which they promised to "pay particular attention to avoid all sharp edges and corners."

They added: "We paint in bright, brilliant colors." Mrs. Timpson's bright, brilliant color is green, as is a lone rungless chair in the writer's collection.† The engaging black-stenciled patterns to be seen on the bed and chest in the

---

* *Toys in America*, op. cit.

† Since these words were written, the bed, chest, and washstand have been "collected."

(306)

FURNISHINGS

Figure 376

catalogue illustration, and on all the pieces in the photograph, were perhaps impractical to illustrate on the minutely drawn chairbacks, but one assumes they were present.

Although the bed in the photograph has curving feet instead of the flat ones in the catalogue, and though there are a few other minor variations such as the backs of the chairs and the number of drawers (four instead of three), perhaps these minor modifications may be accounted for by the fact that the 1874 catalogue and Mrs. Timpson's painted tin bedroom set represent different years of manufacture.

In 1874 such sets, consisting of "bedstead," bureau, washstand, towel stand, four chairs, looking glass, and mantelpiece, were listed (wholesale) at $15 per dozen.

The parlor furniture, reproduced from the same catalogue, looks, except for the mantelpiece, side chairs, and center table, curiously unrelated in style and manufacture. The more elaborate sofa, armchair, oval mirror, and étagère are similar to European pieces, and it seems possible that the manufacturer assembled a combination in this "set."

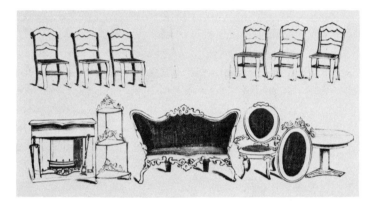

Figure 377

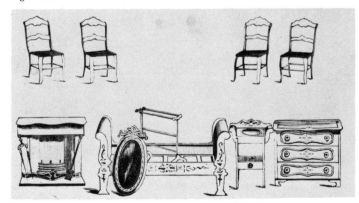

Figure 378

RELATED MATTERS

A FRET-SAWED FURNISHED ROOM

DATE: CA. 1880
HEIGHT: 11½"
    (OF CHAIR): 4¼"
WIDTH: 16¼"
DEPTH: 17"
OWNER: AUTHOR'S COLLECTION

Fret-sawed dolls' house furniture of great delicacy is frequently found in European dolls' houses of the nineteenth century, but the bedroom furniture pictured is peculiarly American. It was made, ca. 1880, from a pattern produced by H. L. Wild of New York.

In a 1953 article about "Fret-Sawed Elegancies," *Spinning Wheel* described the fret-work revival which was initiated in the 'seventies by Mr. Wild who provided patterns (and saws) for making such conceits as steamboats, windmills, and clocks disguised as churches, workshops, and locomotives. He also provided devices for animating these astonishing objects. Since the results are the ultimate in gingerbread ornamentation, the technique was marvelously suited to the making of Victorian dolls' houses and furniture. *Spinning Wheel* reproduced the Wild pattern for a fancy dolls' house, ca. 1880, and ten pieces of bedroom furniture. A few years later, by one of those lovely coincidences collectors cherish, the similar set pictured, plus a room of its own, was found in an Annapolis, Maryland, antique shop. The chest has two drawers instead of three, and the design is not identical, but the forms are the same. Of thin basswood, approximately the thickness of popsicle sticks, the unpainted pieces are fitted together with flat (shaped) pegs and may be readily taken apart for storage. (The brass bail handles on the dresser drawers and the mirror above them were also available at Wild's.)

The room, which was not described in the article, is similarly ingenious. Wooden clips resembling flat, fluted clothespins, and attached in pairs to each of the three walls, slip easily over the base which then resembles wainscot. The fret-sawed window frames, attached in pairs inside and out, with a layer of glass between, have High Victorian lintels and fanciful sash bars. (Those missing in the illustration have since been replaced.) The antique wallpapers on walls and floors are a pleasing supplement.

Figure 379

"MYSTERY" FURNITURE

DATE: CA. 1880'S (?)
HEIGHT (OF CHAIR): 4¼"
    (OF SIDEBOARD): 8"
OWNER: MRS. JAMES TIMPSON (NEW JERSEY)

One should perhaps clarify the fact that the "mystery" houses of Figs. 243–5 are in no way related to the "mystery" furniture herewith, except that (1) the houses were clearly made in the United States, as this furniture may well have been, and (2) the origins of both houses and furniture are, to this writer at least, a mystery.

When Mrs. Timpson sent the picture of her pleasing quintet, she mentioned that it was

Figure 380

different from any she'd seen, and seemed "so like American real furniture" that she was curious to learn what might be known about it. I was obliged to confess ignorance except for ownership of two apparently related sets in two smaller scales, and a similar impression that they might be American. The finish on the wood was aptly described by Mrs. Timpson as "artificially grained to resemble rosewood," and this is so artfully accomplished that one feels obliged to examine it from all angles to avoid the impression that it is veneer. (It is of interest, by the way, to remember that artificial wood graining was a popular decoration for full-sized Victorian furniture.) The shaping of the small pieces is less skillful than the graining, and the result has a somewhat primitive charm suggesting a relatively modest home industry source.

The resemblance between Mrs. Timpson's pieces and the larger of the other two sets may be seen in the chairs; hers, an inch taller, have somewhat more elaborately turned legs and more interesting backs, but the kinship is evident, even to the upholstery. Mrs. Timpson notes that in the cracks where hers is not faded this is "a pretty mauve between rose and lavender," and this color may also be seen on a chair where a sliver of the gilt paper edging (which also trims her furniture) has been lost.

The beading on the pillars of the clock appears to be the same as that of the turned posts on the étagère. In the smallest set, which is more modest in all respects, the plump legs of the sofa (height, 1¾") are identical in shape to those on the big one. The upholstery on the midget set is cotton rather than the velvet of its "betters."

WOOD FURNITURE WITH PAPER UPHOLSTERY

DATE: CA. 1880'S (?)
HEIGHT (OF CHAIR): 3¼"
OWNER: AUTHOR'S COLLECTION

Perhaps it is stretching a point to consider this unassuming set of furniture American made because of the stars-and-stripes "upholstery" on the sofa (Fig. 381). Native wordings and/or decorations often were adopted by exporters, but it seems unlikely that such a patriotic covering of a purely "local" nature would suggest itself to a manufacturer overseas. The simplicity of the

Figure 381

set might also suggest "country furniture" made in the United States.

This remarkable group, in virtually mint condition, was found at an antique show in Washington, D. C., in the 1960's. The neat paper-upholstered seats, a different pattern on each chair over wood, is pristine; evidently this set was never played with. The only other pieces of this furniture I have seen are two worn chairs in Miss Redman's dolls' house. The family friend who presented these to Miss Redman died in 1971 at the age of ninety-five, and the ca. 1880's dating is related to this shred of documentation. (Fig. 118)

FURNITURE BY R. BLISS

DATE (OF PATENT): 1888
HEIGHT (OF TALLEST CHAIR): 5¾"
  (OF ALPHABET CHAIRS): 3¾"
OWNER: AUTHOR'S COLLECTION

The delights of finding dolls' house furnishings in their original boxes have been sufficiently celebrated in these pages. Still, no such discovery was ever more exciting than the one, several years ago, of a set of bedroom furniture with the name "R. Bliss" on the lithographed lid. Without the name, it might have been difficult to think of Bliss as the maker inasmuch as the rather primitive dolls' house shown on said lid bears not the faintest resemblance to a Bliss house.

On the other hand, it might have occurred to a long-time fancier of Bliss houses that Bliss furniture, when and if it did materialize, would be (whatever else) of lithographed-paper-on-wood. Chairs similar to the ones in this set had been in my collection for years, but somehow the Bliss name had never for a moment come into view as the likely manufacturer.

The bed to the marked set was missing, but a bureau, a center table, two side chairs, and a rocker had survived, and in virtually mint condition. Someone had sagely written on the lid, in a corner: "These should be taken care of—they are well on their way to being antiques." (Unfortunately, two additional notations—possibly a name and a date—had been crossed out.)

(310)

FURNISHINGS

Figure 383

Figure 382

This set was in part the key to identifying the Bliss chairs from six different sets.* Another clue, which helped to identify other Bliss sets, and especially, to assist with their dating, was supplied, in 1971, by a perceptive antique dealer from whom I bought by mail a set of furniture similarly made but considerably larger in scale, and in a very different style. How she managed to discover the faint outlines of a patent date, pressed into the cardboard of the small cradle shown, is impressive indeed. Somehow she had, though the date is difficult to locate, even when one knows where to look, and she included it in her advertisement: "June 26, 1888." This astute dealer contributed more than a footnote to Bliss history, withal unknowingly (and I regret having misplaced her name). See Plate 7.

Her discovery set off a search for patent dates on other pieces. Among several possible Bliss sets only one such date was discovered, and, most fortuitously, it was on a drawer in the marked Bliss box, definitely relating, because it was the same 1888 patent date, the two sets. The date was impressed in the cardboard bottom of the lone drawer in the bureau. There were also two patent numbers, a different one on each side of the drawer.*

---

* All have turned legs of unfinished wood, and wooden seats. The two largers chairs have wooden backs. The chair second from right has a rare combination back of wood and cardboard.

* Perhaps one of these patents relates to the construction of the drawers; these are cardboard with wooden fronts, a combination of materials also found on chairs (wood with cardboard backs), store counters, and other pieces. There is a type of metal joint on drawers and boxes which may relate to one of the patent numbers. Reference is made in the Bliss 1901 catalogue to a set of furniture with "the same features of tenoning [as] employed . . . in our other sets."

Figure 384

(311)

Not only did this discovery establish the second set as Bliss, but it also served to identify a third, identical to the second, but smaller in scale, which had been acquired many years before on Maryland's Eastern Shore. These sets are decorated with scenes of children at play, mostly at the seaside, a setting especially beloved of Victorian illustrators. These are lithographed in the familiar Bliss blue, surrounded with red and gold embellishments. The same colors are also to be seen in the Bliss house with the lithographed interior, and on the pieces of alphabet furniture shown in the house.

The furniture in the marked Bliss box is also composed of reds, blues, and golds, but with the emphasis on the reds, and with a very different type of decoration. A bust of a boy or girl, each different, decorates the back of each chair or drawer. On the small dresser that contains the helpfully patent-marked drawer, there is a head of a girl where one might expect a mirror.

The patent date, by the way, is not all the information this small drawer has to offer. Its lithographed front, in the lower-left-hand corner, beneath a small boy in a sailor suit, bears the model number of the set: "494." This corresponds not only, as it should, to the number on

Figure 386

the box lid, but also to Bliss bedroom furniture advertised in the R. Bliss 1901 catalogue and referred to as a "handsome set of chamber furniture . . . 7 pieces."

None of the furniture in the catalogue is illustrated (except for a box lid), but a description is given of the companion parlor furniture (No. 493). "A set of furniture in 9 pieces . . . piano, sofa, table, chairs, etc., handsomely lithographed in neat designs and colorings." Reference was also made to the "strong pasteboard box 10″ by 8¾″ with a beautifully lithographed label," and to the "25¢ size."

All other furniture advertised in the 1901 Bliss catalogue is "ABC furniture." This catalogue was unknown to me in February 1970, when an Ohio collector wrote to ask if I knew anything about such furniture. However, the 1901 catalogue describes several sets. (Again, only the box lid is illustrated.) These include "ABC Parlor Furniture No. 322 . . . adorned with beautiful lithographs embellished with bronze. The chairs, sofa, etc., have the alphabet upon them. 50¢." Bedroom furniture Nos. 298 and 299 included bureaus and commodes with "drawers which open" and "a handsome oval mirror in the bureau . . . the prevailing color

Figure 385

being blue with gold trimmings." These bedroom sets came in a fifty-cent size (in a box 11½" by 9¼"), and a dollar size (box: 16½" by 11½").

Also described was ABC Furniture No. 489: "something beyond the ordinary style lithographed in fine new colors with an embellishment of bronze." This was a parlor set with chairs, table, and sofa.

There are two incomplete sets of alphabet furniture in the writer's collection. The first has the typical Bliss blue decorations of children at play, with the alphabet in red, and all embellished with "bronze." The second set, with the identical shapes, is decorated in a totally different manner, and with very different colors. In a sort of Art Nouveau style, this is a subtle blending of pink, yellow, and pale blue. As the photograph shows, the only representational figures consist of a simple fruit pattern with green foliage and the letters themselves in dark brown. The letters are arranged in the same manner on both sets, and it is quite a project to find the entire alphabet. There are two letters on each chair, and the sofa has the lion's share: On the back are "A" and "B"; on the seat, "C," "D," and "E"; on the arms, "P" and "Q" and, on the sides, "S" and "R." In the more complete set of the two "N" and "O" are missing, and perhaps were on a table since the customary table is missing from the set.

The only model numbers discernible on any of the pieces are a quite unnoticeable "217" on a lithographed strip beneath the keyboard of the piano, and an almost invisible "264" on a similar strip beneath the sofa. The same number is on the sofa in the alphabet set. The discrepancy between the two numbers is difficult to account for; perhaps Bliss stopped making one piano model and substituted a simpler one. (I have seen a snapshot of an ABC piano of more elaboration, with brackets, and so forth, involving additional bits of wood trim. This was lent by Mrs. Cramer, the Ohio collector who was seeking information about her ABC furni-

Figure 387

ture. Her piano, incidentally, did not come with her furniture, but was acquired separately.)

However one accounts for the small discrepancy, the "217" on the piano serves to identify as Bliss still another set of parlor furniture. This beautiful and rare parlor set (color Plate 6) also came in its original box. As the illustration reveals, the "upholstery" is not only of an unusual pattern, but the shapes of the pieces are rare, including chairbacks of both wood and cardboard, and such High Victorian accoutrements as tufted (lithographed paper-on-wood) bolsters on the sofa. The piano is identical in shape to the one in the ABC set just described. The lithography on the front is also the same, but the "W, X, Y" and "Z" on the top of the Art Nouveau piano is not present on this one. However, the number "217," to be found under the keyboard of the ABC piano, may be seen in the identical position here.

This is puzzling inasmuch as here, too, the original lid exists, with the model number "202." What is more important, of course, is the clue the piano and sofa supply to help identify as

Bliss this lovely "Parlor Furniture for Doll House," as its beguilingly lithographed lid describes it. This lid has the same blue and gilt paper rim that is to be found on the Bliss unmarked box lid shown in Fig. 386. It is surprising that I have never seen so much as another chair in this pattern—the set was a premium in an 1895 *Youth's Companion*.*

The unmarked lid is a small tale in itself, and a final fragment in the Bliss furniture puzzle. When the set with the patent-dated cradle was advertised, something—perhaps the fact that the dealer had taken the trouble to notice and advertise the date—caused this collector to express to her an interest in toys in their original boxes. There had been no thought that *this* set might still be in its original box, and, therefore, great was my pleasure and surprise when she replied that she hadn't the box of the set she was mailing, but that she was enclosing the lid!

This extraordinary lid says only "Bedroom Furniture." In view of the multiplicity of beds (and occupants) provided by the artist, even these two words appear unnecessary. In any case, it was not till this summary of the furniture was in progress that a thorough search discovered one other notation on the box lid—a model number. Perhaps the fact that these numerals were printed in gilt on blue, and were seemingly a part of the pattern, had caused them to be elusive for so long. The number is "295," and though it is not to be found in the 1901 catalogue, the lid itself is the 11½" by 16½" ($1) box size advertised there for ABC sets "298" and "299"—numbers, needless to say, not far away from "295."

A study of Bliss dolls' house furniture, one concludes, is best taken up by collectors fond of solving puzzles.

---

* On the lid is a reference to "8 pieces," and, surprisingly, nine are present. The *Companion* advertises and illustrates nine, including the piano, and one suspects that the latter, with its discrepant number, was an addition, at some point, to the original set.

PRE-WORLD WAR I FURNITURE FROM GERMANY

DATE: LATE VICTORIAN TO WORLD WAR I
HEIGHT (OF CHAIR): 4⅛"
OWNER: MRS. PIXIE GROSSMAN PREWITT (CONNECTICUT)

These pieces happen to be from "Englewood," * but their duplicates, with variations, are to be found in many collections of old dolls' houses. They were obviously made over an extended period of time—possibly beginning in the 'nineties and unquestionably extending to 1914 inasmuch as catalogue illustrations of that date are known (and a few are shown).

The bedroom pieces came with the house (Englewood), having been added to it by the second-generation owner, and these include not only the bed and the marble-topped washstand, but the chair with the rush seat. The dining-room pieces were added by Mrs. Prewitt's mother in recent years, and it will be noted that the chairs have plain wooden seats.

This furniture was made by the firm of Gebrüder Schneegass of Waltershausen in Thuringia, whose 1914 catalogue we were permitted to examine through the courtesy of Mrs. Henry Erath of F. A. O. Schwarz. The firm was established in 1845. In the 1914 issue, with entries in French, English, and Spanish as well as German, the identical chair with rush seat may be seen, identified as a "cane chair," and it could be obtained in red, yellow, and white, with or without arms, 9 by 5½ cm. The plain-seated (plank-bottom?) chair is listed under "kitchen-furniture of maple, raw" and the size indicated is 10½ by 6½ cm. The dining-room table, which is translated in the catalogue as a "telescope-table," was available in the same colors, and it is amusing that in the "conditions of sale" the finishes are further described as "polished like mahogany, or in yellow cherry tree. Bedrooms also in white."

* Fig. 79.

7/203 | **8/203**
rot *rouge* red *encarnado* | gelb *jaune* yellow *amarillo*

bestehend aus: 1 Büffet, 1 Ausziehtisch, 1 Serviertisch, 1 Lederbank, 3 Stühlen, 1 Armstuhl, 1 Schaukelstuhl, 1 Büstenständer

composés de: 1 Buffet, 1 Table à coulisses, 1 Table à servir, 1 Banc en cuir, 3 Chaises, 1 Chaise à bras. 1 Fauteuil à bascule, 1 Pilier pour bustes

consisting of: 1 Side-Board, 1 Telescope-Table, 1 Serving-Table, 1 Leather-Bench, 3 Chairs, 1 Arm-Chair, 1 Rocking-Chair, 1 Bust-Stand

compeniéndose de: 1 Buffet, 1 Mesa con prolongación, 1 Mesita, 1 Banco forrado de piel, 3 Sillas, 1 Sillón 1 Mecedora, 1 Columna para figuras

Carton 58×40 cm . . . . p. dz. sh ~~58~~/—
2043/—

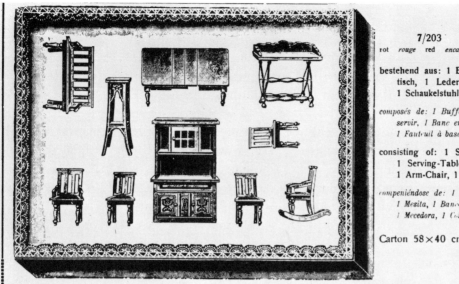

Figure 388

Figure 389

7/105 | **8/105**
rot *rouge* red *encarnado* | gelb *jaune* yellow *amarillo*

bestehend aus: 1 Vertikow, 1 Sofa, 2 Sessel, 4 Stühlen, 1 Schaukelstuhl, 1 Tisch, 1 Schreibtisch, 1 Trumeau, 1 Standuhr, 1 Marmortisch, 1 Büstenständer

composés de: 1 Verticow, 1 Sofa, 2 Fauteuils, 4 Chaises, 1 Fauteuil à bascule, 1 Table, 1 Bureau, 1 Trumeau, 1 Pendule, 1 Table de marbre, 1 Pilier pour bustes

consisting of: 1 Vertikow, 1 Sofa, 1 Arm-Chair, 4 Chairs, 1 Rocking-Chair, 1 Table, 1 Wirting-Table, 1 Trumeau, 1 French-Clock, 1 Marble-Table, 1 Bust-Stand

componiéndose de: 1 Armario para cubierto, 1 Sofá, 2 Sillones, 4 Sillas, 1 Mecedora, 1 Mesa, 1 Mesa de escritorio, 1 Espejo para vestir, 1 Reloj para puesto, 1 Mesa de marmol, 1 Columna para figuras

Carton 63×45 cm . p. dz. sh ~~84~~/—
3513/—

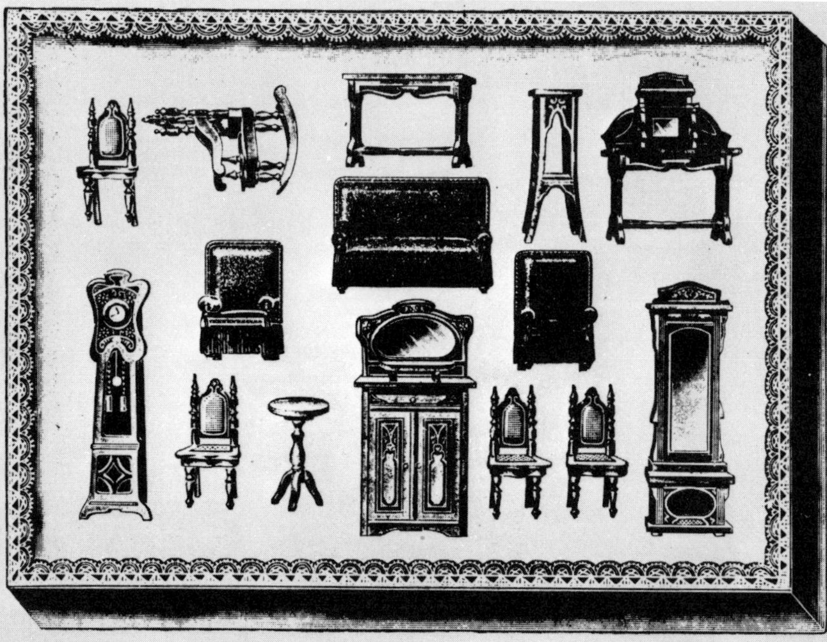

There were also two scales in dining-room tables. One was 7½ by 17 cm. and the other was 8 by 20½ cm.

Although a marble-topped buffet with similar legs is shown in the catalogue, it has a mirrored door above with a small shelf at each side, rather

RELATED MATTERS

than the open shelves between doors as shown here, and there is a drawer between the marble top and the lower doors. There are no finials at the corners. Although two marble-topped washstands are shown, and one, like Mrs. Prewitt's, has a splashboard, they are not of the same style. Nor are any of the beds similar to the one pictured. A mirrored armoire, or wardrobe, however, has similar ornamentation to that of the headboard, with three circular openings rather than one. Unquestionably, all were made by the same firm, but perhaps some items had been discontinued.

All of Mrs. Prewitt's dining-room pieces bear the familiar red-and-white circular labels which G. A. Schwarz, the Philadelphia brother, seemed to place on every piece of dolls' house furniture he sold. These, with the well-known address of 1006 Chestnut Street, appear to have, as I've mentioned elsewhere, great staying power. For years I had been making rather ineffectual efforts to learn how late the firm was at this address, information which would have provided a cut-off date, though it would not, of course, have established how early the furniture was made.

Finally, through the courtesy of Miss Florence Redman, a former Philadelphian, I learned that "Gustavus Schwarz, Toys"* was listed at the Chestnut Street address from 1860 through 1917!

In the summer of 1972, F. A. O. Schwarz's Antique Toy Department had for sale a dolls' house bedroom set of this same Schneegass furniture with the most rare label of the Baltimore Schwarz brother on several of the pieces. This read "Henry Schwarz, Toys, 15 E. Baltimore St., Baltimore." (The set included a bed and washstand similar to the ones in the

* In the Philadelphia City Directory of 1865, it was "Schwarz, Gustavus A., fancy goods"; by 1867, the more familiar "G. A."

Figure 390

(316)

FURNISHINGS

illustration, plus a "dresser" with mirror and a cheval glass.)

Henry Schwarz, at the age of twenty-eight, was the first Schwarz brother to come to the United States. He arrived in New York in 1848 and then moved to Baltimore where he started his business on Howard near Baltimore Street. He moved nearly a quarter of a century later to 15 East Baltimore Street where he continued till his death in 1903. According to *Playthings*, the toy trade magazine, the firm was continued by family members after his death, and a 1904 issue refers to a new address to which the firm moved after the old was "burned out" in a "recent fire." Therefore it was possible to date the bedroom pieces with the label as no later than 1903, although identical ones may well have been made later, and similar* ones were still being advertised in the Schneegass catalogue in 1914.

"NO. 3 BACHELOR'S PRIDE"

DATE: 1898
HEIGHT: 11¾"
WIDTH: 9¾"
OWNERS: JUDGE AND MRS. W. FRANKLIN FARNSWORTH (CALIFORNIA)

Having included in these pages an architect's model, perhaps one may be forgiven for including a patent model, especially one as astonishing as this.

At least this little gem *appears* to be a patent model; it can safely be said that it is "a patent*ed* model," inasmuch as it is labeled on its top,

"No. 3 Bachelor's Pride, Patented Jan. 8, 1898 by L. W. Rhoads, 490 N. Fourth St., San Jose, Cal." Mr. Rhoads' inspiration is well named; except for a roof, this is a complete apartment for the most exacting Edwardian bachelor, and I for one have never before heard (and possibly never may again) of a fireplace which converts to a bed.

Figure 391

Figure 392

---

* Instead of the cut-out circle in the bed, for instance, there was, as the Schneegass catalogue illustration shows, a pressed cardboard embellishment mounted on the frame. Similar ornamentation is usually found on other later pieces, including the cheval glass—described by Schneegass as a "standing-glass." (The translations of some of the terms are not unlike those found in some Japanese instructions for knock-down toys, in recent years!) Catalogue illustrations courtesy F. A. O. Schwarz.

Especially a fireplace with hand-set blue and white simulated tile.

There are drawers for clothing, dishes for eating, and a toilet set (jug, basin, chamber, etc.) in lieu of plumbing.

Although I had hoped to find my way once more* to the terrible reaches of Crystal City, a literally outlandish location encircled by concrete highways rather than crystal, to which the Patent Office was moved in recent years, and to look up this patent, I failed to do so.

Patents, needless to say, have been taken out on many strange objects which have never gone into manufacture. Since this is one of the stranger, it seems unlikely that this curious but undeniably handy combination was ever made in full size, or that this miniature version was intended as a salesman's sample.†

This, however, may be as suitable a place as any to mention the mystification on the part of many collectors—and dealers—with respect to the difference between a salesman's sample, an apprentice piece, and a dolls' house piece. I have alluded to this elsewhere, and must here add the patent model. Salesman's samples are usually larger in scale than dolls' house furnishings, and are relatively rarer, but many toy furnishings, because of impeccable detail, have been mis-called salesman's samples. Elsewhere I have confessed to my own confusion regarding a small brass bed in perfect scale and style, with a removable wire spring of similar perfection. The evidence seemed overwhelming that this small marvel was a salesman's sample till I saw it illustrated in F. A. O. Schwarz's 1913 Christmas Review as "Brass, 6 inches @ 1.25" and "8 inches $1.75" (and in enamel for less!).

PETER PIA COMPLETES A PUZZLE

DATE: 1900
HEIGHT (OF ROOM): 9″
   (OF SIDE CHAIR): 2¾″
WIDTH: 11″
DEPTH: 9½″
OWNER: AUTHOR'S COLLECTION

Many long years ago, the advertisement shown for "Folding Parlor Room, No. 1" was discovered in Montgomery Ward's 1900 catalogue, and the advertisement was duly illustrated in the 1953 and 1965 editions of *A History of Dolls' Houses*.

Perhaps six years ago, this collector walked into an antique shop in New York State, and found the most charming of surprises; one of these rooms, the folding bedroom, rested upon a table, waiting to be "collected." The fragile cardboard walls were intact: The advertisement had promised that the corners, "doubly hinged with book cloth," were "warranted to stay bound." Miraculously, they had.

And every piece of the delicate "white metal furniture" was present and in mint condition—a collector's dream. Fragile prongs still supported the mauve cardboard seats of the rocker and side chair, as well as the card that held the small homemade mattress and pillows on the bed. The easel, with a framed sepia print of cows, continued to work perfectly on its adjustable stand. Most astonishing of all, the "neatly designed mantel fireplace with real glass mirror" still hung by its two prongs to the small openings in the fragile wall.

---

* Of a number of patents ordered on a previous trip, and paid for in advance, most were returned marked "Cancelled" with no explanation—and no refund.

† Mrs. Farnsworth notes that when this piece was pictured in a 1967 issue of *California*, the *Sunday Tribune Home Magazine*, it was referred to as a salesman's sample. She agrees that such a usage was unlikely.

FURNISHINGS

Figure 393

Figure 394

Figure 396

Figure 395

(319)

It seemed miraculous indeed that such a piece of ephemera had survived, and complete with the directions for setting it up. These instructions were themselves of interest inasmuch as they were intended for each of the four rooms in "Dolly's Folding House," and listed the furnishings which belonged in each.* All rooms but the kitchen were supplied with a mirrored mantel and an easel. As an accessory in full-sized houses, the latter had been brought from the artist's studio into the parlor during the "artistic" craze of the 'eighties and 'nineties, and this toy-maker brought it into the dining-room and bedroom as well. Only the kitchen was without this most late-Victorian of accessories. The latter contained a "range," a table, and two chairs, and, according to the directions, a different background: A small hand at the bottom of the instruction sheet admonished: "Be sure you get room with wainscott [sic] for kitchen set No. 4."

The other rooms, to judge by the bedroom, and by Montgomery Ward, are modestly printed with pink floral wallpaper, a beige-patterned carpet, and an assortment of pictures on the walls (more cows above the fireplace) and the lower part of the mantel. The four panes of the arched windows are cut through to the red brick exterior walls.

It is true that the Montgomery Ward illustration shows a table with bulbous legs rather than the settee indicated,† but one is grateful for its presence inasmuch as it helped to fit a final piece into a dolls' house researcher's puzzle. The name Peter F. Pia had been haunting this one's files for a number of years. The McClintocks‡ mentioned that Pia had begun making pewter toys in New York in 1848, and that the business "was still being actively carried on more than a hundred years later." * Because so many tons of "pewter" toys, or "soft-lead" or whatever a layman without a knowledge of metallurgy may choose to call them, were imported from Europe, it was difficult to know which were made by Pia, which by other American makers, and which had come from abroad.

For many years, there has been in the writer's collection a set of metal furniture with scenes of Columbus' arrival in 1492, and I had known that these were made for the Columbian Exposition, but had not known by whom. In the spring of 1972, the 1905 file of *Playthings*,† the toy trade magazine, provided the answer to this, and, in addition, the final piece to the puzzle of the maker of the folding room pictured. The *Playthings* illustration will already have revealed the discovery, but there was the table with the plump legs‡ and four chairs exactly like the ones in the Montgomery Ward advertisement four years earlier. The news columns in early *Playthings* issues were always circumspect about revealing manufacturers' identities, perhaps fearing a flood of requests for equal space from rival makers, but here, as can be seen, the maker's name was prominently mentioned below the illustration, although, if only the surrounding news story were consulted, this was a deep, dark secret.

The latter refers to the "good, steady demand for these sets made up in pewter," and makes note of the "dining-room set" illustrated.

---

* In addition to the easel and mantel, the parlor contained "1 settee, 1 centre table and 2 chairs"; the dining-room, "1 dining-table and 4 chairs"; the bedroom, the pieces to be seen in the photograph.

† Unfortunately, catalogue illustrations and descriptions are not invariably reliable. One other variation should be noted. The bedroom furniture is not "decorated in gold." Perhaps this set dates from a different year.

‡ *Toys in America.*

* However, no firm was listed under the name of Pia in the 1973 New York phone book.

† These early files, as explained elsewhere, had been elusive.

‡ It is hard to believe that this table is made of metal rather than wood. Those legs would have required a great deal of metal unless they were hollow. It seems more likely that the correct table was absent and that the illustrator took a wooden table for his model.

FURNISHINGS

"Each set is packed neatly in a box, 4 inches long by 4 inches wide," the reporter continues. This makes one wonder whether Pia marketed the furniture in the cardboard rooms as well as in boxes, or whether some of it was sold to another manufacturer (or to Montgomery Ward) who added the room-like packaging. *Playthings* also alludes to parlor sets, and mentions that these "vary in the number of pieces, some having four and other larger ones having seven."

In any case, it was gratifying to be able to identify the furniture in the folding room, as well as the perambulators with their parasol tops* and some of Pia's other cherished contributions to the dolls' houses of the past.

Figure 397

THE "ORIENTAL COZY CORNER"

DATE: 1903+
SIZES: 18", 21", AND 24"
MAKER: GEO. H. BUCK (BROOKLYN, N. Y.)

Having insisted for many years that "everything which has ever been made in full size has also been made in miniature," this collector is

*Offered by the Attleboro Premium House as a premium in 1904. (See Fig. 397).

always delighted with each new bit of evidence which appears in support of this theory, but rarely is overwhelmed. The latter state, however, was attained in 1971 when, combing the early files of *Playthings*,* the toy trade publication, the ultimate in dolls' equipment was discovered: Upon a page of the June 1903 issue, there suddenly loomed an advertisement for the "Oriental Cozy Corner." Even the description, "A Real New Bunk for Dolly," could not dim the luster of this discovery.

In a delectable book† which is required reading for all decorators of Victorian dolls' houses, Frances Lichten alludes to "the craze for the Turkish Cozy Corner [which] ran like a forest fire through the homes of the nineties." Tucked into alcoves and under stairs, such nooks were "the ultimate nineteenth century manifestation of the taste for the picturesque. . . . A house was indeed out of date which did not boast at least a modest semblance of this Oriental idea."

A dolls' house of the 'nineties, it is now abundantly clear, was also, if it lacked a Cozy Corner, "indeed out of date." When Geo. H. Buck of Brooklyn, N. Y., began manufacturing his miniature version, there was no excuse.

From "Buck's trimmed metallic Beds" (in ten different sizes), with their bedding and draperies, it had been an easy step to the Cozy Corner.

"Buck's latest invention," the advertisement boasted. "Original and attractive and the only toy cozy corner on the market. Perfect beauties made in three sizes complete with spears, battle axes, fairy lamps, Oriental draperies and sofa cushions." (A later ad also mentions "Turkish emblems.")

*One might have made this discovery a quarter of a century earlier if the Library of Congress run of these invaluable trade journals which were studied at that time had included the first few volumes. One is grateful for the cooperation of Geyer-McAllister Publications in New York who have made these early files available.

†*Decorative Arts of Victoria's Era*, op. cit.

RELATED MATTERS

Figure 398

Additional details were to be found in the news columns of the same *Playthings*: "The framework is of wire in black Venetian iron finish. The whole toy folds up completely and comes packed one in a pasteboard box. Several sizes are made to retail from one dollar upwards."

Only one possibility remains to make a dolls' house researcher's world complete: the finding of one of Mr. Buck's Cozy Corners, complete or partial. Failing that, one battle ax, one fairy lamp, a sofa cushion, or even a fragment of an Oriental drapery would be welcome. Mr. Buck went on advertising his Cozy Corners in *Playthings* till 1905, so presumably a number were sold. Somewhere in some storage trunk, folded flat, between a crazy quilt, perhaps, and a velvet lambrequin, and smelling pungently of moth balls, one of these miniature reminders of Eastern atmosphere for Western households may still lurk.

The printed illustration is vague but convincing, and it is reproduced. An illustration of a full-sized "Oriental Booth" shown in an 1896 issue of *Ladies' Home Journal* may serve to reinforce it.

As a sort of postscript, it seems pertinent to mention that the notion of a *packaged* cozy corner was not limited to miniature versions for the toy trade.

In England, in 1894,* Cozy Corners were advertised by an Oxford Street firm. Godfrey Giles & Co. offered "Our Patent Cozy Corner" which they suggested as "Elegant and Comfortable additions to any room, either with or without recesses, Angles of Staircases, Landings &c." Even if these could not be packed in a pasteboard box per Mr. Buck's, they could "be made to fold into small compass and required no fixing."

* In *The Country Gentleman's Catalogue,* republished by the Garnstone Press, London.

Figure 399

(322)

FURNISHINGS

A PARLOR SET MADE IN CINCINNATI

Date: ca. 1910
Height (of chair): 4"
Owner: author's collection

Nothing is more satisfying to a fanatical collector (a classification this one has never denied) than to find a set of what he collects in its original box. When such a set bears an identifying label, a thing infrequently found on dolls' house furniture, a collection's satisfaction can be quite *annoying*.

Undoubtedly, I have annoyed more than one non-collector with more information than he cared to have about this parlor set, still in its original red pasteboard box with a most informative label on the side. In sizeable print, this reads: "American Toy Furniture," and, in somewhat smaller letters, "One Parlor Set No. 205." Sandwiched between these two lines, in modest type, is the information one always longs for but seldom receives: "Manufactured by STAR NOVELTY WORKS, Cincinnati, Ohio U.S.A."

The chairs and sofa are upholstered in blue cotton in a pleasing shade, and all the pieces are of brightly varnished "dark oak." * The set had been in my possession for years when a two-inch illustration in a 1910–11 R. H. Macy catalogue provided the only missing information—the date of manufacture. In the tiny photograph, the celebrated New York department store advertised the identical parlor furniture, neatly sewn into its 12" by 16" box, and available in the fall of 1910 for 98 cents (plus 40 cents postage). My

* The center table is covered with a "lace" cloth obviously added by the original dolls' housekeeper.

Figure 400

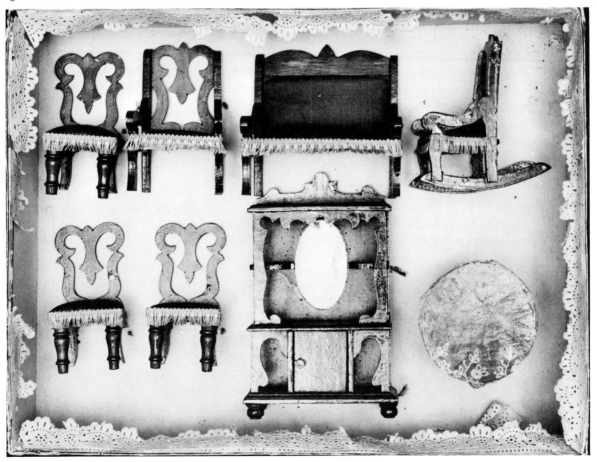

own pieces long ago had been cut from their moorings by the forever anonymous original young owner, and the photograph made it possible to reassemble the furniture in the box exactly as it had been when new. (This discovery meant as much to me as Columbus' meant to him.)

Macy indicated that "other furniture sets, for bedrooms, dining-rooms and parlors," were also available "from . . . 24¢ to $4.49." Presumably these were from other manufacturers as well as Star. In any case, the "No. 205" which identified this parlor set is tantalizing. Collectors are never satisfied, and this one wonders what sets or toys bore the previous 204 numbers.

THE HOUSE OF TYNIETOY

DATE: 1920–50
HEIGHT (OF DESK): 3¾"
    (OF TABLE): 2¾"
WIDTH (OF DESK): 3¾"
    (OF TABLE): 1¾"
OWNER: MRS. JAMES TIMPSON (NEW JERSEY)

"Over ten years ago," a Tynietoy catalogue* of dolls' houses and dolls' house furniture begins, "two women, both lovers of antique colonial furniture, saw an opportunity to popularize its beauty by making artistically perfect, made-to-scale dolls' furniture. Equipped with a

* Lent by, with illustrations reproduced through the courtesy of, Mrs. Preston Weatherred of Texas.

child's circular saw, they opened a tiny shop in the tiniest state in the Union."

Although the catalogue is undated, it is evidently ca. 1930,* inasmuch as it was in a 1920 issue that *Playthings* described the "Toy Furniture Shop" in Providence, Rhode Island, as "an innovation," and referred to the "exhibit and sale" of colonial dolls' houses and furniture, which was to be seen "any day from 10 to 6 in the Handicrafts Club at 227 Benefit Street." Ten years later, according to the catalogue, there were "fifty expert craftsmen making Tynietoys." The firm was still in business as late as 1950.

As early as 1923, the venture was well established. In that year, *House Beautiful* described two furniture collections in Providence "just across the street from each other . . . one noted the country over for its priceless examples of seventeenth century cabinet making . . . the other [the Toy Furniture Shop] . . . becoming almost as well known" for reproductions ("many of its best pieces") which it owed "to the great collection across the way."

The two ladies who launched this highly popular line (highly popular while it was being made, and highly "collectable" today) were Mrs. Marion I. Perkins and Miss Amy Vernon II, referred to in 1920 as the "promoters of the shop." An additional role was credited to Mrs. Perkins: "The colonial dolls' house is an exact

* Since writing these words, I have discovered, on a wholesale price list which came with the catalogue, "Terms: 2/10/30 F.O.B. Factory."

Figure 401

FURNISHINGS

reproduction of an old New England Colonial house and the miniature articles of furniture designed by Miss [sic] Perkins for the tiny rooms are exact reproductions of fine old colonial furniture."

In 1920, the "tiny high post beds, chests of drawers," and the "real rush bottom Colonial chairs" were painted in any color desired," and the beds had curtains to harmonize. Mrs. Timpson's charming "18th century" work table (with "old fashioned silk bag" beneath) and her secretary (both shown in the photograph) may be of later vintage, but in the 1923 *House Beautiful*, many of the familiar groupings were to be seen. The firm catalogue referred to reproductions of Hepplewhite, Sheraton, Chippendale, and other early American designed furniture. It is hard to believe that knife urns (in the writer's collection) complete with knives, 1750 style, and available in mahogany or maple finish, were, in 1930, $1.50 the pair.

Especially in view of its quality, the furniture was remarkably inexpensive. Pieces could be bought both individually and in "suites." In the 1930 catalogue, an "Empire Sleigh Bedroom" with bed, bureau, and chair was available for $6.35 in green or yellow, and for $6.55 in mahogany! (The 20 cent difference is difficult to account for.) In 1925, "complete furnishings for the library" were advertised (12 pieces) for $21. This included a pair of Georgian bookcases, listed at $2.75 each, a Colonial looking glass ($1), and a table lamp with decorated parchment shade (75 cents). "All furniture," said the advertisement, was "Southern mahogany finish —metal parts of solid brass exquisitely fashioned. Doors and drawers open and shut."

The furniture in a 1950 Tynietoy list is individually priced, and many pieces cost little more than they did in 1930.

Because there are many intriguing pieces, it is impossible to do the collection justice in a brief summary. The historic furnishings include a "tilt stand, round, mahogany finish; copy of one from which George Washington had tea," and a square piano in "light mahogany finish" which is a reproduction of "the first piano imported to America by John Jacob Astor."

Painted Tynietoy furniture in pink or pale green, including a cheval mirror (left rear), a poster bed, and several styles of chairs may be seen in the nursery. The same bed, two-drawer chest, and rocker were shown in F. A. O. Schwarz's 1923 catalogue.

It is of interest that the iron refrigerator marked "Alaska," part of the Tynietoy kitchen, was made by Hubley. Of course, many accessories, including an oil "Perfection" heater

Figure 402

RELATED MATTERS

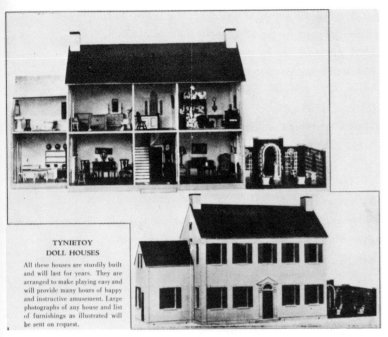

Figure 403

(sold in 1930 with furnishings for "Maid's bedroom"), were not made by Tynietoy.

Of special note is a black metal "French" phone, in the writer's collection, which is marked Tootsietoy and has attached, by a cord, a small phone book marked Tynietoys on the back and, on the front, "Telephone Book. Fall, Winter, Spring, Summer." Inside, phone numbers and an address are printed: "Toy Furniture Retail Department, 44 College Street" * on the first page; and "Toy Manufacturers Toy Furniture Shop, 31 Market Square," on the last. There are also pages headed "Gift Shops," "Wholesale Gifts," and "Wood Workers" at one or the other of these two addresses. The phone is too large for either Tynietoy or Tootsietoy furniture, but the phone book is in perfect scale.

Tynietoy dolls' houses were available in various architectural styles, and were considerably more costly than the furnishings. Even by today's standards they were not inexpensive. The "colonial mansion," which was called a manor

* In the 1950 price list, only a Post Office Box number is given as Tynietoy's address.

house in 1923, was listed *wholesale* in 1930 for $145, without garden, $170 with garden. (*Furnished* with garden, it was $267; and the sum for the contents, just under $100, would be a bargain today, to say the least.) Actually, the mansion would be considerably more costly today, if anyone were to attempt to reproduce it. Six feet, two inches wide (2'8" tall and 1'5½" deep), this contained nine rooms, three halls, and a pantry, and, as they say, listen to this:

House painted white with green shutters, gambrel roof. French doors opening onto brick terrace with marble curbing, shrubs, sundial and a real fountain. Cornice and baseboard in all rooms. Bonnet top doorcasings on first floor, mahogany stained doors with brass doorknockers. Chair rail and old fashioned scenery (scenic) paper in music room. Palladian window in hall. Windows non-breakable. Balustrade stairway to third floor. Wired for electricity. Front removable, attached with hooks.

And then there was the garden!

Other models available in 1923 were a "Nantucket type with a captain's lookout," "a quaint two-room cottage that should please the very young doll couple," and the manor house ("with eleven rooms, a kitchen wing and a formal garden"). In the 1930 catalogue, in addition to the colonial mansion, there was a New England town house (with a footscraper on the doorstep), and the Nantucket model was still available, along with the two-room cottage which was now referred to as a "South County Farm House." Also for modest budgets, there was a "four-room village house." The five-room Nantucket house came with hollyhocks painted on front and side, a rain barrel and trough, and a ladder "with which to reach [captain's] walk."

It seems worthy of mention that there were other types of toys: An "Old New England Farm," a "Garage with Automobile" (which seems to have been designed to harmonize with any of the houses), and a "Peter Pan Theater."

FURNISHINGS

MINIATURE OBJECTS IN THEIR ORIGINAL BOXES

Owner: Mrs. Blair Whitton (Connecticut)

There are many kinds of collectors, but to those who collect from a historical point of view, nothing is more satisfying than finding objects in their original boxes—or sewn onto their original cards. The ultimate example of the latter is the four-room French house with its original furniture still sewn in (see Fig. 289), but every one of the items illustrated herewith, shown through the courtesy of Mrs. Blair Whitton of Connecticut, is rare indeed.

Even when there is little information, or none, on the container, as in the case of the lovely Bristol* tea set with its original tin tray

* Called opaline in France.

Figure 404

Figure 405

Figure 406

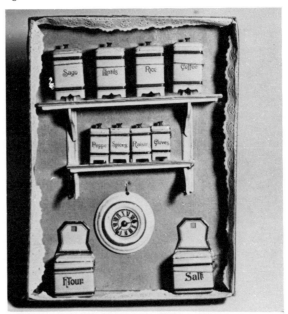

Figure 407

(327)

Figure 408

and oval wooden box, it is gratifying to see the service complete as it appeared at the time of its purchase. But it is even more rewarding when there is information on the box lid, as there is, for instance, on that of the wooden dinner service for six, which not only identifies the contents in several languages, but illustrates the pieces to be found inside the box, and how a table at the time might have appeared—including the length of the cloth and the style of the table itself. Even the candles are present in their sticks, along with one of the vases of flowers. (Probably there were originally two, as in the illustration.) The tureen is 1″ tall; the dinner plate ¾″ in diameter.

Although it is probably later, the tea set on its round tray is even more satisfying to those of us who collect facts as well as objects. Again the tea service is pictured on the lid as it might have appeared on a tea table of its day, with the correct number of pieces exactly represented, but the lid also contains the name of a manufacturer, "A. Lerch" (a starting point for some future researcher), and a country, Germany. Even though the service is known to be German, with "Theezeug" in larger letters than those of the other languages to help substantiate this, it is comforting (as a cup of tea) to have a specific "Made in Germany" spelled out for us. Since, as is well known, such identification was required after 1891, the three words also serve to narrow the range of years during which the set might have been made. Similar tea services were very likely manufactured earlier than 1891, but not this one.

The tin kitchen set, with spice rack, endearing spice tins, flour and salt boxes, and hanging clock, offers printed information only on the tins themselves, and the fact that this information is in English is, of course, no real clue to where the set was made: In addition to the assorted languages with which such items as the tea and dinner sets described above were manufactured for export, others were marketed with one language—that of the country importing the item. With sizeable outlets both in Great Britain *and* the United States, the probable German maker of this kitchen set had enough prospective customers to warrant the making of tins with exclusively English labels. (The clock's diameter is 1¼″.)

Objects sewn into boxes or onto cards are sometimes even more desirable than ones *packed* in their original containers because no doubt can exist about a lost item or a replacement. When they survive, such "mint" groupings serve to identify pieces which may enable their owners to complete partial sets. The "Pets' Cooking Set" is a pleasing example. The skillet in this set is 2¾″ long, and the manufacturer is well known. At least it seems likely that Mr. Ralph Dunn, an English toymaker who, ca. 1909, began advertising a series of "Pets' Stores" as an attempt to make a dent in Germany's monopoly of such toys, is the manufacturer. (In six years, nine million of his stores were "opened up.")

The other items on cards, pictured with the "Pets'" set, are considerably less informative than the examples which have been described, but even the smallest—the crumb tray and brush—offers a beguiling look at the packaging practices of times past.

FURNISHINGS

MINIATURE OBJECTS

OWNER: MRS. EVELYN ACKERMAN (CALIFORNIA)

Although this metal "Colonial Tea Set" is "late," pieces from it occasionally are found with sets of older vintage, and it seems helpful to include this illustration not only for the increasing number of collectors who are furnishing dolls' houses and rooms of the 1930's, but for the information of antiquarian collectors who may not be aware of the relative recency of this set.

Unlike earlier box lids, which often are infuriatingly silent, this one, as the two illustrations indicate, tells us all we need to know. Or nearly all: Mrs. Evelyn Ackerman of California, who generously provided the print, points out that the 1934 copyright may refer merely to the box, and that the set may have been made abroad. This seems unlikely, but some future dolls' house historian may wish to check this possibility out with the patent office.

The sugar bowl is ¾" tall and the tray, somewhat over-scale for "inch-to-the-foot" collectors, is four inches in diameter.

A postscript must be added: Since the words above were written, a set which later must have yielded the identical molds was found illustrated in a 1913 issue of *Woman's World*. In a full-page advertisement which offered a two-foot rag doll named Golden Locks and Her Twins plus "one of Golden Locks' Own Chocolate and Tea Sets," along with a year's subscription to the Chicago publication—all in exchange for a mere fifty cents—a photograph of Golden Locks' chocolate set was shown. The cups and saucers appear to be of a pattern identical to Mrs. Ackerman's, but the sugar bowl and chocolate pot have lids (with tall finials) usually missing, and the 1913 set has no tray. The twenty-three pieces proudly shown included the six cups, six saucers, six spoons, and two lids.

This appears to be an instance in which molds are disposed of and later offered by a different company, with minor variations.

Figure 409

Figure 410

Figure 411

RELATED MATTERS

DOCUMENTED MINIATURE ILLUMINATION BY MAERKLIN

OWNER (OF CATALOGUE): MR. AND MRS. BLAIR WHITTON (CONNECTICUT)

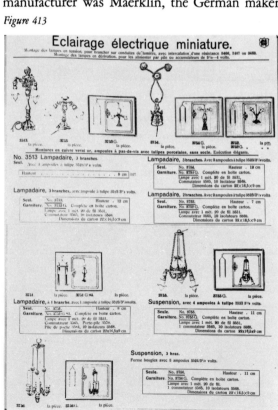

Figure 412

Of all the miniature objects from dolls' houses of the past to which antiquarian collectors are most partial, perhaps none are more coveted than the brass chandeliers and lamps fitted, in the Victorian era, with Bristol globes; and in the Edwardian, with pointed light bulbs sheathed with bristol or porcelain shades.

These were found in houses both in the United States and abroad, and although this collector has managed to retrieve a goodly variety of these bewitching fixtures over the years, and has sought toy catalogues (with small success) for more than twenty-five, I had no idea, till the 1909 and 1919 catalogue pages shown were generously lent to me, that the manufacturer was Maerklin, the German maker

Figure 413

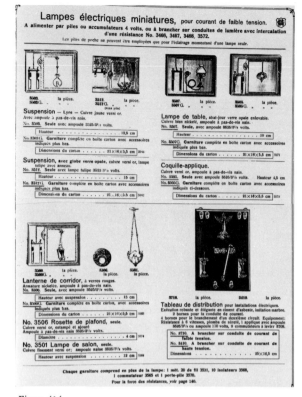

Figure 414

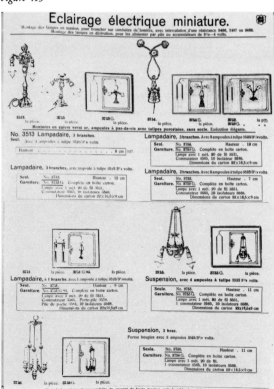

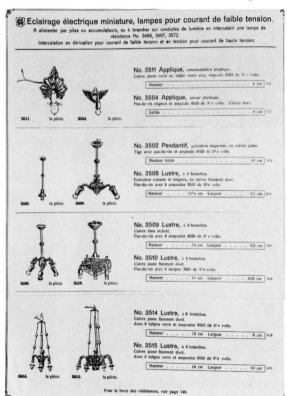

Figure 415

(330)

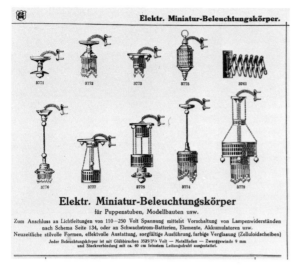

Figure 416

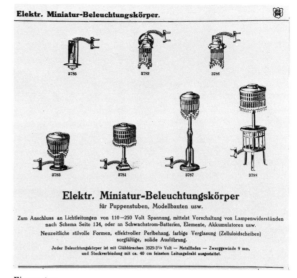

Figure 417

of so many luxury toys, magnificent ships and trains among them, all of them meticulously detailed. Nor did I realize that many of the familiar styles were later wired for electricity, and advertised—as these pages indicate—as early (or should one say "as late"?) as 1909.

There are also styles not previously encountered, such as No. 3756, the model with electrified candles, and No. 3753G, the marvelous newel post light with "porcelain tulips" to hold the bulbs.

It has been of particular interest to discover how the maker described the metal, still astonishingly golden as a rule, even after many decades. This glittering brass, one can now infer, was "finely gilded" to maintain its golden finish (if the translation from German to French is more reliable than catalogue translations from German to English sometimes are). Other, lesser styles, it appears, were of gilded copper; and there were also copper ones in a nickeled finish.

For anyone fortunate enough to find any of these fixtures, the catalogue information about voltage, and other electrical details, should be helpful, even though "la force des resistances" is on a page not shown here.

The writer's collection includes the electric fixture shown in Fig. 412 which corresponds to No. 3514 in the catalogue. Some gaslight fixtures in the same collection were obviously converted to electricity by turning them upside down, and replacing the gas globes with "tulips" containing bulbs. I have mentioned elsewhere that this process was evidently reversed with respect to a chandelier found in its rare original box. The box, stamped "Germany," bears a label which says "Elect. Chandeliers," with the "Elect." inked out, suggesting that it may have been boxed in the transitional period when both types were available, and that this one may have been mismarked.

It is also informative to see the Maerklin catalogue pages of 1919, one with metal chandeliers, and one with sconces and lamps; most of the shades decorated with beaded strands, and all of them supplied with small plugs which are not to be seen on the 1909 models. The latter appear to have fine wire as lightly sheathed as some of the miniature electric fixtures of the 'twenties (also by Maerklin?), of the type attached to a cumbersome battery by small round paperclips; their powers of illumination, seemingly, of a highly ephemeral nature.

Chairs

In choosing the illustrations to be shown in color following page 338, an effort has been made to select those which may be of most value to the collector. Because, during the Victorian era,* sets of dolls' house furniture were manufactured, both in the United States and abroad, by innumerable companies, and in what seems an infinitude of patterns; and because a chair, more than any other piece in a set of furniture, may serve to represent the complete set, more than two hundred chairs, in color, are offered here.

The selection, because it is culled from one collection (the writer's) is, to some degree, arbitrary, but an effort has been made to present this assortment in somewhat definable groupings, according to country or type, and within a sort of flexible chronology, which it is hoped will be useful.

On the other hand, the black-and-white illustration which accompanies these first paragraphs comprises a small gallimaufry. The pair of upholstered chairs in Queen Anne style, which may be the oldest of the lot, was found years ago at an antique show, with nothing to suggest a date. They were duly installed in a Georgian house, the oldest in the writer's collection, and the chair on the right, with handsomely carved legs (not entirely discernible in the photograph), was believed to be more authentic than the one on the left, the legs of which seemed more fanciful, and possibly a replacement. In any case, the two chairs were thought to be one-of-a-kind, and therefore it was with real wonder that, while revisiting the Shelburne Museum in the summer of 1972, I saw the very chair shown on the left, with similar upholstery, and identical "replacement" legs. It *is* possible that a one-of-a-kind set was split, with one chair going to Vermont and one coming to Maryland, and others—perhaps—going elsewhere. It is not easy to believe that more than a few of these were made. Nor is it easy to date the chairs, which clearly have a good deal of age, always difficult to pinpoint in handmade pieces.

The other chairs in the illustration include the side chair with cut velvet seat, of a Classic Revival style, which appears to date from the early nineteenth century, and the unusual Biedermeier rocker at the right, with its original mauve silk upholstery and gilt paper edging in almost mint condition. The Chinese chair in the center, with its incised decoration, is apparently intended to represent teakwood. It is part of a rare dining-room set in the Tiffany-Platt house. The three remaining pieces, of a shimmering gilt metal which appears to tarnish only under the direst circumstances (and seems to be neither brass nor solid gold!), have red silk seats. The most remarkable of the trio is, of course, something more than a chair, and it is known by many names—tête-à-tête, "S" chair, conversation chair—but my favorite definition was provided by the noted Italian writer Mario Praz, in his monumental *Illustrated History of Furnishing*,*

---

* The majority of chairs illustrated are from ca. 1860–1910, with a few earlier and some later examples.

* George Braziller, New York, 1964.

CHAIRS

Figure 418

who calls this a *confidante,* and adds that, when there is a third seat, it becomes an *indiscrète!**

(The numbers in the following text for color plates refer to the chairs in the order of left to right.)

CHAIRS MADE IN AMERICA
(See Plate 7)

With only one exception, the makers of the chairs shown in this grouping can be identified as American. (In the bottom row, chair (3) is only "suspected" of U. S. origin.)

The earliest here are the iron chairs, (1), (3), and (4), in the top row and (2) and (4) in the bottom row, all to be seen in the 1872 illustrated

* There is a miniature example in the Farie dolls' house, now in the United States, in the collection of Mrs. George Canfield of Connecticut. (This is part of the set of Empire furniture presented by the Empress Eugenie.)

price list of Stevens & Brown of Cromwell, Connecticut. Chairs (1), (3), and (4) were also shown in the 1869 catalogue of Ellis, Britton & Eaton of Springfield, Vermont. The painted tin chair, bottom row (1), was also common to the two New England firms, illustrated in the office set of Ellis, Britton & Eaton, in 1869, and in the chamber set of Stevens & Brown, in 1872. The green tin side chair, (4) in row two, was made by a contemporary, Althof, Bergmann of New York, and is shown as part of a chamber set, in the firm's 1874 catalogue.

Two commemorative chairs are the wooden Carver chair in the top row (2), a "Fac-Simile" of the one brought over on the *Mayflower* by the first governor of Plymouth Colony; and the ornate lead chair (2), in the middle row, which resembles no actual chair, but is part of a set of sofa and chairs impressed with a scenic representation of the landing of Columbus, made for the Columbian Exposition of 1893, by Peter F. Pia of New York. Pia also made a chair similar to the

(333)

one in horseshoe pattern (4), middle row, but the horseshoe in the Pia model does not permit the ribbon lacing of the example illustrated. The latter was "Manufactured by Adrian Cooke Metal Works, Chicago, Ill.," as a printed card under its faded pink plush seat relates, along with the information that it is "The 'Fairy' Furniture," that it is "INDESTRUCTIBLE," and that it is made of "an alloy of aluminum and white metal." The rocker, first row, is of similar make, but I do not know positively by whom it was made.

In row two, the wooden chair (1) with blue upholstered seat was manufactured in Cincinnati by the Star Novelty Works, ca. 1910.

MORE AMERICAN CHAIRS
(See Plate 8)

These chairs, early and late, were, most of them, undoubtedly (and the remainder possibly) made in the United States.

There is no doubt about the three lithographed paper-on-wood chairs, (2), (4), and (5) in row one, made by our old friend R. Bliss. The paper-seated chair (2), in row two, is one of a group described on page 310. In the same row, the two metal chairs, (3) and (4), were made by Peter F. Pia, who possibly also manufactured the three "pewter" specimens in row three. Also in that row, (4) is part of a set of table, chairs, and settee with a seller's label on the settee. (The label reads: "From Frank Cousins' BEE-HIVE, 172 Essex Street, Salem, Mass.")*

In addition to the horrendous "overstuffed" armchair of wood (in a shade that outdoes crimson), there are three other chairs from the 'twenties: the iron Kilgore potty chair, (5) in row two, and the two metal Tootsietoy chairs, (2) and (3) in row three.

STILL MORE AMERICAN CHAIRS
(See Plate 8)

Bentwood chairs, made by a variety of manufacturers, are generously sprinkled through the catalogues of Sears Roebuck and Montgomery, Ward, and similar houses at the turn of the century and before. Though I have no evidence that they were made in the United States, their retail history has suggested inclusion with this group. They were turned out in many qualities, usually in sets containing three other chairs, a sofa, and a table. The dining-room chairs (2), (3), and (4), below them, also enjoyed a considerable vogue among subscribers to mail order catalogues: (2) appears to be identical to a chair which is shown with a boxed dining-room set made by the Star Novelty Works, Cincinnati, Ohio, and simple furniture of this type was also made by such American toy makers as Whitney-Reed and others.

Considerably later in date, the remaining chairs pictured have already come into their own with collectors. The iron ladderback (1) in row three was made by the Arcade Manufacturing Co. of Freeport, Illinois, beginning in the late 'twenties, and the remaining chairs illustrated are by Tynietoy of Providence, Rhode Island, who made copies of "colonial" pieces, beginning in 1920.

"BIEDERMEIER"
(See Plate 9)

In the November 1972 issue of *Antiques*,* there is a most intriguing quotation, taken from

---

* Some fascinating research on the label was accomplished in behalf of this writer by her friend Mrs. Donald Marion, of Newburyport, Massachusetts, but like many things intended for inclusion in these overstuffed pages, this has had to be omitted for want of space and time. It is hoped that an opportunity to explore this material will be found in future.

* Clues and footnotes. Quoted from the Dedham *Patriot* in the *Commercial Advertiser*, April 28, 1837, Vol. 40, p. 1.

CHAIRS

Figure 419

an 1837 publication: "We yesterday examined an elegant piece of furniture veneered with marble paper in imitation of rosewood," it begins, and it goes on to describe the perfection of this process. Since this reference, needless to say, is to "life-sized" furniture, it is fascinating to relate it to the lovely "imitation rosewood" dolls' house furniture made during much of the nineteenth century, and so coveted by collectors today.

There are many ways of describing this charming "Biedermeier" furniture which Vivien Greene prefers to call the dolls' Duncan Phyfe. It has occasionally been mentioned in Victorian publications as "imitation ebony and gold," a reference to the engaging variety in which gilt inlay is imitated on printed papers, and so firmly affixed to the wood that I have never seen so much as an edge lift from a small foundation. Mrs. Greene, who has found the original catalogues, is bringing out a book about this "beautiful Waltershausen furniture" which, as she has pointed out, was made "in hundreds of designs, and was exported in many thousands of crates to England as well as to the Continent,"* and, one might add, to the United States.

It seems of more than passing interest that in the 1914 catalogue of the Waltershausen firm of Gebrüder Schneegass, a chair very similar to (1) in row one is shown. The Saxon firm, founded in 1845, may not be the one whose catalogues Mrs. Greene has discovered,* but the possibility may be worth noting.

Not all the pieces have printed paper designs. Some, such as (1) in row three, are hand-stenciled, or painted, in a simple gilt pattern. The Victorian Gothic chair with its crimson velvet upholstery, (2) in row two, is less commonly found than the rococo shapes above it. The upholstered pieces are to be seen in silk (blue, rose, violet, or green), as well as cut velvets. A rare variation is the seat woven of a gossamer and indescribable material in row three (2). Another rare example, to the right of this "cane"-seated chair, has a red-leather upholstered seat embellished in a gold pattern. The armchair to this set is shown alone (Fig. 419), to exhibit its decorated profile. Unfortunately the bit of braid meant to cover the front seam is missing.

Perhaps the rarest chair is the one to be seen in black-and-white, with its article of convenience (not the original, however) inside, a handsome alternative to indoor plumbing. See Fig. 420.

* She dates the furniture as from 1820.

Figure 420

* *Discovering Antiques*, BPC Publishing Ltd., 1971.

RELATED MATTERS

GERMAN CHAIRS BY GEBRÜDER SCHNEEGASS
(SEE PLATE 9)

There is hardly a dolls' house to be found anywhere, in the United States or abroad, from the years surrounding the turn of the century, in which one or more of these German chairs of "yellow cherry" is not to be discovered. Three from the 1914 catalogue of Gebrüder Schneegass, of Waltershausen in Thuringia, may be specifically seen in row two, (1), (2), and (4), the latter two described as "cane chairs." Some of these were made in the identical style over a long period of years, and some may be seen in the catalogue pages shown on page 315.

As the painted chair, (5) in row one, suggests, there were alternative finishes to the "yellow cherry," and most pieces were available in white, as here, and red, as well.

IMPORTED UPHOLSTERED CHAIRS
(SEE PLATE 10)

Like the "yellow cherry" chairs, the upholstered side chairs were imported, most of them undoubtedly from Germany, and the variations in style, but especially in upholstery materials, are multitudinous. Silk, cotton, and velvet, prints and solid colors, are all represented, but even leather, (1), bottom row, and (5), top row, and a skillful paper imitation of leather, (1), middle row, are represented.

One non-upholstered chair, (4), middle row, crept into the group; this chair warrants singling out inasmuch as many dolls' houses made in the first and second decades of the twentieth century contained such pressed cardboard furniture, found in several scales and colors; red, as here, or white.

CHAIRS MOSTLY FROM FRANCE
(SEE PLATE 10)

Well aware of the pitfalls which may result from saying even that "most" of these chairs were made in France, one hereby goes out on a limb! Those that came with French rooms appear to be unmistakable, and include (3), (4), and (5) in row one, (1) and (6) in row two, and (5) and (6) in row three.

As explained, on page 289, the chair with "ormolu" mounts, (4) in row three, I now realize was, despite its Empire styling, made in Saxony. Also (1) in row three, with its purple paper upholstery, is part of a set that came from Belgium years ago in its original wooden box, with a maker's mark on the paper lining of the box. This bears the monogram with "L" and "D" superimposed on "C," possibly the emblem of Louis Delachal, a Paris toy maker who, according to the Colemans,* was active ca. 1890–1904.

Evidence linking the remaining chairs to France is largely circumstantial. Disputants are welcomed.

FAUTEUILS
(SEE PLATE 11)

Gebrüder Schneegass, who show in their ubiquitous 1914 catalogue a chair almost identical to (1) in row one, describe it in four languages. Of most interest here is the reference in English (armchairs), and the reference in French (*fauteuils*).

Most of the chairs here seem to belong in the category of *fauteuils*, and it is possible that more than one of those illustrated was made in France. The tufted example in blue, (3) in row three, arrived with several companion chairs from Belgium, but could conceivably be French. In

---

* *The Collector's Encyclopedia of Dolls*, Crown, 1968.

green checked velvet, the angular chair, (2) in row three, came in a pair of rooms from Vienna, and if it is not Austrian, is probably German.

The most interesting is the pair of chairs which combine to form a loveseat. There is undoubtedly a proper bit of nomenclature for this unusual duo (which is rare in full size as well as in miniature). Surviving pairs presumably become separated; if some of these were reunited, they might prove to be less rare than one supposes.

A GROUP OF METAL CHAIRS
(See Plate 11)

The chairs here assembled have in common the fact that all are of metal. A few, such as the English parlor chair, (2) in the top row, with "W. Avery & Son, Redditch" stamped beneath, are upholstered. The two mid-nineteenth-century chairs, (2) and (4), bottom row, have removable upholstered seats. (They are identical, but the missing cushion on (4) helpfully reveals the pattern hidden on the other.)

The engaging painted chair, (3), middle row, is believed to be Regency, and is one of the earliest in our "miscellany." The painted chair, (5), top row, with pierced seat, is of the type Vivien Greene* identifies as manufactured in Furth. In the bottom row (3), the elaborately pierced "filigree" example is of the genre made by the firm of Babette Schweitzer of Diessen am Ammersee, in Bavaria, founded in 1799, and still in operation.

A GROUP OF METAL CHAIRS
(SMALLER SCALE)
(See Plate 12)

The three imitations of bentwood rockers (top row) include (3), a version made by the same French manufacturer who produced the side chairs, (1) and (3), in two divergent scales in the bottom row, as well as (5) in row two. "Made in France" is nearly always molded in the bottom of each of these pieces, which are ca. 1910.

Chairs (2) and (4), row two, are of special interest inasmuch as they were part of a large collection of painted metal dolls' house furnishings made in Mexico in the first quarter of the twentieth century. (These, a rather crude but interesting imitation of European models, included sewing machines, typewriters, etc.) The lyre-back chair, perhaps intended for a music room, is marked "Made in U.S.A. Pat. Pend."

The chair of the relatively untarnishable gilt metal mentioned earlier, (1), row two, may be dated by its chairback, impressed in a glorious Art Nouveau floral pattern.

SPECIAL PURPOSE CHAIRS
(See Plate 12)

A small sampling of chairs made for special purposes, beyond the ordinary requirements of parlor or dining-room, include several intended for the nursery. Described as a "baby-chair," (2), top row, may be seen (with legs less elaborately turned) in the 1914 Gebrüder Schneegass catalogue, and was obtainable not only in white, as here, but also in red and yellow. The yellow, (2), bottom row, was presumably made with simpler legs, as in the catalogue.

The three filigree baby chairs, bottom row, include (1), a dual-purpose piece which lowers into a table-and-chair combination; (3), an adjustable chair on wheels which can be lowered to make a rocker;* and (5), a highchair. (The tray is missing.)

---

* *English Dolls' Houses of the 18th and 19th Centuries.*

* A life-sized highchair in the writer's household, patented in 1881, performs this very trick.

RELATED MATTERS

One of the most interesting chairs, (3), top row, is hinged, and is intended for use either as a kitchen ladder or as library steps. (It came with a German kitchen, ca. 1895.) Chairs (4) and (5), top row, fold, and (5), which is German, came accompanied by three others in a set which includes a folding card table. The lyre-back chair, (1), top row, was part of a whole set of music room furniture, including a music rack and piano; the iron desk chair, (4), bottom row, which may have been made by Kilgore, swivels.

CHAIRS FOR CONSERVATORIES, PIAZZAS, AND GARDENS
(See Plate 13)

Because every proper Victorian house had a piazza, a conservatory, or a garden, or all three, it is not surprising to see the variety of furniture which was available for such oases in miniature. When he was so abruptly uprooted, the bisque-headed gentleman in his wire chair could have been relaxing nowhere else but in a conservatory with a black-white-and-rust tiled floor.

Two of the earliest chairs shown include a painted settee, admittedly not a chair (but it somehow crept in), made by Stevens & Brown, and illustrated in their 1872 catalogue. Although it is described as a "toy sofa," it seems more appropriate as a garden bench. To its right, the painted tin chair is part of an endearing set for conservatory or garden. There are two chairs, a matching bench, and a circular plant stand with a pierced rim. (A duplicate of the latter may be seen in the garden of the Brett house.)

The three examples of rustic chairs, middle row, (2), (3), and (4), are expressions of the romantic taste which even crept indoors. Chair (2) is made of bamboo, and was of a type turned out in varying qualities by various makers, on both sides of the turn of the century.

Since wicker, reed, and willow were also popular in bedrooms and parlors some of the miniature versions illustrated here may have been intended for indoor use. Advertised as part of a set of "fine reed furniture" by F. A. O. Schwarz in the 'twenties, the green chair, (1), middle row, was also available in blue or orange. Imitation wicker, (1) and (5), bottom row, was obtainable in pressed cardboard, also during the 'twenties. This, unquestionably, was to furnish the innumerable "sunrooms" of the period.

The wicker chair, top row, (5), is part of a set I believe may have been handwoven from a description in an Edwardian magazine. In the bottom row, (2) is one of an English pair exquisitely made by hand, and may be as early as mid-nineteenth century.

The folding chair, (6), top row, was made in a number of fabrics with adjustable backs, and one is advertised in the faithful Gebrüder Schneegass 1914 catalogue. (It was obtainable "raw," or painted in red or yellow.) A different sort of folding chair, of slatted wood, (4), top row, was also made, more typically, as a bench.

KITCHEN CHAIRS
(See Plate 13)

Kitchen chairs are, as a group, undistinguished. Dolls' house kitchens seem often to have made do with cast-offs, though most of the ones shown here were simple styles specifically made for kitchen use.

Chairs (2), (3), and (5), top row, and (4) and (5), bottom row, are of metal; (2), bottom row, is of the pressed cardboard shown in red with the upholstered chairs. The blue and white wooden chair, (1), top row, is from a German kitchen of the 1920's, as its style might also proclaim. The two unpainted wooden chairs, lower row, (1) and (3), are frequently found in

(338)

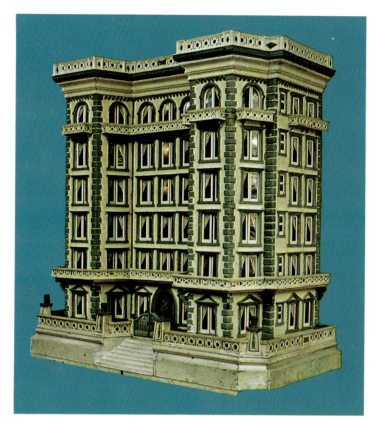

A six-story building from New Jersey, dated 1903 on the cornice, and said to be a copy of an Asbury Park hotel. Height: 33″ (See page 100.)

Five row houses from East Baltimore, two rooms each, with wallpaper. Width: 56″ (See page 158.)

PLATE 1

A French house, with the original furniture still sewn in! Height (not including spire): 34″. (See page 245.)

Detail of two of the four rooms in the French house. Height of chair: 3¼″

Classic three-room Bliss house. Front and left side swing open. Height, not including chimney, 20½″ (See page 227.)

A house by Converse of Winchendon, Mass. Height (not including 3″ chimney): 19¾″ (See page 253.)

PLATE 2

A grocery store by R. Bliss, patented in 1895. Height (not including chimney): 9½″ (See page 229.)

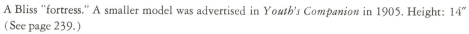

A Bliss "fortress." A smaller model was advertised in *Youth's Companion* in 1905. Height: 14″ (See page 239.)

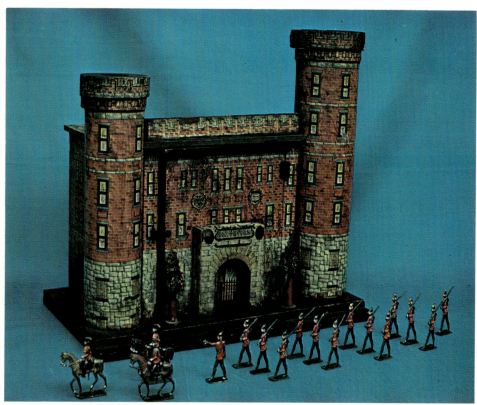

PLATE 3

Bliss Fire Station No. 2, with matching lithographed pumper, "Niagara." Height: 19½" (See page 233.)

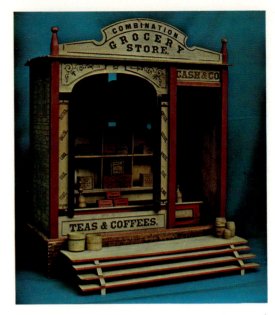

A "Combination" grocery store by Stirn and Lyon of New York, patented in 1882. Height: 21¾" (See page 209.)

Dunham's Cocoanut Doll House, with lushly lithographed interiors. Height: 29" (See page 212.)

A stable made by R. Bliss. Numerous styles were available. Height (not including cupola): 14" (See page 237.)

PLATE 4

The lid of the box in which *Dolly's Playhouse* came "knocked down." Size of lid: 12¾" x 21"

Dolly's Playhouse by McLoughlin. Made over a period of more than two decades. Height: 18" (See page 248.)

A McLoughlin folding house, 13" square and 1" thick when folded. (See page 249.)

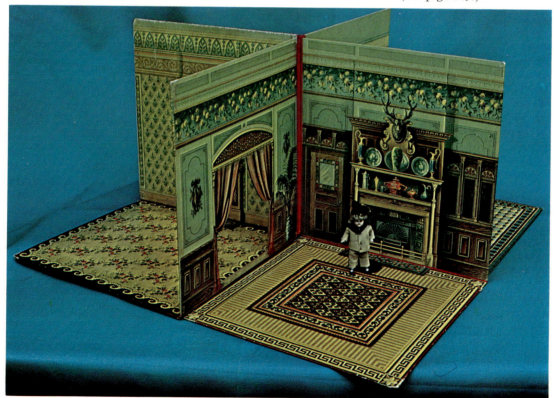

PLATE 5

Bedroom furniture by R. Bliss in original box. (The bed is missing.) Height of chair: 4″ (See page 310.)

An unmarked set of parlor furniture believed to be Bliss. Height of chair: 3⅞″ (See page 313.)

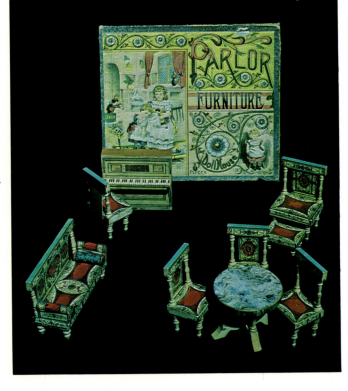

PLATE 6

A chamber set advertised by Stevens & Brown in 1872. Height of chair: 4⅛″ (See page 298.)

Chairs by Bliss made of lithographed paper-on-wood. (See pages 311 and 334.)

Chairs "Made in America," including three iron examples (top row) advertised as early as 1869. Height of (1), top row: 3¾″ (See page 333.)

PLATE 7

More American chairs, including three of lithographed paper-on-wood by R. Bliss. (top row.) Height of (3), middle row: 2¾″ (See page 334.)

Still more American chairs, including four bentwood variations (top row). Height of (1), top row: 4¼″ (See page 334.)

PLATE 8

"Biedermeier" or "imitation rosewood" chairs made for generations in many styles in Waltershausen, Germany. Height of (1), first row: 4⅜" (See page 334.)

German chairs by Gebrüder Schneegass of Waltershausen, Germany. Chairs (1), (2) and (4), lower row, may be seen in the firm's 1914 catalogue. Height of (4): 4⅛" (See page 335.)

Imported upholstered chairs; with one exception, (4) in the middle row, which is of pressed cardboard. Height of latter: 3⅞″ (See page 336.)

Chairs mostly from France. (4), bottom row, with "ormolu" mounts, was made in Saxony, despite its Empire styling. Height of latter: 3½″ (See page 336.)

PLATE 10

"Fauteuils." These upholstered chairs with arms are mostly from the Continent. (5), top row, may be seen in the 1914 Schneegass catalogue. Height of latter chair: 4⅞" (See page 336.)

A group of metal chairs, some upholstered. The English parlor chair (2), top row, has "W. Avery, Redditch" stamped beneath. Height of latter: 4½" (See page 337.)

PLATE 11

A group of metal chairs (smaller scale) including three versions of bentwood rockers. Height of French chair (1), bottom row: 2¾″ (See page 337.)

Special purpose chairs include folding chairs (4) and (5), top row, and the wooden chair which becomes a ladder (3). Height of latter: 4½″ (See page 337.)

PLATE 12

Chairs for conservatories, piazzas and gardens. Included are iron and rustic furniture for gardens; wicker for indoors. Height of (1), middle row: 3¾" (See page 338.)

Kitchen chairs of wood, metal and pressed cardboard. Height of (1), top row: 4¾" (See page 338.)

PLATE 13

One-of-a-kind chairs were often home-made. (1), top row, is one of an English set of wheelback windsors of great delicacy. Height of latter: 4⅛″ (See page 338.)

"Another melange." An assortment, including a peasant chair from a Danish set (1), top row. Height of latter: 3⅞″ (See page 339.)

PLATE 14

A bisque dolls' house family in which the glass-eyed children resemble their glass-eyed mother rather than their "bisque-eyed" father, nanny and housekeeper. Height of father: 6½" (See page 346.)

Composition-headed dolls house dolls'. Height of gentleman in top hat (including hat): 6¼" (See page 344.)

PLATE 15

An assortment of very small "mignonettes," believed to be French. Height of judge: 2¾" (See page 348.)

A pair of rare bisque ice skaters wearing metal skates. Height of skater at left: 4" (See page 347.)

PLATE 16

CHAIRS

the kitchens of German dolls' houses, and were evidently made over a long period of time. The blue and white metal chair, (4), bottom row, is part of a most appealing kitchen set which includes a table, cupboard, and benches.

ONE-OF-A-KIND CHAIRS
(See Plate 14)

Victorian ladies feathered their nests with all manner of decorative objects made by themselves. Some of their handiwork is to be seen in these one-of-a-kind chairs. The feathered example, (1), bottom row, is part of a set (which includes even a feathered cupboard with a workable door), said to have been made for the 1870 Paris Exposition. The quill chair, (2), top row, is clearly a defeathered relation. The chair with seat and back of woven thread, (2), bottom row, is of the most gossamer weave; (5), bottom row, is from a set woven of wool on straight pins.

The wheelback Windsor, (1), top row, is one of a set with saddle seats, made in England, exquisitely and obviously long ago. Made with similar delicacy, the painted "fancy chair," (3), bottom row, came with the same Georgian house, and must have been fashioned by the same skilled hand.

The fret-sawed chair, (4), bottom row, is European. Fret-sawed chairs of somewhat less delicacy were part of a fret-saw revival in the United States in the 'eighties.

The chair with the petitpoint slip seat, (4), top row, is one of a set known to have been made for Queen Mary's dolls' house at Windsor. Many more pieces were received than could be used, and this is said to have been among the "rejects" later disposed of.

Beaded chairs, made usually on wire, were also a popular type for home-crafting, but one in the writer's collection (from a set which includes a beaded fireplace and a beaded dog) was too small in scale to illustrate with the other chairs shown.

ANOTHER MELANGE
(See Plate 14)

Herewith is another jumble of chair types, some of which didn't quite classify, and some of which "escaped" from other groupings.

The peasant chair, (1), top row, may serve to represent the great variety of peasant chairs to be found, even today, especially in Bavaria. This one comes from a Danish set.

The chair with pink silk seat, (3), row two, is part of a set of two-toned wood, unvarnished and inlaid, of a type obviously made over a period of decades. A page of this furniture, including the identical chair, is to be seen in a mid-nineteenth-century German catalogue. Chairs in a very similar style, but obviously from very different makers, may be seen in row one, (2) and (4), and in row three, (4). The unvarnished wooden chair, (5), top row, has incised decoration on the seat, and I believe it to be early—from the mid-nineteenth century at the latest.

A most unusual, but unfortunately unphotogenic, chair is to be seen in row three, (2). This is from a set with designs resembling the papier-mâché with mother-of-pearl inlay so beloved of the Victorians. How the effect is achieved here is difficult to ascertain, but it is unmistakable.

(339)

Dolls' House Occupants

It is likely that, almost without exception, the inhabitants of American dolls' houses are immigrants. It is well known that the bisque "dolls' house dolls" of the late nineteenth and early twentieth centuries were natives of Germany, and that their ancestors (of wood or porcelain extraction) had crossed the ocean before them.

The elegantly dressed lady of the house, as well as her cook and parlor maid; her distinguished-looking husband, as well as his chauffeur; all emigrated to the United States in the 'eighties and 'nineties, many of them arriving on the same ships which brought crates of furnishings to the American dolls' houses they inhabited. The ladies with their well-coiffed bisque hair-dos, the gentlemen with their bisque mustaches, their servants, suddenly (as these words are written) in fashion again with their bisque sideburns, look like little people;* they are well proportioned and well dressed, and when they can be found in their original clothing, they add immeasurably to the warmth and vivacity of the chambers they occupy.

When the term "dolls' house doll" is mentioned, this relatively recent group is perhaps the one which springs most readily to mind, along with glass-eyed, be-wigged bisque cousins made by the well-known Thuringian firm of Simon & Halbig; but small dolls of all materials and persuasions, needless to say, have populated the dolls' houses of the past. A doll needs only to be suitably short to qualify.

One longs to know what the "Lilliputian dolls" advertised in the *Independent Gazeteer* of Philadelphia of May 6, 1785 were like. For this earliest of American references to dolls of dolls' house size, which were for sale with other dolls and toys, including "two new houses with fine gardens" at John Mason's shop, I am indebted to the account of a friend in England, Mary Hillier.*

This engaging reference is especially welcome in view of the absence of the original dolls and furnishings from the Van Cortlandt baby house, the only eighteenth-century American example on record. The early part of the nineteenth century, however, is well represented: Generations of dolls accompanied the Brett house to the Museum of the City of New York,† and a few may be glimpsed in the rooms. Several lovely dolls may be seen in another fine American baby house—the Voegler at West Chester.

In any case, virtually all dolls' house people, including "old families" considerably "older" than the bisques, emigrated to the United States, and all of them are related to the dolls' house people in houses across the sea. There were the peg-jointed dolls, such as Queen Victoria and her governess dressed to represent celebrated personages of their time, and which were made with variations for more than a century in the Grodner Tal. (Formerly part of Austria, and now Italy.)

---

* The wedding in miniature, from a 1907 issue of *McCall's*, demonstrates the accuracy of this resemblance. It is necessary to look closely to determine that the bridal party consists of dolls. See Fig. 421.

* *Dolls and Dollmakers*, G. P. Putnam's Sons, 1968.

† Most are in storage; if all were installed in the house, it would appear that a sizeable ball or reception were in progress!

Figure 421

Figure 422

Figure 423

Figure 424

In a charming book about trades, C. L. Matéaux* describes the making of these "jointed wooden Dutch dolls" in the "Southern Tyrol . . . [in] the busy little toy-making town of St. Ulrich." Matéaux wrote:

There are rooms upon rooms quite filled with these dolls, of every size and style, small and large, painted and unpainted; their sizes vary from tiny atoms scarcely an inch long, to huge figures of nearly a yard in length, most of them jointed and the great part uncoloured, and just as they came from the hands of the carver . . . some sizes are more popular than others, a very favourite length being about two inches; of this size one of the great doll-merchants of St. Ulrich buys thirty thousand a week during the

* *The Wonderland of Work*, Cassell & Co., New York, London, and Paris, 1884.

(341)

whole year. The makers of this kind of toy can turn out about twenty dozen a day, the painting being quite an after-concern, with which the carvers have nothing to do.

These dolls, Clara Matéaux reported, could "be bought for anywhere . . . from a farthing upwards." According to the Colemans,* who quote a somewhat earlier (1875) account of wooden doll-making in St. Ulrich, the larger jointed woodens were made with ball type joints and the smaller ones with peg joints. It is the latter, needless to say, which are of interest here. A rare early example with porcelain head (secured by a peg) and porcelain limbs is 3⅝" tall.† Another group of "peg woodens" in early if not "original" clothing may be seen below her (page 341) including the one with "Tuck comb" under a net cap at left.

The dolls that Kate Greenaway bought with her pocket money, at mid-century, in London's famous Lowther Arcade, were not identified as jointed woodens, but the evidence strongly suggests that they were, especially significant being the information (given by her biographers)* that her Royal Family "was completed by the princes and princesses at a farthing apiece." Her Majesty, Queen Victoria, cost a halfpenny, and so did Prince Albert. Her Majesty's garments are not described, but His Royal Highness wore a white gauze shirt trimmed with three rows of cerise satin and, for further distinction and identification, a red ribbon tied across his shoulder and under his left arm. These garments "could only be removed by an actual disintegration," and this, of course, is also true of the clothes of their descendants, the late Victorian dolls' house dolls whose realistically designed garments are sewn on.

The princes and princesses made do with "dresses from the gauze bonnet linings" just then going out of fashion, and such scraps of net and ribbon as had proved usable. The Royal

* *The Collector's Encyclopedia of Dolls*, op. cit.

† Author's collection, as are all groupings of dolls' house dolls unless otherwise mentioned.

* M. H. Spielmann and G. S. Layard, Adam & Charles Black, 1905.

Figure 425

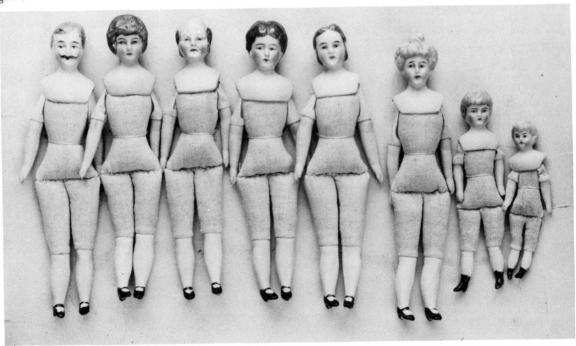

Family, by the way, did not occupy a dolls' palace, but a toy cupboard in Kate's bedroom which was well furnished, even though "furniture was hard to come by at a farthing (pocket money) a week." It took twenty-four weeks to obtain a six-penny piano, but "once Aunt Aldridge came to town and presented the dolls with a work table." ("Unhappily, so great a piece of good fortune never again befell.")

The Colemans point out that beginning in the late 1870's "the commercial concept of a doll family appeared in advertisements, although the ingenuity of much earlier generations had provided families of dolls that were distinguished by their clothes and relative size." They further refer to the fact that "some of the bisque dolls' house dolls have cloth bodies* and some bisque bodies," and that "many of them have molded hair and shoes that help to date them, although the same molds were often used for many years."

The subject of these variations in dolls' house heads and limbs is a study in itself, and I know of at least one book being written on this subject which should be a delight.

The late Martha Thompson, the beloved doll maker, once published an illustration of a dolls' house man dressed for the opera. He was in his original box (cardboard, not opera), and Mrs. Thompson expressed regret that the firm which made the doll neglected to inscribe its name "somewhere." "Not even on the boxes in which they came," she wrote, "is there a clue."

Shortly before this summary went to press, it was arresting to discover in the collection of Mrs. Cecil St. C. King, a discerning dolls' house collector from Arlington, Virginia, a bisque Negro butler in his original lace-edged cardboard box. His glass eyes† sparkled in his

---

* I am grateful to Mrs. Joseph Andrews of Virginia whose dolls' house family, with cloth bodies still sewn onto their original card, and waiting to be dressed, is reproduced nearby.

† These rare eyes do not appear to be set in like the glass eyes of other dolls' house dolls, but bear, at the least, a sort of glaze which make them look "glassy."

Figure 426

bisque head, his towel was in proper position over his arm, and, wonder of wonders, there was a label at one end of the box bearing a name—Kellner—and an assortment of hieroglyphics such as "(50 af a/m) NO 29/2," etc. Obviously, this was not a shop label, and being certain that Kellner was the maker, and this a great discovery, I took the matter up with doll scholar Dorothy Coleman. However, it was her belief that Kellner may have been a distributor, or middleman, rather than a manufacturer. Proof will have to await further investigation.

The Colemans, incidentally, list a number of makers of dolls' house dolls, including Heinrich Schmuckler who, they record, "specialized in such dolls from 1895 to 1925+." They also list Matilde Sehm who "made dressed dolls' house dolls," as well as Ernst Winkler, Alfred Pensky, Friedmann & Ohnstein, Elizabeth Bürchner, Grete Cohn, Schindhelm & Knauer, and Welsch & Co.

In the writer's collection is a small Kestner girl in her original box. She is five inches tall, which would be out-of-scale for the child she is clearly meant to represent, but other dolls believed to have been made by Kestner were made in dolls' house scale, and it seems not unlikely that many a Kestner doll has inhabited many a dolls' house.

In 1972, the Pyne Press issued a 1927 Kämmer & Reinhardt catalogue* found by Margaret and Blair Whitton, and among many pages of dolls, there is one fascinating page of dolls' house dolls. The catalogue was printed in four languages; and in English these were identified as "Highly Original Character Dolls," and described as "light as a feather, wire frame, felt cloth dressed, cloth faces." At least one doll, a coachman, came with a "biscuit" (bisque) head, and all the dolls were made in various sizes, from approximately 3¾" to 9".

It is evident from the catalogue illustration, (not shown here) that the cloth faces described are treated in a way that resembles a highly detailed composition. The strange little group below, including the shifty-eyed gent at the left, may be of this material.

* Princeton, N. J. With an introduction by Dorothy S. Coleman.

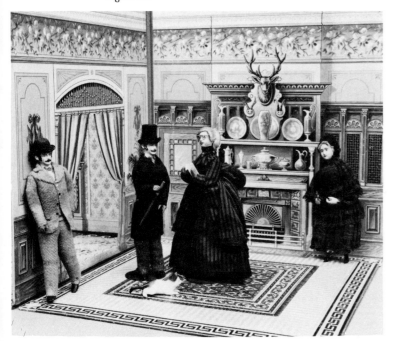

Figure 427

Figure 428

Curiously, in 1927, no families appear to be available from this maker;* at least there were no mothers, fathers, grandparents, or children listed. Instead, the "professions and trades" are represented: "The only practical and beautiful dolls of good value for: Motor cars, trams, trains, workshops, kitchens, shops, fire brigades, cannoniers [soldiers, presumably] and sailors, and many others."

(Dorothy Coleman points out a reference in this catalogue to the succession by Kämmer & Reinhardt to Simon & Halbig whose glass-eyed dolls with wigs, as mentioned previously, are often found in dolls' houses.)

* In a 1928 catalogue by the same firm (reprinted by Pat Schoonmaker), most of the same dolls are shown, with the addition of three sets of bisque-headed dolls' house families, including domestics. These are described as "Doll-Chamber dolls, little dolls dressed for all functions or professions moveable with wire in legs and arms, can sit and alone stand." (There were evidently problems about obtaining English translations in Germany in 1928.) Actually the reference appears to relate to both the dolls dressed for "professions" with composition heads and wired limbs, as well as to the bisque heads.

The bisque maid (shown with a "flapper" in the Tootsietoy living-room) seems to be identical to a maid illustrated in one of the family groups in the 1928 catalogue. (Her missing lace collar appears to be the only variation.)

DOLLS' HOUSE OCCUPANTS

Figure 429

Figure 430

(345)

Although I have reproduced elsewhere the illustration of dolls' house dolls advertised in F. A. O. Schwarz's 1913 "Christmas Review," it seems to bear repeating in this context. It will be noted that there was a size range of five to seven inches, and servants are shown in a greater array than "gentlemen and ladies."

An assortment of female domestics of different eras is shown in Fig. 429. Some of its members pose rather anachronistically (especially the Georgian rag doll with her fierce expression, and the peg wooden with missing cap, both in the bottom row) for a turn-of-the-century photographer. The variety and quantity of dolls' house domestics to be found is not surprising when we consider a sentence written by A. J. Downing* in 1850: "Having already defined a cottage to be a dwelling so small that the household duties may all be performed by the family, or with the assistance of not more than one or two domestics, we may add that a villa is a country house of larger accommodation, requiring the care of at least three or more servants."

The domestics shown in the crescent moon photograph are exclusively female. Two butlers, one black and one white, may be seen in Fig. 428 along with another distaff member (in a gorgeous apron. Undoubtedly, unlike her two companions, she is home-dressed). The black butler does not have the glass eyes to be seen on Emily King's splendid fellow. Her butler also has some gold "braid" on his livery which this man lacks, and it seems possible that the vintage rather than the maker may be different.

A quartet of chefs (surely about to break into song) may be seen in Fig. 431. The chef at the right holds his original platter, and though his cookery doesn't appear to be as appetizing as once it was, his rare molded chef's hat is pristine, prescribing for eternity even the angle at which such headgear was worn. Next to him is a pastry cook, a term which somehow comes to mind without evidence! He is probably French, and it would be of interest to know if the manner in which his apron is turned up at one corner is typical, as chefs' hats are, of a special school of cookery. An identical chef in a smaller scale (in the writer's collection) has an apron turned up in the same way.

There is less to be said about the gentleman with the false beard who looks like a department store Santa Claus, and came from Austria complete with wooden spoon. The fourth chef, very Teutonic, is bearing up bravely though he's lost his hat.

The dolls' house family, (Plate 15) shown in front of the entrance to their lithographed house, has been brought together in relatively recent years. The glass-eyed children came together many years ago, along with the maid holding a feather duster, and they bear a glass-eyed resemblance to their glass-eyed mother rather than to their bisque-eyed father, Nanny, and housekeeper. The latter has her original bunch of keys at her waist.

* *The Architecture of Country Houses*, op. cit.

Figure 431

DOLLS' HOUSE OCCUPANTS

Figure 432

Figure 433

Dolls' house housekeepers complete with keys are not impossible to find, but the dolls' house dolls on ice skates are the only ones known to me (Plate 16).

A different sport is represented in the person of the lady in the bathing suit and cap. She, too, is rare, and because, at the time of her purchase many years ago, her feet had been amputated above the ankle (undoubtedly in some bizarre accident that does not bear investigation), she has always been displayed in a cracker jar, in fish sand (into which, in the picture shown, she is "beyond her depth"). Her cap is removable.

An earlier and rare pair of glass-eyed dolls may be seen in Fig. 432. The grandfather in his robe and cap is especially engaging.

The anachronistic street incident, in which a doll intended to represent Amelia Earhart Put-

Figure 434

Figure 435

nam descends from the dirigible *New York*, offers an opportunity to introduce dolls from different walks of life—and even different eras! The gentleman in white tie, the lady in leg-o'-mutton sleeves with her under-sized son, the motorist with molded goggles, the golfer, and the—I think—zoo keeper, share with the small dog a degree of surprise at the goings-on—and well they might.

An assortment of very small dolls' house dolls, believed to be French, are photographed in a small French parlor. Their hostesses stand aside in some bewilderment while these mignonettes,* a judge (dressed as for a Daumier legal print), coachman, nurse, constable, and—of all things—Scotsman pose in her parlor. All bisque, and fully jointed, they are approximately $2\frac{1}{2}''$ tall.

* The name in France for "little dolls."

PART 4

CONTEMPORARY MATTERS

The Philosophy of Restoration, or, the Horrors of Urban Renewal in Miniature

One who writes on the subject of dolls' houses receives two types of "fan" letters. The first usually begins: "Dear ———: I love your books. Please tell me where I can find (1) 'Grandmother So-and-So's Dolls' House Furniture,' or (2) an antique dolls' house."

The second type of letter, far more appealing to receive, inquires about the restoration of an old dolls' house already in the writer's possession, and about the degree of restoration "permitted." Even when such advice is solicited, it seems somewhat presumptuous for anyone to give "permission"—to decree what a dolls' house owner may or may not do with an object he has chosen (or possibly inherited). However, just as collectors of iron toys, for example, have evolved over the years certain guidelines about re-painting their treasures,* similar guidelines have come to exist among many dolls' house collectors with a feeling for the past, and for its patina.

One definition of patina offered by Webster is "a surface appearance, such as a coloring or mellowing, of something grown beautiful, especially with age or use." It is sad but true that even museums and historical societies do not all honor this definition with respect to *all* of their collections. Sometimes, it is one minor official put in charge of several areas who does not particularly revere one of those areas. I know of one great historical society which has permitted green-and-white paint to be spread, with great generosity, over an important small collection of dolls' houses,* and therefore it is less surprising that a small private museum with which I am also acquainted has repainted its houses to such a degree that any touch of antiquity has been lost. I know of another historical society where a fine old dolls' house has been repapered with "Contact."

It is only fair to mention here that this collector has not been blameless, and has never quite recovered from a youthful error: permitting the walls of the South Jersey house (Figs. 83-4) to be repainted, after the house was found dirty and neglected, in 1945, in an antique dealer's barn. Not only were the original paint colors of the rooms covered when they might have been cleaned, but small smudges on the walls, evocative smudges, which told of minus-

---

* They don't, of course, or the value goes down, and many of these collectors are hard-headed businessmen. Others, needless to say, love their toys, and find beauty in a coat of worn paint, which suggests the years of pleasure the object has conferred on its owner(s).

* It should be mentioned that some of the misfortunes which have befallen museum collections were the misguided miniature "urban renewal" projects of curators long departed.

Figure 436

THE PHILOSOPHY OF RESTORATION

cule sconces long gone but once lighted there, were obscured forever.

(In atoning for this miniature sin, the South Jersey's owner now probably "goes too far," and was, to cite a tiny example, overly pleased in recent months with the very small inspiration of placing moth flakes in a miniature trunk full of clothes. The moth flakes were modern, it is true, but this small touch of olfactory authenticity gave great pleasure.)

In the several years in which this book has been in preparation, a file of notes relating to restoration has been growing for inclusion in this brief section. This had been left till the last, and shortly before the manuscript was completed, Audrey Johnson's delightful book *Furnishing Dolls' Houses** appeared. This clearly will become the Bible for the hordes of dolls' house enthusiasts who are presently building a far-flung network (related only by measurements) of miniature architecture of heroic though diminutive proportions. The author's drawings and instructions for making carefully researched copies of old dolls' houses and their furnishings are sufficiently irresistible (almost) to inspire even so fanatical an antiquarian as this collector to take saw and paste-pot in hand.

More to the point, Audrey Johnson's book contains a concise and informative chapter on "The Restoration and Care of Old Dolls' Houses" which is required reading for every antiquarian collector. Although some of the products recommended have British trade names, which may require "translation" into American ones, Mrs. Johnson's materials and methods, some of them obviously abetted by her knowledge as an illustrator, are so much more comprehensive than the informal suggestions offered in the following paragraphs that her chapter is highly recommended as a necessary supplement.

After the preceding remarks, it seems almost superfluous to define the "philosophy" to be expounded here, and I shall add only a few words; that this philosophy, which can be summarized as "laissez faire," is dedicated to leaving an old dolls' house as much as possible as it originally must have been, with cleaning, replacing missing bits, repainting only if the original is hopeless, the basic tenets.

(*MINIATURE*) HOUSE CLEANING

If the diversified staff of domestics shown in Fig. 429 might be activated, and put to work on furnished dolls' houses in need of cleaning, each might be armed with an old toothbrush (life-size), a tool recommended as supplemental to a supply of clean cloths for such work. The toothbrush is especially helpful for such "heavy duty" jobs as scrubbing moldings and carvings inaccessible with a damp cloth.

For dampening the cloth itself, there are several plausible alternatives to the old standby of water and mild soap. The first of these, to be preceded, needless to say, by a thorough dusting, resulted from an antique dealer's startling but effective tip for cleaning Victorian game boxes. It has proved to be so effective for restoring delicate lithographed lids, that it is unhesitatingly recommended for wooden dolls' houses and, needless to say, for commercially made ones of lithographed cardboard. The name of this product, "Ajax Floor and Wall Cleaner," sounds thoroughly unsuited to the delicate task of cleaning dolls' house woodwork, much less antique lithographed paper, but in a mild solution, it works like a charm. A spoonful in a cup of lukewarm water (swooshed about) should be tested sparingly on a cardboard box lid; one may proceed with greater confidence on wood.*

Neither this, nor soap and water, would do more than clean, and I have not yet tried a

---

* G. Bell & Sons, Ltd., 1972.

* Since these words were written, this product seems to have disappeared from the market, but a similar cleaning agent may do as well.

concoction, offered by Audrey Johnson, which sounds positively palatable, and is of a nature which must also feed the dry wood. This recipe (receipt sounds more in keeping!) consists of "2 dessertspoons of turpentine, 2 dessertspoons of linseed oil, 2 dessertspoons of vinegar and 1 teaspoon of methylated spirit." These are mixed together, applied with "a soft clean cloth," and followed with a "good beeswax polish." Before offering this delectable method, Mrs. Johnson suggested a process of dealing with woodworm, but this type of infestation is one of the few not found in the United States (although with the number of English dolls' houses which have been finding their way across the Atlantic in recent years, such a problem may be imminent).

PAINTING

Many peculiarities of individual dolls' houses enter into the process of repainting. When an old house has obviously been repainted, and to its disadvantage, perhaps the simplest restoration is to apply paint remover in a relatively obscure spot, and when the original color has been found, to match it as carefully as possible. (Mrs. Johnson, in a chapter about crafts, offers well-informed advice about the types of paints proper to use.) In restoring the "Six Story Building from New Jersey," (see Fig. 112) the painting problem was especially acute since water had obviously dripped down one side, and bits of coigning and other trim had fallen off, along with flaking paint. The trim that remained bore an irreplaceable patina with a tracery of infinitesimal cracks, as delicate as those in a spider web. It was difficult enough to match the precise shade of green; this was finally supplemented by mixing the color with artist's oils, but the new trim will have to await additional aging to resemble the tracery of the old. All areas which were reasonably presentable were subjected only to cleaning; the new bits of trim, along with neighboring members, were painted as well as cleaned.

Painted exteriors, including roofs and walls of commercially made houses, especially those from abroad, often flake. A well-informed antique dealer and collector from Minnesota mentioned that artist's fixative, painted with a brush over such areas, preserves painted finishes of this type.

WALLS

One of the most evocative and appealing elements the interior of an old dolls' house may offer is an assortment of wallpapers. Engaging ones made in tiny patterns especially for dolls' houses are often found in mid-nineteenth-century houses, especially those from England. Two irresistible rooms in an English dolls' house of this period * not only contain such papers, but nearly all the pictures and mirrors hang where, it is evident, they have hung for decades. Proof of this is offered by two exceptions: one missing picture in each room has left an oval indication of where it once hung, and where, exactly as it might have in an actual room, the paper has darkened (rather than faded) around it.

In the same house, before it left England, an inconsiderate hand had painted over another pattern, in a neighboring room (vestiges may be seen beneath the velvet lambrequin on the corner mantelpiece), and unless some remarkable product is invented which will remove paint from wallpaper, there it will remain. However, there is an alternative to the bright yellow the room is presently painted and which, when time permits, will be substituted. An old wallpaper may be mounted on cardboard the size of each room wall, and tacked lightly into position. In that way, if a more desirable wallpaper, or other happier alternative, ever comes to hand, the papered panels may be removed with ease.

* Author's collection. (Fig. 436)

THE PHILOSOPHY OF RESTORATION

When wallpapers seem hopelessly damaged, this method of restoration is only one possibility. Another, suggested by Mrs. Johnson, is to copy missing pieces, using watercolors or other paints. (This presupposes that the restorer, like Mrs. Johnson, is an artist!) She also suggests a similar technique—artists' pastels—to obliterate "common brown streaks of damp," and further recommends "a P.V.A. fixative . . . in aerosol form" * to fix wallpapers.

As for layers of old wallpapers, Vivien Greene's fingernails are famous for having discovered lovely early examples under many layers. Sometimes it is possible to remove such layers by wetting them thoroughly, and permitting them to soak for a brief period, but this has hidden dangers and must be done with great care to avoid removing the original layer as well. When sufficient segments of a pretty paper remain, it is well to keep in mind that pictures hung and furniture arranged with sufficient ingenuity can cover a multitude of sins.

Nothing can remove the character of an old dolls' house more readily than repapering with modern substitutes, no matter how suitably miniature and charming. A trained eye can spot these even on a photograph. If all else fails, it is sometimes possible to glue well-scaled segments of a print too large in its entirety, to a plain wallpaper (a ceiling paper should serve well), after mounting this on cardboard, as previously described. This is also a satisfactory method of extending a paper of inadequate size. Another way of making a small amount of an old wallpaper go farther is to provide a chair rail or dado, with the paper above and paint below.

Border paper given many years ago by the late Miss Faith Bradford to the writer may be seen in Fig. 402. After undesirable parts were cut off the strip, the remaining sections were applied vertically to the walls, in almost perfect proportion to the widths a full-sized paper-hanger would hang in the same manner. A narrow strip previously cut out of the "life-size" border was then used as a miniature border at the top of the room.* Papering a miniature room in this manner appeared to be as time-consuming as papering a big one, but perhaps the difficulties were owing to inexperience!

If the original wallpaper in an old house is entirely unsalvageable, and no "roll" of the proper scale and vintage is at hand, painting the walls is a feasible alternative. Painted walls, after all, are traditional, and though wallpapers are charming, they are not the only solution. Care should be taken to avoid shrill colors and shiny enamels, and to find shades which are representative of the era of the house.

LIGHTING

As one who "takes on" about the proper restoration of old dolls' houses, and who puts great store by original condition, this collector may well be accused of inconsistency with respect to a habit of installing electricity in houses which, beyond an occasional miniature candle, timorously lighted, or a Lilliputian oil lamp, illuminated with kerosene and infinite caution, had never known lighting. Most antique dolls' houses made do by day with such sunlight as might filter through their curtained windows and by night with such lighting as the room containing the dolls' house afforded.

Of installing electrical fittings in antique houses, I can only plead "guilty." However, if the lighting is subtly accomplished, it seems to me infinitely preferable to bore a few holes, and to insert a few wires,† rather than to focus a

---

* An artist's fixative of the type used to fix pastels.

* Since this was a house (1920's) made from a nondescript cupboard, the paper was applied directly to the walls. It probably would have been simpler, and have required fewer acrobatics, to apply the paper to cardboard and then tack it in, as suggested for older houses.

† The wires can be removed and the holes readily obliterated if a future owner so desires.

modern spotlight on a room which had never been exposed to such obtrusive illumination. Or to be able to perceive its contents only dimly. In many years of having houses wired, I have always made every effort to conceal the source of the lighting, including the bulbs themselves. Sometimes this is possible with the aid of the construction of the house itself, if the façade conceals a corner where a small socket can be hidden from view, or contains a strip at the top and front of a room to which it can be fastened. When such aids are not available, I have occasionally resorted to opaque plastic covers in Italianate bracket shapes, installing one in an upper front corner of a room to conceal the fixture and bulb. (Fig. 131)

The type of fixture and bulb has varied over the years, and some methods have been experimental. Bulbs wired in series, as on some Christmas trees, were not scorned, in the early years, for houses with sufficient rooms to contain the proper number. Cumbersome transformers were coped with for those with insufficient rooms. A year or two before this book was completed, toy train bulbs, transformers, Christmas tree lights, and other relatively unsatisfactory methods of illuminating dolls' houses seemed no longer bearable, and, one afternoon, this collector (to whom the secrets of electricity will always be a mystery) spent several hours on the telephone attempting to track down a type of miniature lighting another collector had mentioned, one which had been designed for dolls' houses. The type of lighting I'd set out to locate was never found, but one phone call led to another, and the final phone call led to a type of lighting I had not considered before, and one which I have been using ever since, and have recommended to numerous collectors.

Basically, this involves the small bulb which lights a radio dial, and its advantages are numerous. The bulbs give off almost no heat, and they offer the additional advantage of long life (after all, radio dials receive much use and cannot pause for frequent replacements of so minor a nature). Most important, these bulbs cast a warm and delicate light. In the "Six Story Building from New Jersey," the ancient wiring (presumably 1903, the date on the cornice) was removed, and eighteen of these small fixtures and bulbs were substituted, giving an almost fairy-tale effect to the premises. Special sockets, in several varieties, are made to hold the small bulbs, and the source I know is a firm called Lafayette Electronics.* Presumably there are other firms engaging in the manufacture of electronic parts for radios, who will have similar bulbs and fittings for dials.

All dolls' house collectors find pleasure in discovering various improvements, and happening upon improvisations, and this one must confess to an especial delight in having worked out (with the technical assistance of a family friend and carpenter who did all the work) this type of dolls' house lighting.†

DOLLS' HOUSE OPENINGS

The manner in which a dolls' house opens is, of course, of great interest to collectors. Some houses swing open on hinges at front, sides, or back; a few (and these are most unsatisfactory from a collector's point of view, as they must also have been from a child's) lift off in sections beginning at their rooftops. Now and then a house is found which, except for windows, doesn't open at all. Others are entirely uncovered at the back or front.

---

* Who, if they have a run on these fittings in future, may wish to know that not all of them are illuminating radio dials. Various styles of sockets have been used, and a recent style obtained from Lafayette is marked "Drake LH 22/1." The only mark on the bulbs is SYL 120 V (presumably Sylvania).

† In October 1972, the Essex Museum, Salem, announced an expenditure of $600 to install special "fibre-optic" lighting in the Bessie Lincoln House because "light bulbs are too hot and much too big."

THE PHILOSOPHY OF RESTORATION

Especially with this last type of house, a means of protection from family pets, small hands, and dust becomes essential, and the most satisfactory protection I have found, which permits clear viewing along with its other advantages, is a sheet of Plexiglas (¼" thick or ⅛" thick according to the size of the piece needed), which can be applied to the house in a variety of ways. Sometimes it is possible to attach a strip to the bottom of the rooms as well as to the top, to support a sliding panel, or panels, of this material. Another method is to suspend the panel from a projecting hook (fastened to the upper portion of a room). Occasionally, a small magnet can be attached to the outer projection of a room to help keep the Plexiglas in place.

The back of the South Jersey house which originally opened in three cumbersome sections, with antique latch fastenings, has been removed (but carefully preserved) and replaced with doors made of ¼" plastic, which have been fitted with small locks (one for each of two sections) and a key. This use of Plexiglas can also be adapted to houses with façades, and fitted in such a way that the façade can be closed over Plexiglas set in slightly, to furnish covers for individual rooms.

With experiment, this inoffensive material can be adapted to protective usages in a variety of ways.

HOUSE FURNISHINGS

CARPETS

Floor coverings often remain in dolls' houses when all else is gone, but if these, too, are missing, excellent substitutes can be readily provided. Pieces of old velvet (if one is a purist), or new velvet in antique colors (if one is less fussy), mounted on cardboard which has been cut to the shape of the room, make admirable carpets.

Small rugs from old dolls' houses (often for sale with other miniature lares and penates), appropriately arranged on the floor of even a carpeted room, help to augment the lived-in appearance which dolls' house decorators find so desirable! The small "cigarette" rugs, in Oriental patterns, given away as cigarette premiums prior to World War I, are especially suited to Edwardian rooms, and even to elegant ones of the 'twenties.

CURTAINS AND DRAPERIES

It is always desirable to find an antique dolls' house with its original curtains and draperies, even when the rest of its furnishings are dispersed. Sometimes these are in need of laundering, and a gentle swooshing in a mild solution of liquid Ivory or Lux, or something comparably mild, would be beneficial to many of the small, grimy net curtains which frequently are to be found in late-nineteenth-century dolls' houses.

Draperies which may contain dyes are another matter, and one must be careful. Mrs. Johnson makes this suggestion: "Wet a piece of white cloth and squeeze a corner of the curtain in it." She advises dry cleaning if any "loose die" shows. She also mentions the "life-size" eighteenth-century draperies at Uppark, the home of the celebrated baby house of the same name, and the liquid in which these curtains have been "washed regularly," made from "a pink-carnation like plant called soapwort." A member of the family who came from Uppark to lecture at the National Gallery of Art in Washington in the 1960's recounted the discovery of this unusual cleaning agent and its remarkable properties for cleaning delicate fabrics.* Obviously, it would be suitable for the most gossamer.

It may be useful to go one step beyond Mrs. Johnson's advice with respect to drying minia-

---

* The name of the product is "Saponin." At the time, it was to be marketed in the United States.

ture curtains (after thorough rinsing): "flat on absorbent paper so that they retain their shape." A "life-size" domestic once undertook to launder a few pairs of miniature curtains for me. After they were washed, she carefully smoothed out the folds for drying, and it was not till they were dry that I realized, too late, that the original folds were gone forever, and the resulting squares were stiff and difficult to arrange. In describing the making of new curtains, Mrs. Johnson suggests a procedure that may be applied to this problem as well: She illustrates a method of pinning the folds into place on a flat surface and then "fixing" them with hair spray. She also mentions that curtains can be "pinned or glued to the wall, or hung on string or wire or elastic. . . ." I've been told that the meticulously arranged curtains in the Thorne rooms were glued onto glass the size of the window, with the duplicate glass then set into place in the window opening.

Although Mrs. Johnson mentions curtain rods made of doweling and covered with gilt paper, with a fancy gold bead at each end, I have found satisfactory the plebeian wire coat hanger cut to size and suspended between two cup hooks. If old lace is used for the curtains, the effect is sufficiently pretty, and the coat hanger sufficiently invisible, to make this method acceptable. (On the other hand, among my favorite miniature possessions is a set of Victorian brass extension rods with brackets so perfectly engineered that after many long years, they still grasp and release the rods with ease; and suspend the curtains with the aid of a row of minuscule matching clamps with infinitesimal springs and with brass rosette tops!)

FURNITURE

For cleaning old dolls' house furniture, another trick borrowed from the Thorne rooms might be mentioned. This is the well-known method of attacking the dust with water-color brushes, tools of a proper delicacy especially for antique upholstery which is beginning to show its age.

MISCELLANEOUS

All other suggestions for cleaning (and/or repairing) furnishings are of a miscellaneous nature, odds and ends gleaned over the years: one relates to cleaning tin; and this was recommended to a Georgia collector with a tin dolls' house, of which many Victorian examples are known to have been manufactured (and a few of which have survived). But the method is also applicable to cleaning tin furniture, such as the early pieces made by Althof, Bergmann, or Ellis, Britton & Eaton, among others.

This tip, found in a column about antiques, was in answer to a question from a collector of tin trays who'd had bad luck with warm sudsy water (using a mild detergent). A thin layer of warm Vaseline applied to the tin, and permitted to stand "for at least 24 hours," with the excess then wiped away with a soft cloth or tissue, was recommended for cleaning "any painted piece of tin—old or new." The writer promised that this method would not only prevent rust, but would brighten the paint. She advised a gentle rubbing with 0000 steel wool for stubborn rust spots.

Another aid relates to cleaning, of all things, dressed dolls' house dolls. This was provided by a friend (and fellow collector) in England, Mrs. Magdalena Byfield, who mentioned that to clean such a doll and her clothing, she placed her, fully dressed, in a bag of Fuller's Earth which, every now and then, she gave "a good shake."

The final suggestion relates to repair and requires no talent at all—only a cooperative jeweler. From time to time, for the repair of metal pieces, especially for the fragile ones of lead, I am given the name of an effective glue (which I promptly mislay). Other collectors speak well of the results to be gained by soft solder, but the most successful mending project of this sort which has ever been my lot was

THE PHILOSOPHY OF RESTORATION

achieved by a department store jeweler years ago, who mended an "important" lead chandelier, one with workable wicks and blown globes. Not all jewelers are willing to do such work, but if one perseveres, there is much of a fragile nature which can be salvaged.

Because this collector has found little time to restore dolls' houses, and has been obliged to depend largely upon other people, when they can be found, for such restoration, I must mention again that the preceding paragraphs are intended not as a comprehensive summary but, rather, as a sort of traveling bag of tips picked up here and there on the collecting road, and intended only as a small bonus in a book which was written with other purposes in mind.

Contemporary Craftsmen

While today's maker of dolls' houses and their furnishings is outside the primarily antiquarian limits of these pages, the great revival in miniature crafts, has, like the revival of all handicrafts, become so widespread, and is so vital a part of the miniature scene, that not to touch upon it, at least, might be comparable to writing about the ocean and neglecting to mention a tidal wave. A tidal wave in progress . . .

In looking through some old publications, it was surprising to discover that even in the remote year of 1946, *Cranford Miniatures*, a Pleasantville, New York, firm no longer in existence, reported, in a semi-monthly newsletter sent to customers, that their mailing list at that time numbered "over four thousand names." Inasmuch as the tidal wave of miniaturia which engulfs us in the 'seventies was scarcely a whitecap in 1946, it is almost frightening to think of what figure might be reported now. That great entrepreneur of miniaturia, John Blauer of San Francisco, who should know, has stated that, following dolls, now number two in collecting intensity, and coins and stamps, number one, "miniatures" have become the number three collecting pursuit. Along with the craft revival, a part of this may be owing to the multitude of doll collectors, in former years entirely preoccupied with dolls, who have turned to collecting smaller ones, and to furnishing homes, or at least rooms, in which to house them.

Whatever the reasons, the sheer variety of furniture and accessories being made today is almost unimaginable. To begin to summarize the makers and their wares is a subject for another book; it is possible in the limited space here to list only a handful of the leading craftsmen and suppliers, and briefly to summarize their marvelously diversified specialties. Alphabetically, and most miscellaneously, they include:

BLAUER, JOHN M. THE MINIATURE MART. 883 39th Avenue, San Francisco, Calif. 94121. Mr. Blauer is as celebrated for his own remarkable collection, which includes a handsomely furnished forty-room castle known as Maynard Manor,* as for his wide stock of miniature accessories. For $1.50,† Mr. Blauer

---

* Although I had hoped to include at least one illustration of Mr. Blauer's marvelous castle, space limitations forbid. It must be mentioned, however, that the Manor contains more than 3,000 treasures (a word used literally here), including such items as "a set of 36 gold knives, forks and spoons in a fitted case, and a tiny gold jewel cask, made by Fabergé, [both] . . . among items sold to a Paris dealer by a Russian noblewoman after the revolution." Many pieces are from the celebrated collection of Jack Norworth, who was as well known for his collection of miniatures as for the fact that he wrote "Take Me Out to the Ball Game" and "Shine on, Harvest Moon." (John Blauer acquired the entire Norworth collection.)

† All information about catalogues, etc., is of course subject to change.

will supply a catalogue in which three hundred examples of his wares, all inch to the foot, are illustrated. After receiving one of his thick catalogues in September 1971, this fanatically antiquarian collector wrote to tell him what a revelation it was: "after seeing all you offer in your present catalogue, I'm *almost* beginning to wonder why I've been collecting miniature antiques for all these years—it's clear that *almost* everything I have is being made, and more...."

The catalogue in question included everything from a folding lorgnette (50 cents) to one of Mr. Blauer's fine room settings (for people who prefer not to assemble their own) at $1,500. Several types of chandeliers and of fireplace mantels (the latter made from what he refers to as "hydra-castings") are illustrated.

CHESTNUT HILL STUDIO. Box 38, Churchville, N. Y. 14428. Everything required to grace miniature rooms of the quality of Mrs. Thorne's is obtainable from this firm, founded by the late Reta Cowles Johnson, a retired New York advertising executive, in 1947. Carefully researched and meticulously crafted, the emphasis here is on furniture, but accessories of similar quality and variety are obtainable as well, ranging from Bohemian ruby lustres, $1\frac{1}{4}$" high,

Figure 438

with prism drops, to a China Trade Punch Bowl with eagles of deep blue both inside and out. Chestnut Hill, in its 1971 catalogue, offered five completely furnished rooms "inspired by outstanding American interiors." These include a James River Drawing Room (ca. 1760) and a Philadelphia Ballroom (French Empire 1820–30) containing, among other fine pieces, a square piano, a harp with thirty-eight strings, and—most irresistible of all—a borne (Fig. 438). (The

Figure 437

latter a circular sofa—this one surrounding a center column surmounted by a flower-filled urn—is only the second miniature specimen known to me. An antique example is in the "Sanitary Fair" dolls' house in Wilmington.)

Architectural elements (windows, doors, fireplace mantels, and panelling), miniature silver and petitpoint rugs in Oriental patterns are also available, but perhaps the most remarkable furnishings supplied by Chestnut Hill relate to fabrics. These include draperies and upholstered pieces not only of "the most elegant fabrics with textures and patterns suitable" to one inch scale, but also of correct designs for the period of each piece.

(Chestnut Hill also furnishes a catalogue, for $1.50.)

DEVEREUX, TOM. 5701 N. Sheridan Rd., Chicago, Ill. Mr. Devereux is well known for the beautiful furniture he makes, as well as for his own collection of miniature rooms. He also creates such accessories as chandeliers, and will also make pieces to order, such as lacquered Chinese furniture. (As these words were written, he was in the process of making furniture of the Ming Dynasty for two Virginia collectors, Mrs. Raymond Norris and her daughter, Miss Marshall Norris. He will also make furniture of the Ch'ing dynasty!)

GRAY, JOSEPH H. "Atoms of Art." 112 S. College Way, Auburn, Calif. 95603. Formerly based in Chicago, Mr. Gray, who has been a celebrated purveyor of miniaturia for many years, has been known for stocking such unusual items as minuscule tubes of toothpaste, and workable tools (wrenches and such), made with the utmost realism and skill. (A list is obtainable for twenty-five cents.)

THE PEDDLER'S SHOP. 12408 E. 46th Terrace, Independence, Mo. 64050. An excellent source of miniature hardware and other materials for embellishing both dolls' houses and miniature furniture. In addition to such brass items as pulls, hinges, catches, frames, and an assortment of miscellaneous embellishments, Ellen Krucker, the proprietor, stocks special papers for wall coverings, chandelier parts (including crystal beads for making one's own), and even "Castle Decor." (One page of her catalogue is laden with brass hatchments, swords, and other emblems and objects for the surprising number of builders of castles—who prefer their battlemented structures made of something more tangible than dreams or sand. An illustrated catalogue is $1.)*

PRESCOTT, MRS. B. Box 177, Warrenville, Conn. 06278. Mrs. Prescott's custom-made miniature furniture, in the customary inch-to-the-foot scale, is well known. She has been specializing in recent years in reproductions of Victorian furniture, but is also known for tester beds, tall chests, and Windsor chairs of an earlier period. (Twenty-five cents to Mrs. Prescott for a list and photos.)

VALENTINE, BETTY. 114 New State Road, Manchester, Conn. 06040. Mrs. Valentine makes exquisite miniature furniture, some of the

Figure 439

* Since these words were written, Miss Krucker has become Mrs. Blauer. With their firms merged as well as themselves, all inquiries should be sent to Mr. Blauer's address.

CONTEMPORARY CRAFTSMEN

most perfect reproductions of antique pieces I have ever seen. Mrs. Valentine will send a list (S.A.S.E.), and she also makes furniture to order. Sometimes she creates her own settings, but the Federal hallway pictured was a collaborative effort, combining Mrs. Valentine's furniture and a background created by Diane Sayers, 111 Groveland Street, Haverhill, Mass. 01830, another gifted craftswoman. (Fig. 439)

THE VILLAGE SMITHY. Alfred Atkins. 73 Kensington Road, Bronxville, N. Y. 10708. Mr. Atkins, as the name of his establishment suggests, works in metal, and his wrought-iron objects, which include eighteenth-century-style chandeliers, spiral staircases, and fencing by the foot, are to be found, very probably, nowhere else. Mr. Atkins, who is a former free-lance commercial artist, has discovered a most unusual branch of the miniature tree. (The latter, undoubtedly a spreading chestnut, as *Nutshell News* has aptly considered.)

WHITTON, MRS. MARGARET. Hut Hill Road, Bridgewater, Conn. 06752. For $1, Mrs. Whitton, a well-known doll dealer, will send a twenty-four-page catalogue in which more than two hundred pieces (furniture and accessories), scaled one inch to the foot, are illustrated.

WILLOUGHBY'S EIGHTEENTH CENTURY. P. O. Box 918N, Los Altos, Calif. 94022. Willoughby's advertises Queen Anne furniture, wallpapers, fabrics, paintings, silver, panelling, etc., along with a "historical catalogue describing the furnishings and ambience of the Eighteenth Century" ($1.50). Both catalogue and wares are highly recommended by several collectors of impeccable taste.

From time to time, various dolls' house groups have been established, and a number of these, like the doll clubs (which have their own vast "Federation of"), founded in 1972 an association of their own; the California-based "N.A.M.E." (National Association of Miniature Enthusiasts). Membership includes a subscription to the *Miniature Gazette*, a quarterly publication. The address is P.O. Box 2621, Brookhurst Center, Anaheim, Calif. 92804.

There have been other publications, from time to time, to offer news of the flourishing fancy. Two current quarterlies are the English-based *International Dolls' House News*, edited by Miss Felicity Locke, and *Nutshell News*, which in 1972 moved its headquarters from New York to California (because its editor, Mrs. Gordon MacLaren, moved there!)*

Of those craftsmen and purveyors of miniaturia who have been listed, most are occupied in full-time enterprises, in which their wares are sold to the public. In considering the contemporary scene, however, this fails to touch upon the public itself—the many collectors who are also craftsmen, building houses and/or furniture, or incorporating old pieces into skillful backgrounds of their own devising. A few have been included in other sections of this book, largely builders and furnishers of houses in architectural styles which otherwise would not be represented in these pages. (An example is Mrs. Andrews' replica of a 1735 general store and post office in Virginia.)

To choose one "contemporary collector," † to represent those whose works are not to be found in these pages, is a formidable task, and perhaps a presumption, but I shall risk such a choice and briefly salute Mrs. Alice C. Steele of West Cummington, Massachusetts (on the Berkshire trail), whose miniature representations of New

---

* Miss Locke retired with the Summer, 1973 issue. "The Dolls House Society" has taken over. Address: Circulation Manager, I.D.H.N., 56 Lincoln Wood, Haywards Heath, RH16 1LH, Sussex, England. The address of *Nutshell News* is 1035 Newkirk Drive, LaJolla, California 92037.

† I wish also at least to allude to the work of Mrs. Homer (Betty Ann) Twigg of Bethesda, Maryland, who, using the name of "Elspeth" not only makes miniature rooms of lovely perfection but provides printed instruction for other makers.

Figure 440

England life have brought pleasure to many visitors over a period of years. Mrs. Steele began collecting antique miniatures more than half a century ago, and, with a true feeling for the past, as well as an actual recollection of a bit of it, has, with the help of her husband, Frank Steele, a retired cabinetmaker, displayed her collection in more than two hundred authentically designed rooms, all in the usual one-inch-to-a-foot scale.

Until recent years, a number of these were open to the public as "Tiny Old New England," an exhibition of Americana in miniature. Perhaps what is most characteristic of Mrs. Steele's work is that the nostalgia which infuses it is not limited to objects; occasions as well as interiors are represented: a Masonic Hall, a church food sale, a country auction—even an "old-time funeral in a home parlor." The original group was bought by the late Mrs. Homer Strong of Rochester, and it is hoped that it will be on view again when the Strong Museum is re-opened.

In the photograph of one of the "scenes" from that group, "The Quilting Party," the three chairs which may be seen are quite properly New England made. The dolls are an assortment of china-heads and bisques and are, of course, immigrants. Mrs. Steele has written that most of her rooms are replicas of actual ones members of her family once occupied in Hampshire, Franklin, and Berkshire counties. "Everything is old if it is humanly possible to have it so, and the dolls in the rooms represent the people who inhabited the rooms."

The artist, who is past eighty, has been continuing her work, making rooms for Mr. and Mrs. Raymond Schmitt of Moodus, Connecticut, who have been restoring an industrial village. (One of the rooms she was working on in 1972 was a copy of a parlor, with stenciled walls which were found under many layers of wallpaper "right here in Cummington ten years ago.") She has also given seventeen rooms to the Kingman Tavern Museum of Cummington, of which she is one of seven commissioners.*

Unlike the Thorne rooms, which are the result of the arts and the ingenuity of many makers, Mrs. Steele's rooms are entirely made by herself.

* The commissioners manage the museum, which belongs to the town, and is open on Saturday afternoons, and by appointment, during "the warm weather."

APPENDICES
A BRIEF BIBLIOGRAPHY
MUSEUMS WITH DOLLS' HOUSES
INVENTORY OF WHEELER DOLLS' HOUSE
INVENTORY OF FAIR-Y VILLA
NOTE ON METRIC SYSTEM
SCALE PLAN OF HAYES HOUSE NO.1
SCALE PLAN OF HAYES HOUSE NO. 2

INDEX

A BRIEF BIBLIOGRAPHY

This is intended only as a sampling of books about dolls' houses and related subjects. Most have been consulted in preparation for this volume; others are included as a guide to those who wish to delve further into such matters. Many volumes relating to nineteenth-century decorative arts and architecture were also studied; many of them are footnoted in the text. Such museums as the Victoria and Albert in London and the Rijksmuseum in Amsterdam have issued pamphlets about their dolls' houses and toys, over the years, in various editions, some of them presently obtainable. Although the contents of these are largely outside the scope of this book, this is mentioned for the information of collectors who may wish to seek them out. Various catalogue reprints and related materials are indicated elsewhere in these pages. For a more comprehensive bibliography prior to 1965, see *A History of Dolls' Houses*.

BARENHOLTZ, EDITH F. (Ed.) *The George Brown Toy Sketch Book*, Princeton, N. J.: The Pyne Press, 1971.

COLEMAN, EVELYN, ELIZABETH, and DOROTHY, *The Age of Dolls*, Washington, D. C., 1965.

———. *The Collector's Encyclopedia of Dolls*, New York: Crown, 1968.

FRASER, ANTONIA, *A History of Toys*, London: George Weidenfeld and Nicolson, Ltd., 1966.

FREEMAN, RUTH and LARRY, *Cavalcade of Toys*, Watkins Glen, N. Y.: Century House, 1942.

GREENE, VIVIEN, *English Dolls' Houses of the Eighteenth and Nineteenth Centuries*, London: B. T. Batsford, Ltd., 1955.

GRÖBER, KARL, *Children's Toys of Bygone Days*, translated by Philip Hereford, London: B. T. Batsford, Ltd., 1928.

——— and Metzger, Juliane, *Kinderspielzeug aus alter Zeit*, Hamburg: Marion von Schröder, 1965.

HERTZ, LOUIS H., *Handbook of Old American Toys*, Wethersfield, Conn.: M. Haber, 1947.

HILLIER, MARY, *Dolls and Dollmakers*, New York: G. P. Putnam's Sons, 1968.

HOLME, GEOFFREY, *Children's Toys of Yesterday*, London: The London Studio, Ltd., 1932.

HOSMER, HERBERT H., *Four Dolls' Houses*, South Lancaster, Mass., 1964. (pamphlet)

HOWARD, MARIAN B., *Homes for Paper Dolls and Kindred Paper Toys*, Miami, Florida, 1953.

JACKSON, MRS. F. NEVILL, *Toys of Other Days*, London, 1908.

JACOBS, FLORA GILL, *A History of Dolls' Houses*, New York: Scribners, 1953 and 1965.

———. *A World of Doll Houses*, Chicago: Rand McNally & Co., 1965, and Gramercy Publishing Co., 1973.

——— with Estrid Faurholt, *A Book of Dolls and Doll Houses*, Rutland, Vermont: Charles E. Tuttle Co., 1967.

JACKSON, MRS. F. NEVILL, *Toys of Other Days*, New York: Scribners, 1908.

JOHNSON, AUDREY, *Furnishing Dolls' Houses*, Newton Centre, Mass.: Charles T. Branford Co., 1972.

LATHAM, JEAN, *Dolls' Houses: A Personal Choice*, London: A & C Black Ltd., 1969.

MC CLINTOCK, MARSHALL and INEZ, *Toys in America*, Washington, D. C.: Public Affairs Press, 1961.

MC CLINTON, KATHARINE MORRISON, *Antiques in Miniature*, New York: Scribners, 1970.

———. *Antiques of American Childhood*, New York: Clarkson N. Potter, Inc., 1970.

MOORE, COLLEEN, *Colleen Moore's Doll House*, New York: Doubleday & Co., 1971.

MURRAY, PATRICK, *Toys*, London: Studio Vista, Ltd., 1968.

REMISE, JAC, and FONDIN, JEAN, *The Golden Age of Toys*, Greenwich, Conn.: New York Graphic Society, Ltd., 1967.

SYMONS, HARRY L., *Playthings of Yesterday*, Toronto: The Ryerson Press, 1963.

MUSEUMS WITH DOLLS' HOUSES

The following is a list of museums in the United States and Canada in which dolls' houses, shops and their furnishings and/or related toys may be found. This is only a selection: A form letter inquiring about such collections was sent to more than a hundred museums and historical societies. (Several thousand more were not circularized.) Many of the hundred failed to reply; of those which did, collections vary widely in quality as well as quantity. The word "found" is used advisedly. Many collections are in storage; some of them are available only at specified times of year.

Arizona
    Phoenix: Art Museum
California
    Buena Park: Mott Miniatures
    Oakland: The Oakland Museum
    San Francisco: John Blauer's "Maynard Manor"
    Santa Ana: The Charles W. Bowers Memorial Museum
Colorado
    Denver: The Art Museum
Connecticut
    Cheshire: Cheshire Historical Society Museum
    Fairfield: Fairfield Historical Society
    Litchfield: Litchfield Historical Society
    Old Lyme: Lyme Historical Society
    New London: Lyman Allyn Museum
    Washington: Historical Museum of the Gunn Memorial Library
    Wethersfield: Isaac Stevens House, National Society of the Colonial Dames of America
Delaware
    Wilmington: Historical Society of Delaware
District of Columbia
    United States National Museum
    Smithsonian Institution
Florida
    Homosassa: Doll Museum
    Silver Springs: Early American Museum
    Winter Haven: Museum of Old Dolls and Toys
Georgia
    Savannah: Juliette Gordon Low Birthplace

Illinois
    Chicago: Art Institute
             Chicago Historical Society
             Evanston Historical Society
             Museum of Science and Industry
Indiana
    Fort Wayne: Allen County-Fort Wayne Historical Museum
    Indianapolis: Children's Museum
    Richmond: Wayne County, Indiana Historical Society
Maryland
    Baltimore: Baltimore Museum of Art
               Maryland Historical Society
    Hagerstown: Washington County Historical Society
    Westminster: Historical Society of Carroll County
Massachusetts
    Ashburnham: Ashburnham Historical Society Museum
    Boston: Children's Museum
           Society for the Preservation of New England Antiquities
    New Bedford: Old Dartmouth Historical Society
    Newburyport: Historical Society of Old Newbury
    Norwood: Historical Society
    Plymouth: Plymouth Antiquarian Society
    Salem: The Essex Museum
    Sandwich: Yesteryear's Museum
    South Lancaster: The Toy Cupboard Museums
    Wenham: Wenham Museum
    Worcester: Worcester Historical Society
Michigan
    Dearborn: The Ford Museum

MUSEUMS WITH DOLLS' HOUSES

Michigan (cont.)
    Detroit: Children's Museum
             Detroit Public Schools
    Manistee: Manistee County Historical Museum

Minnesota
    St. Paul: Minnesota Historical Society
          Ramsey County Historical Society

Missouri
    St. Louis: Missouri Historical Society

New Jersey
    Freehold: Monmouth County Historical Association
    Newark: The Newark Museum

New Mexico
    White City: Museum

New York
    Garden City: Nassau County Historical Museum
    New York City: Metropolitan Museum of Art
              Museum of the City of New York
              The New-York Historical Society
              Van Cortlandt Museum
    Rochester: The Strong Museum (not open as of Spring 1974)
    Stony Brook, Long Island: Suffolk Museum and Carriage House
    Southold, Long Island: Southold Historical Society
    Utica: "Fountain Elms" (House Museum)

Ohio
    Cleveland: Cleveland Museum of Art
           Western Reserve Historical Society
    Fremont: The Rutherford B. Hayes Library
    Lebanon: Warren County Museum
    Milan: Milan Historical Museum
    Port Clinton: Ottowa County Historical Museum

Oregon
    Portland: Portland Junior Museum

Pennsylvania
    Douglassville: Mary Merritt's Doll Museum
    Philadelphia: Germantown Historical Society
             Independence National Historical Park Collection

Pennsylvania (cont.)
    Philadelphia: Morris House, Germantown
    Pittsburgh: Museum of Modern Art, Carnegie Institute
    Stroudsburg: Monroe County Historical Society
    West Chester: Chester County Historical Society
    York: Historical Society of York County

Rhode Island
    Newport: Newport Historical Society
    Providence: Rhode Island Historical Society

South Dakota
    Custer: Mabel D. Gurney Collection, Custer State Park
    Woonsocket: "Stuart's Castle"

Vermont
    Bennington: Bennington Museum
    Fairlee: Walker Museum
    Manchester Depot: The Enchanted Doll House
    Shelburne: The Shelburne Museum
    Woodstock: Woodstock Historical Society

Virginia
    Richmond: The Valentine Museum
    Williamsburg: The Abby Aldrich Rockefeller Collection
    Woodlawn Plantation

Washington
    Seattle: Museum of History and Industry

Wisconsin
    Fort Atkinson: Fort Atkinson Historical Society
    Madison: State Historical Society of Wisconsin
    Milwaukee: Milwaukee Public Museum
             Milwaukee County Historical Society
    Superior: Douglas County Historical Museum

Canada
    Ontario: Bruce Mines: Public Museum
    Cornwall: Stormont, Dundas and Glengarry Historical Society Museum
    Dundas: Dundas Historical Society Museum
    Oakville: Oakville Historical Society
    Toronto: Black Creek Pioneer Village

INVENTORY OF WHEELER DOLLS' HOUSE

Newark, 1882. (See page 87 and Figs. 91 and 92.)

FRONT HALL

Stand with marble top supporting tall mirror
Gilt dish on stem for calling cards
Runner carpet
Gilt umbrella stand with two umbrellas

PARLOR (*left of door*)

Blue carpet with daisies
"Mahogany" & gilt piano with separate keyboard cover*
Sofa upholstered in white material with colored flowers
Arm chairs upholstered to match sofa
Straight chairs upholstered to match sofa
Round center table on three legs
Three leaf Japanese paper screen
Tall pier glass with gilt frame
Three flowering plants in white pots
Lavender & white jardiniere
White metal mantel & fireplace
Metal fire tongs, poker & shovel
Rectangular gilt framed mirror
Gilt candlestick with blue candle
Embroidered blue sofa cushion
Gilt chandelier with 6 white glass globes
Wooden secretary with 7 drawers & cabinet, cabriole legs
Photo album with gilt cover and clasp
2 sea shells
Photo of Schiller
Gilt flower stand with lavender plant
Gilt mantel clock
Candlestick and blue candle
Four gilt window cornices

* All of the "mahogany" and gilt furniture referred to here is clearly the "Biedermeier" from Waltershausen.

Four pair white net curtains
Seven gilt curtain pins, bouquet shaped

DINING ROOM (*right of door*)

Round "mahogany" table with two leaves & extra support for extension
Six "mahogany" & gilt chairs upholstered in white with colored pattern
Rug with red, blue, yellow, black stripes
Gilt chandelier with three white glass globes, 1 extra globe
"Mahogany & gilt" sideboard, marble top, 2 cabinets
"Mahogany & gilt" china closet with mirror door
Pair of wooden candlesticks painted white w. stripes & flowers, original candles
Candlesticks & candles similar to above but no floral decorations
Pair of vases with flowers matching above candlesticks
Gilt repousse dish with handles
Round gilt wall plaque
Metal epergne with glass container for flowers
3 metal knives, 3 spoons, 2 forks
Tiny footed dish, white with floral decoration
Two plates to match footed dish
Gilt framed picture of landscape with windmill
Gilt framed picture of water mill in landscape
Gilt high chair
Gilt clock
Two forks
Two plates
One knife
One spoon
One footed dish
Two pair white net curtains
Four gilt curtain pins
Two brass curtain rods

INVENTORY OF WHEELER DOLLS' HOUSE

KITCHEN

Stove with 4 loose lids & stove pipe
Kettle with lid
Coal scuttle
Two pair fire tongs & shovel
Mantel & fire place with open grate
Brass 3 legged pot
Red metal tea pot with lid
Wooden table
Two plates holding cake & blue grapes
Kitchen cabinet containing rolling pin, tub, 4 plates, washboard, potato masher, dish with foot
Two tin dishes holding pie & pudding
Blue & white checked linoleum floor covering
Three half-length dotted Swiss curtains
Green tin dish
Light wood chair with arms
Black wood chair without arms
Gilt clock
Negro cook doll

BACK HALL

Yellow metal refrigerator containing 2 tin shelves, cake of ice, 3 dishes of food

UPSTAIRS SITTING ROOM

Rectangular "oak" table
Metal student lamp with white glass globe & container with lid
Oak sofa upholstered in white material with flowers
Four chairs upholstered same as sofa
Oak desk with two drawers, center cabinet & shelves
Gilt ink stand
Pair of metal candlesticks with white candles
Metal clock surmounted by equestrian statue, under glass dome
Metal fender
Tan carpet with flowers
Gilt filigree waste basket
Gilt leaf candlestick with candle
Gilt framed picture of girl and dog
One pair white net curtains
One pair curtain pins

ALCOVE

Oak dresser with center cabinet, side shelves, mirror
Gilt bird cage with parrot
Round metal container with 3 metal plants in red pots
One pair white net curtains
One pair curtain pins

BEDROOM (*over Dining Room*)

Mahogany & gilt bed with mattress, pillow, gold & buff velvet spread and pillow sham
Gilt cradle with pad, blue silk cover, pillow, & lace edged pillow slip
Four straight chairs upholstered same as bed spread
Tan flowered carpet
Mahogany & gilt dresser with marble top, 7 drawers & long mirror
Round pin cushion
Folding fan
Clock with enamel back
Wardrobe with 2 shelves & mirror door
Gilt framed picture showing fitting of Cinderella's shoe
Gilt framed picture of girl & boy
Chamber from inside commode
Vase of flowers
Two pair curtains
Four pair curtain pins

BACK BEDROOM

"Mahogany & gilt" bed with mattress, blue silk spread & blue pillow sham
Black arm chair with blue silk upholstered seat
Black straight chairs with blue silk upholstered seats
Wardrobe with mirror door
"Mahogany & gilt" dressing table with mirror & marble top
Picture—oval "cameo" in metal frame
Carpet, white ground with figures
Glass tumbler
White bowl
Glass carafe
White glass pitcher
Three pair white net curtains

BATHROOM

Dressing table with 1 drawer
Marble topped table for washing
Black slop bucket
Glass carafe
Glass tumbler
Oak mirror
Square wooden toilet
Brown fur rug with blue felt backing
Two window shades
Tin bath tub
Chamber, white with red design
Bowl, white with red design
Pitcher, white with red design

INVENTORY OF WHEELER DOLLS' HOUSE

Two dishes with covers, same design
Black arm chair with blue upholstered seats, same as those in back bedroom
Two black straight chairs with blue upholstery
Covered dish with red design

FRONT STEPS

Two low pottery stands for plants or trees

TO BE PLACED ANYWHERE

Little girl doll, china, in slip, dress & hat

White china cup
Sprays of heather for vases, & artificial evergreen

Two red satin portieres (doorways between parlor and hall, & upstairs sitting & bed rooms have rods & rings)
Total number of curtains:
   19 pairs white net
    3 dotted Swiss
Total number of curtain pins:
   13 quatrefoil
    7 bouquet-shaped

INVENTORY OF FAIR-Y VILLA

Belonging to Mr. Fair-Child, N. Y.—C. O. Jones, Printer, 76 Cedar St., 1864
(See page 87.)

KITCHEN

1. Beebe's Range in good order
2. Sink
3. Large Table
4. Small Table
5. 4 chairs
6. Dresser
7. Copper Stew Pan
8. Quart Measure
9. Iron Ladle
10. Pail
11. Cuckoo Clock
12. Iron Skimmer
13. Cleaver
14. Dutch Oven
15. Flour Scoop
16. Iron Shovel
17. Frying Pan
18. 2 Skillets
19. *(no entry in original)*
20. Funnel
21. Match Box
22. Broom
23. Firkin
24. Pair Candlesticks
25. Tea Kettle
26. Waffle Iron
27. Dust Pan
28. Dust Brush
29. 2 Market Baskets
30. Swill Tub
31. Sieve
32. 2 Cake Moulds
33. Cullender
34. Tin Skimmer
35. Coffee Mill
36. Bake Pan
37. Wooden Ladle
38. Rolling Pin
39. Tray with Knives, Forks & Spoons
40. Japan Tray
41. Smoke Beef Board
42. Grater
43. 3 Stone Jars
44. Castors
45. 3 bottles
46. 2 Tumblers
47. 6 Plates
48. Bowls
49. Iron Pot

DRAWING ROOM

50. Aubusson Carpet
51. 5 Gilt Cornices
52. 5 Pr. Blue Satin Curtains
53. 5 Pr. Lace Curtains
54. Transparencies in Windows
55. Sofa—5 Chairs covered with blue satin
56. 2 Jardinieres
57. Mantel & Glass Complete
58. Blue Satin Valence
59. Set Fire Irons
60. Glass Screen
61. Gilt Chair
62. Gilt Camp Stool
63. Clock
64. Pair Vases
65. Pair Statuettes

INVENTORY OF FAIR-Y VILLA

66. Corner Bracket Gilt
67. Gilt Basket with Flowers
68. Statue of Guardian Angel with velvet cone base
69. Etagère
70. Sofa Table
71. Foot Stool
72. Pier Table & Glass
73. Picture—Copy of Murillo Ascension
74. Pair Side Lights
75. Chandelier
76. Basket of Flowers
76. Jewel Casket
77. Battledore & Shuttlecock
78. Miniature Engine
79. Opera Glass
80. Miniature Cradle
81. Carcel Lamp
82. Pair Silver Candlesticks
83. Snuffers & Tray
84. Chinese Ivory Basket
85. Gilt Inkstand
86. Miniature Chair
87. Gilt Basket
88. Card Plate
89. Pair Candlesticks
90. Ivory Dog

HALL—FIRST FLOOR

91. Door Mat
92. Herrings Safe
93. Stove
94. Coal Scuttle & Hod
95. Ash Shovel
96. Chandelier
97. Oil Cloth

DINING ROOM

98. Velvet Carpet
99. 5 pr. Red Silk Curtains
100. 5 pr. Lace Curtains
101. 5 Cornices
102. Mantel & Glass Complete
103. Set Fire Irons
104. Clock
105. Pair Statuettes
106. Fire Screen
107. Engraving black walnut frame
108. Writing Table with blotting book, pair candlesticks, stick sealing wax, pair scissors, knife, seal, pen, inkstand, paper knife
109. Sideboard with Soup Tureen, 6 plates, 2 compotiers, fruit dish, salt cellar, pair candlesticks, liquor stand, Decanter, 2 wine glasses
110. Six chairs covered with velvet
111. Dinner table with Soup Tureen, 6 plates, Hand-bell, pr. candlesticks, salt cellar, gravy boat, casters, 2 decanters, 6 wine glasses, soup ladle, 6 knives, 6 forks, 6 spoons, 2 wine coolers, with 2 bottles champagne
112. Foot Stool
113. Side Table
114. Tray
115. Tea Set
116. Silver Tête-à-tête set
117. Chandelier

HALL—SECOND FLOOR

118. Oil Cloth
119. Key Safe
120. 2 Armchairs

BEDROOM

121. Green Velvet Carpet & Rug
122. 2 Black & Gold Cornices
123. 5 pr. muslin cornices
124. Marble mantel
125. Set Fire irons & stand
126. Pr. Bellows
127. Clock
128. Pr. Vases
129. Mirror
130. Corner Bracket
131. Statuette (Samuel)
132. 2 Chairs
133. Work Table furnished
134. Single wash stand
135. Basin & Pitcher
136. Soap Dish
137. Tumblers
138. Duchess Toilet Table
139. Hand Glass
140. Hair Brush
141. Croton Water Wash Stand
142. Water Bottle
143. Tumbler
144. 2 Toilet Bottles
145. Bed Canopy & Curtains
146. Mattress
147. Pair Pillows
148. Pr. Linen Sheets
149. Pr. Linen Pillow Cases

INVENTORY OF FAIR-Y VILLA

150. Blanket
151. Marseilles Quilt
152. Afghan
153. Watch Case & Watch
154. Table
155. Candlestick
156. China Figure
157. Tête-à-tête set
158. Fur mat

NURSERY

159. Brussels Carpet & Rug
160. 5 pr. Muslin Curtains
161. 5 Cornices
162. Mantel Piece
163. Set Fire Irons with Stand
164. Ash Brush
165. Bellows
166. Bedspread
167. Mattress
168. Pr. Linen sheets
169. Pillow cases
170. Blanket
171. Marseille Quilt
172. Cradle with lace & silk curtains
173. Bureau
174. Mirror
175. Cuckoo Clock
176. Pr. Candlesticks
177. Pot Pomade
178. Pr. Scissors
179. Hair brush
180. High Bureau
181. Transparency
182. Bird in cage
183. Table
184. Gold fish globe
185. Basket knitting
186. 4 chairs
187. Rocking Chair
188. Infant's chair
189. Taper
190. Pr. Statuettes
191. Iron Wash Stand with basin
192. Soap dish & Water can
193. Picture framed
194. Piece Oil cloth
195. Infant's Bath tub
196. Infant's Basket

197. Soap Dish
198. Sponge

COOK'S ROOM

199. Bedstead
200. Mattress
201. Pillow & Case
202. Pr. Cotton Sheets
203. Blanket
204. Quilt
205. 4 chairs
206. Dressing Table
207. Wash stand furnished
208. Bureau
209. Wardrobe
210. Carpet

WAITER'S ROOM

211. Bedstead
212. Mattress
213. Pillow & Case
214. Pr. Sheets
215. Blanket
216. Quilt
217. Washstand
218. Basin & Pitcher
219. Bureau
220. Mirror
221. Wardrobe
222. 2 chairs
223. Carpet

TRUNK ROOM

224. Trunks
225. Hat boxes

BATH ROOM

226. Oil cloth
227. Bath tub
228. Sitz bath
229. Foot tub
230. Water can
231. Shower bath
232. Towels (?)
233. 3 pr. muslin curtains
234. 3 cornices
235. Oil skin cap

INVENTORY OF FAIR-Y VILLA

EXTERIOR

236. 6 Hanging baskets filled with choice plants
237. Mat
238. Perambulator

FAMILY CONSISTS OF:

Mr. & Mrs. Fair-Child
Elsie & Ida—their two little girls aged 9 & 7 yrs.
Frank aged 5
Willie aged 3½
Bobbie aged 2 yrs.
Minnie, the baby aged 6 months
Adele, the French Nurse
Rose Downing, the Cook
Patrick Mahoney, the Waiter

Made by Mrs. Henry Chauncey and exhibited at her residence, 25 Waverly Place. Sold to Alexander Van Rensselaar for $500 and offered for sale by him at Union Square Fair Building.

A NOTE ON THE METRIC SYSTEM

With more and more countries adopting the metric system, and with many schools and other institutions in the United States also turning from inches to centimeters, it seems pertinent to include at least a brief reference to the relationship of the two sorts of measurement:

Since a centimeter is equal to about one-hundredth of a meter, or about two-fifths of an inch, a chair three inches high would be, in metric terms, about seven and one-half cm. A meter, the fundamental unit of length in the metric system, is equivalent to 39.37 U. S. inches, corresponding, more or less, to the height of a dolls' house of average size.

A brief table follows:

Inch = 2.54 centimeters
Foot = .3048 meter
Yard = .9144 meter

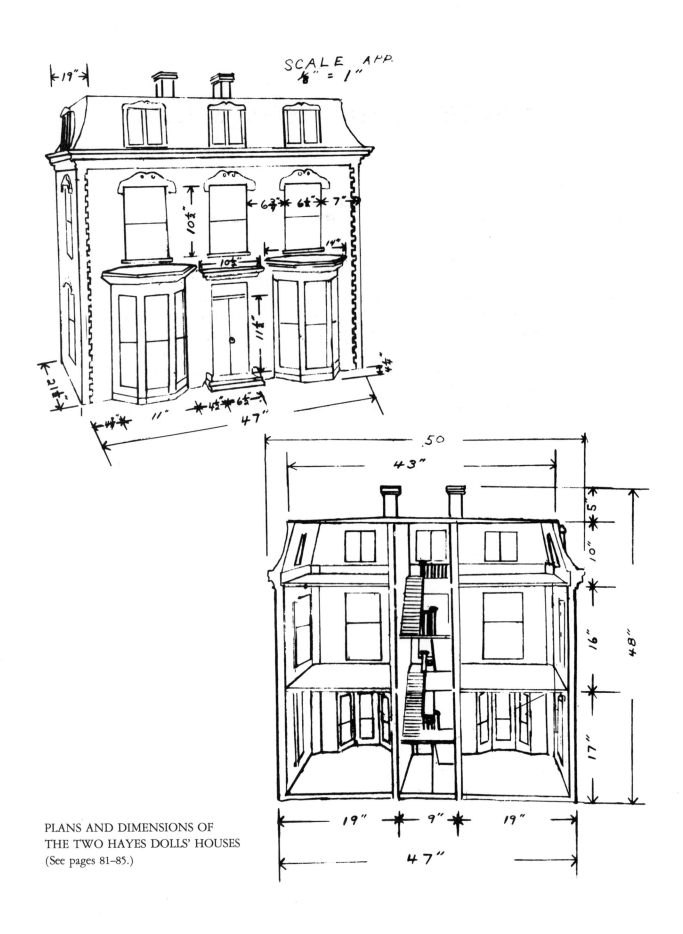

PLANS AND DIMENSIONS OF
THE TWO HAYES DOLLS' HOUSES
(See pages 81–85.)

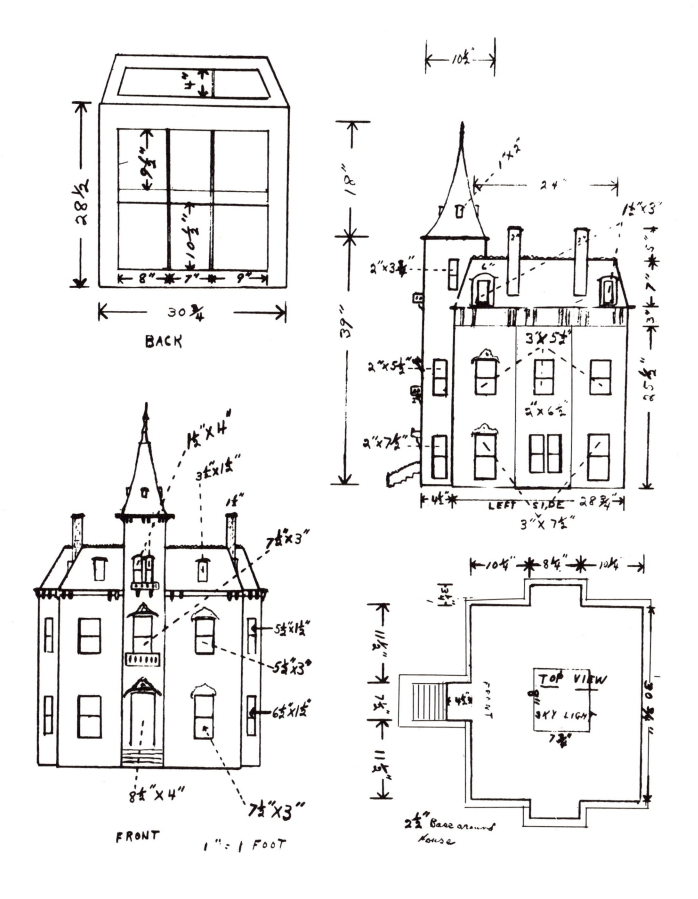

A NOTE ON THE INDEX

Exact headings of the subjects discussed in the text are listed, within quotation marks, among the entries (i.e. "A Brooklyn Sandstone.") The listing of page entries—sub-headings such as references to architectural elements and to furnishings are selective, and to some degree random, inasmuch as a comprehensive subject index might form almost a book-length manuscript.

A

Abby Aldrich Rockefeller Folk Art Collection, 120–5
ABC furniture, 312–14
Ackerman, Evelyn, 329
Adams, Henry, 6
Adrian Cooke Metal Works, 334
Adults, dolls' houses for, 70
Adirondack cottages, 226, 235–7
African safari (Schoenhut), 261
Albany, dolls' house from, 137–8
"Albert Schoenhut's Bungalows (And Such)," 267–9
Alexandria, dolls' house from, 6
Allen County–Fort Wayne Historical Museum, 169–73
Allyn, S. C., 272
"Altoona, A House in," 98–9
Amateur Work, 201
"American Grocery in Scotland, An," 211–12
"Amish Farmhouse, An," 92–3
Anderson, Bart, 71
Andrews, Mrs. Joseph, 163–4, 343, 363
Angione, Genevieve, 207
Antique Toy Collectors of America, 227, 295
Apartment houses, 102, 252, 258
Apprentice pieces, 318
Aquarium, 213
"Arcade Laundry Room, Etc., An," 274–6
Arcade Manufacturing Co., 274–6, 334
Archer, Janet Pinney, 114
"Architect's Model from Philadelphia, An," 80–1
Architecture, Federal, 18, 62–6
"Architecture from Frederick, Maryland," 149–50
Armories, 222, 236, 239, 269
Art gallery, miniature, 74–6
Art Nouveau clock, 266–7; furniture, 313, 337
Asbury Park, 100–2
Ashburnham (Mass.) Historical Society Museum, 212–13
Aspidistra, 213, 215
Astor, John Jacob, 325
Athol, Massachusetts, 264–5
Atkins, Alfred, 363
Attleboro Premium House, 321
Austrian bronze, 108
"Authoritative Colonial Copy, An," 60–1
Avery, W. & Son, Redditch, 337
Awnings, 229, 234, 265, 282
Ayre(s), cabinetmaker, 35–6

B

Babette Schweitzer, 337
"Baby" chairs, 260, 337
Backstairs, 12
Bailey, Mrs. James Douglas, 96–7
Baker's cocoa, 211
"Bakery (1904) from New Jersey, A," 102–4
"Baltimore, A Colonial Revival Mansion from," 153–5
"Baltimore, Five Row Houses from," 158–9, Pl. 1
Baltimore, houses from, 4, 6, 133, 153–5, 158–9, 176
Baltimore Museum of Art, 176
"Baltimore's Sellers Mansion," 146–7
Bamboo furniture, 338
Band, Percy, 203

INDEX

Banks, Mrs. Robert, 135–6
Barenholtz, Edith, 293
Basement, 109, 111, 175; door, 136
Bathing suit, doll in, 347
Bathroom, 56, 87, 106, 129, 132
Baxter prints, 204, 219
Beacon, New York, 272
Beaded furniture, 339
Bed, French metal, 102
Bedroom furniture, 24, 71, 141, 316, 310–14
Belles, Laurence L., 274–6
Belleville, Illinois, 167
Belvederes, 76, 81, 133, 144, 158, 175
Bentwood rocker, 267, 334, 337
Berger, Meyer, 113
Berkeley Square, 299
Berkey & Gay, 275
"Bessie Lincoln House, The," 34–6, 38, 356
"Bessie Mitchell's Xmas, 1879," 133–5
Beverly, Massachusetts, dolls' house from, 36–8
Biddle, Miss, 76
Biedermeier furniture, 10, 25, 112, 119, 171, 289–91, 298, 299, 300–1, 332, 370, Pl. 9 (*See also* Waltershausen, Dolls' Duncan Phyfe)
"Bingham Dolls' House, The," 177–8
Black Creek Pioneer Village, 203
Blackie and Sons, 290
Blauer, Ellen Krucker, 362
Blauer, John M., 9, 195, 360–1
Bliss, R., 7, 214, 224–40, 252, 253, 264, 269, 310–14, 334, Pl. 2; church by, 228; furniture, 135, 310–14, Pl. 6, 7; stables, 237–9, Pl. 4
"Bliss Fire Station No. 2," 233–4, Pl. 4
"Bliss Fortress, A," 239–40, Pl. 3
"Bliss, R., Furniture by," 310–14, Pl. 6
"Bliss, a Grocery Store by," 229–30, Pl. 3
"Bliss Houses, Unmarked," 231–33
"Bliss Warehouse, A," 230–31
Boathouses, 8
Boger, Louise Ade and H. Batterson, 24, 300
Bolton, Hon. Frances P., 177
Books, miniature, 19, 112
Borne (circular sofa), 361
"Bowling, Hall," 157–8
Bradford, Faith, 5, 355
Brandt, William, 98
Brass bed, 318
Brass extension rods, 358
Breininger, Lester P., Jr., 99
"Brett House, The," 5, 108–13, 338, 340
Brett, Rev. Dr. Philip Milledoler, 108

"Brewster Cupboard House, The," 25–6
Brewster family, 25
Briggs, Rose, 26
Briner, William, 194
Bristol glass, 69, 112, 327
"Brooklyn Sandstone, A," 119–20
Brooklyn, dolls' houses from, 119
Brown, George, 293; Toy Sketchbook of, 293
Brownstone houses, 113, 119, 135, 180
Brush, Anna, 136
Bubb, J., 69
"Buck's Folding Doll Tent," 251–2
Buck, George H., 251–2, 321–2
"Buffalo, A Mansion from," 125–7
Building dolls' houses, 178, 201, 353, 360, 363
Bulfinch, 15
Bungalows, 253–4, 267
Burns, Robert, 112
Butcher, James W., 274
Butler Bros., 254, 264–5
Byfield, Mrs. Magdalena, 358

C

Caldwell, L. W., 144
Callicott, Mrs. Claude, 138, 141, 252
"Camp Dewey," 236
Campbell, Mrs. B. R., 272–4
Canada, dolls' houses of, 9, 196–204
Candy box furniture, 25
Candy box horse, 237
"Cane"-seated chair, 335
Canfield, Mrs. George, 333–4
"Cape May, A Cottage from," 96–7
Captain's walk, 27, 30, 36, 38–9, 65, 122, 326
Cardboard, dolls' house of, 250
Card table, by Hersey, 291
"Carnahan Sisters' Christmas Present, The," 169–173
"Carpenter Gothic," 188
Carpets, 85, 357; Aubusson, 20; Brussels, 45, 156, 249; needlepoint, 21, 71
Carroll County, Historical Society of, 143–4
Carver chair, 333
"Casa from Spain, A," 240
"Cass Grocery, A," 264–5
Cass, N. D. Co., 253–4, 264–5
Cast-iron furniture, 275, 333; autos, 276
Castles, fittings for, 362
Cats, affinity of owners to dolls' houses, 149
Ceilings, beamed, 60
Centennial, Philadelphia, 80, 121, 306
"Central-chimney houses," 61

(384)

INDEX

Chair rail, 66
Chairs, 10, 24, 41, 301, 311, 314, 325, 332–39; Pl. 7–14
"Chairs for Conservatories, Piazzas and Gardens," 338, Pl. 13
"Chairs Made in America," 333–4, Pl. 7
"Chairs Mostly from France," 336, Pl. 10
Chamberlain, Benjamin H., 41–4
"Chamberlain House at Wenham, The," 41–4
Chambermasters, 282
"Chamber Set from Cromwell, Connecticut, A," 298
Chamber sets, tin, 295, 298, Pl. 7 (See also bedroom.)
Chandeliers, 17, 25, 119, 330–1, 359; beaded, 39; with workable wicks, 46, 53, 245, 294; reproduction, 361
Chanler, Mrs. Winthrop, 6
Charleston, South Carolina, dolls' house from, 6
Chart, Mrs. Betty, 231–2
Chatauqua, 251
Chefs (dolls), 346
Chess set, 20
Chester County Historical Society, 70
Chestnut Hill Studio, 361
Cheval glass, 32, 294, 302, 317
Child Life, 276
Children's Museum, Boston, 57
Chimney, graduated, 139, 161; hooded, 158; kitchen, 141; "outside," 139
China Trade Punch Bowl, 361
Chinese chair, 332; furniture, 119
"Chinese Chippendale," 24
Chippendale settee and chairs, 21
"Christmas 1893 in Milwaukee," 178–181
Christmas Gardens, 158, 162, 217
"Christmas Present, Albany, 1900, A," 137–8
Christmas tree fences, 79, 91 (South Jersey)
Churches, 87–9, 196–7; Bliss, 228; "Gothic," 212; Mission, 193
"Church from Ile D'Orléans, A," 196–7
Cigarbox wood, 100
"Cigarette" rugs, 357
"Cincinnati, A Parlor Set Made in," 323–4, 334
Cissna & Co., W. A., 230, 232, 234
"Civil War P. O. W. House, A," 144–5
"Civil War Residence, A," 29–30
Classic Revival (chair), 332
Claytor, Mrs. W. Graham, Jr., 99–100, 234
Cleaning dolls' houses, 353–4; tin, 358
Cleveland children, 81
Clocks, Gothic, 296; Hotchkiss, 184; under glass bell, 294
Closet, coat, 279; broom, 153
Coachman (doll), 348
Coal yard, 11, 222
Cobb & Drew, 26

Cobb family, 299
Coddington, Verdelle Flynn, 217
Coleman, Dorothy S., Elizabeth A. and Evelyn J., 241, 267, 271, 296, 336, 342, 343
Coleman, Dorothy Smith, 247, 266, 284, 343, 344
Coleman, Kathleen Moore, 189
Colombia, dolls' house furniture from, 9
Colonial baby houses, 106–8, 139–40
"Colonial Revival Mansion from Baltimore, A," 153–5
"Colonial Revival from Massachusetts, A," 53–4, 122, 153, 177
"Colonial Tea Set," 329
"Colonial Toy House," 251
Columbian Exposition furniture, 320, 333
"Combination Doll Mansion," 207–9
"Combination Doll Villa," 207
"Combination Grocery Store," 207, 211
"Commercially Made Colleen Moore Castle, A," 280–1
Compton, Mrs. Mildred, 185
Confederate Prison, dolls' house built in, 29–30
"Connecticut, A Haunted House from," 46–8
"Conservatories," chairs for, 338
"Contemporary craftsmen," 360–4
Converse of Winchendon, 214, 224, 252–6, 261–4, Pl. 2
Converse, Morton E., 252, 264
Convertible high chair, 260
Cook, Catherine, 260
Cook, Mrs. Dorothy, 232
Cornices, 21, 72, 120
"Cottage—Dated December 1901, A," 138
"Country Auction," 363
Country store, 211
Cousins, Frank, 334
"Cozy Corners," 169, 251, 321–24
Crackerjack prizes, 276
Craft revival, 9, 360
Craigie House (See Longfellow-Craigie House.)
Crandall's Patent Building Blocks, 296
Crane bathroom fixtures, 275
Crane house, 12
Cranford dolls' houses, 51
Cranford miniatures, 360
Creekmore, Mrs. E. F., 151
Cremer, W. H., 10
Cresson-Dickey baby house, 7, 15
Cresson, Sarah Emlen, 64
Cricket on the Hearth, 282
Cromwell, Connecticut, 298
Crowninshield, 18, 21
Crumb tray and brush, 328
Cummington, Massachusetts, 363–4
Cunninghams, 166

(385)

INDEX

Cupboard-type house, 165
Cupola, 27, 42–3, 56, 80 (*See also* Belvedere)
"Currier & Ives Country House, A," 203–4
Curtain rods, 133, 358; pins, 87
Curtains and draperies, 8, 57, 72, 87, 249, 357

D

Danaher girls, 137
"Dandy Toy House by Grimm & Leeds, A," 250–1
Danenhower, Ethel Mitchell, 135
Davidson, Marshall, 53
Davis, Elizabeth L., 146
Davison, Mrs. Louise Dickey, 63
Dayton Journal-Herald, 272
Decker, B. A., 166
Delachal, Louis, 336
Delano & Aldrich, 274
Delaware, Historical Society of, 74
Denver Art Museum, 5
Devereux, family, 21; Eliza, 21
Devereux, Tom, 361
"Dexter Mansion, The," 26–9
Dexter, Lord Timothy, 27
Dickens, Charles, 282
Dickey, Mrs. Cresson, 64; John Miller, 64
Dirigible "New York," 348
Doble, Mrs. Frank C., 297
"Documented Miniature Illumination by Maerklin," 330–1
Dodge, Eliza, 24
"Doll Mansions by Stirn & Lyon," 207–9
Doll, peg wooden, 24, 340, 342
Doll room, 290
Doll samplers, 121, 195
Dolls, 10, 24, 70, 112, 165, 175, 181, 184, 185, 189, 266–7, 280, 294, 329, 340–8, 363, Pl. 15, 16
"Dolls' Duncan Phyfe," 10, 112, 300 (*See* Biedermeier.)
"Dolls' House Occupants," 340–8, Pls. 15, 16
" 'Dolly's Playhouse' by McLoughlin," 248–50, Pl. 5
"Domville House, 1899," 199–202
Doolittle, Mrs. Lytton W., 32–34
Door plates, 19, 42, 56, 87
Doors, sliding, 12
"Dorothy Coleman's Dolls' House," 266–7
Downing, A. J., 143, 177, 346
Dowst Manufacturing Co., 276
Draperies, 21, 43, 72, 357
Drury, Mrs. Saxbam E., 299
DuBois, Mrs. Delanne Lopeman, 38, 162, 269
Dundas Historical Society Museum, 199
"Dunham's Cocoanut Doll House," 212–14, Pl. 4
Dutch door, 111

Dutcher, Edward B., 17
"Dyckman Street Copy in Tin, A," 130–1

E

Easel, 320
Educator crackers, 265
Ehrich Bros., 211–12
Eighteenth century, dolls' houses of, 3, 106–8, 139–40; work table of, 325; reproductions, 363
"Eleanora's House," 161–2
"Electric fixtures, 119, 330
Electrifying dolls' houses, 355
Elevators, houses with, 57, 104, 258
Elizabeth Bennet-Percival Collection, 196–8, 202
Ellis, Britton & Eaton, 35, 124, 296, 297–8, 302–3, 333
"Ellis, Britton & Eaton: A Tin Office Set," 297–8
Ellis, Joel, 35
"Elsa Mannheimer House, An," 219–21
Elspeth, 363
Elton, R. H. & Co., 248
Embossed floral scraps, furniture with, 247
Empire furniture, 24, 70
Empress Eugenie, 333
Englar, Mrs. Clayton, 155–7
"Englewood, New Jersey, A House from," 72–4, 314
English baby house, 9, 66–8
English half-timber design dolls' house, 273
"English Houses, A Series of, in America," 282–6
Erath, Mrs. Henry, 314
Essex Institute, 18, 20, 356

F

Fabergé, 360
Fairchild, Mrs. Richard, 165
Fairfield Historical Society, 29, 54, 60
"Fairy Doll-house," 228
Fairy lamps, 321
Fairy Toy Works, 169
"Fair-y Villa," 11, 373–6
Fallon, Mrs. Myrtes, 6
Fanlights, 18, 54, 68
Farie dolls' house, 333
"Farm Property by Converse," 261–4
Farms, 7, 261–4
Farnsworth, Judge and Mrs. W. Franklin, 194–5, 317
"Farnsworth's ca. 1860 Reproduction, The," 194–5
Fauteuils, 336, Pl. 11
Fawcett, Clara, 178
Feather furniture, 339
Federal Architecture, 18, 62–6
"Federal Baby House from Philadelphia, A," 62–6
Filigree furniture, 102, 162, 337

INDEX

Firegrates, 69
Fire marks, 62–3
Fireplaces, 18, 43, 66, 107, 141, 175, 317, 318
Firetool holders, 66
Fish-scale shingles, 127, 133, 151
Fitzgerald, F. Scott, 189
"Five Bliss Stables," 237–9
"Five Row Houses from East Baltimore," 158–9, 217, Pl. 1
Flagpole, 100, 156, 187
Fleishmann's Yeast, 265
Floor cloths, 66, 108
Floor coverings for dolls' houses, 55, 60, 66, 108, 357, (See also carpets.)
Floors, inlaid, 132; pegged, 124; timbered, 60
Folding chair, 338
Folding dolls' houses, 208–9, 249, 260–1, Pl. 5
"Folding Parlor Room, A," 318
"Folk Art at the Shelburne Museum," 17–18
Food shop, 218
Footscraper, 326
Forbes Litograf Co., 224
Ford, Allen Price, 181
"Formidable Series of Mystery Houses, A," 215–18
Fort, toy, 223 (See armories)
Fort Wayne Public Library, 169–70
"46 Hunt, Beverly, Mass.," 36–38
Fountains, 76, 326
France, chairs from, 336–7; doll rooms of, 247; dolls of, 348; furniture from, 104, 245–7; houses of, 9, 214, 244–5, 245–7, 256, 258–60, 279; milliner's shop from, 215; parlor from, 348; schoolroom, contents of, 184; stores, 218
Francis, Field & Francis, 292, 294
Fraser, Mrs. Robert W., 12, 59–60
Frau Negges, 11
"Frederick, Maryland, Architecture from," 149–50
Freeport, Illinois, 276
"French-Canadian Cottage, A," 202–3
"French House with Sewn-in Furniture!, A," 245–7, 327, Pl. 2
French seaside villa, 245
"Fret-Sawed Furnished Room, A," 308
Fret-sawed furniture, 308, 339; house, 151
Friedmann & Ohnstein, 343
Frigidaire, 275
Funeral (miniature), 363
"Furniture from Matthew Vassar," 298–9
"Furniture by R. Bliss," 310–14

G

Gardens, 108, 175, 209, 260–1, 269, 326, 340; chairs for, 338; formal, 76, 326; roof, 60; walled, 245
Garland, Mrs. Moira, 285–6
"Gay Nineties" Mansion, 153
Gebrüder Schneegass (See Schneegass)
Georgia, house from, 147
Georgian dolls' house, 68
Germany, chandeliers and lamps from, 331; dinner service from, 328; dolls' houses of, 178, 180, 214; furniture of, 9, 10, 55, 57, 181, 188, 245, 258, 298, 314–17, 334–5, 335–7
Gerry, Elbridge T., 113
"Gertrude's House from Halifax, Mass.," 56–7
Gibson, Mrs. C. H., 18
Giles, Mrs. Ashby, 28, 273
Girl Scouts, 147
Girls' Own Paper, The, 178
Glasson, Mrs. George, 264
Glover, Deborah Anna, 30
Goelet, Peter, 113
"Golden Gate Residence, A," 188–9
"Golden Locks' Own Chocolate and Tea Sets," 329
Golfer (doll), 348
Gordon, Elizabeth, 51
Gothic, clocks, 296; church, 212; furniture, 300; Revival, 245
"Governor Johnson Doll Mansion, The," 140–1
"Governor Ramsey Doll Mansion, The," 173–5
"Graddon Family's Parlor Set, The," 289–91
Grant, General U. S., 74
Gray, Joseph H., 362
Greek Revival, 70
Greek statues, 219
Green, William H., 221–4
Greenaway, Kate, 342
Greene, Vivien, 10, 34, 70, 112, 290, 300–1, 335, 337, 355
Greenough family, 106
"Grimm & Leeds, A Toy House by," 250–1
Grindstone, 124
Griswold, Mrs. Woodward H., 133–5, 297
Gröber, Karl, 125
"Groceries at Numbers '6' and '8'," 270–2
Grocery stores, 221, 229–30, 264–5, 270–2
Grodner Tal, dolls of, 340
Grossman, Mrs. John H., 60, 169, 181, 299
"Group of Metal Chairs, A," 337
"Group of Metal Chairs, A (Smaller Scale)," 337

H

Haddonfield, N. J., 76
Hamilton, Ontario, 199
Hand-crafted houses, furnishings, 178, 201, 219
Hanna, Mrs. John H., 149
Hanna family, 172
Harding sisters, 92; Miss Constance, 149
Hardware and Woodenware Corp., 223

INDEX

Hargrave, Colleen Moore (*See* Moore, Colleen.)
Harms, Madeline A., 102
Harnish, Mrs. Herb, 172
Harper's Bazar, 128 (sic)
Harps, 17, 112, 361
Harrell, Mrs. John, 188–9
"Haunted House from Connecticut, A," 46–8
Hawkins, Mrs. Herbert, 215, 217
Hayes, Fanny, dolls' houses of, 81–5
Hayes Museum, 4, 5
Hayes, Mrs. Webb C., 83–4, 289; Rutherford B., 81, 175
Hersey, Caleb, 292; Samuel, 32, 291–2
Hertz, Louis, 7, 262, 294
"High Victoriana from Massachusetts," 38–9
"Hill-Gray House, The," 167–9
Hill, James J., 167
Hillier, Mary, 340
Hill's Alphabet Blocks, 296
Hingham, Mass., 291–2
Historic preservation in miniature, 3, 12
Hobby horses, 224
Hodge, Charles M., 27
Hollywood architecture, 192
Homans family, 106
Home-made furniture, 178
Hopkinson, William, 79
Hosie, Miss Elinor, 63–5
Hosmer, Herbert, 282
Hot Point stove and heater, 275
Hot water heater, 104, 129, 132
Hotchkiss patent clock, 184 (*See also* clocks.)
House Beautiful, 324–5
House cleaning (miniature), 29, 353–4
"House of Tynietoy, The," 324–326
"House with a Coincidence, A," 242–4
Howard, Ethel, 153
Howard, Marian, 249
Hubley Manufacturing Co., 275, 325
"Hudson River Bracketed," 126
Hughes, G. Bernard, 282, 284
Hull & Stafford, 292–4
Humpty Dumpty Circus, 267 (*See also* Schoenhut.)
Hunt sisters, 36
"Hustler, The," 230
Hyland, Mrs. William, 167

I

Ice skates, dolls with, 347, Pl. 16
Ideal Toy and Novelty Company, 271
Ile D'Orleans, 196
Illumination, miniature, 119, 245, 330–1, 335–6, 359, 361

Imitation graining, 309
Imitation rosewood, 10, 309, 335. (*See also* Biedermeier, Waltershausen.)
Imported dolls, 340
Imported dolls' houses and shops, 9, 244–5, 266, 271
"Imported House with a Walled Garden, An," 244–5
Imported toys, 320
"Imported Upholstered Chairs," 336
Independence Hall, model of, 29
Independence Hall National Park, 62
Indianapolis, Children's Museum of, 184
International Dolls' House News, 282, 285, 363
"International Style, The," 278
Inventories, 87, 370–72, 373–76
"Iron Parlor Set: Vermont, Connecticut or Ohio, An," 301–5, 333
Iron toys, 351
Italianate cornice, 120
Ives preacher, 87–8
Ives, Blakeslee & Williams, 87

J

James River Drawing Room, 361
Japanned tin furniture, 292 (*See also* tin.)
Jefferson, Thomas, 111
Jennings, A. Elizabeth, 54
"John Howard Payne Salt Box, The," 129–30
Johnson, Audrey, 353
Johnson, Reta Cowles, 361
Johnson, Governor Thomas, 140
Johnstone, Beatrice Johannah Grieb, 95
Judge (doll), 348
"Juliette Gordon Low House, The," 147–8
Juliette Gordon Low Birthplace, 147

K

Kammer & Reinhardt, 344
Kane, Mrs. Richard R., 140, 157–8, 161–2
Keith Company, 5
Kellner, 343
Kestner doll, 343
Kilgore, 9, 334, 337
"Kimball House," 127–8
King, Mrs. Cecil St. C., 160, 215, 343, 346
Kingman Tavern Museum, 364
Kitchens, 43, 107, 132, 212, 275, 284, 320; summer, 140
Kitchen, chairs, 338, Pl. 13; ladder, 337; tin set, 328
Knapp, Mr. and Mrs. Raymond, 15–17, 217, 258
Knife urns, 325
Komlosy & Company, 7, 8
"Kueffner Civil War Cottage, The," 167

INDEX

Kueffner, Walter, 167
Kuntz, Charles, 88

L

Lacquered furniture, 24; Chinese reproduction, 361
Ladies' Home Journal, 178, 272, 322
Lakin, Eleanor V., 139
Lambrequins, 45, 135, 249
Lamps, 331
Lancaster, Osbert, 12, 87, 126, 272
Laundry room, 274; tubs, 129, 132
LaVove, Mrs. Arthur, 193
Law, Mrs. Elyse, 242
"Lawler House from Lowell, Mass., The," 52–3
Lawler, Dr. William P., 52
Leather-upholstered chair, 335
Leeds figures, 68
Leeds Toy House, 250–1
Leominster, Mass., 212, 221
Lerch, A., 328
Lewis, Mr. Clifford, III, 63
Lewis, E. D., 74
Lewis, Elizabeth Bennet, 198–9
Library steps, 337
Lichten, Frances, 249, 301, 321
Lighthouses, 7, 97
"Lighthouse without a Light, A," 97
Lighting, dolls' house, 119, 245, 355–6; miniature fixtures, 119, 245; outside, 76, 79, 155 (*See also* illumination; chandeliers.)
Lightning rods, 204
Lincoln, Bessie, 20
Lincrusta, 103
"Lindens, The," 185
Linens, miniature, 20, 135, 172, 294
"Linwood," 155–7
Lippit, Gov. Henry, 33
Litchfield Historical Society, 299
"Lithographed Apartment House, A," 252
Lithographed paper-on-wood furniture, 104, 310–314; houses, 221, 229, 249, 252–3; papers, 224, 244, 268, 279
"Little Toy Town Grocery Store," 265
Lock, presence of, 17, 37, 48, 65, 73, 80, 119, 141, 159
Locke, Felicity, 282, 363
"Longfellow-Craigie House, The," 48–51
Long Island, dolls' houses of, 106, 121, 129, 133–5
Longworth, Alice, 5, 81
"Lord Dolls' House, The," 57–8
Lord, Mrs. Frederick T., 57
Lost America, 180
Low, Juliette Gordon, 147–8
Low, Will, 138

Lowther Arcade, 342
Luck, Barbara, 124
"Lutheran Church in Pennsylvania, A," 87–9
Lyme Historical Society, 133, 297
Lynes, Russell, 251, 267

M

Maass, John, 279
MacLaren, Mrs. Gordon, 137–8, 217, 243, 363
"Maclise House in Oakland, The," 186–7
Maclise, James, 186
Macy, R. H., 323
Maerklin, 33
Mahoney, Mrs. William Redd, 172–3
"Maine Cottage, A," 38
"Maison Mère, La," 198–9
Mannheimer, Elsa, 173, 175, 218–21
Manor house, 326
"Mansard in Missouri, A," 175–6
Mansard roof, 21, 30, 36, 44, 56, 76, 85, 127, 175
Marble-topped furniture, 72, 188, 315–16
Marbleized paper, 155
Marchman, Watt, 81
Marion, Frieda, 27, 28, 29, 59, 212, 334
Marshall Field, 258, 280
Martin and Co., 7, 8
Maryland Historical Society, 140, 155
"Mary's House," 59–60
Maslin, Georgiana Davey, 119
Mason and Converse, 252
Masonic Hall, 363
"Massachusetts, High Victoriana from," 38–9
Massachusetts, houses from, 15, 35–6, 38–9, 53–4, 56
Mateaux, C. L., 341
Maunder, Mrs. William S., 221
"Maynard Manor," 360
McClintock, Marshall and Inez, 248, 253, 256, 278, 291–2, 303–4, 306, 320
McClinton, Katharine Morrison, 106
McHenry, Julia, 144; James Howard, 144
McIntire, Samuel, 15
McKennon, Mrs. J. W., 216
McLoughlin folding houses, 249, 260–1, Pl. 5
"McLoughlin Folding House with a Garden, A," 260–1
McLoughlin, John, 228, 248–250, 260–1
Measurements, 4–5, 251 (*See also* scale.)
Meat market, 222
"Mediterranean Seaside Villa," 240
Mert, Joe, 194
Metal furniture, 260, 274–6, 276–8, 337, Pl. 11, 12 (*See also* tin and iron.)

(389)

INDEX

"Metal House from Upstate New York, A," 128–9
Metal houses, 128, 130 (*See also* tin.)
Metric system, note on, 377
Mexico, miniature furnishings from, 9, 337
"Michigan Cottage, A," 181–2
Mid-Atlantic Region, dolls' houses from, 62–105
Mid-West, dolls' houses from, 165–85
Mignonettes, 348, Pl. 16
Milan Historical Museum, 165
Milwaukee County Historical Museum, 178
Milwaukee Public Museum, 178
Milwaukee, dolls' house from, 178–181
Miniature Gazette, 363
"Miniature Objects," 329
"Miniature Objects in their Original Boxes," 327
"Minnesota Farmhouse, A," 182–4
Minnesota Historical Society, 126–173
Miss Gray's House, 285
"Miss Mannheimer's Mercantile Establishment," 218–19
Missouri Historical Society, 175–6
Missouri, dolls' houses from, 175–6, 184–5
"Missouri House in Indiana, A," 184–5
Mitchell, Bessie, 133–5; Mrs. Ernest, 135
Mitchell, Mrs. Helene A., 240
Model T, 254
"Modern Jack's House," 234–5
Moe, Mrs. Donald, 249
Moline, Illinois, dolls' house from, 177–8
Montgomery Ward, 248, 267, 318
Monticello, 111
Montreal, churches of, 197–8
Moore, Colleen, 11, 189–92, 280
Moosehead, 213
Morgan's Hand Sopolio, 210
Morse, Mrs. Hazel F., 213
Mother-of-pearl inlay, 339
Motorist (doll), 348
Mount Vernon, 7, 51
Mouse house, 34
Mumm, Marguerite, 182–3
Munn, David C., 102
Murphy, Bernard J., 276
Murray Hill, 296
Murray, Patrick, 211
Muse's heads, architectural, 180
Museum of Childhood, Edinburgh, 211
Museum of the City of New York, 108–13, 113–15, 294–5
Museum of Science and Industry, Chicago, 189
Music room furniture, 337
Mutual Assurance Company of Philadelphia, 63
" 'Mystery' Furniture," 308–9

" 'Mystery' Houses, A Formidable Series of," 215–19
"Mystery houses," 90, 132, 215–19

N

"Nag's Head, A Cottage from," 150–1
Nantucket dolls' house, 326
National Association of Miniature Enthusiasts, 363
National Cash Register, 272
National Novelty Corporation, 225–6, 235–6, 238
National Trust for Historic Preservation, 3
Navajo rug, 253
Needlepoint, 21, 41, 71, 112, 221
Neo-Classical house, 111
"Newark House Dated 1882, A," 85–7
Newark Museum, 86
Newburyport, 26–7
Newel post, 39; light, 331; ornament, 43
New England, dolls' houses of, 4, 7, 15–61, 40
New England town house, 326
"New Jersey, A 1904 Bakery from," 102–4
"New Jersey, A Six-Story Building from," 100–2, Pl. 1
"New Jersey Mansion and Garden, A," 76–8
"Newport stable," 239
New Rochelle, House from, 131–3
New York, Museum of the City of, 108, 111
New York state, dolls' houses of, 4, 106–38, 243
Noah's arks, 260
Noble, John, 108
Nolan, Michael P., 133
North Carolina, house from, 150
"Norwalk, Ohio, A House from," 165–7
Norwood, Mass. Historical Society, 57
Norworth, Jack, 360
"No. 3 Bachelor's Pride," 317–18
"Nuremberg of America," 253
Nurse (doll), 348
Nutshell News, 138, 243, 362, 363
Nylander, Richard, 24

O

"Oakland, The Maclise House in," 186
Oakland Museum, 186–7
Observatory, 236
Office furniture, 297
Ohio, dolls' house from, 165–7; school house from, 184
Old Newbury, Historical Society of, 26
Old Ordinary (Hingham, Mass.), 292
"One-of-a-Kind Chairs," 338, Pl. 14
Opaline, 327 (*See also* Bristol.)
" 'Oriental Cozy Corner', The," 321–2; 251
"Oriental villas," 125

INDEX

Original box, doll in, 343; original boxes, furniture in, 236, 247, 310, 313, 323, 327–9, 331
"Original," definition of, 294
Ormolu mounts, 289
"Our New Clergyman," 87–8
Outhouse, miniature, 108
"Over-stuffed" chair, 334

P

Palladian, 15; window, 68; -windowed house, 282
Palmer, Fanny, 203
Parlor sets, 32, 289–91, 294, 301, 307, 312–13, 318–21, 323–4, Pl. 6
"Parlor Set Made in Cincinnati, A," 323–4
Patina, 351
Paris Exposition of 1870, 339
Parquetry floors, 216–17
Patent clock, 184; model, 317, range, 275
Patent date, cradle with, 311; mirror with, 302
Patent Office, 318
Paul of Boston, 21
Pawtucket, Rhode Island, 224, 226
Payne, John Howard, 129
Pearson, Eric, 17
Peasant furniture, 339
Peddler's Shop, The, 362
Pedestal table, 292, 294
Peg wooden dolls, 342 (*See also* dolls.)
Peirce, John, 15
Pennsylvania Cupboard House, 294
Perambulators, 321
Percival sisters, 197, 203
Perfection heater, 325
Perkins, Mrs. Marion I., 324
"Peter Goelet Brownstone, The," 113–15
Peter Pan Theater, 326
"Peter Pia Completes a Puzzle," 318–20
"Petite Princess furniture," 192
Petitpoint upholstery, 71, 339
"Pets' Cooking Set," 328
"Pets' Stores," 328
Pewter toys, 320, 334
Philadelphia, 62, 80, 93, 104, 340
Philadelphia ballroom, 361
Philadelphia Evening Bulletin, 105
"Philadelphia, A Puzzling Pair from," 93–4
Philadelphia Tin Toy Manufacturing Co., 292
"Philadelphia Town House, A," 79–80
Philbrick, Mrs. Lawrence S., 20
"Philippine Mahogany Mansion, A," 133
Photography, miniature, 21

Pia, Peter, 9, 278, 318–21, 333–4
Piano, 28, 41, 57, 343
Pianoforte, square, 20, 32, 361
Piazzas, 49, 51, 56
Pickering-Dodge-Devereux Baby House, The, 21–25
Pickering, Lucia, 21
Pierce family, 126
Piscataqua, 15
Pitts, ZaSu, 256–7
Pittsburgh, house from, 90
"Plainfield, New Jersey, A House from," 89–90
Plant stands, 247, 338
Platform rocker, 169
Platt family, 116
Playthings, 7, 86, 225, 226, 235, 238, 248, 250, 269, 317, 320, 321–2, 324
"Pleasure Dome, A," 125
Plexiglas, for dolls' house openings, 79, 357
Plymouth Antiquarian Society, 25
Plywood, invention of, 48, 122
Porte-cochère, 161
Portières, 43, 129, 169
Portsmouth Atheneum, 15
Portsmouth (N. H.), 15, 30
"Portsmouth, New Hampshire, A House from," 30
Potty chair, 334
Powers, Mrs. Patsy, 46–8
Praz, Mario, 332
Prescott, Mrs. B., 362
Pressed cardboard furniture, 258, 267
Prewitt, Pixie Grossman, 72, 314–16
"Pre-World War I Furniture from Germany," 314–17
Price family, 70–1
"Pride of Jersey Tomatoes," 210
Printed-on-wood houses, 253
"Prison" houses, 90, 216–17
"Providence, A Historic Replica from," 32–4
Providence, Rhode Island, houses from, 32–4, 40–1, 45, 324–6
Pumper "Niagara," 233
Pure Food Law, 265
Putnam, Amelia Earhart, 347
"Puzzling Pair from Philadelphia, A," 93–4

Q

Quackenbush children, 296
"Queen Anne Cottage, A," 160–1
Queen Mary's dolls' house, 145–6, 155, 173, 199, 202, 299, 339
Queen Victoria, dolls' house of, 282
Quill furniture, 339
"Quilting Party," 363

INDEX

R

Radio dials, bulbs for, 356
Rag doll, 329
Railroad station, 269
Rain gutters, 30
Ramsey County Historical Society, 167
Ramsey dolls' house, 126
Ramsey, Gov. Alexander, 173
"Ramshackel (sic) Inn of ZaSu Pitts, The," 256
Ranch-type house, 194
"Rare Biedermeier Pattern, A," 300–1
"Rare Eighteenth Century Tidewater House, A," 139–40
Ray, Katryna Hoffman, 299
Ray, Mrs. A. M., 177–9
"Realy (sic)-Truly Doll House," 255
"Realy-Truly Doll House Furniture," 255
"Red Robin Farm," 262–3
Redman, Miss Florence, 104, 310, 316
Reed church building blocks, 212
"Reed" furniture, 338
Reed, W. S. (Toy Co.), 212, 221
Regency chair, 337; furniture, 68
"Regional Architecture from York, Pennsylvania," 91–2
Repainting dolls' houses, 354; toys, 351
Repairing metal furnishings, 358
Replacing damaged wallpaper, 355
"Replica" houses, 7, 20, 32–4, 125–7, 144, 155
Reproduction, Colonial, 60, 325
Reproductions, furnishings, 360–64; houses, 60–1, 164, 194, 325
Restoration, 351–359
Revi, A. C., 99
Rhoads, Mrs. Daniel, 87, 92, 98
Rhode Island, dolls' houses from, 40–42, 44–5
"Rhode Island Mansard, A," 44–5
"Rinaldo," game of, 209
Ring tree, 294
Robsjohn-Gibbings, T. H., 279
Rocking horse, 223–4, 255–6
Romaine, Lawrence B., 292–3
Roosevelt, President T., 261, 263
Roosevelt Stock Farm, 261–3
Rosa, Salvator, 76
Rosenberg, Dr. Fritz, 5
"Rosewood" furniture, 300–1 (*See also* Biedermeier, Waltershausen.)
Ross-Ross, Mrs. Philip, 199–203
Roth, Leonard, 80
Rothermel, Peter Frederick, 75
Royal Baking Powder, 210, 265
Rustication, 215
Rustic chairs, 338

Rutgers College, 111
Rutherford B. Hayes Library, 81, 84

S

"S. K. Mumm Extra Dry," 210
"Sailor's Church in Montreal, The," 197–8
St. Louis, dolls' houses from, 175–6, 185
St. Ulrich, 341
Salem, cabinetmaker of, 18, 21, 35–6; house, copy of, 20; silversmith, 41
Salesman's samples, 74, 274, 318
Salisbury dolls' house, 282
Salt box house, 129–30
"Samuel Hersey of Hingham," 291–2
Samuelson, Lady, 282–4
San Francisco, dolls' houses from, 186–8
"San Francisco Bay Architecture," 187–8
"Sanitary Fair House of U. S. Grant, The," 74–6, 361
"San Quentin, A House by 30780," 197–8
Sappington, Gertrude, 153
Savannah, Georgia, 147
Saxony, Furniture of, 10, 290 (*See* Waltershausen, Biedermeier.)
Sayers, Diane, 362
Scale, 5, 315
Schindhelm & Knauer, 343
Schmitt, Mr. and Mrs. Raymond, 364
Schmuchler, Heinrich, 343
Schneegass, Gebrüder, 21, 28, 181, 188, 243, 267, 314–17, 335–8, Pl. 9
Schoenhut, 224, 261, 264, 267–70, 280
"Schoenhut Railroad Station, A," 270
"Schoolhouse from Ohio, A," 184
Schoonmaker, Pat, 344
Schramm, Mrs. Jean, 216
Schwarz, F.A.O., 102, 121, 172, 185, 216–17, 218, 271, 273, 314, 317–18, 325, 338, 346
Schwarz, G. A., 105, 291, 316
Schwarz, Henry, 158, 316–17
Sconces, 331
Scotsman (doll), 348
Screens, window, 183
Scull, Mrs. Luther, 244–5
Sears Roebuck, 262
Seaside architecture, 30, 96, 127, 130, 151, 227, 240, 245
"Second Empire Renaissance," 126
Secretaires, 119
Sehm, Matilde, 343
Sellers, Mathew, 147
"Semi-Detached Houses from Washington, D. C.," 159–60
"Series of English Houses in America, A," 282–6

INDEX

Servants, 346
"Set of Early American Tin, A," 292–4
"Seven Dolls' Houses of Colleen Moore, The," 189–92
"1780 House from Massachusetts, A," 15
"1735 Reproduction from Virginia, A," 163
Seville, Spain, townhouse from, 242
Sewn-in furniture, house with, 245–7
Shaw, Miss Helen, 63
Shelburne Museum, 17, 256–7, 332
" 'Shell Parlor Suit'—1876," 305
Shippen, Edward, 64
Shutters, 90, 91, 93, 147
Silber & Fleming, 284, 286
Silhouettes, framed, 112
Silsbee, Marianne Cabot Devereux, 21
Silver, 41, 72, 112; tea set, 42, 171
Simkin, Colin, 203
"Simmons" bedroom furniture, 275
Simon & Halbig, 340
Simonelli, Mrs. M. A., 305–6
Singer Sewing Machine, 9
Skylight, 84
Skyscraper, 7
Sleigh bed, 24
Sloan, Samuel, 125, 175
"Small World of R. Bliss, The," 224–9
Smith, Mrs. William Mason, 202
Smithsonian Institution, 80, 94
Smyth, John M., Co., 263
Society for the Preservation of New England Antiquities, 19, 21
Soldiers, toy, 222, 239, 269
"Some Flats in Paris," 258–60
"Somerville, Massachusetts, A Mansion from," 31–2, 291, 301
South, dolls' houses from, 139–164
"South Jersey, The," 78–9, 351, 357
"Spanish Casa in Los Angeles, A," 193–4
Spanish Colonial Revival, 277
Spanish furniture, 275
"Spanish" houses, 163, 192, 193, 240–2, 276–8
"Spanish Mansion by Tootsietoy, A," 276
"Special Purpose Chairs," 337, Pl. 12
Spencer, Mrs. J. Harry, Jr., 52
Spinning Wheel, The, 99, 207, 308
Spiral staircases, reproduction, 362
Stables, 7; Bliss, 237–39
Stained glass, 39, 56, 102, 180, 280
Staircases, 18, 53–4, 56, 66, 91, 101, 114, 125, 145, 168, 174, 180
Star Novelty Works, 323, 334
State of New Jersey Library, 102
Steele, Alice C., 363–4; Frank, 363
Steinmetz, Mrs. George Evans, 125–7, 217

Stettheimer dolls' house, 5
Stevens & Brown, 41, 43, 124, 166, 293, 295–6, 298, 302, 333, 338, Pl. 4
Stevens Castle, 6
Stickley, Gustav, 267
Stiles, Mr. and Mrs. Alfred H., 258
"Stirn & Lyon, Doll Mansions by," 207–9
"Stirn & Lyon, Groceries," 209–10, Pl. 4
Stirn & Lyon, 212; folding house, 208–9; villa, 212
Stock farms, 261–4; car, 264
"Stockbroker's Tudor from Beacon, New York," 372–4
Stoop, 136
Stores, 7, 200, 221, 264, 271 (*See also* grocer's, milliner's, etc.)
Stove, iron, 26, 53; "Bay State," 43; Franklin, 28; pot-bellied, 184
Strombecker furniture, 60, 280
Strong, Mrs. Homer, 128, 217, 363
Strong Museum, 4, 12, 30, 76, 125, 127, 128, 146, 214, 217, 231–3, 260–1, 270–2, 300, 363
"Sudbrook House: A Maryland Villa," 143–4
"Suffolk, Virginia, A House from," 151–3
Sunderland, Mrs. Thomas, 273
Sunstein, Mrs. Charles G., 66, 129
Swan, Malcolm, 101
Swivel chair, 337

T

Taylor, Henry Hammond, 60
Tea service in original box, 328
Tefft, Thomas A., 33
Telegraph office, 270
"Telescope-table," 314
"Tennessee Villa, A," 141–3
"1074 from New Rochelle," 131–3
Tent, 209, 251
Tester bed, 17, 26, 71, 119, 124, 292
Tête-a-tête, 332
"Texas Stucco, A," 162–3
Thayer, Joan L., 218
Thompson, Martha, 343
Thor washer and ironer, 274–5
Thorne rooms, 358
Thornton, Mrs. B. H., 93, 102–4
Thuringia, 267
"Tidewater House, A (Rare Eighteenth Century)," 139–40
Tiffany family, 116
"Tiffany-Platt House, The," 31–2, 116–19, 332
Timpson, Mrs. James, 30, 79, 89, 130, 297, 306–7, 308–9
Tin, cleaning of, 358
Tin dolls' houses, 128, 130; furniture, 292–8, 294–7, 206–7, 333; kitchen, 212; kitchen set, 328
"Tin Parlor Furniture from New England," 294–7

INDEX

"Tiny Old New England," 363
Tippet, James S., 256
"Toledo Brand Durable Iron and Steel Toys," 303
Tombstones, 46
Tool shed, 124
Toothpaste, miniature, 362
Tootsietoy, 9, 161, 193, 255, 277–8, 280, 326, 334, 344
Towel rail, 298
Tower Toy Guild, 291
Tower, William S., 291–2
"Toy Crofters, The," 272
"Toy Furniture Shop," 324
Toys, dating of, 296
"Toy Town Bungalows," 254
"Toy Town of the U. S.," 256
"Toy trust," 225, 238
Toys and Novelties, 291
"Tramp Art House, A," 99–100
"True Prison House from Pittsburgh, A," 90–1
Tuckerware, 71
Turkish Cozy Corner (*See* Oriental Cozy Corner.)
"Turn-of-the-Century House from Pennsylvania, A," 94–6
"Turn-of-the-Century Interior, A," 54–5
Tuscan Villa, 133
Twigg, Mrs. Homer L., 363
Twin dolls' houses, 172
Tynietoy, 274, 324–26, 334

U

Uihlein, Mrs. Joseph E., Sr., 180
"Ultimate in Gingerbread, The," 214–15
"Uneeda Biscuit Boy," 271
"Uneeda Kid," 271
Union Manufacturing Company, 293
"Unmarked Bliss Houses," 231–33
Upholstered chairs, 336, Pl. 10
"Upholstered House, An," 45–6
Uppark, 357
Utrecht, Dolls' House at, 6

V

Valentine, Betty, 362
Valentine Museum, 151
"Van Cortlandt Baby House, The," 3, 15, 62, 106–8, 340
Van Cortlandt Museum, 106, 139
"Vanished Houses of Whitney-Reed, The," 221–24
Vassall House (*See* Longfellow-Craigie House.)
Vassar, Matthew, 298
Venetian blinds, 72
Vermont Novelty Works, 296
Vernon, Amy, II, 324

Vestibule, 30, 215
Vickerman Baby House, The," 66–9
Vickerman house, firegrates from, 69; furnishings from, 69
"Victorian Gothic from Illinois, A," 177–8
"Villa de Sales," 145–6
Village Smithy, The, 362
Villas, 143
Virginia, houses from, 44–5, 120–5, 163–4
"Virginia, A 1735 Reproduction from," 163–4
"Voegler House in West Chester, The," 70–2, 340

W

Wagstaff clock, 71; Thomas, 71
Wainscoting, 68, 103, 132, 172
Walker Museum, 270
Wallpapers, 8, 26, 55, 85, 87, 130, 145, 354–5; scenic, 16, 70
Waltershausen, 10; furniture, 20, 112, 290, 298–9, 300–1, 335 (*See also* Biedermeier.)
Wanamaker's, 226, 250–1
Warehouse, Bliss, 230–1
Warren, Annie Crowninshield, 18–20
"Warren House at Salem, The," 18–20
Washington (D. C.) Dollology Club, 121
"Washington, D. C., Semi-Detached Houses from," 159–60
Washington's tomb (in miniature), 7
Watercolor brushes (for miniature dusting), 358
Water cooler, pewter, 245
Watertown, New York, 128
Wayne County, Indiana Historical Society, 40
Weatherred, Mrs. Preston, 324
Weathervane, 27, 80, 263
Webb, Mrs. J. Watson (Electra Havemeyer Webb), 18, 206
Wedding in miniature, 340
Wedgwood medallions, 16
Weeks, Allen, 40
Welch, Denton, baby house of, 68
Welsch & Co., 343
Welton, Mrs. Courtenay S., 144
Wenham Museum, 41, 297
West, dolls' houses from the, 186–95
Western Reserve Historical Society, 177
"West 69th Street Brownstone, A," 135–7
Wheelback windsor, 339
Wheeler, Mrs. John R., 44, 48–51
"White House Dolls' House (I), The," 81–4
"White House Dolls' House (II), The," 84–5
Whitney-Reed (Chair Co.), 11, 214, 221–4, 236, 334
Whittier house, 51
Whitton, Blair, 87, 344
Whitton, Mrs. Blair (Margaret), 90–1, 194, 229, 268, 303, 305, 327–9, 330, 362

INDEX

Whitwell, Frederick Silsbee, 21–25
Wholesale grocery, 222
Widow's walk, 48, 74, 153 (*See also* Captain's walk.)
Wicker furniture, 338
Wild, H. L., 308
Wilde, Oscar, 279
Willard, Mrs. Howard, 242–3
"Williamsburg, The Imposing House in," 4, 5, 120–5
Willoughby's Eighteenth Century, 363
Wilson, Marianne Van Rensselaer, 6, 45–6, 61, 120, 131, 215
Winchendon, Massachusetts, 252–6, 265
Winchester, Alice, 301
"Windowphanie," 56, 89, 272
Window shades, 43, 54, 60, 97, 158, 186
Windows, method of glazing, 28
Womack, Mrs. Chester, 270

Woman's World, 329
"Wood Furniture with Paper Upholstery," 309–10
Woodman, Mrs. Charles M., 41
"Woodman House from Providence, The," 40–1
Woodward & Lothrop, 261, 266
Worcester Art Museum, 282
Wrought-iron reproductions, 362

Y

"York, Pennsylvania, A House from," 91–2
Youth's Companion, The, 230, 239, 301, 314

Z

ZaSu Pitts, 256–7
ZuZu ginger snaps, 271
ZuZu Kid, 271